APPLYING MULTICULTURALISM

APPLYING MULTICULTURALISM

An Ecological Approach to the APA Guidelines

Caroline S. Clauss-Ehlers
Scott J. Hunter
Gayle Skawennio Morse
Pratyusha Tummala-Narra

AMERICAN PSYCHOLOGICAL ASSOCIATION

Copyright © 2024 by the American Psychological Association. All rights reserved. Except as permitted under the United States Copyright Act of 1976, no part of this publication may be reproduced or distributed in any form or by any means, including, but not limited to, the process of scanning and digitization, or stored in a database or retrieval system, without the prior written permission of the publisher.

The opinions and statements published are the responsibility of the authors, and such opinions and statements do not necessarily represent the policies of the American Psychological Association.

Published by
American Psychological Association
750 First Street, NE
Washington, DC 20002
https://www.apa.org

Order Department
https://www.apa.org/pubs/books
order@apa.org

Typeset in Charter and Interstate by Circle Graphics, Inc., Reisterstown, MD

Printer: Gasch Printing, Odenton, MD
Cover Designer: Anne C. Kerns, Anne Likes Red, Inc., Silver Spring, MD

Library of Congress Cataloging-in-Publication Data

CIP Data has been applied for.
Library of Congress Control Number: 2020044390

https://doi.org/10.1037/0000348-000

Printed in the United States of America

10 9 8 7 6 5 4 3 2 1

*To my great, great grandfather Bernard Doran Killian,
an immigrant to the United States, whose role as a journalist,
politician, and friend of Abraham Lincoln supported social justice.
His legacy is an inspiration.*

*And to Olliver, who was born during our multicultural guideline
development process. Ollie grew as our guidelines grew—each process
mirroring the other. And of course, to Olliver's big sisters,
Izzy and Sabrina, and to their friends, with hope that these
guidelines will pave the way for their generations.*
—CSCE

*To my colleagues and trainees, as we engage more fully our world
and its demands.*
—SJH

*I dedicate this book to my daughter, Catherine Ann Morse,
the brightest light in my life!*
—GSM

*To my maternal grandparents, Kakarla Subba Rao and Lakshmi,
who emigrated from India to the United States with curiosity and courage,
and invited us to join them on a life-changing journey.*
—PTN

Contents

Foreword: The Last Page and Dreams of the Future and the Weight of the Past—Joseph E. Trimble   ix
Acknowledgments   xv

I. FOUNDATIONS OF MULTICULTURAL PRACTICE   1
   1. An Introduction to the *2017 Multicultural Guidelines*   3
   2. The Layered Ecological Model of the Multicultural Guidelines   21

II. A BIDIRECTIONAL MODEL OF SELF-DEFINITION AND RELATIONSHIPS   47
   3. Recognizing the Fluidity and Complexity of Self-Identity and Social Dynamics: Multicultural Guideline 1   49
   4. Understanding and Avoiding Psychologists' Biases: Multicultural Guideline 2   69

III. UNDERSTANDING COMMUNITY, SCHOOL, AND FAMILY CONTEXT   85
   5. The Cultural Significance of Language and Communication: Multicultural Guideline 3   87
   6. The Impact of Social Capital: Multicultural Guideline 4   101

IV. CONSIDERING THE INSTITUTIONAL IMPACT ON ENGAGEMENT — 115

7. Recognizing Institutional Barriers and Systemic Marginalization: Multicultural Guideline 5 — 117
8. Promoting Culture-Centered Interventions and Advocacy: Multicultural Guideline 6 — 135

V. PSYCHOLOGICAL PRACTICE WITHIN A DOMESTIC AND INTERNATIONAL CLIMATE — 153

9. Understanding Globalization's Impact on Psychology: Multicultural Guideline 7 — 155
10. The Intersection Between Development and Biosociocultural Context: Multicultural Guideline 8 — 181

VI. OUTCOMES — 199

11. Conducting Culturally Informed Work in Psychology: Multicultural Guideline 9 — 201
12. Applying a Strength-Based Approach to Psychology: Multicultural Guideline 10 — 219

VII. FUTURE DIRECTIONS IN MULTICULTURAL PSYCHOLOGY — 239

13. Where Do We Go From Here? Looking Towards the Future in Multicultural Psychology — 241

Afterword—Lynn Pasquerella — 271
References — 273
Index — 309
About the Authors — 331

Foreword

The Last Page and Dreams of the Future and the Weight of the Past

Sometimes when I'm reviewing a manuscript or opening the first pages of a long-awaited book I often want to skip to the end to read what the authors concluded, where they believe the field is headed, how the story really ended, or what their data mean for the welfare of some special population. When I read the first section of this book, *Applying Multiculturalism: An Ecological Approach to the APA Guidelines,* my curiosity won, and I turned to the last page to find out what the authors wanted the reader to do with the guidelines, information, and recommendations they were presenting concerning the future of multicultural psychology. I was excited by what I read.

The tale of challenge and change of diverse populations in United States psychology is remarkable in its uniqueness—for it is the tale of people who endured enslavement, colonization, segregation, isolation, internment, discrimination, and blatant forms of oppression and exclusion. It is a tale in which racism, sexism, classism, colonialism, lookism, sizeism, heterosexism, ethnocentrism, colorism, nativism, cisgenderism, ableism, ageism, and xenophobia routinely fan the fires of aversion, antipathy, hostility, and loathing. It is the tale of people who were objects of a concept and ideology—scientific racism—that was integral to the justification of their oppression and exclusion. It is the tale of a scientific discipline that embraced that concept, contributed to its legitimacy, and simultaneously struggled against it.

I am deeply indebted to Molly E. Trimble, who provided skillfully worded editorial comments and suggestions through draft versions of the Foreword. I am extremely grateful for her time, effort, and thoughtful assistance.

It is also the tale of people who had faith that the discipline of psychology could somehow make an important difference in diverse cultural communities. It is the tale of people who, less than a lifetime ago, were being documented by that discipline as innately inferior human beings and who are now that discipline's major transformational force for a psychological science, practice, and ideology appropriate for the multicultural and global realities of the 21st century. It is quite simply a tale of wonder.

This tale also is a primer for the value and significance of cultural diversity. In contrast to popular conceptions, diversity is not simply a matter of appropriate representational numbers of persons of color in the service of a colorblind society. It includes the intersection of race, ethnicity, ethnocultural identity, status, and gender. It includes the lived experiences of racism, biculturalism, marginalization of nondominant groups. Diversity is a transformational and revitalization change strategy that recognizes the unique benefits to all of multicultural/multiracial experiences and perspectives. In psychology, that change is resulting in a substantive broadening of knowledge and skills serving to significantly expand the range of psychological practice and research.

Nevertheless, important barriers continue to exist to the full participation of persons of color in psychology. These include continuing multicultural and diverse inequities in student and faculty recruitment, retention, training, and curricular representation. Much more substantial barriers and ethnic/racial underrepresentation exist in the discipline's two major knowledge "gatekeeper" functions: (a) editors of scientific and professional journals in psychology and (b) federal and foundation grant administrators of psychological research. These gatekeeper functions undoubtedly will be the next target of the focused and coordinated action that consistently has been demonstrated by psychologists of color and their allies. For access to these functions is essential for a transformed psychology in North America.

Indeed, psychology in North America and worldwide is undergoing a significant paradigm shift. The shift from a once dominant Eurocentric psychology toward a multicultural/multiracial diverse psychology is characterized by (a) recognition of the unity of spirit, mind, body, and behavior; (b) development of new terminology, concepts, and methods that are more appropriate for and respectful of communities of color and diverse populations; (c) increased use of multidisciplinary knowledge and methods; (d) research questions and professional practices that recognize the individual's embeddedness in a variety of cultural/historical and social/ecological systems; and (e) increased emphasis on psychologists' social responsibility, including the need to incorporate advocacy and service into research, educator, and practitioner roles. This is the future of ethnic minority psychology—as well as the future of psychology, certainly within the United States, North America, and worldwide.

Understanding the meaning of race, ethnicity, and the minority experience is a challenge that requires conceptual and methodological tools. Despite the findings of the Human Genome Project that race does not appear to have a biological basis, race and ethnicity are constructs or categories that continue to be an integral aspect of our social fabric. Racial and ethnic categories are used to establish political and social structures, and these categories in turn are the result of social, historical, and political processes that continue to influence and define the experience of ethnic minorities, as well as that of nonethnic minorities. It is often difficult to separate ethnicity and race from socioeconomic status and the experiences of migration, acculturation, and discrimination. At times, the issue of race and ethnicity may serve as a proxy for other variables (e.g., socioeconomic status, ethnic identity, acculturation, acculturative stress, racism, discrimination, sexism, homophobia, xenophobia). The challenge ahead is to move away from simplistic categories of race, ethnicity, and diversity toward the development of constructs that reflect the true complexity of culture, ethnicity, and diversity and their relationship to psychological phenomena. Another challenge rests on focusing efforts in the study of prevention and remediation to the consequences of racism, oppression, and discrimination. This monumental book and corresponding guidelines offer conceptual and methodological tools that move the field closer to the consideration of more complex and ecologically valid constructs that underlie notions of diversity, race, and ethnicity.

Despite a growing and compelling body of work that argues against a universal approach to the study of human behavior, too many graduate programs, scholars, practitioners, and researchers carry out their affairs as though a universal approach was appropriate. Perhaps one reason for this pattern is the absence of a comprehensive resource on critical issues to be considered in studying and understanding the psychology of ethnic minorities. *Applying Multiculturalism: An Ecological Approach to the APA Guidelines* is a comprehensive and much needed resource for professionals, scholars, and educators seeking to incorporate diversity into their training or work. This book challenges the false notion that diverse ethnic minorities are alike and highlights differences within racial and ethnic minority groups.

There are, however, important similarities for certain ethnic minority groups that share a legacy of oppression, genocide, slavery, colonization, and/or conquest. The counterpart of these legacies, such as resistance, survival, endurance, and resiliency in the face of overwhelming odds, merits serious study as these processes can point the way to culturally effective prevention and remediation strategies.

A consideration of the legacies of genocide, slavery, conquest, oppression, and discrimination is basic to understanding the social and psychological processes linked to stress, health, well-being, and behavior. Conceptual models of human behavior must incorporate the legacies of oppression, discrimination, and the strength inherent in resistance, resilience, and survival to fully appreciate the unique experiences specific to ethnic minorities. This book examines common historical experiences as well as differences among ethnic minorities and explores ways such experiences are critical to the teaching, research, and practice of racial and ethnic minority psychology. To punctuate the profound depth of each of the guidelines, well-crafted case studies are provided illustrating the difficult struggles diverse people experience in their daily lives.

Through the use of guidelines and narrative the book presents us with numerous challenges. One challenge most assuredly will press the vigor, intellect, and wit of those bent on advancing an inquiry into intersectional ethnic and racial identity. The number of ethnic and racial groups in North America is increasing not declining; the U.S. is not a melting pot as some often characterize it. The populace does not appear to be assimilating at the rate demographers and sociologists once predicted. All over the world geopolitical boundaries are changing as a result of political turmoil, colonialism, and globalization, consequently individuals are changing their ethnic allegiances and identities as their boundaries are rearranged or they move from one environment to another.

Multicultural psychology and diversity are in desperate need of structure and order. There is a pressing and growing need for a comprehensive resource for students, investigators, and practitioners to critically evaluate the debates, concepts, issues, and approaches to the psychological study of race and ethnicity. To accomplish orderliness and structure scholars are challenged and encouraged to engage deeper into the topic to sort out and challenge the discrepancies and incongruities. For example, a good starting point for a probing inquiry is the emergence of a multiracial or multiethnic classification category. In cultural and ethnic comparative research researchers typically rely on monoethnic or monoracial categories to test hypotheses about the contribution one's cultural lifeways and thought ways make to some outcome variable or variable domain. What deep or surface cultural attributes will a multiethnic and diverse category permit? If a researcher is interested in discovering rich cultural, racial, ethnic, and diverse contributions to a cognitive learning style, for example, how will the contributions be disentangled from one's multiethnic worldview or orientation?

Other healthy challenges await the reader of this book. One has to do with the complex diverse cultural backgrounds and their identity and identification characteristics. Ethnic identification and diverse ethnic transformations are not solely private acts. People typically construct their identities within the context of their biological background and the sociopolitical context in which they are socialized. People often construct autobiographies to place themselves in the social order and seek out settings and situations for confirmation. Often diverse ethnic and racial identity declarations, especially those of mixed-ethnic background require external validation and thus the judgments of others play a key role in the transaction. Hence, we find people constructing their identity and self-image to fit preferred sociocultural contexts and constructing the situations and contexts to fit the preferred image. Identity is transformative, with evolving views of self—people change and their identities and sense of self change. The intersection of diverse cultural identities leads to new multicultural challenges as outlined and illustrated in this book.

Applying Multiculturalism: An Ecological Approach to the APA Guidelines is wonderfully organized and thoughtfully constructed. It is a formative, comprehensive, engaging book that will be a major source for understanding the complexities of establishing progressive guidelines for the practice, teaching, and study of multicultural psychology. With its wealth of interesting material and a clear accommodating style anyone who delves deeply into these chapters will emerge a more informed student, researcher, practitioner, and consumer of psychology. The chapters are written with authority, clarity, confidence and pull together the rich story of the meaning of ethnocultural relationships to personal and community well-being framed in a contextual ethnographic perspective.

The authors encourage the reader to think deeply about the realities of diverse ethnocultural groups and how practice and research can be effectively and sensitively provided and conducted. The book extends the growing body of social and behavioral science literature on diverse ethnocultural groups and will become an excellent reference for students and practitioners who work with multicultural clients. The authors are to be highly commended for compiling this impressive exploration of an important and complex topic. If anyone is curious about the depth and scope of the mental health topics covered in *Applying Multiculturalism: An Ecological Approach to the APA Guidelines*, it should be kept close by as a reference and a resource. I recommend reading the book from cover to cover, rather than skipping to specific chapters, to get a full appreciation for its profound depth and relevance. I recommend the reader start on the first page to get a full appreciation for the rich depth and relevance of the explicit direction on the last page: to lift the weight of the oppressive, repressive past and forge an enlightened inclusive dream of the present and future.

—*Joseph E. Trimble, PhD*

Acknowledgments

Caroline S. Clauss-Ehlers expresses gratitude to the many mentors whose support has helped pave the way for this work and to the students who will bring the next generation of multicultural scholarship forward.

Scott J. Hunter thanks his students, interns, and fellows for always reminding him of the importance of diversity and intersectionality.

Gayle Skawennio Morse acknowledges the support of colleagues at Russell Sage College, who are the finest and kindest group of professionals she has ever worked with! Their support has sustained her through the years and especially during this strange COVID time.

Pratyusha Tummala-Narra is grateful to her clients, students, and colleagues who continue to inform and shape the important ways in which our profession advances understandings of multicultural issues.

Our writing team thanks Christopher Kelaher for his encouragement and support in moving this book forward. Many thanks to David Becker for his thoughtful feedback and editing skills that further strengthened this book.

PART I FOUNDATIONS OF MULTICULTURAL PRACTICE

1 AN INTRODUCTION TO THE *2017 MULTICULTURAL GUIDELINES*

Ours is a diverse society. To be a multiculturally responsive helping professional, educator, researcher, and consultant in the 21st century means being open to and engaging with the diverse identities presented by clients, students, research participants, and consultees. Relationships between and among reference group identities have a profound influence on an individual's self-definition and experience. Introduced as an important consideration by Crenshaw (1989), *intersectionality* broadly helps us understand how reference group identities such as race and gender intersect with one another. Crenshaw argued that "Black women are sometimes excluded from feminist theory and antiracist policy discourse because both are predicated on a discrete set of experiences that often does not accurately reflect the interaction of race and gender" (p. 140). She further stated, "Because the intersectional experience is greater than the sum of racism and sexism, any analysis that does not take intersectionality into account cannot sufficiently address the particular manner in which Black women are subordinated" (p. 140). A central task for 21st-century students, trainees, and psychologists is to be open to hearing, understanding, and then grasping how reference group identities

https://doi.org/10.1037/0000348-001
Applying Multiculturalism: An Ecological Approach to the APA Guidelines, by C. S. Clauss-Ehlers, S. J. Hunter, G. S. Morse, and P. Tummala-Narra
Copyright © 2024 by the American Psychological Association. All rights reserved.

intersect with one another and the impact intersectionality has on the lives of clients, students, research participants, and consultees with whom we work (Cho et al., 2013; Crenshaw, 1989).

To provide a framework for these issues, the American Psychological Association (APA) published *Multicultural Guidelines: An Ecological Approach to Context, Identity, and Intersectionality, 2017* (hereinafter referred to as *2017 Multicultural Guidelines*; APA, 2017c). This volume is intended as a user's guide for that document (please see the description of the Task Force, described later). Our aim with this user's guide to the *2017 Multicultural Guidelines* is to assist you in thinking about how development unfolds across time and in connection with intersectional experiences and identities, contributing to rich lives with impact and meaning. For helping professionals at the start of the third decade of the 21st century, advances in research and clinical scholarship lend themselves to an evidence base that supports a contemporary psychological approach that "incorporates human differences across their varied elements" (APA, 2017b, para. 3).

The purpose of this user's guide is to encourage practitioners, educators, students, trainees, researchers, and consultants to discover the ways in which the *2017 Multicultural Guidelines* can support efforts to be multiculturally responsive and attuned to the varieties of human experience that exist. Appreciation, understanding, and willingness to learn about the multicultural backgrounds of individuals, families, couples, groups, research participants, organizations, and communities are critical to our work as clinicians, educators, researchers, and consultants.

To this end, each of the 10 guidelines is described in detail in a single chapter, expanding on the information provided in the *2017 Multicultural Guidelines* (see Table 1.1 for a list of the guidelines). These chapters each

TABLE 1.1. The *2017 Multicultural Guidelines*

Guideline no.	Guideline
	Level 1: Bidirectional Model of Self-Definition and Relationships
1	Psychologists seek to recognize and understand that identity and views of self can change and that the interaction between the two is dynamic. To this end, psychologists appreciate that intersectionality is shaped by the multiplicity of the individual's social contexts.
2	Psychologists aspire to recognize and understand that as cultural beings, they hold attitudes and beliefs that can influence their perceptions of and interactions with others as well as their clinical and empirical conceptualizations. As such, psychologists strive to move beyond conceptualizations rooted in categorical assumptions, biases, and/or formulations based on limited knowledge about individuals and communities.

TABLE 1.1. The *2017 Multicultural Guidelines* (Continued)

Guideline no.	Guideline
	Level 2: Community, School, and Family Context
3	Psychologists strive to recognize and understand the role of language and communication through engagement that is sensitive to the lived experience of the individual, couple, family, group, community, and/or organizations with whom they interact. Psychologists also seek to understand how they bring their own language and communication to these interactions.
4	Psychologists endeavor to be aware of the role of the social and physical environment in the lives of clients, students, research participants, and/or consultees.
	Level 3: Institutional Impact on Engagement
5	Psychologists aspire to recognize and understand historical and contemporary experiences with power, privilege, and oppression. As such, they seek to address institutional barriers and related inequities, disproportionalities, and disparities of law enforcement, administration of criminal justice, educational, mental health, and other systems as they seek to promote justice, human rights, and access to quality and equitable mental and behavioral health services.
6	Psychologists seek to promote culturally adaptive interventions and advocacy within and across systems, including prevention, early intervention, and recovery.
	Level 4: Domestic and International Climate
7	Psychologists endeavor to examine the profession's assumptions and practices within an international context, whether domestically or internationally based, and consider how this globalization has an impact on the psychologist's self-definition, purpose, role, and function.
8	Psychologists seek awareness and understanding of how developmental stages and life transitions intersect with the larger biosociocultural context, how identity evolves as a function of such intersections, and how these different socialization and maturation experiences influence worldview and identity.
	Level 5: Outcomes
9	Psychologists strive to conduct culturally appropriate and informed research, teaching, supervision, consultation, assessment, interpretation, diagnosis, dissemination, and evaluation of efficacy as they address the first four levels of the *Layered Ecological Model of the Multicultural Guidelines*.
10	Psychologists actively strive to take a strength-based approach when working with individuals, families, groups, communities, and organizations that seeks to build resilience and decrease trauma within the sociocultural context.

begin with a case illustration that highlights key concepts from its respective guideline, followed by discussion questions for readers to consider and a review of relevant literature. Then, these chapters provide important, practical considerations for applying each guideline in four fields: clinical practice, teaching and training, research, and consultation.

Like the *2017 Multicultural Guidelines*, this book principally uses nonbinary pronouns, with the exception of case illustrations and quoted material. And like the *2017 Multicultural Guidelines*, this book advocates for a more diverse and inclusive population of psychologists.

INTRODUCTORY CASE ILLUSTRATION: YOU THE READER

This introductory case illustration asks you to focus on yourself and your experience. We encourage you to consider next steps in your own personal and professional development. We invite you to consider the following reflection questions: As you think about your life and who you are, what factors influenced your interest in psychology? What made you want to be a helping professional?

Do you remember an early experience where you felt different from those around you (Clauss-Ehlers, 2006b)? Perhaps you felt you stood out, weren't accepted, or were discriminated against. Looking back on this early experience of difference, consider the impact it had on your development. What impact did it have on your interpersonal relationships and your sense of self?

You may feel challenged when thinking about articulating a vision for your life, given the realities of the larger current political climate and environmental risks. Every day—as we write this and as you read it—we are bombarded with news of rollbacks of previous civil rights gains, decimation of the Voting Rights Act, police brutality, health and mental health care disparities (specifically at this time related to COVID-19), the policy shift currently taking place that bars trans persons from military service, the burning of Black churches and escalating gun violence by White supremacists, the housing of asylee children from Central America in cages, a policy of forced separation of asylum-seeking families at the southern border of the United States, the gradual and progressive legal blocking of women's and girls' right to choice over their body integrity, and just recently, the attempted mandated inclusion of a citizenship question in the 2020 Census. It takes immense effort to envision the future when every day can feel like a stark fight for the most vulnerable amongst our communities and ourselves.

As you think about the next steps in your life, how do you see yourself growing as a person? Is there anything from reading through the list of the *2017 Multicultural Guidelines* that resonates with your life story? If so, what factors do you feel capture your experience? What factors are missing that we need to consider to move us forward in the future? What do you envision your contribution will be as you move forward in your current professional role or in your next role as a professional?

Discussion Questions Related to You the Reader

Questions for Undergraduate Students

1. What has prompted your interest in psychology?
2. To what extent does the psychology field reflect how you define yourself?
3. To what extent does the psychology field speak to the experiences of your community/communities?
4. What changes would you like to see in the psychology field?
5. How would you like to contribute to those changes?
6. How do you view your role as an advocate?

Questions for Graduate Students

1. Do you find the psychology field to be currently responsive to your reference group identities and their intersectionality? How so and/or how not?
2. Has your training been focused primarily on a Western model of psychology? How so and/or how not?
3. In what ways can you learn more about cross-cultural approaches to psychology?
4. Are there areas of training in which you would like to gain more experience? What are those areas? How can you pursue that learning?
5. To what area(s) of psychology do you see yourself contributing the most? The least?
6. Where do you see yourself contributing as an advocate?
7. How are you pursuing your interests in the psychology? What barriers stand in your way? Who in your network can collaborate with you to overcome those barriers?

(continues)

> **Discussion Questions Related to You the Reader (*Continued*)**
>
> ***Questions for Professionals***
> 1. How do you engage with the profession as a multiculturally responsive psychologist?
> 2. Are there areas where you feel you could learn more and gain more training? What are those areas? How can you pursue additional training in them?
> 3. How did your training prepare you to be engaged in the field as a multicultural practitioner? How did it not?
> 4. How can you address barriers to multicultural training moving forward?
> 5. What is the role of cultural humility in your life?
> 6. What is the role of advocacy in your life?
> 7. As you envision the next 5, 10, 15, and 20 years of your career, what kind of professional do you want to be? How do you see yourself contributing to the psychology field?
> 8. What kinds of training opportunities do you see yourself providing the next generation of psychologists?

BACKGROUND ON APA'S MULTICULTURAL GUIDELINES

In 2002, the *Guidelines on Multicultural Education, Training, Research, Practice, and Organizational Change for Psychologists* (*2002 Guidelines*) were adopted by APA's Council of Representatives as APA policy. The attention given to these original multicultural guidelines underscored the seminal contribution they made to the profession and to society (APA, 2002, 2003). Their support also indicated that the field was ready to further multicultural scholarship and practice as a priority. Certainly, this has been the case. Between 2002 and 2017, the field saw tremendous growth in multicultural scholarship and practice.

APA guidelines are generally considered to be in effect for 10 years (APA, 2019b, pp. 13–14, Association Rule 30-8.3). As this time frame was reached with the *2002 Guidelines* and the evidence base for multicultural psychological science expanded, the APA's Board for the Advancement of Psychology in the Public Interest (BAPPI) put out a call for membership for two separate task force groups. BAPPI decided to convene two task force groups because of advancements in scholarship related to race/ethnicity and additional reference group identities in the years since the initial guidelines. The objective for the

Task Force on Re-Envisioning the Multicultural Guidelines for the 21st Century was to consider scholarship across a range of reference group identities and the intersectionality between them. This task force was charged with

> [reviewing] the diversity scholarship across the full expression of all aspects of human diversity with the goal of developing "pan" or "umbrella" guidelines that capture the universal concepts that are common across the experiences of diverse groups. The hope is by reviewing this broad cross section of literature focused on various identity groups that the authors will be able to create a framework for diversity guidelines that position psychology going forward. (APA, 2015a, para. 4)

The goal of the APA Task Force on Re-Envisioning the Multicultural Guidelines for the 21st Century was to review scholarship specific to race and ethnicity, given that the *2002 Guidelines* were largely focused on these two variables. In tandem, the Task Force on Guidelines Focused on Race/Ethnicity was charged with "[reviewing] the abundant literature published since 2002 on race and ethnicity and determin[ing] a new framework of guideline statements that organizes the totality of scholarship both within psychology and from other disciplines about race/ethnicity" (APA, 2015a, para. 5). We (along with BAPPI) view the work of these two task force groups as complementary to one another, with reciprocal guidelines that further the role of multicultural psychological practice and scholarship.

We also recognize the important multicultural work being done in related helping professions. This work includes the American Counseling Association's (ACA) *Multicultural and Social Justice Counseling Competencies: Guidelines for the Counseling Profession* (Ratts et al., 2016), the *Standards and Indicators for Cultural Competence in Social Work Practice* (National Association of Social Workers, 2015), and the American Psychiatric Association's *Cultural Formulation Interview* (American Psychiatric Association, 2013a), as well as work by other professional groups (e.g., APA, 2017a).

OVERVIEW OF THE *2017 MULTICULTURAL GUIDELINES*

The book as a whole is based on the work of the Task Force on Re-Envisioning the Multicultural Guidelines for the 21st Century, who wrote the *2017 Multicultural Guidelines*. Task Force membership included Caroline S. Clauss-Ehlers (Chair), David Chiriboga, Scott J. Hunter, Gargi Roysircar, and Pratyusha Tummala-Narra. The document that emerged from our work as a task force, *Multicultural Guidelines: An Ecological Approach to Context, Identity, and Intersectionality, 2017* (i.e., *2017 Multicultural Guidelines*), addressed the multicultural science that has evolved since the publication of the *2002 Guidelines*.

The *2017 Multicultural Guidelines* speak to the profession's recognition of the important role that multiculturalism plays with regard to how individuals and groups define themselves. The 2017 revision views an intersectional, ecological approach as central to our understanding as helping professionals. Our hope is that this user's guide to the *2017 Multicultural Guidelines* will walk you through developmental and contextual antecedents of identity and structural institutional factors, such as racism, that have an impact on human experience. We encourage you to consider how the *2017 Multicultural Guidelines* can be acknowledged, addressed, and embraced to engender more effective models of professional engagement.

As mentioned in the description put out by BAPPI, the *2017 Multicultural Guidelines* address reference group identities broadly while considering contextual factors and intersectionality. This broad approach is responsive to current trends that focus on contextual factors and intersectionality between and among the reference group identities. The variables considered in the *2017 Multicultural Guidelines* include ethnicity, gender identity, race, ability status, socioeconomic status, sexual orientation, religion and spirituality, age, culture, immigration status, education, and employment. However, it is important to note that other variables or subsets of these variables may intersect to have an impact on an individual's experience and are encouraged to not be ignored.

KEY CONCEPTS IN MULTICULTURAL PSYCHOLOGY

This book presents three key organizing concepts. We hope they will guide you in reading and understanding the material. The key concepts are additive in that they augment important dimensions to the way in which we as students and professionals think about our work and roles. These three organizing principles are described in more detail in the sections that follow.

The first key concept involves the inclusion of a domestic and transnational focus. This focus accounts for that fact that most of the globe does not make up the 5% to 7% of research participants who are reflected in articles published in APA journals, a group described by transnational feminist scholars as the Global Minority (L. H. Collins et al., 2019). Adding a transnational focus urges us to engage in research, practice, and training endeavors that include what transnational feminist scholars describe as the Global Majority, the 93% to 95% of people across the globe who are not represented in research and practice efforts.

The second key concept is a focus on cultural competence and cultural humility. Cultural competence is important because of the knowledge and skills it applies to being multiculturally responsive in our work. At the same time, cultural humility is an acknowledgment of the important roles of empathy and advocacy that are required for working multiculturally. Through cultural humility we understand cultural competence as a lifelong process that we are engaged in and by which we seek to truly understand another person's experience. Taken together, this approach says that the end goal of our work is not just being culturally competent; it is also striving toward competence and constantly learning about what lives hold for our contemporaries. Having both cultural competence and cultural humility allows one to make this lifelong commitment to being multiculturally responsive to the needs of those with whom we work as well as in our own self-awareness.

A third key organizing concept is a focus on bidirectional relationships. This book encourages bidirectional relationships between client, student, research participant, and consultee and the practitioner, educator, researcher, and consultant. A bidirectional relationship includes a give and take between the parties. The idea is not that the professional is doing something to the party receiving services. Instead, both parties are jointly influenced by each other. This consideration of a mutual exchange is, for many, a paradigm shift in how we view our work as psychologists.

Domestic and Transnational Focus

Increasingly, ours is a globalized world. Although the *2017 Multicultural Guidelines* come from the APA, our approach incorporates a domestic and transnational focus that recognizes members of a society do not exist alone. Wherever we engage in professional practice, there are always transnational elements to our work as psychologists. As stated by L. H. Collins et al. (2019),

> As globalization spreads connections and increases mobility, psychologists are called on to diagnose and treat clients, help with disaster responses, consult on research, assist communities, and work with a wider range of populations in settings both inside and outside their home countries. (p. 3)

Being responsive to globalization involves being aware of what is happening beyond our own borders. For instance, one area related to globalization and the work of psychologists is the increase in forced migration around the world (UNHCR, 2019). *Forced migration* is "a process where people have to leave their homes and homelands due to situations such as political instability, human rights abuses, torture, war, and other factors" (Clauss-Ehlers, 2019a, p. 330). It has increased to the point that the United Nations High

Commissioner for Refugees described it as a "global trend" (UNHCR, 2019). The Pew Research Center (Budiman, 2020) reported that the United States has more immigrants than any other country across the globe. In 2018, the U.S. foreign-born population was 44.8 million (Budiman, 2020). According to a 2020 Pew Research Center publication, immigrants make up 13.7% of the U.S. population, compared with just 4.8% in 1970 (Budiman, 2020).

And yet, despite this global reality, the psychology field appears to have lagged behind, as shared by L. H. Collins et al. (2019). More psychological research is needed including populations that are not represented in the literature, country experiences that are not given voice in the literature, and issues that lack intervention and an evidence base (Clauss-Ehlers, 2021b; Clauss-Ehlers, Weist, et al., 2020). Such issues include the importance of our understanding the global context of poverty (Iotti & Jungert, 2020); the status of educational access for women and girls (Pasquerella & Whitehead, 2020); the impact of COVID-19 on global mental health (Clauss-Ehlers & Tummala-Narra, 2022); systemic racism (Clauss-Ehlers, 2021a; Demby & Miraji, 2020); the need for greater support for LGBTQ+ communities (Gowin et al., 2017); human trafficking (Chuang, 2020); communities affected by war (Musisi & Kinyanda, 2020); the need for greater support for people with diverse ability statuses (S. J. Hunter, 2021); mass incarceration, including the incarceration of youth (Jensen et al., 2021); and immigration trauma (Tummala-Narra et al., 2021), among many other pressing concerns. Given these global trends, it is imperative that our work incorporates a transnational context. A key addition to this book that differs from the *2017 Multicultural Guidelines* is an intense focus on working with communities from a transnational perspective. This book approaches domestic and transnational work from a frame that values bidirectional relationships and cultural humility.

Cultural Competence and Cultural Humility

Table 1.2 presents key approaches related to cultural competence and cultural humility, in chronological order starting with Sue and colleagues' (1982) description of cultural competence and ending with the revised *2017 Multicultural Guidelines* published in *American Psychologist* in 2019 with the article titled "APA Multicultural Guidelines Executive Summary: Ecological Approach to Context, Identity, and Intersectionality" (Clauss-Ehlers et al., 2019). As shown in Table 1.2, cultural humility was first introduced by Tervalon and Murray-García (1998).

Debate exists in the field about whether we should practice cultural competence or cultural humility (Blume et al., 2020; Garcia et al., 2017).

TABLE 1.2. Conceptualizations of Cultural Competence and Cultural Humility

Focus of approach	Sources	Key descriptors
Cultural competence	Sue et al. (1982) Sue et al. (1992)	Cultural awareness Cultural knowledge Cultural skills
Cultural humility	Tervalon & Murray-García (1998)	Lifelong commitment to: "Self-evaluation and self-critique" "Redressing the power imbalances in the patient-physician dynamic" (p. 117) "Developing mutually beneficial and nonpaternalistic clinical and advocacy partnerships with communities on behalf of individuals and defined populations" (p. 117)
Multicultural competence grounded in a social justice approach	Vera & Speight (2003)	"Macrolevel analysis of issues of multicultural competence" (p. 269) "Definition of multicultural competence centered on social justice" (p. 270) Multicultural advocacy
Cultural competence via cultural adaptation research	Bernal & Domenech Rodríguez (2012)	Culturally adapted interventions Culturally adapted evidence-based practice Culturally adapted clinical approaches
Cultural humility	Fisher-Borne et al. (2015)	"Acknowledges power differentials between provider and client" p. 165) "Challenges institutional-level barriers" (p. 165) "A move from a focus on mastery in understanding 'others' to a framework that requires personal accountability in challenging institutional barriers that impact marginalized communities" (p. 165)
Cultural humility	Foronda et al. (2016)	Attributes: "Openness, self-awareness, egoless, supportive interactions, and self-reflection and critique" (p. 210) Antecedents: "Diversity and power imbalance" (p. 210) Consequences: "Mutual empowerment, partnerships, respect, optimal care, and lifelong learning" (p. 210)
Cultural competence that incorporates cultural humility	APA (2017a); Clauss-Ehlers et al. (2019)	"Cultural competence as a lifelong process of reflection and commitment" (APA, 2017a, p. 8)

Note. Approaches are presented in chronological order.

Much of this debate has centered on the view that cultural competence implies that once mastery is achieved, the work of the multicultural professional is complete. The concern is with the idea that once a person is competent, or considers oneself to be so, there is no need to continue to be accountable (Fisher-Borne et al., 2015). Other critiques of cultural competence are that the concept tends to focus on acquiring knowledge about cultural competence rather than self-awareness and reflection, that the term doesn't have enough of a focus on social justice, that a "cultural competence script" can promote stereotypes, and that cultural competence does not adequately address institutional inequities (Campinha-Bacote, 2018; Fisher-Borne et al., 2015; Tervalon & Murray-García, 1998). In contrast, cultural humility addresses the importance of self-reflection, self-evaluation, being open to feedback, addressing systemic inequities, engaging in critical theory that explores power relationships, and being aware of power imbalances (Campinha-Bacote, 2018).

At the heart of cultural humility is a "lifelong commitment to self-evaluation and self-critique, to redressing the power imbalances in the patient-physician dynamic, and to developing mutually beneficial and nonpaternalistic clinical and advocacy partnerships with communities on behalf of individuals and defined populations" (Tervalon & Murray-García, 1998, p. 117). It incorporates the idea that one is always engaged in learning. Material is never mastered; rather, the development of knowledge, skill, and self-awareness is an ongoing process. Cultural humility includes understanding power differentials within the helping relationship. It incorporates the role of advocacy.

The *APA Dictionary of Psychology* (APA, n.d.-a) defines *advocacy* as

> speaking or acting on behalf of an individual or group to uphold their rights or explain their point of view. An individual engaged in advocacy is called an advocate, of which there are two general types: A case advocate represents a single individual, and a class advocate represents a whole group.

For example, a clinician who advocates for additional school-based counseling services as part of a student's individualized education program is a case advocate. A student who advocates for additional mental health benefits offered by a university health center is a class advocate. Being an advocate is a critical role for psychologists, who have training and unique areas of expertise that can influence public policy (e.g., the provision of mental health care services, consultation regarding how to build an equitable and diverse workforce). As psychologists, we can provide the general public with an awareness of psychology and what professional psychologists do. We can encourage high school students and undergraduates from diverse backgrounds to develop an interest in the field, thus creating a pipeline of future professionals who represent a diverse workforce (APA, 2020a, 2020b). Psychologists engage in advocacy efforts when they share their expertise, raise awareness, advance the field, and garner funding (APA, n.d.-b). At the same time, as trainees and psychologists, we can encourage others to engage in self-advocacy and efforts directed toward the issues they care about.

We take a "both/and" rather than an "either/or" view of cultural competence and cultural humility. This view acknowledges both concepts as complementing each other and as jointly important. Throughout this book, we encourage you the reader to think about how cultural competence applies to your work and role while acknowledging that such applications may change and shift as you develop greater awareness and insight (Yancu & Farmer, 2017).

Bidirectional Relationships

Historically, the field of psychology viewed the role of the professional psychologist as the expert in responding to the needs of patients. This idea is very much founded on a medical model that looks at the doctor (i.e., the expert) as the person treating the ills of the patient. The bidirectional relationship at the heart of the *2017 Multicultural Guidelines* moves away from this unidirectional medical model of the expert "treating" the patient; medicine, too, has moved directly toward a bidirectional, patient-centered collaborative care model (Siegler, 2019). Instead, the bidirectional relationship reflects mutuality, or a give and take, within the context of a professional relationship, whether as practitioner, educator, consultant, or researcher. Ongoing growth and accountability applies to both parties involved in the relationship and its progression. Within the research domain, in a bidirectional relationship, the social scientist doesn't simply take data and knowledge from the community being studied. Rather, within the context of a bidirectional relationship, the social scientist partners with the community, giving something back and co-creating knowledge jointly (Cabassa & Baumann, 2013).

Within the context of the bidirectional relationship, the multiculturally responsive psychological professional and the client, student, research participant, or consultee acknowledge and address structural barriers and systems that have an impact on experiences. In this book, we urge educators, researchers, consultants, and practitioners to consider the larger institutional barriers that have an impact on institutional engagement, or a lack of it. For example, the racial/ethnic health disparities that have emerged during COVID-19 (Centers for Disease Control and Prevention, 2020), along with ongoing incidences of police brutality toward people of color (Elliott & Bowman, 2020), tell us that we need to look beyond individual instances of inequity and racism to acknowledge and address how systems perpetuate oppression. The bidirectional relationship is a paradigm shift from the idea of psychologists "doing" something to someone else. Instead, psychologist and client are addressing something together.

A REFLEXIVITY ORIENTATION TO THE BOOK

When the task force finished writing the *2017 Multicultural Guidelines*, we wanted to create a user's guide that would help undergraduates, graduate students, trainees, early career professionals, and mid-career and seasoned professionals to engage and use the material presented. One of our goals as a task force was to make sure that we presented the evidence base that informed the guidelines. It was critical to show how the literature and research generated since the *2002 Guidelines* supported each guideline in the *2017 Multicultural Guidelines*. A difference between our user's guide and the *2017 Multicultural Guidelines* is that, while research is presented, this user's guide is more focused on how to incorporate and engage the material in our everyday lives as clients, clinicians, students, trainees, educators, research participants, researchers, consultees, and consultants.

Each chapter in this user's guide focuses on a specific guideline. After a brief introduction, we present a case illustration that highlights the main aspects of the guideline, with discussion questions at the end of each case to encourage you to engage actively with the case material. After case presentations, each chapter provides detail about how the guideline may be relevant to our work as psychologists, with sections that consider how the guideline of focus applies to practice, education (e.g., training experiences), research, and consultation.

Reflexivity

Before providing an overview of the book's contents, we thought it would be helpful to provide an orientation to the reflexivity work that is central to becoming a multiculturally responsive clinician, researcher, educator, student/trainee, and consultant. We believe that reflexivity work is a critical aspect of building cultural competence and cultural humility. Our hope is that you engage with us in reflexivity work related to who you are as a student, trainee, or professional. There are many paths to self-awareness; we present a few ideas that we hope will guide you as you absorb the material presented in the pages that follow.

Being self-reflective is an important part of cultural competence and cultural humility. As you read through the chapters that follow, we encourage you to think about how what you are learning reflects your own background and experience. How do the *2017 Multicultural Guidelines* sit with you? What are the ways in which they may or may not reflect your experiences? How does your own awareness better inform your ability to understand the work of a multiculturally responsive psychologist?

A second concept is active listening. By "active listening," we mean not just listening to information but truly taking it in. Active listening requires moving from listening to hearing in a way that fosters understanding or fosters your ability to ask questions that seek to promote understanding. One way to listen actively as you read this user's guide is to hear the perspectives being presented, such as the voices of the people presented in case studies.

Empathy is another central concept for cultural competence and cultural humility. So much of what we can offer as psychologists involves empathy. We are being empathic when we want to know more about someone else's perspective. When we have empathy, we are committed to trying to understand someone else's emotions and experiences. Empathy can serve as a bridge, helping us to have and to hear difficult conversations in our attempt to understand where a person is coming from. Self-awareness and active listening help us be empathic.

Being open to learning throughout the lifespan is another important process to keep in mind while reading this book. Whether you are a student or professional, you will always have things to learn. This is good news, as it means that you are engaged in a dynamic process of understanding the world around you and considering how psychology as a field connects with that world. Being open to learning can take many forms. For a student, whether undergraduate or graduate, it might involve exploring what interests you and identifying the area of psychology you are interested in pursuing. For a predoctoral or postdoctoral trainee, being open to learning might involve responding to training and supervision in active ways, such as engaging and questioning. For a professional, being open to learning might involve incorporating new perspectives and being informed by the work that you do in innovative ways. Certainly, the bidirectional relationship that is central to our approach suggests that individuals in a professional role are also informed by clinical, student, research, and consulting interactions. The bidirectional relationship reflects that being open to learning is a two-way street: We can be as informed by those with whom we are working as we are by the work we are doing.

Another aspect of knowing one's self to keep in mind while reading this book is to strive to be nondefensive in your openness to learning. It is natural to be defensive and respond to uncomfortable material in ways that suggest, "That's not me. I'm not like that." In pushing beyond these initial responses, we can work toward having more self-awareness about our own behaviors, thoughts, and reactions. We can have more awareness about how our own sense of privilege and power might play out in clinical, research, consulting, and educational interactions. In working through defensiveness, we can see the larger contextual, institutional nature of racism, sexism, homophobia, ageism, xenophobia, classism, and ableism.

Working through defensiveness may also involve acknowledging areas of growth, rather than seeing these areas as weaknesses. Identifying areas of growth can help us respond to things we need to work on in our professional and personal lives. Just as our clinical work invites clients to change and view themselves in different ways, acknowledging and working through areas of growth can encourage us to get to a different place. As you read through the chapters that follow, you might find some content is familiar but that other content is unfamiliar and challenging. The goal is for you to be aware of that dynamic and not to run away from what registers as unfamiliar and scary.

At the same time, we think it is important to identify strengths that you bring to the bidirectional relationship and your understanding of the *2017 Multicultural Guidelines*. The strength-based focus of this book takes us away from a traditional disease-driven model. Just as the *2017 Multicultural Guidelines* encourage a strength-based approach, so do we encourage you to think about the positive qualities you bring to clinical, teaching, consulting, and research encounters.

Finally, this book encourages you to apply the *2017 Multicultural Guidelines* to your work and learning. An applied approach is important. These ideas don't simply remain ideas; rather, the application of concepts makes them come alive. It is what makes them relevant. We hope that in applying the *2017 Multicultural Guidelines,* you can see how they resonate with the experiences of those with whom you are working and your own experiences in these interactions. At the same time, you may find gaps or areas that don't resonate. These are important also, as they set the stage for upcoming work and future areas to consider.

ORIENTATION TO THE BOOK'S STRUCTURE

This book is divided into seven parts to facilitate your learning. Part I, Foundations of Multicultural Practice, includes this chapter, as well as Chapter 2, which provides an understanding of the theoretical framework and corresponding ecological layers that form the foundation for the guidelines. The theoretical framework for the *2017 Multicultural Guidelines* incorporates a five-level model in which each layer is nested within another. These layers move from the micro level, which focuses on the bidirectional relationship, to the larger societal context and ultimately focus on building resilience and responding to trauma as part of outcomes in our work. Our hope is that you approach Parts II through VII of the book from this theoretical standpoint.

Parts II through VI are each dedicated to a level from the layered ecological approach described in the *2017 Multicultural Guidelines* and in Chapter 2. Each chapter focuses on one of the 10 multicultural guidelines. As described earlier, each chapter includes a case illustration and discussion questions, a literature review, and practical applications for clinical practice, teaching and training, research, and consultation.

Part II, A Bidirectional Model of Self-Definition and Relationships, presents guidelines that correspond with Level 1: Bidirectional model of self-definition and relationships. This first level of the ecological model is concerned with mutuality in the context of a professional relationship, whether that involves the practitioner/clinician, educator/student, researcher/research participant, and/or consultant/consultee. Chapter 3 focuses on Guideline 1, with an emphasis on identity formation and the intersectional nature of identity development. Chapter 4 discusses Guideline 2 with its focus on conscious and unconscious biases that helping professionals bring to clinical work and how these have an impact on the therapeutic relationship.

Part III, Understanding Community, School, and Family Context, presents Level 2 guidelines that reflect the community, school, and family context. Chapter 5 focuses on the cultural significance of language and communication that are emphasized in Guideline 3. Language is viewed as a complex interaction that involves verbal and nonverbal domains of communication. Chapter 6 focuses on Guideline 4, which specifically addresses the impact of social capital on the experiences of clients, students, research participants, and consultees. This chapter discusses how disparate experiences of social capital promote inequities, for example communities having differential resources allocated to them.

Part IV, Considering the Institutional Impact on Engagement, includes chapters that reflect Level 3 guidelines. This third level of the ecological model examines how the surrounding context has a systemic impact on engagement with institutions. Level 3 guidelines underscore the institutional barriers that prevent engagement. Chapter 7 emphasizes key themes presented in Guideline 5, such as structural stigma and disparities in legal, educational, and health care systems. Chapter 8 follows from Chapter 7, focusing on the important role of systemic advocacy, as well as prevention and intervention initiatives, key themes presented in Guideline 6.

Part V, Psychological Practice Within a Domestic and International Climate, includes chapters related to the layer of the ecological model addressing domestic and international climates. This fourth layer of the model examines how the nature of domestic and international climates affects the preceding three levels of the model. To this end, Chapter 9 encourages practitioners, educators, researchers, and consultants to understand the impact of globalization on psychology, as presented in Guideline 7. Chapter 10 focuses on understanding life transitions within a biosociocultural context, a theme that is central to Guideline 8.

Part VI, Outcomes, focuses on the fifth and last level of the ecological model: outcomes. Chapter 11 discusses Guideline 9, encouraging psychologists to engage in culturally responsive teaching, research, practice, and consultation. Chapter 12 takes a strength-based approach to the work of psychologists, presenting culturally informed ways we can increase resilience and decrease trauma.

Finally, the book concludes with Part VII, Future Directions in Multicultural Psychology. Chapter 13 presents benchmarks to consider as we move toward the future of multicultural psychology and the subsequent *Multicultural Guidelines* that will build upon this work and incorporate advances in research, practice, teaching models, and theoretical approaches that have developed since the *2017 Multicultural Guidelines*. We look forward to this day, as it will reflect a continued advancement of practice, teaching, research, consultation, and theoretical models.

We now encourage you to begin your journey by reading Chapter 2. That chapter, "The Layered Ecological Model of the Multicultural Guidelines," starts us on this journey with a presentation of the theoretical orientation to the *2017 Multicultural Guidelines* and a description of the ecological model.

2 THE LAYERED ECOLOGICAL MODEL OF THE MULTICULTURAL GUIDELINES

After our introductory chapter, Chapter 2 provides you with an overall foundation for understanding the *Multicultural Guidelines: An Ecological Approach to Context, Identity, and Intersectionality, 2017* (hereinafter referred to as *2017 Multicultural Guidelines*; American Psychological Association [APA], 2017c) and its use of a *layered ecological model,* through the application of Uri Bronfenbrenner's (1977, 1979) developmental-socioenvironmental theory that addresses the range of transactional ecological influences that impact social, emotional, behavioral, and cognitive functioning across the lifespan. At the end of this chapter, you will have a strong understanding of the five ecological layers that are associated with the *Multicultural Guidelines'* overall model and how each of the two guidelines associated with each layer supports a process that builds on itself, culminating in a structural approach to engaging the multidimensional facets that define multiculturalism and its applicability to professional psychological practice. We anticipate that by the end of the chapter, you will have a solid sense of how the guidelines apply to the work of psychological professionals, across the array of demands that occur while conducting clinical work, research, education, and consultation

https://doi.org/10.1037/0000348-002
Applying Multiculturalism: An Ecological Approach to the APA Guidelines, by C. S. Clauss-Ehlers, S. J. Hunter, G. S. Morse, and P. Tummala-Narra
Copyright © 2024 by the American Psychological Association. All rights reserved.

within clients' communities. Each Multicultural Guideline discussed will be illustrated through the application of our ecological model to a case study, including the one discussed initially here.

Consider for a moment that you are a community mental health clinician working with a family dealing with recent losses secondary to the COVID-19 pandemic that has impacted the world in 2020 and beyond. This family consists of multigenerational members, many of whom immigrated to the United States from Latin America. Several family members have required supportive interventions for exposure to the virus and their subsequent development of physical symptoms. You have been asked to work with the granddaughter, Alicia, who is identified as the key member guiding the management of the family's health care and associated needs. Alicia is seeking assistance with her increasing level of anxiety arising from both her immediate family's needs, particularly those of her grandparents, who are in the group considered most at risk for contracting and becoming ill from the virus, and her role as one of the main support coordinators for her broader family system. One of your first tasks is to assist Alicia in making sense of the network of care being required and how its coordination is affecting her, the individuals within the family system she is responsible for supporting, and the community that they are engaged with socially and professionally. Your client feels overwhelmed by the challenges she is facing, which include connecting family members with the correct sources of support and intervention, from community-based health to the main hospital system that will accept this family for care. Central to these challenges is the management of communication, given that not all members of the family are English-speaking. You find yourself considering these multiple layers of interaction and how they will ultimately not only affect the availability of care for key family members but also influence the level of support Alicia herself needs.

This brief vignette opens our discussion of the multiple levels of engagement that communities and their members must consider. To best appreciate the complexities, as well as the transactional considerations at play, we turn to Bronfenbrenner's (1977, 1979) ecological theory. This theory presents a detailed conceptualization of developmental influences across people's lives and serves as a model of the multilevel interactive relationships that support how individuals and systems codevelop, through their interactions, mutual influence, and concurrent considerations (see Sameroff, 2009, for a more detailed discussion about how these relationships are transactional in their influence and effect). With this developmental model regarding humans and their mutual engagements, Bronfenbrenner described how individuals develop and become members of their communities and society within the systems (e.g., environmental contexts) that surround and engage them, from the microsystemic proximal level to the distal macrosystems that provide organization and engagement across the lifespan. Adapting this model to guide how we conceptualize multicultural influences and identities, we developed the five layers of our ecological multicultural model to replicate Bronfenbrenner's five concentric systems, defined next.

The first layer is the *microsystem*, which comprises the near (proximal) network of influences and support systems with which an individual, couple, family, or group of peers engage and interact. These include the broader family, neighborhood, work setting, educational or vocational setting, and religious/spiritual institutions, as well as the local community resources that house health care and rehabilitative services.

The second layer is the *mesosystem*, which consists of the relational interactions between individuals, groups, and structures that support and sustain the broader community. Relevant to the mesosystem are reciprocal engagements that occur between individuals and their communities, and the systems with which they interact regularly, such as their community center, places of worship, or the broader educational system.

Next is the third layer, the *exosystem*, or the array of broader systems that define a society's structure and that engage and apply the laws and values that organize the society. Components of the exosystem include state and federal governments and a society's legal system, including the policies and legislation these component structures enact and enforce.

The *macrosystem* is the fourth layer, which Bronfenbrenner (1977) described as comprising cultural and social norms, applicable political structures, and their inherent considerations within a society; the macrosystem incorporates the community or society's general worldview and the set of interdependent societal demands that are made by the broader community and stem from its needs. This level is deeply associated with the experiences of privilege and oppression that exist within a society, and it is the macrosystem that provides the overarching structure of life for a community or society, ideally addressing these inequities. The experience of privilege and oppression that exists within the macrosystem impacts all members of that specific society to varying degrees.

The fifth layer of our multicultural ecological model is the *chronosystem*, which is concerned with the changes and transitions that affect the lives of a society's members across time. Changes in the chronosystem radiate through the underlying four levels just discussed, from the *microsystemic* (e.g., a family's experience of challenge given alterations in employment or housing) to the *macrosystemic* (e.g., patterns of immigration and emigration

24 • Foundations of Multicultural Practice

TABLE 2.1. Examples of Bronfenbrenner's Ecological Systems

Systems	Examples
Microsystem	Comprised of the individual's family, friends, neighbors, school/place of employment, place of worship, organizations (e.g., community and corporations), and cohorts (e.g., clubs or cultural groups).
Mesosystem	Comprised of the interaction between various microsystems. For example, how an individual's family interacts with the school system. This system becomes increasingly complex as more systems inevitably interact with one another.
Exosystem	Comprised of the policies and procedures for various microsystem organizations as well as large, government-run organizations (e.g., Medicare, Medicaid, Social Security).
Macrosystem	Comprised of the federal government as well as a nation's values, beliefs, attitudes, methods of effecting change (e.g., through military, political, or financial practices).
Chronosystem	The influence of the passage of time on all subordinate systems. For example, as a person ages, they experience changes at the biological level. Another example is the change in national mores because of shifts in individual and organizational beliefs and policy changes because of major events (e.g., mass trauma such as a disaster or terrorist attack; coronavirus epidemic).

Note. These lists of examples are not all-inclusive and are based on an ecological model of development (Bronfenbrenner, 1979; Bronfenbrenner & Ceci, 1994).

within a community). Bronfenbrenner added the chronosystem to his original model over time, in recognition that the transactions that occur between individuals and systems take place within a time frame developmentally (see Bronfenbrenner, 1995; Sameroff, 2009). Table 2.1 presents examples of the five ecological layers.

CASE ILLUSTRATION—DRS. ROBERTO AND CLAUDIA: COMMUNITY BASED INVESTIGATIONS OF PARENTING AND RESILIENCE IN IMMIGRANT FAMILIES IN TWO URBAN MIDWESTERN LATINX COMMUNITIES

Drs. Roberto and Claudia, professors in a community psychology program at a local urban university in the U.S. Midwest, serve as principal investigators for a study addressing ecological and contextual variables that influence cognitive and emotional development in a community of youth growing up in two Latinx communities in their city. They are specifically interested in which interacting factors (i.e., parenting style, community involvement, relational attachments among the youth and their families, positive vs. negative peer relationships, and educational mentorship) promote developmental resilience for these youth. Together with their team of graduate and undergraduate research assistants, Drs. Roberto and Claudia are working closely with community members, consultants, and local programs situated within the two communities, to foster a collaboration that will support and better define their understanding of how family and community influence effective developmental outcomes. They are employing a complex mixed-methods (i.e., quantitative and qualitative psychosocial and neurocognitive assessments, and examination of biological markers) approach to studying the intersection of and interaction between aspects of cognitive, behavioral, and prosocial development. The communities they are engaging with for this research are made up principally of Mexican and Latin Caribbean immigrants, most of whom have been residing in the city for an extended period of time and are affiliated with social and communal networks that foster immigrant family stability. Many of the families they are engaging with are multigenerational, with original immigration of family members having taken place up to 30 years in the past. In order to embed their work within a culturally supported approach aimed toward intervention, the investigators have organized their study and its goal ecologically. They believe that this will allow them to better understand and share the levels of influence and interaction that emerge from their work with and within the community. This can allow for the identification of sources of resilience across the generations studied.

Their research hypothesis is drawn from Bronfenbrenner's ecological model, which they believe can serve as an organizing approach for identifying systems that promote risk and resilience. They assert that this is necessary for guiding an understanding of the families and their experiences and to more effectively address the needs of these families within their community systems. The researchers are especially interested in how immigration and subsequent patterns of acculturation may influence and change patterns of parenting and attachment within the community across time, particularly as the families become embedded within broader social structures in the urban United States. A significant goal is to identify key points of influence and stress and the intersectional considerations that emerge with community members' identities across generations within the community. The researchers are particularly aware that they are embarking on a complex approach to their research, one that requires a strong organizational structure and model for interpreting the layered ecologies of the families and the systems they interact with within the community.

Working with two senior graduate students, Drs. Roberto and Claudia recently brought a set of mothers and fathers from each of the two communities into small focus groups at two of the main community centers. They asked these groups about parenting styles, how these have been learned, and what has become more challenging with parenting approaches they used across time, given their experience with the broader community systems that support their children, like the public and parochial schools they attend. In smaller, subset interviews with the individuals' families, the researchers also discussed involvement with such programs as the Department of Child and Family Services (DCFS) and with medical primary care providers. At the core of these discussions were concerns around particular parenting interactions, approaches, or styles of engaging with their children that may have led to concerns about, or even reports of, neglect or abuse, or that contributed to negative feedback from teachers, counselors, or pediatricians, when meeting with the parents. Several of the parents revealed stories about being reported by teachers or medical providers to DCFS for potential child neglect and abuse, arising from suspicions of an overreliance on corporal punishment that could be perceived as abuse and the reliance on children in the family to serve as primary caregivers in response to parents' challenging work schedules. Another group of parents were quite vocal about their interactions with schoolteachers and administrators, particularly regarding expectations for home-oriented guidance and support with educational demands, and they expressed their own worries about how they could meet these expectations in light of their work schedules and, for a number of the parents, their own language barriers to assistance, given that English was not their primary language.

With this information, the team began to organize what they had heard in the focus groups, the subgroups, and individual interviews. They used this information to begin to map out the potential networks across the varied layers of community and government that families were required to negotiate and interact with and to delineate how these served as potential sources for either guidance or challenge. During a subsequent focus group, the team presented their organizational efforts to key community representatives, specifically, individuals who serve as the go-between support for families regarding school and medical care, to discuss how they could best conceptualize together these layered interactions and their ramifications. This, the researchers hoped, would allow them to begin to structure a series of directed questions concerning community-oriented parenting practices and expectations and how they intersected with broader systems of care and educational support, whose answers would inform efforts at intervention across these systems, improving communication and collaboration between families and the schools and medical care providers.

Discussion Questions Related to Drs. Roberto and Claudia

1. Considering the five layers proposed by Bronfenbrenner as components of a community's particular ecology, how might you begin to consider particular questions for the parenting focus groups yourself? What might be most pertinent to you to learn, in order to build a model of parenting that is transactional in its considerations for these communities? Are there specific systems you would seek to find more information about when doing so?

2. What might you anticipate are the greatest challenges for newer immigrants settling into and becoming participant members of their potential community systems? Who would be their initial social supports? (Hint: This question reflects the *microsystem* directly.)

3. Are there specific other systems across the five layers that you would see as important to query the families about when asking questions about their personal parenting styles? Where would you find a focus on relationships most pertinent?

4. What factors might you consider to be most associated with resilience for immigrant families when building their lives in a new country? What might be the different systems and resources they will need to look toward for support with this process? (Hint: This question addresses more directly the *mesosystem*.)

5. Considering both case examples shared with this chapter, the clinician working with their client and the researchers studying local communities, can you identify specific programs that might be effective resources for care and respite? How can these be more readily engaged? (Hint: This question addresses the *exosystem*.)

6. Where might conflict lie for these families when misunderstandings take place about discipline or parenting choices, such as needing to leave one's children home together without parental supervision due to overnight work schedules? (Hint: This question addresses the *macrosystem*.)

7. What would you imagine life has been like, across three generations, where the grandparents were the first to immigrate from the Dominican Republic to a Midwestern U.S. city? What stories might they have told to their children who were born in the United States about their transition and what occurred differently across the two settings? How might this impact the dynamic of parenting across time, with acculturation to the United States? (Hint: This question addresses the *chronosystem*.)

THE FIVE LEVELS OF THE LAYERED ECOLOGICAL MODEL

Kurt Lewin (1936) said, "Every psychological event depends upon the state of the person and at the same time on the environment, although their relative importance is different in different cases" (p. 12). This quote shows how Lewin doesn't look at the individual or the environment separately. Rather, as Heft (2022) contended, Lewin looks at them jointly to examine the relationship between the two. Bronfenbrenner (1995) also considers how individuals and communities interact within a larger ecological context with a focus on varying levels of engagement and interaction, which he labeled the microsystem, mesosystem, exosystem, macrosystem, and chronosystem. Our layered ecological model of the *Multicultural Guidelines*, derived from Bronfenbrenner's model, likewise includes five concentric circles that overlap and interact across the dyadic relationships (both interactional and transactional) that occur between clinicians and clients, students and instructors, consultants and consultees, and researchers and study participants. We discuss each of these relationships, and the transactions that occur within them, as we proceed.

Our book considers how a multicultural approach to the helping professions can be located within an ecological context. By understanding the context surrounding an individual, couple, family, group, or organization, we can explore the influence of surrounding ecological factors on experiences. For instance, in the context of a competitive graduate training program, students may feel unable to take risks to explore counseling styles. Conversely, a graduate program that fosters may encourage students to share and explore areas of growth due to a context of a safe environment (i.e., Sameroff, 2009; see also Bronfenbrenner, 1995; Eriksson et al., 2018; McKown, 2005).

Level 1: Bidirectional Model of Self-Definition and Relationships

The first level of the layered ecological model of the *Multicultural Guidelines* is the bidirectional model of self-definition and relationships. This inner first level focuses on the importance of allowing people to define who they are, rather than having an "expert" define them, and building professional psychological relationships on the basis of respect for that self-definition. As demonstrated in Figure 2.1, two inner circles capture a bidirectional model of self-definition and relationships (APA, 2017c; Clauss-Ehlers et al., 2019). The circle on the left shows the individual's self-definition in their role as client, student–trainee, research participant, or consultee. In other words,

FIGURE 2.1. Level 1: Bidirectional Model of Self-Definition and Relationships

Individual's Self-Definition
- Client
- Student
- Research Participant
- Consultee

⇔

Individual's Self-Definition
- Clinician
- Educator
- Researcher
- Consultant

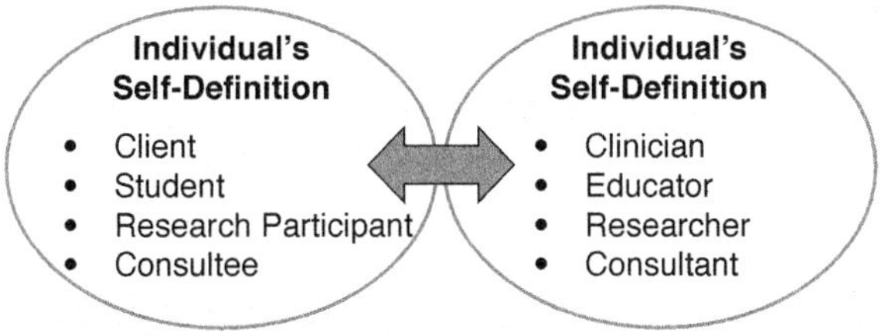

this circle reflects how clients[1] define themselves. It refers to clients' identification with reference group identities (i.e., how identities interact and interconnect with one another to form a person's experience; Crenshaw, 1989; Greene, 2013; see Chapter 3, this volume). The circle on the right represents an individual psychologist's self-definition in their role as clinician–practitioner, educator, researcher, and consultant. This circle refers to their reference group identity of the psychologist and their intersectionality, which in turn influences their self-definition as a clinician–practitioner, educator, researcher, and/or consultant.

The bidirectional arrow in Figure 2.1 overlaps the circles, illustrating the mutuality—and give and take—in the relationship between client and psychologist. Guidelines 1 and 2 are Level 1 guidelines. To further assist and guide you, the guidelines are presented here (see also Table 1.2 in Chapter 1):

Guideline 1. Psychologists seek to recognize and understand that identity and self-definition are fluid and complex, and that the interaction between the two is dynamic. To this end, psychologists appreciate that intersectionality is shared by the multiplicity of the individual's social contexts.

Guideline 2. Psychologists aspire to recognize and understand that as cultural beings, they hold attitudes and beliefs that can influence their perceptions of and interactions with others, as well as their clinical and empirical conceptualizations. As such, psychologists strive to move beyond conceptualizations rooted in categorical assumptions, biases, and/or formulations based on limited knowledge about individuals and communities.

Considering our research case, it is evident that Level 1, the bidirectional model of self-definition and relationships, is quite relevant when considering the broader development and implementation of the research program by Drs. Roberto and Claudia. They have conceptualized their work with the

---

[1]Please note, we use the term *client* to encompass the roles of student, trainee, research participant, and consultee throughout the book.

two communities they are seeking to engage with and learn from as representative from the start of this bidirectional relationship. Their focus groups in particular, as discussed in the case, are put in place to ensure that they are (a) seeking to understand immediately from the community how individuals and families define themselves, and how those definitions are understood within the context of developing an approach to learning about parenting choices when residing in a broader culture than they may have come from; and (b) how power and privilege can be conceptualized from the standpoint of the individuals within these communities, and how they are experienced in the interactions individuals have with the broader members of society across their city, as well as in their relationship with the researchers. For example, when holding the focus groups, it became very clear that for many of the parents, the community systems they interacted with about their decisions regarding parenting were impacted by challenges with communication and mutual understanding. Schoolteachers and administrators were identified as not always able to consider that (for example) work schedules or language barriers could prove troublesome for the parents with regard to ensuring their children were making gains with their learning goals. Similarly, parents reported experiencing challenges in the area of cultural expectations; parents who had not been students themselves in the U.S.-based public educational model were uncertain about its expectations, and they felt they had little guidance, let alone support, given their own immediate needs and language.

This first level of the guidelines recognizes that there are strong cultural and social considerations that must be directly addressed by psychologists in their work with clients, students, consultees, and their research participants. Additionally, psychologists' recognition of their own privilege is key; when exploring these experiences with their clients, psychologists must become attuned to a dual role as both *expert* and *learner*. They may have models from which to organize their knowledge, and expertise to share once an understanding of a situation is in place, but they must also situate themselves immediately within the position of learning what is the lived experience of their clients. Furthermore, they need to come to understand the levels of interaction that occur within the immediate community for their clients, and how the dynamics of these interactions can directly influence the opportunities that their clients have to engage within the systems necessary for daily life.

Taking a bidirectional approach, psychologists, whether as clinicians or researchers, are called upon to immediately recognize the power relationship, and its inherent privilege. They must then step back to allow the expertise of the client about their own experience (of themselves and their life) to guide how they both make sense of the situations being presented and to guide the conceptualization of means of support and change. Psychologists identify the intersectional considerations that are at play with the client, for example, how biological sex and physical identifiers of race, such as physique, color, or speech patterns, influence meaning in collaboration with clients' broader lived experience. Such factors as generational position, social and economic class, gender identification, sexuality, profiles of communication within and across families and communities, and clients' knowledge about where and how to seek assistance and support all work together to define the present and the array of potential future opportunities for each client or research group being worked with.

Clinicians are encouraged to approach an understanding of clients by actively working to hear, explore, and discuss the complexities of experience: learning about who defines the family and the community; where they originated from and how they view their lives as immigrants and residents across time; their physical and social environments; and their engagements with social and community-based systems of support, such as schools, religious facilities, or community programs. Defining the parameters of this ecological niche reveals much about the opportunities and constraints that exist for each client and allows for an understanding of the set of experiences that serve as either supportive and guiding, or challenging to navigate and engage.

Recognizing how both past and present influence clients in their engagements with their ecological niche is also a component of understanding where current opportunities and constraints may be situated. Developmental experiences occur at multiple levels, from the basic biologically driven aspects of growth in cognition and behavior across time, to the emotional and personality aspects of identity, that are formed schematically through proximal (familial) and distal (structural and systemic) interactions that take place with time and maturity. Making sense of the community's key events and goals, at the individual and group levels, in concert with this developmentally framed model, allows the psychologist to understand both what is a strong area of fit for their clients, providing support and successful engagement toward growth, and what proves a mismatch between self and system, contributing to challenge and potential diminishment of opportunity. This knowledge then guides the psychologist to be able to, with their clients, begin to understand the influence of and engagement with the second level: the community, school, and family context.

Level 2: Community, School, and Family Context

Moving from the microsystem, which concerns the individual's experience of themselves and the bidirectional relationships they hold across their daily

32 • *Foundations of Multicultural Practice*

lives, we next discuss the second layer of the model, which surrounds the first level: the mesosystem. This second layer consists of reciprocal relational interactions between individuals, groups, and structures that support and sustain the client's broader community. This level, as suggested in our previous discussion, serves to influence and engage bidirectionally the relationships that we considered in Level 1. Figure 2.2 further illustrates this level and how it both defines and extends the first level. The second level in our model comprises Guidelines 3 and 4:

Guideline 3. Psychologists strive to recognize and understand the role of language and communication through engagement that is sensitive to the lived experience of the individual, couple, family, group, community, and/or organizations with whom they interact. Psychologists also seek to understand how they bring their own language and communication to these interactions.

Guideline 4. Psychologists endeavor to be aware of the role of the social and physical environment in the lives of clients, students, research participants, and/or consultees.

Within this level, as seen with the two guidelines, psychologists are asked to think about the immediate systems that our clients interact with and how these systems' functioning serves to facilitate either collaboration or challenge as a result of the bidirectional influences that occur. Key to these guidelines is clinicians' consideration, with their clients, of how sensitive these immediate systems are to the individual and community, as interactions occur at the local and immediate levels of experience and engagement. For example, it is important to recognize that, with our research case, much of what often influences each individual is layered across the family and its ecological niche, and the experience of the family within the next level of systems that define

FIGURE 2.2. Level 2: Community, School, and Family Context

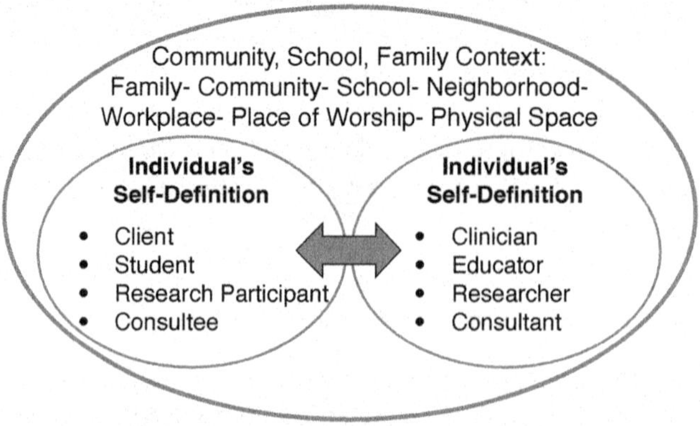

Community, School, Family Context:
Family- Community- School- Neighborhood- Workplace- Place of Worship- Physical Space

Individual's Self-Definition
- Client
- Student
- Research Participant
- Consultee

Individual's Self-Definition
- Clinician
- Educator
- Researcher
- Consultant

the community itself—those organizations, such as schools and direct health care or mental health care settings, and local religious and social networks, that provide a place and setting for supporting cultural, academic, spiritual, and social opportunity.

As part of their efforts to define the ecology of the research participants' lives, initial work by the research team must explore what defines this network. Through the use of questionnaires that were developed through previous foundational research done by the investigators, it was learned that several important local structures were integral for the communities and the research participants individually; these included their local elementary and high schools, specifically the teachers and administrators; the local Catholic parishes attended by the majority of the families; and the community health care centers, where primary care and mental health services were located. From the questionnaire responses by the participants prior to the organization of the focus groups, the research team was able to ascertain that participants experienced a series of important supports and challenges in the range of interactions they had with these principal organizations. These supports and challenges included efforts made by family members in times of stress, such as during the pandemic, to the availability of virtual and in person social opportunities, where participants could share guidance about obtaining necessary care. These supports and challenges included efforts made by family members in times of stress, such as during the pandemic, to the availability of virtual and in person social opportunities, where participants could share guidance about obtaining necessary care.

As we think about Level 2, we recognize that the framework of the *Multicultural Guidelines* provides professional psychologists a structure for understanding the role of the broader community context in the lives of clients and research participants. Moving from the direct interactions at the personal level, Guidelines 3 and 4 remind us, and guide us, to make sense of how educational, vocational, and community-based resources structure lives and contribute to sources of resilience and risk; and how misunderstandings, miscommunications, and failures to recognize and engage with the experiences of power and privilege that situate within this level of the broader ecology of the individual ultimately serve to assist us in making sense of where particular interventions may be required. For example, a middle school teacher's inability to recognize and then consider the implications of a student's struggle with their parents' elementary level of education and lack of experience with broader learning systems, such that they (the parents) cannot effectively help with homework, hampers the student's opportunities with learning. The social stress of such an experience can further affect the student's capacity to make use of potential resources directly and may even lead to a diminished commitment to academic engagement.

Level 2 therefore serves to influence us in our efforts, as multiculturally and ecologically informed psychological practitioners, to attend more effectively to the transactions that occur both within and across the range of our consultees', clients', and research participants' lives. It fosters a necessary foundation for developing a layered understanding of experience, and how that serves to direct and guide choices made or opportunities missed. Level 2 also provides a richer conceptualization of the ways in which individual resilience unfolds, with experiences that are nurturing and supportive, and hence guiding, for clients and their families. Ultimately, though, we must recognize that these structures within Level 2 are themselves influenced by institutional structures that situate around and above them, facilitating what may occur at the broader systems and societal levels. This leads us to Level 3.

Level 3: Institutional Impact on Engagement

The model's third level considers the *institutional context*, the influence of local, state, and federal governmental structures; medical, and behavioral and mental health systems (broadly); the legal systems across the local, state, and federal levels, including law enforcement; and the broader educational systems on individual, family, and community life experiences. Of concern for us as multiculturally informed psychologists is the effect of these institutions, and their policies and actions, on how clients and we ourselves as professionals experience their influence on our daily lives. The impact of these institutions strongly influences how individuals come to see themselves more directly within their society; it also affects the range of relationships we have with each other, as discussed with Level 1. Actions taken, and interactions that occur, at Level 2 of the model are also directly affected by the influences of the institutions represented within Level 3. As such, we are able to consider how each of the four previous guidelines intersect with Guidelines 5 and 6 that correspond to Level 3:

Guideline 5. Psychologists aspire to recognize and understand historical and contemporary experiences with power, privilege, and oppression. As such, they seek to address institutional barriers and related inequities, disproportionalities, and disparities of law enforcement, administration of clinical justice, educational, mental health, and other systems as they seek to promote justice, human rights, and access to quality and equitable mental and behavioral health services.

Guideline 6. Psychologists seek to promote culturally adaptive interventions and advocacy within and across systems, including prevention, early intervention, and recovery (see Figure 2.3).

FIGURE 2.3. Level 3: Institutional Impact on Engagement

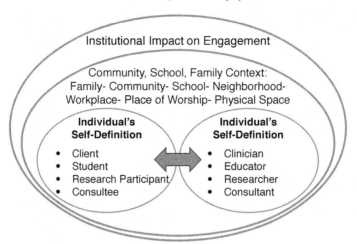

The third level of the model explores the range of contextual factors that support or impede our connections with institutions. Its importance has been particularly evident in the immediate time period we are living through, the COVID-19 pandemic as it has played out across the United States, individual states, and internationally. Additionally, the engagement with a need for greater change regarding the civil rights of persons of color, specifically those representing the Black and Brown communities, has been a significant reminder of the interdependencies on institutional structures and their considerations for our daily lives as we have moved from the death of George Floyd in Minnesota through the initial criminal trial that was held addressing his wrongful death by local police officers (Buchanan et al., 2020; McLaughlin, 2020). Our capacity to think ecologically as multicultural psychologists fosters a process whereby we move from seeing all challenge through a lens of individual choices, such as why there has been a greater degree of reluctance for some Black community members to obtain the COVID-19 vaccinations, to recognizing the history of systemic racism and aggression that Black persons in the United States have experienced related to medical care and treatment (e.g., the Tuskegee experiment and its impact on the lives of Black men in that study, and the forced sterilizations that a significant number of Black women in the United States were subjected to historically). Level 3's focus on the institutional impact directs our gaze from solely individual considerations to ones that are broader in their influence: specifically, how laws, policies, and social contracts (e.g., White supremacism) are a means for restricting individuals' options, or in the case of earlier civil rights legislation, built forward to facilitate stronger opportunities and greater resilience within and across communities.

As we consider our research case, we begin to think about how some of the challenges that were discussed by the parents in the focus group meetings with the team are impacted at an institutional level as much as at the local community level. Parents in particular who described challenges regarding reports to DCFS by either medical providers or their child's teachers were not only struggling with the implications of the decisions made by these individuals regarding concerns about neglect or abuse but also were attempting to make sense at an institutional level with the reality of how laws concerning parenting and discipline are structured and set in place. The majority of states in the United States require that persons such as physicians, counselors, and teachers make a report to the state's case management organization in charge of child safety and family service needs when abuse or neglect is suspected. When a clinician or teacher encounters information or makes an observation (for example) on the basis of an observable bruise that a belt was used for discipline, they are required by law to make a report; it is then up to the caseworkers with DCFS or a similar organization to then determine whether the report is warranted and to then investigate. In some families immigrating from a very different social environment from that of the present-day United States, such a disciplinary action might occur and lead to the report. The family then confronts a set of considerations that are quite different from those in their social and cultural background, and their impact can be quite disruptive. Embarrassment, anger, shame, and frustration are some of the emotions shared with the research team by the parents who had experienced reports to DCFS; the researchers were able, from these discussions with the parents, to parse more directly the transactional impact of these experiences, with regard to concerns about the need to better understand laws that affect parenting and discipline and how to better work between the systems that make the reports, those responding to them, and the families themselves within the community, to reduce challenges around expectations and communication.

By utilizing an ecological approach that explicitly considers the institutions that direct and guide opportunity and choice at a metastructural level, psychologists can more effectively engage with the individuals, groups, and communities they work with to gain a better understand of their areas of vulnerability, as well as their strengths, in tandem with broader social expectations. This then leads us to the next level, where domestic and international considerations come into play.

Level 4: Domestic and International Climate

The fourth level of our model takes into account the broader domestic and international climate that serves as the *macrosystem* that addresses societal considerations impacting our communities and our lives. Within this level, psychologists think about systems of oppression and privilege specifically, and more broadly, about the concepts of human rights and social justice. Our considerations bidirectionally are the influences that serve to foster or suppress human rights for members of an array of communities throughout the world. As with each of the earlier levels, the fourth level encompasses and transacts with Levels 1 through 3, as illustrated in Figure 2.4. Guidelines 7 and 8 correspond with Level 4:

> **Guideline 7.** Psychologists endeavor to examine the profession's assumptions and practices within an international context, whether domestically or internationally based, and consider how this globalization has an impact on the psychologist's self-definition, purpose, role, and function.

> **Guideline 8.** Psychologists seek awareness and understanding of how developmental stage and life transitions intersect with the larger biosociocultural context, how identity evolves as a function of such intersections, and how these different socialization and maturation experiences influence worldview and identity.

In daily life, the macrosystem may act as a distal influence for many individuals, although its influence is increasingly felt when we consider the

FIGURE 2.4. Level 4: Domestic and International Climate

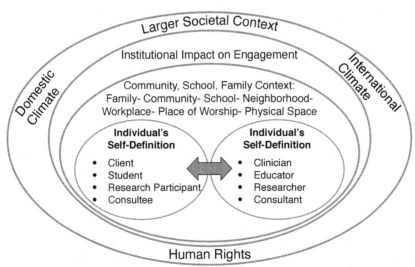

broader impact of economic, transnational, and sociocultural factors that more readily engage our attention on an everyday basis. This system encompasses the mores, scripts, and beliefs that societies hold, and it addresses how we as communities with different social and cultural values interrelate within a now truly global context. Anyone who spends time considering the wealth of information shared through social media and news outlets will regularly confront the transactional considerations that are at play across many of the systems we engage.

Thinking about this specific level in relationship to our research case, we find ourselves directly considering the implications of immigration and the resulting integration of lives that is required in the new home society. Concerns are immediately raised as to how, at the societal level, systems are in place to facilitate and support immigrants and their families, and how they are supported in becoming accommodated to different cultural expectations that exist regarding parenting choices, vocational expectations, academic opportunities, and health care. As you recall, because this study in particular is focused on multigenerational families within the two Latinx communities, the researchers were particularly interested in how to take into account the intersectional considerations that existed across multiple levels of identification for their research participants. This interest included making sense of their attachments to and relationships with their home of origin, and how those factors influence the range of choices they continue to make, even as a family becomes more deeply integrated into their U.S. community with its own cultural values and expectations.

Notably, at this level, we also consider the variations in culture and societal structure in individuals' places of origin. As ecologically minded psychologists, we pay attention to the fact that there are a great variety of differences between and within cultures, given place of origin and time of transition to another setting. Generational differences exist as well, such that we may find that younger members of a community identify themselves and their relationship with their home and background from a different perspective than do older members. Within the United States, discussions have been taking place regularly around generational responses to our political system and demands for its capacity to confront and then repair colonialist, unjust decisions and actions taken in the past. What were once accepted histories are being revised, although there are differing voices from within communities of color concerning how to best seek and then press for consideration of these revisions, and what should happen in response (e.g., progressive vs. traditionalist Democratic Black voting communities). These considerations and their range of implications have a significant impact on the levels below this one; choices made at the individual level are deeply influenced by the awareness of psychologists' global presence and engagement.

Level 5: Outcomes

Our fifth layer of the model is the encompassing layer: Through its emphasis on outcomes, it surrounds and influences the four preceding layers. Within American psychology, this is an active area of emphasis now, as there exists within the profession a strong focus on outcomes-based considerations and evidence for the effectiveness of therapy. Admittedly stemming from a Western values orientation, the emphasis on outcomes is also one drawn from a desire to guide opportunity and choice for members of society and the organizations that structure it, the entities that engage our professional services. However, as applied to the model, we take a different approach to considering outcomes and instead refer to them as the potential processes that unfold and emerge from the layers of the model. These are the products of bidirectional influence, and they may be positive, negative, or neutral in their effect. Thinking ecologically, outcomes are the potential responses, reactions, and sources of knowledge, change, and impact that derive from the array of interactions that take place across the model's levels of influence and transaction. Figure 2.5 illustrates Level 5, and Guidelines 9 and 10 are its representation:

> **Guideline 9.** Psychologists strive to conduct culturally appropriate and informed research, teaching, supervision, consultation, assessment, interpretation, diagnosis, dissemination, and evaluation of efficacy as they address the first four levels of the *Layered Ecological Model of the Multicultural Guidelines.*
>
> **Guideline 10.** Psychologists actively strive to take a strength-based approach when working with individuals, families, groups, communities, and organizations that seeks to build resilience and decrease trauma within the sociocultural context.

The range of outcomes possible through psychological professional practice are directly influenced by the interactions, transactions, and experiences in which psychologists and their clients, students, consultees, and research participants engage, across the levels discussed previously. It is important for us as psychologists to readily consider these transactions across the ecological model's layers, to inform how we understand the possible results that emerge for the individuals, communities, organizations, systems, and structures we work with. More directly, it is our task to make sense of which levels of the model directly or indirectly contribute to, influence, and inhibit desired outcomes, as we guide, support, and effect change and choice.

40 • *Foundations of Multicultural Practice*

FIGURE 2.5. Level 5: Outcomes

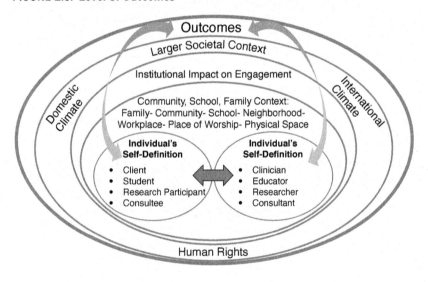

The task of psychology researchers, and of the community based mental health clinician, is ultimately a shared one: to consider how the information that is learned through our professional efforts informs our understanding of the developmental, acculturational, experiential, and decisional actions that are taken or are unable to move forward. Through examining the bidirectional interactions and transactional responses that take place, both in the explorations of concern for the research work being done and when working individually in treatment, the psychologists involved have the opportunity to identify the necessary and pertinent factors, and their interactions themselves, that influence and guide how new opportunities may unfold or how interventions can contribute to a more positive change.

TEMPORAL FACTORS: THE CHRONOSYSTEM

As psychologists, we recognize that all systems are influenced by time—its passage and its accumulated experience. As such, we acknowledge that in our efforts, our construction of an ecological map of the individual, their community, and the systems that influence that community, at both the micro and macro levels, is solely a representation of one moment (or perhaps an accumulated series of moments) in time. Notably, the chronosystem can be considered within the research case we have discussed as a description of the current, past, and potential identification of pertinent contexts; those that have and continue to exert influence, those that are reflective of current demands and how they are met, and finally the range of potential responses that are possible across the levels of interaction that define the complex communities involved in the study. Assessment over time can allow a reconsideration of what has been learned, based on examination and evaluation of the hypotheses that are generated as individuals and collective groups share their specific experiences of choice and response in the past and present.

THE THREE DYNAMIC PROCESSES: POWER/PRIVILEGE, TENSIONS, AND FLUIDITY

When constructing the layered ecological model, the authors were particularly invested in considering the processes that contribute to the experience of trauma for individuals, communities, societies, and cultures and how trauma can be addressed to best engage resilience (APA, 2017c). They identified three dynamic processes that influence the breadth of the model. In Figure 2.6, these processes are located on the dotted line and create a circle, essentially another

FIGURE 2.6. Ecological Model of the Multicultural Guidelines

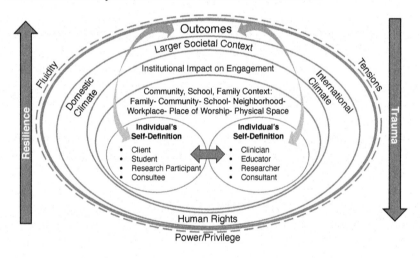

layer, around Levels 1 through 5; this demonstrates their influence across and within the whole model. We include these processes because of their impact on the bidirectional relationship and surrounding ecological levels (APA, 2017c; Clauss-Ehlers et al., 2019).

The first dynamic process, *power/privilege*, represents a continuum of power and privilege that is experienced by participants engaged in psychological efforts, whether as participants in research, students in courses and within supervision, clients participating in treatment or counseling, or consultees in organizations working to effect change. It is further experienced directly by psychologists themselves, in their professional efforts with others. Psychologists strive to attend to the range of social and professional power and privilege they hold within these bidirectional relationships with their clients, students, research participants, and consultees. They consider how those working with them experience them as "experts" and what influence that has for the engagement and transactions that occur within their collaborative work. The bidirectional emphasis of the model encourages psychologists to engage in cultural humility, while also considering the necessary challenges that define a need for structural humility (i.e., "the capacity of health care professionals to appreciate that their role is not to surmount oppressive structures but rather to understand knowledge and practice gaps vis-à-vis structures, partner with other stakeholders to fill these gaps, and engage in self-reflection throughout these processes"; Downey & Gomez, 2018, p. 217) in response to the organizations and institutions they represent (Metzl & Hansen, 2014). Psychologists in the end recognize readily that our clients are in fact the experts of their own lives and experience; we use empathy and cultural humility in our efforts to share space and time with these clients (Clauss-Ehlers, Sood, & Weist, 2020; Garcia et al., 2017).

The second dynamic process involves the *tensions* that exist between and among Levels 1 to 5 of the model. Tensions may arise between and within concentric circles, as well as within the bidirectional relationships that occur at each level. As psychologists, it is important that we recognize these tensions and their dynamic and contextual nature. They may not result solely from issues occurring at one level of the model, but instead, can exist across multiple sources of intersection and interaction between and within the levels. Through our professional efforts with our clients, students, mentees, research participants, and consultees, we are in a position to identify and engage tensions across the levels. This engagement fosters a more efficacious and dynamic process within our own work; it allows for the consideration of depth and breadth in the range of influences that occur, as opposed to situating at the surface.

TRAUMA AND RESILIENCE

A related process outcome is the idea of increasing resilience and decreasing trauma. Very well addressed throughout the psychological literature, *resilience* can be defined as a "process, capacity, or outcome of successful adaptation despite challenges or threatening circumstances . . . [the achievement] of good outcomes despite high risk status, sustained competence under threat, and recovery from trauma" (Masten et al., 1990, p. 426). This is illustrated in Figure 2.6, where there is an upward-facing arrow labeled *resilience* on the far left and a downward-facing arrow labeled *trauma* on the far right.

As applied to the layered ecological model of the *Multicultural Guidelines*, it is important to consider the role of contextual level factors and how they intersect with individual level factors, to contribute to both resilience and potential trauma. Resilience is often described as the ability to overcome hardship. At a basic level, this approach concerns an individual's ability to meet and overcome challenges. For the book's purpose, and in keeping with the *Multicultural Guidelines*, resilience is viewed in a cultural context. Cultural resilience considers how larger sociocultural factors surrounding the individual can support proactive responses to adversity. In this way, resilience is viewed as the intersection between individual traits and the ecological context (Clauss-Ehlers & Wibrowski, 2007). In tandem, while trauma is global in its experience, and it is identified as a vulnerability for a significant portion of the world's populations, our role as psychologists is to understand and address the contexts that contribute to trauma, with the goal of achieving, through trauma-informed responses and interventions, a broader capacity for resolution within the community that supports our clients, consultees, students, and research participants (Clauss-Ehlers, Sood, & Weist, 2020).

As we return to both of the case examples discussed at the beginning of the chapter, the goal of resilience as the model for the clinical work undertaken with Alicia and the research being conducted by Drs. Roberto and Claudia and their team is drawn directly from the consideration of these overarching influences across the layered ecological model. By thinking through the experiences of challenge, their potential for traumatic impact, and how they are resolved through the micro to macro, to the chronosystem interactions that envelope the lives of the participants in psychological practices, we come to see that this model provides a strong foundation for engaging effective strategies for intervention and collaboration, a foundation that is multicultural in its orientation and elaboration, and ecological at its core.

CONCLUSION

This discussion and application of the layered ecological model lays the groundwork for the subsequent chapters. Each chapter that follows focuses on a specific Multicultural Guideline, starting with Guideline 1 in Chapter 3. As you read, we encourage you to refer back to Figures 2.1 to 2.6, to visualize how the model fits with the guidelines and fosters a stronger conceptualization of the intersecting considerations that serve as a foundation for the guidelines overall. Case presentations aim to make the applicability of the guidelines come alive for our readers. Discussion questions are designed to encourage critical feedback and conversation about the complex topics raised in the pages that follow.

PART II: A BIDIRECTIONAL MODEL OF SELF-DEFINITION AND RELATIONSHIPS

3
RECOGNIZING THE FLUIDITY AND COMPLEXITY OF SELF-IDENTITY AND SOCIAL DYNAMICS
Multicultural Guideline 1

Guideline 1. Psychologists seek to recognize and understand that identity and self-definition are fluid and complex and that the interaction between the two is dynamic. To this end, psychologists appreciate that intersectionality is shaped by the multiplicity of the individual's social contexts.

Multicultural Guideline 1 is the first guideline in Level 1 of the ecological model presented in *Multicultural Guidelines: An Ecological Approach to Context, Identity, and Intersectionality* (hereinafter referred to as *2017 Multicultural Guidelines*; American Psychological Association [APA], 2017a). Level 1 guidelines emphasize a bidirectional model of self-definition and relationships. Multicultural Guideline 1 recognizes that a person's identity formation and how a person identifies with regard to sociocultural location are fluid and complex. Identity formation is a lifelong process that takes shape through developmental shifts and milestones (e.g., biological, psychological, social, cultural) and through interpersonal interactions within various contexts. Multicultural Guideline 1 further calls for psychologists to deepen understandings of the intersectional experiences and identities of individuals and how identity is influenced by a sense of connection and disconnection in

---

https://doi.org/10.1037/0000348-003
Applying Multiculturalism: An Ecological Approach to the APA Guidelines, by C. S. Clauss-Ehlers, S. J. Hunter, G. S. Morse, and P. Tummala-Narra
Copyright © 2024 by the American Psychological Association. All rights reserved.

different contexts, such as families; ethnic, racial, and religious communities; peers; friends; schools; workplaces; and social media. Importantly, attending to intersectionality implicates an analysis of power, privilege, marginalization, and oppression accompanying specific sociocultural locations.

Theories of identity development in psychology are largely based on European American cultural values, and, therefore, it is important to recognize potential bias that shapes clinical practice and empirical inquiry into one's psychological development, including identity formation (Hays, 2016; Tummala-Narra, 2016). Sociocultural assumptions and stereotypes influence theory, clinical practice, training, research, and consultation. Stereotypes and distorted perceptions can also be internalized by individuals and communities and thus contribute to challenges to identity formation and to psychological distress. Avoiding overgeneralizations or simplistic categories of various groups and communities is critical to developing more nuanced, sophisticated understandings of psychological experience, identity formation, and mental health.

Multicultural Guideline 1 emphasizes the heterogeneity of experience among individuals in any particular sociocultural group. Whereas sociocultural groups have shared experiences, such as those reflecting culture, migration history, religion, language, and discrimination, individuals have unique relationships with and experiences of their sociocultural contexts. As such, individual and group identities develop through the influence of multiple interacting individual, interpersonal, and social factors. Listening to individual narratives of sociocultural context and modifying existing theoretical paradigms in clinical practice, training, research, and consultation accordingly is an important step in recognizing identity as self-defined (Seeley, 2005; Tummala-Narra, 2016).

CASE ILLUSTRATION–CYNTHIA: A VIETNAMESE AMERICAN WOMAN COPING WITH TRAUMA AND ANTI-ASIAN RACISM

Cynthia[1] is a 45-year-old Vietnamese American cisgender woman who was referred to me (Usha) after experiencing depressed mood for more than 3 years. Cynthia had trouble concentrating at work for several months, and after her friend suggested that she see a therapist, she reached out to me. Cynthia's husband, Ron, has been supportive of her seeking help. Upon first meeting me, Cynthia stated that she no longer found her work interesting

---

[1]In the case illustration, all appropriate steps have been taken to disguise the identities of the individuals discussed.

and that she "was going nowhere" in her company. She had never before met with a therapist and was unsure about how therapy might help her with her depressed mood and feelings of hopelessness. She also reported feeling guilty for having these feelings, as she did not want to burden her husband or her friends, and she did not want to be ungrateful for having a job when so many people had lost their jobs during the COVID-19 pandemic.

Cynthia's parents settled in the United States in the aftermath of the Vietnam War, and she was born in an urban area in the United States. She is the oldest of four children, and she feels close to all her siblings. Her father passed away when she was 16 years old, after which she carried the responsibility of taking care of her younger siblings, as her mother worked very long hours and struggled to provide for the family's needs. Cynthia's mother passed away about 5 years prior to our initial meeting. Cynthia worked to fulfill her parents' dream of finding safety and security in the United States. She worked hard in school and "stayed out of trouble," mostly by avoiding socializing with peers who "didn't take school seriously" or used substances. She and her siblings were very aware of the trauma and hardships that her parents had endured in Vietnam and in the United States. For example, her father had witnessed the murder of his cousin during the war. After arriving in the United States, Cynthia's parents had difficulty finding steady work; eventually, her father found work as a cook in a restaurant and her mother cleaned houses and worked in a grocery store. Her parents coped with limited financial resources as well as linguistic and cultural barriers while adjusting to life in the United States. They had little time or space to grieve their separation from loved ones in Vietnam. Although her parents did not reveal many details of their own hardship, Cynthia was aware of her parents' stress, as her family faced food insecurity and racial discrimination when people yelled racial slurs at them and told them repeatedly to "go back to your country."

Cynthia attended a local community college, transferred to a 4-year university, and completed her bachelor's degree. While attending a predominantly White university, she often felt as though she were on the outside looking into a world of economic and racial privilege with unfamiliar cultural norms and expectations. She recalled in one of the sessions, "I didn't really know how to talk to White people. I was mainly interacting with other Vietnamese kids my whole life, and here I didn't know what to say to White kids." At the same time, Cynthia felt alienated among other Asian Americans on her campus, as many of these students had more economic resources than she did. She spoke about the impact of stereotypes about Asian Americans on her adjustment to college: "I don't really feel like I'm some model minority.

I grew up poor, and I don't feel like some other Asians, but I know how important education was for my family. We just worked hard, but this stereotype makes it seem like every Asian is just born smart or something." Cynthia struggled in college to find friendships where she felt that she could be her whole self.

Cynthia also worked part-time throughout college and helped to support her family financially until her youngest sibling graduated high school. She has been successful in her career, and she met her husband, Ron, who is Filipino American, at a previous workplace. She and Ron have been married for 10 years, and she described him as kind and supportive. While Cynthia has felt proud of her ability to take care of her family, she shared in therapy that she has felt exhausted in recent years, particularly since her mother passed away. She remains close to her siblings but feels depleted by their challenges with securing work and positive relationships. At work, she feels as though she is taken for granted by her colleagues and that she has to work much harder than they do to be recognized or valued. Additionally, although she felt connected to her Vietnamese culture and language earlier in her life, losing her mother made it increasingly difficult for Cynthia to connect with her Vietnamese heritage. Over the past several years, she has felt disconnected from her family and friends.

She has also felt more anxious about her safety and that of her family after the election of Donald Trump and the onset of the COVID-19 pandemic, due to growing violence against and harassment of Asian Americans. In fact, she reported a recent incident in which a person in a grocery store pointed to her and said, "It's your people. You did this. You brought the virus. It's your fault!" Cynthia shared with me, "I was stunned. I felt like my heart was breaking. What would my parents think if they saw how cruel people in America are?"

Cynthia's traumatic stress related to racism was compounded by the loss of her parents and the cumulative effects of financial strain and caring for her family. In psychotherapy, although she spoke about these traumas and losses, she worried about my reaction to her sharing negative feelings about her family and her workplace. She worried that an Indian American therapist might view her as not being grateful or betraying her family if she spoke about her negative feelings about relatives, her Vietnamese heritage, or American society. She commented, "I don't want to sound ungrateful." In these moments, I responded, "I am wondering if you think that I may be evaluating you somehow, and if talking to another Asian American person is bringing up these feelings for you." She replied by letting me know that it felt difficult to confide in anyone and that she sometimes felt negatively judged by other Asian Americans. She also expressed that she rarely felt like her whole self in any single context (i.e., Vietnamese American, Asian American, or mainstream American).

In psychotherapy, Cynthia and I focused on working through her grief and traumatic stress and explored how she might begin to take risks in more freely expressing her feelings about various aspects of her identity. Engaging in this exploration entailed my willingness to share with her my own limited knowledge about her Vietnamese experience, even though I could relate to the experience of being a racial minority and an Asian American woman. Gradually, Cynthia began to reveal how she really felt about various aspects of her identity and how her Vietnamese identity had transformed over the course of her life in the context of her relationships with family, friends, and husband and her experiences in school and work. Her family's traumatic displacement from Vietnam and experiences with poverty and racism together shaped her identity as a Vietnamese American woman. In our work together, Cynthia started to engage in a more honest dialogue about her experiences of racism without feeling as though she had to qualify her expressions of distress and grief by having to "feel grateful." She also started to discuss her experience of racism in her workplace, which was a major barrier to expanding her career goals and to being valued by her colleagues, and how racism affected her identity and well-being throughout her life.

Discussion Questions Related to Cynthia

1. What were your reactions in reading Cynthia's story? Did aspects of her experience resonate with you?
2. How do you imagine that Cynthia's parents' experiences as refugees influenced Cynthia's identity development?
3. How do you think that Cynthia's experiences of racism have shaped her identity?
4. In what ways has Cynthia's identity shifted over time?
5. How do you understand Cynthia's connection to her Vietnamese identity and feelings of difference from other Asian Americans?
6. How do you understand Cynthia's identity formation from an intersectional perspective?

LITERATURE REVIEW

Identity has been thought to reflect an experience of *subjective self-sameness* (Erikson, 1950; Mann, 2006) that is formed over context and time. It has been noted that identity is influenced by individual, interpersonal, social, and structural factors. One's identity is shaped by age, generation, gender, ethnicity, race, religion, spirituality, language, sexual orientation, social class, disability status, national origin, immigration status, and experiences of privilege and marginalization (APA, 2017a; Crenshaw, 1989; Hays, 2016). Group identity and social identity encompass a person's affiliation with and connection to a sociocultural group, such as a racial or ethnic group or community (Helms & Cook, 1999; Phinney, 1996). Individual identity and group identity vary significantly across people who identify with one or more sociocultural groups and can shift over the course of a lifetime (Hays, 2016; Tummala-Narra, 2016).

Identity transforms across generations as well, in that various interpersonal contexts and sociopolitical conditions affect the ways in which identity is experienced and expressed (APA, 2017a). For example, the coming-out process for a gay adolescent boy may be affirming within a family context and a sociopolitical context that are supportive of him, and, therefore, he can secure safety and a sense of belonging. However, this process can be traumatic for an older adult gay man who, while growing up, was prohibited from talking about sexuality or his sexual orientation with his family and peers who had homophobic attitudes and who currently lives in a sociopolitical context in which the safety of LGBTQ+ people is continually threatened. As such, social attitudes toward sexual orientation and other aspects of identity and social location have important implications for how individual and group identities are formed (Belkin & White, 2020; Drescher, 2009).

Relatedly, identity for people with minority status (e.g., racial, religious, and sexual minorities; LGBTQ+ people; economically marginalized people; undocumented immigrants; people with disabilities) develops within the parameters of social oppression (Tummala-Narra, 2016). Exposure to violence, harassment, discrimination, and bias, particularly from early childhood onward, influences identity development and the freedom to explore who one truly is. Stereotypes and the internalization of stereotypes illustrate the role of social oppression on identity development. For instance, as noted in Cynthia's case, the model minority stereotype, as applied to Asian Americans, is a positive stereotype. At its root is the assumption that all Asians and Asian Americans are innately intelligent, academically successful, and economically privileged (Peterson, 1966). Importantly, these perceptions coexist alongside stereotypes of Asians as carrying a virus, exotic, unattractive, and socially awkward. Nevertheless, all these stereotypes can be internalized by first, second, and later generations of Asian Americans through widespread messages in mainstream U.S. context (e.g., schools, workplaces, neighborhoods, media, social media).

Ample evidence suggests that the internalization of these stereotypes has detrimental effects on mental health (e.g., depression, suicidal ideation, anxiety, body image) and identity formation among Asian Americans (Kiang et al., 2016; Tummala-Narra et al., 2018; Yoo et al., 2010). Furthermore, as in the case of Cynthia, assumptions about the homogeneity of Asian Americans contribute to a masking of challenges and barriers faced by Asian Americans. The model minority stereotype, for example, minimizes and dismisses the mental health distress; social, economic, and cultural barriers; and racism faced by Asian Americans (P. Y. Kim & Lee, 2014; Yoo et al., 2010). This stereotype further perpetuates social divisions among racial minorities by inaccurately differentiating Asian Americans from other racial minority groups in the United States and thus contributing to structural inequities and racism directed toward all racial minority groups (Peterson, 1966). As such, it is important to consider that stereotyping and discrimination have multiple layers of impact on identity, including intrapsychic experience, interpersonal relations, and social attitudes.

Stereotyping can further impede the ability to define one's own identity (Nadal et al., 2015). For example, a Black/White multiracial person may have close emotional connections with both sides of a family and yet be perceived by others as Black or African American due to phenotype (e.g., darker skin tone, hair texture). Racialized perceptions of others can become internalized and can diminish a person's ability to develop identity on one's own terms. The internalization of stereotypes can also contribute to how one approaches interactions with people from different sociocultural groups. For instance, people with physical disabilities may be perceived by others as less able to care for themselves than how they experience themselves internally and therefore may be treated by others as though they are less able to engage productively at school or work (Olkin et al., 2019). Such false perceptions contribute to reductionistic views of human beings and ignore the complexity of psychological experience and identity. Additionally, language that is used to describe one's identity can be critical to developing identity in the context of freedom and choice. For instance, using gender pronouns that accurately reflect a person's internal experience facilitates affirmation of identity and self-definition (APA, 2015b).

Multicultural Guideline 1 suggests that we expand our understanding of intersectionality as a central aspect of identity development. In her seminal work, Crenshaw (1989) proposed a framework of intersectionality as way of recognizing Black women's simultaneous struggles with racism and sexism and how these separate but intertwined forms of discrimination produce injustice and systemic barriers for Black women. It is important to note that identity reflects experiences of various social locations that are shaped by structural power (Cho et al., 2013). Intersectionality theory (Crenshaw, 1989) proposes that "social identities are mutually constitutive" and that "marginalization experienced at the individual, interpersonal, and structural levels are inseparable" (Shin et al., 2017, p. 458). Shin and colleagues (2017) underscored that an intersectional lens allows examination of not only multiple identities but also the structural inequalities that shape "complex relationships between privileged and marginalized social identities" (p. 459). Relatedly, Cole (2020) stated, "Rather than being primarily a descriptor of multiple identities, intersectionality is an analytic framework exquisitely suited for evaluation of adequacy of social policies to meet the needs of multiply marginalized populations" (p. 1039). She further pointed out that an intersectional lens moved beyond the United States and has been used to explore the effects of issues such as religion and caste in India and the impact of colonialism in health care disparities in Australia.

Moradi and Grzanka (2017) developed guidelines for implementing intersectionality responsibly within psychology, including challenging the notion that intersectionality is relevant only to some people or groups. Specifically, they questioned implicit prototypes in multicultural scholarship, such as heterosexual cisgender men of color as an implicit reference group in research on racism and White cisgender gay men as an implicit reference group in research on sexual orientation. They argued that intersectionality research has largely focused on particular areas such as gender/sexism, race/racism, and sexual orientation/heterosexism, ignoring areas such as disability status/ableism, class/classism, transgender identities/cisgenderism, and nationality/xenophobia. The lack of attention to these latter areas is evident, for example, in the scarcity of research exploring the experience of microaggressions against people with disabilities (Olkin et al., 2019). Additionally, Moradi and Grzanka (2017) warned against intersectionality becoming synonymous with multiple minority statuses and highlighted that all people's experiences are shaped by social locations and systems of power. Their important review indicates the critical need to better understand how privilege and marginalization shape one's identity and, more broadly, one's social position in relation to the broader world.

An intersectional lens, as underscored in Multicultural Guideline 1, includes an examination of multiple marginalization rooted in systemic inequality (Crenshaw, 1989; Greene, 2010). For instance, the experience of being marginalized or traumatized within one's own religious community as well as outside of this community can have a profound impact on one's sense of belonging and identity (Tummala-Narra, 2021). A man who is a racial minority and who is sexually abused by an elder in a religious community may be unable to secure safe spaces to talk about his abuse both within his community and with others outside of his community who may stereotype him or his racial group. The ability to access appropriate support across different contexts in these circumstances may be impossible, even though it is critical to a person's safety and health. Nevertheless, securing safe connections in these situations is critical to identity development.

Olkin and colleagues (2019) highlighted the idea that women with disabilities carry at least two identities that are stigmatized or oppressed and that "being an atypical member of two stigmatized groups reduces one's ability to identify with either group fully and can make full acceptance by either group challenging" (p. 758). Identity formation in this example involves both consciously and unconsciously observing whether and how people in each context either provide a sense of inclusion and belonging or dismiss and minimize one's experiences (Tummala-Narra, 2021). Although people who have two or more minority positions navigate different contexts in ways that reflect their resilience, they often do so at a cost to their authentic selves. In other words, psychological shifting across contexts to meet the demands and expectations of others can be emotionally taxing and may contribute to a lack of integration and continuity in the sense of self and identity (Yi, 2014).

It is also important to note that sociopolitical conditions can exacerbate the psychological toll of multiple marginalization. A recent study (Albright & Hurd, 2020) indicated that college students with targeted marginalized identities (i.e., Black/African American/Black American, Latinx, woman, LGBTQ+, Muslim) reported greater emotional distress related to the Trump presidency than nontargeted students reported. Trump's racist, misogynistic, homophobic, and transphobic rhetoric contributed to significant distress for students with a single marginalized identity and even greater distress for students with two or more targeted marginalized identities. Together, scholarship concerning multiple marginalization suggests that exploring identity should involve attention to both the complexity of sociocultural and sociopolitical experiences and the psychological impact of these experiences (Belkin & White, 2020; Ruth, 2012).

APPLYING MULTICULTURAL GUIDELINE 1 TO CLINICAL PRACTICE

Cynthia's experience underscores the importance of exploring complex and sometimes contradictory cultural identifications and a therapists' willingness to engage with painful affective experiences associated with different aspects of the client's identity and social locations. It is critical for practitioners to attune to the client's self-definition of identity and the ways in which identity and identity labels may change over time, context, and developmental transitions (APA, 2017a). For example, a recent study with transgender adults, gender-diverse adults, and adults with transgender histories indicated that many participants experienced a lack of respect for their identities when they were misgendered in psychotherapy and when their therapists either minimized the significance of gender identity or overemphasized gender identity by assuming that it was the source of their distress and ignored their presenting concerns (Morris et al., 2020).

In the clinical intake process, the client's identity should not be based on assumptions made by the therapist. Therapists often assume racial identity of clients based on perceived phenotypes. For instance, a therapist might assume that a new client is African American based on the client's skin color and hair texture, when in fact the client identifies as Haitian American. This type of mislabeling can retraumatize clients who routinely experience an erasure of their identities. Therefore, it is critical that therapists inquire about how clients define various aspects of their own identities.

Research and clinical scholarship indicate that therapists of all backgrounds can find it challenging to engage with different aspects of a client's identity. For instance, Kivlighan and colleagues (2019) found that therapists' racial–ethnic competence varied as a function of the client's gender, suggesting that intersectionality of clients' gender and race required close attention in the therapeutic relationship. Their findings call attention to the impact of gendered racism in clients' lives, which can be overlooked by a therapist who focuses solely or primarily on race and racism. They further noted that "seeking cultural opportunities with openness and curiosity may prove helpful in order to facilitate discussions of the impact of multiple intersecting systems of oppression" (Kivlighan et al., 2019, p. 127; see also Owen et al., 2016). Therapists can initiate discussions about social inequities and oppression with their clients and explore the ways in which these factors interact with personal histories and circumstances (Adames et al., 2018; Tummala-Narra, 2016). An intersectional framework can further help to depathologize clients' distress that is rooted in structural oppression (Adames et al., 2018).

A therapist's attunement to the complexity of the client's identity requires a willingness to bear the unknown and refrain from drawing conclusions regarding the client's full range of experiences based on any single aspect of identity (Belkin & White, 2020). It also requires awareness of the problem of "intersectional invisibility" (Olkin et al., 2019, p. 758; see also Purdie-Vaughns & Eibach, 2008): Individuals with multiple marginalized social identities face challenges in that they may not be fully seen or accepted within any particular sociocultural group or community. For example, Cynthia's experience of racism contributed to challenges in being accepted in predominantly White contexts, and her experiences growing up in poverty were largely invisible to others who perceived her as a model minority. When therapists focus on only one aspect of a client's identity, they not only formulate a client's concerns with an incomplete understanding of the client's identity but also risk further marginalizing critical experiences of the client (Greene, 2010). In therapeutic work with Cynthia, it was important that I, as her therapist, inquired about and explored Cynthia's experiences of racism and social class throughout the course of her life, as these experiences continued to shape her identity, sense of belonging, emotional stress, and relational life.

Stereotypes and assumptions about different sociocultural groups can play important roles in the ways in which therapists listen to their clients' identities and respond to and work through microaggressions and impasses in psychotherapy (Baumann et al., 2020; Mazzula & Nadal, 2015; Owen et al., 2014; Spengler et al., 2016). The influence of stereotypes is evident in transference and countertransference dynamics that are embedded in the client's and the therapist's sociocultural identities and social locations (Comas-Díaz, 2012; Tummala-Narra, 2016). For example, a client who is a racial minority may assume that a therapist who is White may not be able to understand experiences of racism, even though the therapist may have endured religious discrimination. In other instances, a White therapist may assume that a multiracial client who "passes" as White does not consider race to be a significant issue, or a therapist who is a racial minority may assume that a client from a similar racial and cultural background has experiences identical to those of the therapist. These attitudes and behaviors can be based on stereotypes that contribute to reductionistic views of identity. Therefore, a therapist's ability to recognize a lack of knowledge or limitations in understanding a client's experience due to the therapist's own life experiences and perspectives can be critical to developing a sense of trust in the therapeutic relationship. For instance, as Cynthia's therapist, I took an approach of transparency when disclosing that I was limited in my knowledge of the experiences of Vietnamese Americans, although I shared an experience of being an Asian American woman and a racial minority.

Additionally, the therapist's choice of certain techniques in psychotherapy and other interventions should be guided by a consideration of social, political, and historical contexts. For instance, Baumann and colleagues (2020), in their exploration of therapist self-disclosure while working with clients who are sexual and gender minorities, aptly noted, "Self-disclosure and expression are particularly significant in work with a community for whom 'outness' and internalized stigma are complex realities" (p. 247). My disclosure about my own cultural background (i.e., Indian American) and about my limited knowledge concerning Vietnamese American experiences facilitated Cynthia's experience of me as an authentic person. This self-disclosure allowed for Cynthia to experience her therapist as someone willing to engage in discussions about sociocultural identity. Such disclosure indicated to Cynthia that the therapeutic space was one in which she could begin to share her own experiences of race, culture, gender, and social class, among other aspects of her identity and social location. This type of disclosure is especially important when considering that, most often, Cynthia felt that these experiences were invisible to others. As such, it is important to consider the contextual factors associated with a particular aspect of identity when formulating and implementing therapeutic techniques such as self-disclosure. Therapists should further consider collectivistic coping strategies, specifically the ways in which a client can secure support from others (e.g., family, friends, partners, clergy, consciousness-raising groups, affinity groups) who may contribute to positive identity development and well-being (Lewis et al., 2017; Yeh et al., 2006).

Psychotherapy can provide a space in which various aspects of the client's identity can be explored, particularly when therapists recognize and engage with the influence of their own identities and experiences of social oppression, marginalization, and privilege (Greene, 2010; Tummala-Narra, 2021). Such self-inquiry and self-examination can prepare therapists to listen and attune to their client's complex identities and to the role of intersectionality in identity development and structural barriers faced by clients. Identity work can entail the therapist's own personal transformation as they work with clients to discover and work through clients' conflicts and stress related to identity. Furthermore, as no single psychotherapy experience can address all aspects of a client's identity, it is critical for therapists to attend to what is most significant to the client (Adames et al., 2018; Ruth, 2012). For example, for some clients, it is important to explore stress or conflict related to social class background during a specific time in their lives, whereas for other clients, it may be more important to address a conflict related to religious or spiritual background. At different points in her work in therapy, Cynthia felt that talking about her social class background was more urgent that discussing her family's experiences of trauma and loss. It was important that I respect Cynthia's choice to explore a specific issue at any given moment, even while recognizing that each aspect of identity was intertwined with other aspects of identity and life experience.

Nevertheless, as Ruth (2012) noted, therapists can meet patients "with empathy, without judgmentalism, and with even hovering attention to the diverse aspects of their experience and identity" (p. 173). Additionally, as mentioned earlier, intersectionality and multiple intersecting identities are applicable not only to individuals with minority status; rather, they are inherent to identity development for all people. As such, culturally informed psychotherapy engages with intersectional identities and intersectionality as a core part of experience among both majority-and minority-status therapists and clients.

Finally, cultural humility is an essential aspect of approaching identity and intersectionality in psychotherapy and clinical interventions more broadly. *Cultural humility* refers to a "lifelong process of self-reflection, self-critique, continual assessment of power imbalances, and the development of mutually respectful relationships and partnerships" (Gallardo, 2014, p. 3) and to a process that is characterized by "openness, curiosity, lack of arrogance, and genuine desire to understand clients' cultural identities" (Owen et al., 2016, p. 31). Ample evidence now indicates that therapists' cultural humility is associated with a strong therapeutic alliance, improved attunement to power dynamics and sociocultural bias, and better psychotherapy outcomes due to more appropriate diagnosis and treatment planning (APA, 2017a; Owen et al., 2016). Recent scholarship also indicates that psychologists should explore how cultural humility is experienced by minority-status therapists who cope with ongoing sociocultural oppression such as racism, xenophobia, sexism, homophobia, and ableism (Moon & Sandage, 2019).

APPLYING MULTICULTURAL GUIDELINE 1 TO TEACHING AND TRAINING

Cynthia's experience raises questions regarding cultural competence in teaching and training in psychology. While graduate training in psychology includes a required course on diversity, the content and focus of these courses vary considerably. Furthermore, multicultural topics are addressed in different ways during clinical supervision and in the theoretical approaches of different clinical training sites. There is no standard approach to teaching and training in clinical practice or research with regard to issues of diversity and social justice. Multicultural Guideline 1 emphasizes that training programs expand their curricula to include diverse perspectives on human development, identity, mental health, and healing; take a strength-based approach that considers cultural and individual resilience and psychopathology; and provide opportunities for students, faculty, and supervisors to engage in ongoing learning with regard to the impact of sociocultural context on individuals, families, and communities.

Cynthia's experience highlights the need for additional training in specific areas such as immigration, refugee trauma, and the diverse experiences of racial and ethnic groups (e.g., Asian Americans), as well as training regarding intersectionality, such as that of race, gender, culture, and social class. Her experience also illustrates the need to integrate diversity and social justice, including the influence of social policies and sociopolitical conditions on identity and mental health, throughout psychology training curricula rather than locating these issues within a single course. Culturally competent practice and research that examines the complexity of identity should consider that identity is shaped by various aspects of development that are typically addressed in courses such as developmental psychology, psychopathology, neuropsychology, and social psychology, yet these courses are not often integrated with broader diversity curricula in training programs. This lack of integration can contribute to the marginalization of diversity and social justice in training and, consequently, can limit psychologists' abilities to effectively conceptualize and implement culturally informed practice, research, and consultation.

Multicultural Guideline 1 calls for increased attention to teaching and training in intersectionality. Research indicates that greater cognitive complexity allows for the ability to address multiple factors in practice (Anders et al., 2021). When students and faculty engage in regular discussions of multiple ecological factors that shape identity, including structural inequities, they can become more skilled in assessing how context influences one's identity. Ongoing dialogues about identity labels and language can help students and faculty become more familiar with the importance of self-definition of identity. It is important to note that faculty should initiate these dialogues, such that the responsibility of education concerning identity does not fall as a burden to students who identify with one or more sociocultural groups.

Clinical supervision, in parallel to psychotherapy, can reproduce stressful and traumatic dynamics related to identity and social location. Specifically, supervisors can dismiss race, culture, immigration, gender, sexual orientation, religion, social class, and disability status and other aspects of identity in conversations regarding clients' and supervisees' experiences. Both supervisees and supervisors may focus on topics that feel comfortable to them. The attempts to minimize differences or avoid certain aspects of identity can be rooted in feelings of shame or incompetence (Griffin et al., 2020; Tummala-Narra, 2004; Watkins et al., 2019). These dynamics can also occur in the classroom if instructors avoid or minimize the role of sociocultural context on identity formation, failing to recognize cultural bias in theories of development and psychopathology within psychology (Bhatia, 2019).

Graduate programs can benefit from faculty, supervisors, and students engaging in training on how to discuss issues of diversity and social justice in ways that respect multiple perspectives, backgrounds, and degrees of experience (D. E. Davis et al., 2016). Programs can include training on how to address microaggressions in clinical practice and within training institutions (e.g., graduate program, practicum, internship site). Although many programs train students about racial microaggressions, they tend not to provide education regarding other types of microaggressions, such as those against people with disabilities, transgender and nonbinary people, and people who identify as religious (Morris et al., 2020; Olkin et al., 2019). As a result, many students and faculty who are negatively affected by microaggressions disengage from dialogues concerning diversity and social justice. It is important that training programs develop structures that allow for discussion of cognitive, affective, and behavioral impacts of microaggressions and their implications for identity development (Owen et al., 2014).

It would also be beneficial to integrate literature on topics that may produce conflict in perspectives among students and faculty. For example, the topics of religion and spirituality and political ideologies, although relevant to identity formation for students, faculty, clients, and research participants, tend not to be addressed, as they may be perceived to lie outside the purview of scientific psychology. However, religious, spiritual, and political aspects of identity are critical to many people across the world and have important implications for one's sense of self and relationships with others. Developing self-awareness and integrating discussions of these areas in training programs would be important (Sandage et al., 2020; Solomonov & Barber, 2018).

APPLYING MULTICULTURAL GUIDELINE 1 TO RESEARCH

Multicultural Guideline 1 highlights the idea that researchers should engage in several practices to ensure that participants' experiences are accurately represented in empirical studies. In research, as in clinical practice, identity can be understood as complex and fluid. Research questions and methodologies can address the complex identities and intersectionality of participants. For example, research surveys can include space for participants to provide their own definitions of their identities, such as those associated with race, gender, religion, social class, sexual orientation, and disability, rather than requiring forced-choice responses regarding identity (APA, 2017a). It is also critical for researchers to move away from comparing sociocultural groups based on identity labels and instead explore similarities and differences in experiences across and within sociocultural groups. For instance, rather than analyze differences on depressive symptoms between White participants and Latinx participants (i.e., racial categories), a researcher might measure life experiences associated with depressive symptoms within and across these two groups (Helms et al., 2005). It would be more appropriate to measure acculturative stress experienced by White participants and Latinx participants because those experiences may account for differences in depressive symptoms. It is equally important to examine subgroup differences to avoid broad-based generalizations and stereotypes about sociocultural groups when interpreting research data.

Researchers can also conduct studies with participants who have multiple marginalized identities, such as transgender women of color. Multiple marginalization is especially important when considering that attuning to intersectionality allows researchers to recognize the ways in which theoretical models are influenced by social, economic, and political conditions and to develop new paradigms that include the experiences of largely understudied and less visible sociocultural groups (Cole, 2009; La Roche, 2021; Trimble, 2007). For example, research in psychology should examine the impact of the COVID-19 pandemic on federal, state, and local policies that affect access to resources, such as appropriate health care for marginalized communities. Furthermore, research should attend to the role of social positions and structural inequities that can influence identity formation (Bowleg & Bauer, 2016; Cole, 2009; McCormick-Huhn et al., 2019). Intersectionality researchers have underscored the importance of examining the ways in which social positions contribute to structural discrimination and that understanding the role of intersectionality in participants' lives is impossible when attention is not given to social inequality and privilege (Bowleg & Bauer, 2016).

Research cannot be effective in informing culturally informed practices if study samples include only participants who are easily accessed by researchers. My psychotherapy work with Cynthia illustrates how her experiences and those of her family members are less visible in psychology research, as few studies address sociocultural identity among second-generation Vietnamese American women. Indeed, research that explores the complex identities of individuals and communities is underrepresented in psychology research (Cole, 2020; Trimble, 2007).

Researchers should expand the range of methodologies used to understand identity and intersectionality. Scholars have noted that quantitative methodologies continue to dominate research in psychology and that the marginalization of other methodologies (e.g., qualitative, mixed-methods) poses challenges to intersectional research (Cole, 2009; Shin et al., 2017). Multicultural Guideline 1 encourages psychologists to use multiple methodologies to avoid "a false binary regarding qualitative and quantitative methods" (Shin et al., 2017, p. 467). Qualitative and mixed-methods approaches may be especially well suited for understanding identity and intersectionality (Bowleg & Bauer, 2016; Ponterotto et al., 2010). As Cole (2009) noted, reconceptualizing research paradigms to analyze intersectionality does not require new methods but rather requires a focus on "the meaning and consequences of social categories" (p. 176). As such, researchers should inquire as to which participants are included in a particular category, how inequality plays a role in participants' experiences and responses, and what similarities may occur across and within categories (Cole, 2009, 2020).

McCormick-Huhn and colleagues (2019) provided specific recommendations for researchers to engage in intersectional thinking, such as reporting why they are focused on a particular population instead of why they are including a representative sample, justifying choice of measures and considering which subgroups of people a measure may have been validated on, and naming values and limitations of their choices of sample. These recommendations aim to help researchers consider how and why participants at different intersections may be similar or different from each other. McCormick-Huhn et al. further recommended that these shifts in research methodologies be supported by journal practices and grant-making guidelines.

Research concerning identity must attend to critical reflexivity as related to researchers' own perspectives, experiences, and identities (Cole, 2020). For example, it is important to consider how the researcher's racial background and social class may influence the design and implementation of a study and the interpretation of the findings. The concept of reflexivity has typically been a focus in qualitative studies. *Reflexivity* refers to self-awareness and self-reflection that allow researchers to engage with personal biases, including sociocultural biases, throughout the research process, such that participants' experiences remain at the core of data analysis and interpretation (Morrow, 2005; Rennie, 2004). Although reflexivity is typically emphasized in qualitative research, Multicultural Guideline 1 encourages researchers using any design to carefully consider the impact of their own conceptualizations on their studies and to consider how they educate and inform their students about conducting research. Multicultural Guideline 1 does not suggest, however, that researchers with identities and social locations that are different from those of their participants refrain from conducting research with these participants. Rather, researchers should reflect on their own backgrounds, integrate the reflections into their studies and the findings, and report on reflexivity in presentations and publications.

APPLYING MULTICULTURAL GUIDELINE 1 TO CONSULTATION

The emphasis on self-reflection on the clinician's, educator's, and researcher's own perspectives and experiences in Multicultural Guideline 1 is further relevant to consultation. Consultants address both interpersonal and organizational issues concerning identity. They can play critical roles in educating others about the complexity of identity and intersectionality (APA, 2017a). Consultation can occur in clinical, community, research, educational, and organizational settings. As such, addressing issues of identity and intersectionality should be collaborative and tailored to the specific needs of the consultee in a particular setting, with a consideration of the consultant's own perspectives, which may or may not diverge from those of the consultee. Relatedly, it is important for consultants to inform themselves about the social, cultural, and political histories of communities and the ways in which a specific community is uniquely affected by these histories. Consultants should stay open to learning new information from their consultees and should disclose areas of limited knowledge to consultees.

Many institutions lack adequate resources for supervisors to address identity, social location, sociocultural oppression, and intersectionality. Nevertheless, the supervisory dyad or group must consider the intersecting identities of the supervisors and the supervisees as well as the role of power dynamics between the supervisors and supervisees, which can contribute to either a more open exploration of identity or a constricted space that impedes discussions of identity and structural inequalities (Valmas et al., 2020). As such, Multicultural Guideline 1 calls for securing adequate resources and support for professional development of supervisors, particularly as cultural competence and cultural humility entails lifelong learning (APA, 2017a).

Scholars have noted the importance of supervisees being seen and recognized, with mutual recognition of self and identity between a supervisee and supervisor (Watkins et al., 2019). Multicultural Guideline 1 suggests that supervision and consultation be approached with cultural humility, which includes introspection as a key part of interpersonal engagement. Additionally, exploring identity and intersectionality requires a certain degree of vulnerability, and therefore it is especially important that supervisors and consultants attend to their countertransference to ensure that they are not contributing to silencing or dismissing the supervisee or consultee. From this viewpoint, engaging in identity exploration is an interpersonal process in which each participant (e.g., supervisee, supervisor) recognizes that they are influenced by the other (Blasini-Méndez, 2019).

Consultants can avoid broad-based generalizations about sociocultural groups and stay open to learning about the consultee's individual and/or group identities (APA, 2017a; Patallo, 2019). Supervisees or consultees may feel uncomfortable exploring certain aspects of identity and social location because of their history of sociocultural trauma and marginalization. Therefore, consultants are encouraged to navigate their exploration of identity and intersectionality with knowledge and awareness of the effects of sociocultural trauma and marginalization (Patallo, 2019). Consultants are responsible for helping their consultees explore their discomfort by creating a safe space in which issues of power and privilege can be openly discussed.

Hernandez and McDowell (2010) noted that relational safety in supervision is not established at any discrete moment; rather, it develops over time. Importantly, a sense of safety develops as the supervisor and supervisee recognize and take responsibility for their communication with each other, including working through interpersonal mistakes and microaggressions. Relatedly, supervisors and consultants in group and organizational settings can consider how individuals with different identities experience a sense of inclusion in the community. For example, when a student or faculty member is recruited to a university, consultants can assess to what extent the individual's experiences of identity and intersectionality are visible to others in the university. The culture of a group or organization has a significant impact on relational safety (Griffin et al., 2020).

CONCLUSION

Multicultural Guideline 1 indicates that identity is fluid and complex, transforming throughout the course of one's life. Developmental transitions, interpersonal processes, and social structures all influence the ways in which individual and group identities develop. Psychologists should attend to the complexity of identity and intersectionality and examine how structural and interpersonal privilege and marginalization shape one's identity. Multicultural Guideline 1 calls on psychologists to avoid simplistic and overgeneralized approaches to identity development and the experiences of individuals and communities. Addressing the complexity of identity and intersectionality in clinical practice, training, research, and consultation requires listening carefully to a person's self-definition and experience of identity, the psychologist's examination of their own perspectives, and the analysis of power dynamics that influence the experience and expressions of identities. Psychologists' roles include embracing openness and inclusion of new perspectives on identity and intersectionality in clinical theory, assessment, treatment planning, training, research paradigms and methodologies, and consultation. This approach is essential to the development of a collaborative and inclusive profession that honors the lived experiences of individuals from all sociocultural backgrounds.

Chapter 4 builds on Multicultural Guideline 1 and presents Multicultural Guideline 2, which focuses on the idea that psychologists are cultural beings whose sociocultural experiences and perceptions influence their work as clinicians, researchers, educators, and consultants.

4 UNDERSTANDING AND AVOIDING PSYCHOLOGISTS' BIASES
Multicultural Guideline 2

Guideline 2. Psychologists aspire to recognize and understand that as cultural beings, they hold attitudes and beliefs that can influence their perceptions of and interactions with others as well as their clinical and empirical conceptualizations. As such, psychologists strive to move beyond conceptualizations rooted in categorical assumptions, biases, and/or formulations based on limited knowledge about individuals and communities.

Multicultural Guideline 2 is the second guideline in Level 1 of the ecological model presented in *Multicultural Guidelines: An Ecological Approach to Context, Identity, and Intersectionality* (hereinafter referred to as *2017 Multicultural Guidelines*; American Psychological Association [APA], 2017a). Level 1 guidelines emphasize a bidirectional model of self-definition and relationships, and Multicultural Guideline 2 is premised on the recognition that professional psychology involves interactions between individuals who come to the table with a range of ideas, knowledge, and expectations about the social world. Our experiences with our own culture and the cultures of colleagues, friends, and acquaintances with whom we interact on a daily basis may represent and underscore what we believe about differences within and across our communities. These experiences also influence the actions

https://doi.org/10.1037/0000348-004
Applying Multiculturalism: An Ecological Approach to the APA Guidelines, by C. S. Clauss-Ehlers, S. J. Hunter, G. S. Morse, and P. Tummala-Narra
Copyright © 2024 by the American Psychological Association. All rights reserved.

we elect to engage in when encountering or addressing others in our daily lives. Research addressing how multicultural sensitivity and understanding develops has emphasized strongly that a person's cultural experiences form their beliefs about others and influence how they appreciate or dismiss those different from themselves (Sue & Sue, 2016).

Socialization within one's culture defines how people think about gender, age, sex, race, ethnicity, sexual identity, religion and spirituality, social class, and disability status, and it strongly influences the beliefs and biases people hold and present across their lives (Dunham et al., 2013, 2016). Psychologists are as much influenced by these socialization experiences as other individuals are (Tummala-Narra, 2016). These socialization experiences, in turn, contribute to a profile of conscious and unconscious biases that psychologists personally entertain when engaging in clinical and consulting work. They have an impact on how psychologists form an understanding of others' needs and concerns at any given time (Neville et al., 2016; Tummala-Narra, 2016).

These biases also influence how research and teaching unfold—specifically, how we form hypotheses about persons and behaviors and then test them, how data are analyzed and interpreted, and how responses to discussions and assignments within the classroom are considered and graded (APA, 2017a; Haynes et al., 2018). Therefore, it is imperative that multiculturally responsive professional psychologists become aware of and attentive to how their biases and associated perceptions about persons, cultures, and contexts can and do influence their engagement with clients, students, consultees, and research subjects. Psychologists can listen better when they are aware of these biases and understand how they can contribute to misunderstandings and incorrect interpretations that affect service delivery and conceptualizations about self and community. They can respond empathically and as a whole person to what is taking place interpersonally and can remain open to interpretations and findings that may run counter to expectations.

CASE ILLUSTRATION—OMAR: NAVIGATING PROFESSIONAL WATERS AND STAYING TRUE TO SELF

Omar[1] is a graduate student in clinical child psychology. He is starting his first assessment externship at a local hospital near the rural university he attends in Virginia. Omar is an immigrant to the United States from Jordan.

---

[1]In this case illustration, all appropriate steps have been taken to disguise the identities of the individuals discussed.

He came as a young adolescent with his family when his father was offered a position with an engineering firm based in Houston, Texas. Although Omar was raised Muslim, he became less engaged with his religion as he moved through college and into graduate school. Omar came out as a gay man during college and then entered a relationship with his Black/African American/Black American partner, a professor raised in the Baptist tradition, to whom he is now engaged. Although religious identity is not currently a prominent aspect of Omar's self-identity, he is active in his university's Muslim student organization and has coordinated outreach regarding the mental health needs of the Islamic community in the area. Omar is also involved with several other groups that support his gay and immigrant identities.

Omar is excited about working with the pediatric assessment team; he will work primarily with children who have cancer. He is very motivated to gain the skills needed to interview parents and conduct neuropsychological assessments with patients at the medical center.

Omar met with the primary psychologist for the team, Dr. Maier. Before their initial meeting, Omar learned through discussions with peers who had completed the externship that she is a strong professional advocate for the program, and she promotes a culturally sensitive approach to clinical care and training. He describes their interaction as formal and cordial. Dr. Maier indicated that Omar would have the chance to work with her on her leukemia and other blood cancers rotation and, across the year, with several other psychologists and clinicians working in the program. However, Omar also learned from peers that several of the clinicians involved with the program are less positively regarded in terms of their cultural and structural sensitivity. Dr. Soul, one of the White/White American psychologists is an evangelical Christian with conservative political and social views. Given this information, Omar was concerned about working with him. His concerns focused specifically on Dr. Soul's opinions about LGBTQ+ rights and his expressed public support for several recent federal government administrative decisions regarding persons of Muslim faith coming to the United States as immigrants.

Because Dr. Soul coordinates one of the primary rotations that the externship requires that involves working with children with tumors in their central nervous system, Omar asked to speak with Dr. Maier about how best to manage his upcoming practicum experience and reduce potential challenges with stigma and bias. Dr. Maier replied that she would prefer that Omar meet directly with Dr. Soul to discuss their pending work together and to get to know him first. Omar felt that this approach might be adequate, but he was also nervous about how to present himself, given the information that was shared with him. Wanting to be in a safe place as he prepared for the meeting with Dr. Soul, Omar again asked to meet with Dr. Maier. He felt that her feedback would help him to strategize how best to make a strong impression.

Dr. Maier was taken aback at Omar's insistence, and she shared that she did not believe there was any cause for worry. Omar then shared with Dr. Maier what he had heard from fellow students of color regarding the challenges they experienced in their work with Dr. Soul. Dr. Maier responded by saying she was surprised to hear this and noted that she was concerned that she had not previously been told about any discomfort or experiences of microaggressions that Omar's peers described to him, although she acknowledged that Dr. Soul had been open about some of his more conservative social and political viewpoints. She indicated to Omar that she would definitely be available to talk with him, and she encouraged him to share with his peers that they also would be welcome to set up a time to talk with her, to help her understand their externship experiences more fully.

When Omar met with Dr. Soul, he introduced himself directly as a Muslim immigrant from Jordan who is gay. Dr. Soul stated he appreciated Omar's desire to meet with him and share information about himself so that they could have an opportunity to know a bit about each other before the rotation started. Dr. Soul shared that he is eager to work with Omar, particularly with regard to learning from Omar some of the best possible ways to work with patients and families from the Middle East and of Muslim backgrounds. Dr. Soul shared that Middle Eastern and Muslim families are an increasingly large population within the area and that they are being seen with

---

Discussion Questions Related to Omar

1. What reactions did you initially have as you began to learn about Omar's experience?
2. Were there ways that you identified with Omar's concerns? To what extent did his experience resonate with your own?
3. How might Dr. Maier have dealt with the information she received from Omar about students of color having challenges with Dr. Soul?
4. Were you surprised by Dr. Soul's reaction? How so or how not?
5. Did you agree with Dr. Maier's suggestion that Omar speak with Dr. Soul directly? Why or why not?
6. How do you view your role as a clinical supervisor? What learning experiences do you hope to bring to your students?

greater regularity in the program. He told Omar that he was seeking guidance and greater knowledge that would assist him in providing appropriate and thoughtful care.

Omar expressed surprise at the offer to assist. He shared that he would be pleased to discuss cultural differences and differences in religious beliefs and practices, within the scope of providing patient care. The conversation then progressed to expectations for the externship. Omar ended his meeting with Dr. Soul by saying he felt glad they had had a chance to meet to talk about their collaborative work together. His feelings at the end of the meeting were very much in contrast to his earlier fears based on conversations with peers. He now feels more positive and is enthusiastic about starting the externship.

LITERATURE REVIEW

A significant research body has developed in the past 50+ years that has provided us with a strong understanding of how cognitions (i.e., thoughts, beliefs, interpretations, hypotheses) regarding the world and those who form its communities are influenced by setting and time (Fiske & Taylor, 2017). A key focus of the *2017 Multicultural Guidelines* is that the degree of cultural responsiveness and cultural humility a professional psychologist holds influences how they are ultimately experienced by their clients, students, research participants, and consultees. Cultural sensitivity and responsiveness also influence how well a psychologist is able to listen and subsequently to respond to their client's demands and concerns. Clinicians, consultants, supervisors, and educators who are multiculturally oriented are more likely to have positive and engaging connections with clients that reflect an understanding of their experiences (Tummala-Narra, 2016), trainees, and or students (Patallo, 2019). This multiculturally sensitive connection allows a stronger working alliance to unfold (Patallo, 2019).

As clients experience an understanding of who they are in the context of the range of identities and aspects of self that they hold, their capacity for building an effective therapeutic, supervisory, or teaching relationship becomes stronger, and growth and change are more likely to occur (Ponterotto et al., 2010; Tummala-Narra, 2016). More directly, when clients and trainees feel understood and believe that who they are as complete individuals is accepted, they are more likely to trust the efforts made by the psychologist to guide them toward change and accumulated knowledge. It is important to recognize, however, that psychotherapy, supervision and teaching, and other professional psychological consultations are dynamic transactions (Fisher, 2020; Patallo, 2019).

Psychologists and clients come to their work with their internal biases and beliefs (Neville et al., 2016; Ponterotto et al., 2010; Tummala-Narra, 2016). A required part of the shared work in training and ongoing professional development is to confront these considerations. A significant element of psychological practice is predicated on characterizations and categorizations. In psychologists' research, we seek evidence of commonalities and ways to classify behavior and thoughts. We rely on systems of organization that address domains of interest such as intellectual capability, learning capacity, emotional and behavioral regulation, psychopathology, and personality, among others (Haynes et al., 2018). As reflected throughout the *2017 Multicultural Guidelines*, each aspect of human identity is also heavily influenced by context and culture. At risk for all, both in terms of the work that we as psychologists engage in and in the ways our efforts are interpreted and understood, is the impact of implicit bias and stereotyping (APA, 2017a; Neville et al., 2016).

Scholars have shown that implicit and explicit negative attitudes complicate how individuals are regarded daily (Neville et al., 2016; Tummala-Narra, 2016). Categorizations based on gender, race/ethnicity, sexual orientation, religion, age, socioeconomic status, and disability status, among others, are common experiences. These negative categorizations amplify environmental and emotional stress, contributing to significant mental health challenges (e.g., trauma, substance abuse, mood and anxiety disorders) and health disparities (e.g., high blood pressure, heart disease, Type 2 diabetes, obesity, engagement in substance use and abuse). Research has shown that the internalization of such stereotypes regarding aspects of self and community, both as perceived positive (e.g., "model minority" stereotypes experienced by Asians/Asian Americans/Pacific Islanders) and as more directly negative, perpetuates privilege among those deemed not representative of these biased categorizations (Mazzocco, 2017; Spencer et al., 2016). Internalization also contributes significantly to low self-efficacy and regard, as well as poor mental and physical health outcomes, for those who fall within the "rejected" communities (Fryberg et al., 2008; Goodley & Runswick-Cole, 2011; Neville et al., 2016; Spencer et al., 2016; Szymanski et al., 2008).

Addressing categorical biases requires that professional psychologists directly confront stereotyping and negative implicit characterizations (Mazzocco, 2017; Neville et al., 2016). But taking a colorblind approach to addressing difference serves to minimize and negate the variations in human identity and experience, leading to disengagement and denial of self by individuals experiencing such an ideological stance reference. Not only does this negation reduce our client–psychologist collaborations by fostering an experience of disrespect on the part of the client, it also diminishes our own efficacy as psychologists. Privilege of dominant class identity (Wilkerson, 2020) is placed above collaboration, with a commitment to colorblindness offered as an effort to express a belief in the potential of diverse groups, where race and other intersectional characteristics or identifiers are viewed as no longer an issue of significant consideration (i.e., *egalitarian colorblindness*, as proposed by Mazzocco, 2017), and may also be reviewed as something that will be dismantled in the future (i.e., *visionary colorblindness*, as proposed by Mazzocco, 2017) or as an expression of explicit discomfort to be avoided (Mazzocco, 2017; Neville et al., 2016). Ultimately, the outcome privileges the White/White American psychologist at the expense of all trainees, clients, and consultees of different intersectional identities (Hook, Farrell, et al., 2016), and it similarly disrupts the process of research and measurement design (Haynes et al., 2018).

When addressing the implications of Guideline 2, studies have demonstrated that the more we as psychologists engage with issues of diversity and correspondingly become aware of implicit and explicit biases, the less likely we are to take a position of privilege within our professional work (Tummala-Narra, 2016). Through an awareness of norms, beliefs, and values of our clients and communities, the aim is for us to provide a more competent and humble professional practice. Critical to this awareness is our understanding of the sociopolitical influences that sexism, racism, xenophobia, antireligious prejudice, transphobia, cisgenderism, homophobia, heterosexism, classism, ageism, and ableism hold on the acceptance and value placed on others. The ability to address issues of multicultural consideration more effectively has improved dramatically over the last half century (Leong et al., 2010; Ponterotto et al., 2010). As psychology has turned toward a greater engagement with models that are not solely Western in their identification and organization, it has opened to, with some strong guidance by diverse researchers and practitioners, a much broader set of models and theories to understand social and psychological processes (Casas et al., 2017; Ponterotto et al., 2010).

Appreciation for differences in approach and consideration of how development progresses, even with an understanding of the underlying foundational commonalities, has offered a stronger basis for challenging and broadening theoretical approaches. An integration of multicultural considerations in the theoretical approaches available to organize and interpret experience in the context of data considered for these models (e.g., systems, cognitive, behavioral, psychodynamic, humanistic, feminist, integrative) has increased our capacity to make sense of experience and challenge in a more integrated manner (APA, 2017a; Casas et al., 2017; Tummala-Narra, 2016).

The foundation of Guideline 2 is that we as multiculturally responsive psychologists take a critical stance with regard to how we make sense of the world, and the process of making sense helps us to improve the world. People often use theoretical models and approaches in a manner that can readily lead to inherent misjudgments. This vulnerability is something innate in how our brains are constructed (Korteling et al., 2018). It is our task to become deeply aware of the assumptions we hold and to work to modify those assumptions and theories through engagement with others' experiences. Guideline 2 encourages us as psychologists to strive toward an in-depth and ongoing examination that includes reflexivity about our cultural worldviews, experiences, and theoretical conceptualizations. Through engaging in this work, we can better understand how we practice, teach, conduct research, consult, and guide others across our professional lives.

APPLYING MULTICULTURAL GUIDELINE 2 TO CLINICAL PRACTICE

As considered in this chapter's case illustration, the world in which we practice as psychologists comprises a diverse group of individuals from varied backgrounds. Such diverse backgrounds are representative of multiple cultures, racial and ethnic identities, gender identities, sexual orientations, degrees of dis/ability, differences in age and developmental level, and religious affiliations, among others. Omar's experience highlights how we often hold particular viewpoints about others based on these attributes, identities, and affiliations. For instance, Omar's experience demonstrates that it is not unusual for both clinician and client, supervisor and trainee, researcher and research participant, and consultant and consultee to approach the interaction with preconceptions about one another and uncertainties about how that set of preconceptions may play out in the interaction. These beliefs and preconceptions are directly engaged by and promoted across the forms of media with which we interact daily (Wilkerson, 2020), and they reflect embedded considerations regarding differences among ourselves politically and culturally (Mazzocco, 2017; Neville et al., 2016).

According to Guideline 2, a professional dyadic relationship requires that we as psychologists recognize that we and our relationship partners each have complex, multiply determined selves (Fiske & Taylor, 2017). Guideline 2, based on a thorough consideration of the research regarding intersectionality and prejudice, encourages psychologists to recognize their own biases and to be attentive to how they may implicitly or explicitly communicate these biases and beliefs. It underscores the view that, in practice and when working with our clients, it is critical for us as psychologists to be sensitive and open to differences and to how those differences are experienced, and to do so within a framework of humility as we regard our own knowledge of others and their differences and our understanding of how our experiences have guided our conceptualizations of human difference (Fisher, 2020; Hook, Farrell, et al., 2016; Neville et al., 2016; Rattan & Ambady, 2013). For example, Hook, Farrell, and colleagues (2016) asked 2,212 racial and ethnic minority participants about the frequency and impact of racial microaggressions in counseling experiences they have had and looked at how counselor characteristics were related to these experiences. They found that 81.7% of the sample had experienced at least one microaggression from a counselor and that microaggressions were experienced across a range of counselor characteristics. The most frequent types of microaggressions occurred when counselors denied bias or stereotyping based on cultural issues and when they avoided addressing cultural differences and issues. Notably, Hook, Farrell, et al. replicated a finding by Neville and colleagues (2016) that suggested that in the United States, colorblindness was among the most clearly observed category of microaggression as identified on the racial microaggression taxonomy developed by Sue and colleagues (2007). A key component of cultural humility in psychological practice is recognizing that a client's challenges are often based on experiences of how others accept them, engage with them, and attend to their differences (Hook, Farrell, et al., 2016). By building cultural awareness and confronting our own assumptions and beliefs about culture and context, we as psychologists are able to work toward creating a space that prompts growth and change.

From the standpoint of assessment (a common professional practice by clinicians engaged in school, neuropsychological, and forensic practice), an awareness of how measures are vulnerable to potential challenges of validity is a necessity when addressing developmental, educational, or psychological functioning in diverse individuals (American Educational Research Association et al., 2014; Haynes et al., 2018). Haynes and colleagues (2018), in a cogent review, highlighted that

> ultimate considerations in the cross-cultural applicability and sensitivity of psychological assessment measures pertain to their consequential validity . . . that is, will a measure used with persons who differ from those who participated in the original instrument development and psychometric evaluation facilitate appropriate decisions about those persons? Will judgments about sources of distress in their interpersonal relationships, educational attainment, problem-solving abilities, criminal responsibility, and parenting skills be valid and fair when based on the adopted measure? (p. 444)

It is important to determine whether measurement tools have biases built into them, based on mainstream cultural expectations or understanding (e.g., assessments of the Big Five personality traits [Haynes et al., 2018], the Wechsler scales [Geisinger, 2013]). As another example, Kit et al. (2008) examined the impact of stereotype threat on neuropsychological assessment (Steele, 1997). Their literature review highlighted the underlying anxiety that many members of racially and ethnically diverse samples experienced, based on expectations of negative appraisals by professionals, even with measures sometimes thought to be less sensitive to such considerations, such as neuropsychological tests of cognitive functioning. What is noteworthy is the recognition that overt projection of biases can lead to alterations in effort and expectation effects that in turn lead to poorer performance (Haynes et al., 2018).

In addressing these concerns clinically, we need to be open and vigilant regarding the ways in which our assumptions and viewpoints, acquired from our experience and culture, can interfere with our capacity to engage with and understand the people we assess and treat. Engaging a model of cultural humility, framed within a broader understanding of social justice, is a way to limit the challenges that can arise from our biases, assisting us as we work to manage the challenges faced by the individuals and groups we work with regularly. When we understand that measures developed to tap into considerations and models of functioning for a dominant cultural group may likely be challenged in their capacity to be used with diverse members of the community because they were normed on different populations, we can initiate a better process for selecting and developing effective assessment tools that use representative normative samples.

APPLYING MULTICULTURAL GUIDELINE 2 TO TEACHING AND TRAINING

The case illustration of Omar directly addresses challenges that can occur at a training site. This case shows how a student may seek to prepare and obtain clarification about potential difficulties while trying to establish effective training relationships with diverse individuals at a training site. Omar, who is seemingly confident and assertive, sought to clarify questions about the relationships he expected to have with supervisors who differ from him culturally, religiously, and with regard to sexual orientation.

He quickly learned that although peers described negative experiences regarding their supervisors, their concerns had not been addressed directly with the training coordinator. Dr. Maier's surprise was an important clue to Omar that improvements in communication about certain topics and perceived microaggressions were needed. His meeting with Dr. Soul was thus positive—introducing himself and sharing background information enhanced the working relationship. Another positive step forward was Dr. Soul's saying that he, too, was seeking further knowledge. Omar found a greater openness in the upcoming relationship; his supervisor's different background and experiences might have been difficult to navigate had communication not taken place.

Teaching and mentorship are activities that require attention to diversity within the training setting. Educational efforts across ages and developmental levels require that we as psychologists remain aware of and have access to pedagogical guides that amplify our capacity to work with a range of students and mentees, appreciating how our differing backgrounds and sources of knowledge may require direct engagement and discussion. As demonstrated by Omar's experience, communication about experiences and belief systems opens opportunities to build a curriculum that emphasizes the impact of multicultural considerations on learning (Falender et al., 2014). Teachers and mentors are advised to consider the privilege that they represent within their interactions with their trainees and mentees. Cultural humility and holding a multicultural orientation within training are predicated on the need to consider and then clearly address power differentials that can readily have an impact on how guidance and support occur and how what is modeled is understood and appreciated (Abbott et al., 2019; Hook, Watkins, et al., 2016).

Teachers and mentors are further advised to understand that their privileged identities influence how communication may take place bidirectionally (Abbott et al., 2019). By showing an openness to examine self-identity and its biases, coupled with understanding how peers across an array of sociocultural backgrounds may enhance one's own worldview, we as psychologists demonstrate a willingness to enhance competence. By addressing difference, we can learn from it dynamically. This reflexivity forms one of the foundations of a multicultural orientation, with its openness to multiculturalism and to the work required to approach not knowing. Part of this work is accepting that we cannot be knowledgeable about all cultures and experiences while showing respect for others who can guide us to greater understanding and knowledge (Abbott et al., 2019; Hook, Watkins, et al., 2016). Our privilege as teachers is therefore challenged by the need to work collaboratively and openly, taking on our limitations in knowledge and experience directly and understanding that taking an other-oriented interpersonal stance will foster opportunities for shared exploration of culture and a comfort with confronting difference openly (Abbott et al., 2019).

Abbott and colleagues (2019), building on work addressing cultural humility and its impact in psychotherapeutic practice (Hook, Farrell, et al., 2016), set forth a series of considerations for bringing cultural humility to the educational setting for psychologists. They emphasized a need for educators explicitly to "engage in ongoing self-reflection of their personal cultural identities, including critical evaluation of their personal power, privilege, and marginalization" (p. 171), "engage in lifelong learning related to culture, broadly, and culture to which they do not belong, specifically" (p. 172), "allow students to determine which identities are salient" (p. 173), "cultivate a classroom [or mentorship] in which cultural humility can occur and encourage a fluid, developmental approach to understanding culture" (p. 173), "develop assignments and course content in the interest of fostering cultural humility among students" (p. 174), "provide mentorship experiences that honor students' cultural identities" (p. 175), and "demonstrate awareness of limitations of traditional research methods and flexibility with regard to incorporating alternative methods" (p. 176). Pedagogy therefore becomes an iterative process whereby activities within the learning setting as well as in one-to-one supervisory and mentorship engagements "create an environment in which it is safe to engage in deep and critical self-examination without shame or fear" (Fisher, 2020, p. 59). Questioning should be done thoughtfully to guide understanding of how determinations and influences have developed.

Fisher (2020) articulated additional recommendations regarding opportunities to encourage a deeper sense of cultural humility and to build a stronger multicultural orientation for trainees and mentees. Through engagement in supervised training opportunities with diverse, marginalized communities, trainees develop sensitivity as they learn from clients and consultees and build a critical stance regarding their own privilege and its impact on their awareness of themselves as individuals who hold their own marginalities and biases. Direct supervision, through an open process of discussion and engagement with cultural difference, power differentials, and oppression, provides the impetus for reflective engagement with difficult considerations about self and others. Crucial to successful training is the opportunity to learn how to become an advocate for change and to develop broad awareness regarding culture and difference. Modeling and collaborative exploration with trainees will guide supervisees and mentees toward more effective engagement of cultural humility and enhanced efforts within the learning and practicum settings.

APPLYING MULTICULTURAL GUIDELINE 2 TO RESEARCH

Within research, we as psychologists are encouraged to consider the context and implications of our efforts at knowledge acquisition so that we can understand if the hypotheses we are testing are cogent and consistent with addressing a question (or questions) across individual differences as well as group differences. We as researchers also have to understand that engaging with cultural and ethnic differences, as well as differences in gender, sexuality, disability status, and age, may lead to variabilities in response that affect interpretation and understanding of the behaviors, experiences, and presentations of concern. We are specifically encouraged to seek means to develop direct personal engagement with the members of the community with whom we plan to conduct research. This process involves understanding both between-group and within-group differences (Ponterotto, 2010); it also assists us in making sense of the range of diversity that may be present within and across cultural groups. For instance, it is not acceptable for a researcher to base an understanding of Latino/Hispanic/Latinx culture on one research project conducted in Guatemala. In addition, as research that examines depression among Latinx men and women demonstrates, some measures better assess the symptoms that are most commonly shown by women and less often shown by men (e.g., Posner et al., 2001, as discussed in Haynes et al., 2018). Measurement equivalence and invariance are quite important considerations when conducting research on multicultural populations (Haynes et al., 2018).

Overgeneralizing and relying on stereotyped thinking can lead to development of inaccurate hypotheses. These processes can also lead to challenges in developing and implementing models within a broad representation of the community of interest (Haynes et al., 2018; Pelzang & Hutchinson, 2018; Yeager & Bauer-Wu, 2013). Guideline 2 specifies that researchers attend to how research design, method, and analysis are shaped by their worldviews and assumptions. It encourages a collaborative approach when considering cultural differences so as to contribute to culturally informed empirical research (APA, 2017a). Collaboration is necessary at all stages of research—mindfully considering values and ethics when determining the research question and selecting the populations most of interest, determining a design that uses a multimethod approach to assess the communities of concern, and employing a strong multicultural orientation that includes qualitative and quantitative approaches either simultaneously or successively (Yeager & Bauer-Wu, 2013). For example, engaging in focus group meetings with constituents from the community is a well-considered approach to building relationships that foster greater trust and collaboration between the community and research team. Focus group meetings also allow researchers to develop definitions of important cultural and individual-difference variables that are potentially under consideration (Leong et al., 2010).

A mixed-methods approach allows a researcher to identify multiple levels of potential impact or importance of the variables of interest and to select effective assessment of the intersectional components of identity as well as their specific and nonspecific influences (Frisby & O'Donohue, 2018). For example, researchers who examine treatment process and outcome have shown that microaggressions directly influence the development and successful implementation of a working therapeutic alliance (Hook, Watkins, et al., 2016; Owen et al., 2014). To understand the vulnerabilities to particular forms of microaggression more effectively, researchers have developed a combination of quantitative and qualitative investigations to understanding both the timing and the impact of differing microaggressions on client and therapist engagement and collaboration (Hook, Watkins, et al., 2016; Neville et al., 2016).

As an example of one such approach, consider a research clinician who is developing a rehabilitation intervention for persons with cerebral palsy. The researcher makes assumptions about the sample based on the expectation that everyone who has a disability experiences marginalization. After completion of the study, the researcher discovers this misassumption (i.e., an overgeneralization) during discussion with the participants. The researcher then conducts a self-analysis and recognizes a communication error when interacting with research participants. Although the researcher wanted to be seen as empathic, a significant number of participants viewed the researcher as less knowledgeable and potentially less open to the community of interest. The researcher can thus step back and reexamine their biases, reconsidering ways of engaging and learning from the community while revising their approach to the study. This example highlights how imperative it is that researchers explore differing experiences with disability status (or other diversity considerations, including their intersectionality) so that they may become more humbly engaged with the community of interest for the study, diminish their expectations regarding particular beliefs or interpretations, and broaden and challenge those expectations so that they are more effectively able to understand how their approach to the study contributes to understanding the community.

APPLYING MULTICULTURAL GUIDELINE 2 TO CONSULTATION

As we have discussed, the key learning goal connected with Guideline 2 is to recognize our own risks as professionals for engaging with biased or underinformed opinions or for holding overgeneralized viewpoints or approaches that compromise our efforts to support and guide the relationships our consultation work requires. When working in consultation with a group or program, understanding the nature of the system and its underlying composition is a significant first step to becoming comfortable and engaged with the group or organization. This step is particularly necessary when we are tasked with working with programs that are situated within multicultural communities. We can learn about a group through its stakeholders and constituents using a number of actions, including engaging guides or mediators or identifying key constituents who can serve as ambassadors or advocates to address organizational concerns. Holding focus groups and meetings with program members, discussing the project and its goals, and becoming more actively informed about members' organizational considerations can help a consultant understand the community, its needs, and any concerns that may be present.

Finally, as consultants, we need to recognize our own power and how that power privileges and potentially compromises our role. Throughout, considerations regarding cultural humility and the processes necessary for a multiculturally informed engagement will serve to guide how we view and understand different levels of power as they occur across relationships within the consultation setting. Additionally, we as psychologists must take necessary steps to make sense of and be sensitive to our own biases regarding reference group identities. Being open to examining privilege across levels of group structure and allowing for a safe environment to explore the range of individuals' emotional experiences within an organization fosters effective modeling and training for participants.

Notably, practitioners have developed guides that support building a consultation practice that is multiculturally oriented and focuses on identifying barriers to equity in access and opportunity while promoting a social justice framework. For example, a special issue of the APA's *Consultation Psychology Journal: Practice and Research* focused on cultural considerations when providing consultation (Cooper & Leong, 2008). Its articles addressed a series of considerations regarding contextuality within organizations and programs, including where to situate one's understanding of what Pelzang and Hutchinson (2018) discussed as the "sensitivity to structural conditions that contribute" (p. 3) to consultees experiences, perceptions, and existing understanding of the setting. Sue (2008) specifically addressed how to approach diversity issues within consultation and provided guidance regarding the confrontation of organizational systems' elicitation of power and privilege, discussing how it contributes to stereotyped expectations and communications. Sue also included guidance on how to view one's self as a tool to consider intersectional identities and cultural status and how to become more effectively aware of one's worldview and its impact socially and within the context of the consultation. Sue specifically focused on communication and facilitating dialogue, particularly regarding significantly challenging material for the program. Assisting and supporting the engagement of dialogue among and between the key players of the program, and guiding their ability both to respect difference and to gain strong understanding of how it influences their collaborations, requires a comfort with confronting in real time the complexities of diversity and its relevance to the success of the program or organization.

CONCLUSION

Multicultural Guideline 2 presents the pivotal recognition that contextual factors serve to create, from our early development forward, a set of inherent biases about others and our interactions with them. Multicultural Guideline 2 suggests that, as psychologists, we strive to be deeply aware of how our biases serve to influence the ways in which we approach our work, including how we engage with others, approach assessment and diagnosis, structure curricula, develop research studies, and subsequently analyze and interpret data. We best serve clients when we approach them with cultural humility, recognize our own biases, and attend to their multicultural experiences (APA, 2017a; Hays, 2016; Ponterotto, 2010; Tummala-Narra, 2016). This is a lifelong practice.

Chapter 5 builds on the foundation presented by Level 1 Multicultural Guidelines 1 and 2 and focuses on Multicultural Guideline 3, the first guideline in Level 2, which is concerned with the community, school, and family context. Chapter 5 centers on the role of language and communication within a cultural context and includes discussion of nonverbal and verbal aspects of language and the cultural values language represents.

PART III UNDERSTANDING COMMUNITY, SCHOOL, AND FAMILY CONTEXT

5
THE CULTURAL SIGNIFICANCE OF LANGUAGE AND COMMUNICATION
Multicultural Guideline 3

Guideline 3. Psychologists strive to recognize and understand the role of language and communication through engagement that is sensitive to the lived experience of the individual, couple, family, group, community, and/or organizations with whom they interact. Psychologists also seek to understand how they bring their own language and communication to these interactions.

Multicultural Guideline 3 is the first guideline presented under Level 2 of the ecological model introduced in *Multicultural Guidelines: An Ecological Approach to Context, Identity, and Intersectionality, 2017* (American Psychological Association [APA], 2017a). Level 2 guidelines focus on community, school, and family contexts. Multicultural Guideline 3 specifically focuses on the importance of language and communication in our work as mental health professionals. Language is central to what we do, as reflected in the term "talk therapy." Guideline 3 is important because it reflects the heart of what we do in our roles as professional psychologists—communicate with others.

It is important in our work to understand that language, particularly in a therapeutic context, means much more than the words that we speak. Language is a complex, interactive process that "refers to the verbal and nonverbal symbols used to communicate with others" (APA, 2017a, p. 34;

---

https://doi.org/10.1037/0000348-005
Applying Multiculturalism: An Ecological Approach to the APA Guidelines, by C. S. Clauss-Ehlers, S. J. Hunter, G. S. Morse, and P. Tummala-Narra
Copyright © 2024 by the American Psychological Association. All rights reserved.

Clauss-Ehlers, 2006a). Table 5.1 presents four ways that language is defined in the *Merriam-Webster Dictionary* (n.d.). Each definition is followed by relevant questions that might emerge for mental health professionals. These questions are then followed by examples that illustrate how each definition and its application to mental health might show up in our work.

Language is an important pathway to developing rapport and connection in the therapeutic and consultation relationships. Guideline 3 emphasizes how important it is for us to be aware of the language (and language systems) that

TABLE 5.1. Definitions of Language: Applications to the Mental Health Field and Examples/Implications

Definition	Questions raised by definitions in a practice context	Examples of answers to these questions
1a. "The words, their pronunciation, and the methods of combining them used and understood by a community"	1a. What are the languages spoken by the client?	1a. Specific languages such as Spanish, Cantonese, French.
1b. "Audible, articulate, meaningful sound as produced by the action of the vocal organs"	1b. What might be implied by the way clients express themselves?	1b. The psychologist can explore if soft-spoken tone indicates depression, respect for authority, shyness, or feeling intimidated, among other possibilities.
1c. "A systematic means of communicating ideas or feelings by the use of conventionalized signs, sounds, gestures, or marks having understood meanings"	1c. Mental health professionals are trained in a certain language with its own jargon and symbols.	1c. Psychological jargon might alienate the client.
1d. "The suggestion by objects, actions, or conditions of associated ideas or feelings"	1d. What is communicated to clients, perhaps even unknowingly, via gestures used in the session?	1d. It is important to be aware of nonverbal communication in work with clients.
1e. "The means by which animals communicate"	1e. In what ways can animal-assisted therapies help our clients?	1e. Therapy dogs have been used to promote speech and language development among children (Machová et al., 2018).

TABLE 5.1. Definitions of Language: Applications to the Mental Health Field and Examples/Implications *(Continued)*

	Definition		Questions raised by definitions in a practice context		Examples of answers to these questions
1f.	"A formal system of signs and symbols (such as FORTRAN or a calculus in logic) including rules for the formation and transformation of admissible expressions"	1f.	How can we understand the nonverbal communications that we share in our work together?	1f.	In a bidirectional relationship, therapists can seek to understand the linguistic nature of signs and symbols expressed by the clients.
1g.	"MACHINE LANGUAGE"	1g.	What is the role of technology in our communication with clients?	1g.	With the COVID-19 pandemic, there has been a sudden increase in teletherapy as a way to provide services.
2a.	"Form or manner of verbal expression Specifically: STYLE"	2a.	How did you develop your counseling style?	2a.	Specific training styles
2b.	"The vocabulary and phraseology belonging to an art or a department of knowledge"	2b.	Are there specific phrases you feel convey a sense of professionalism?	2b.	Learning specific phrases and terminology
2c.	"PROFANITY"	2c.	How are verbal expressions allowed in your clinical work?	2c.	Encouraging ways to express a range of emotions
3.	"The study of language especially as a school subject"	3.	How can we address the reality that most psychology graduate programs in the United States focus on English as the language in which learning occurs?	3.	Importance of graduate programs to incorporate a second language requirement to meet the shortage of dual language therapists; importance of practica, externship, and internship experiences to provide specific training tracks focused on providing psychological services in a specific language
4.	"Specific words especially in a law or regulation"	4.	What is the language we bring to work with our clients?	4.	We need to be aware of the way we use professional jargon, words for diagnoses, and words to describe functioning that might alienate the client.

Note. This original table is based on the definition of *language* presented in the *Merriam-Webster Dictionary* (n.d.).

we bring to our work as practitioners, educators, researchers, and consultants, while seeking to understand the dynamics associated with language usage for our clients, students, research participants, and consultees. When we do not pay attention to language, we risk missing opportunities for connection and rapport building.

CASE ILLUSTRATION–DONTRELL: THERAPEUTIC LANGUAGE AS A BARRIER TO DEVELOPING RAPPORT

Dontrell[1] is an African American student in the eighth grade. His school is in a neighborhood characterized by low resources. It is difficult to get to his school by public transportation, which is how Dontrell travels to school.

Dontrell was assigned to work with a counselor twice a week as part of his individualized education program (IEP). He had participated in counseling before; he saw a counselor in school during sixth and seventh grades. After reviewing the IEP, the mental health professional assigned to work with Dontrell had a good sense of his experience in counseling, his struggles, and his clinical picture.

Recognizing the importance of establishing a professional relationship, the therapist stopped by the classroom to pick up Dontrell for his first day of counseling. After introducing herself as the psychologist working with his case, the therapist shared that she would be coming into the school to provide Dontrell with treatment for his psychopathology. Dontrell's response was silence, which the therapist interpreted as the client listening and understanding the parameters of treatment. At the end of the session, the therapist thanked Dontrell for meeting with her. Believing that the session had gone well, the therapist felt that she and Dontrell had begun to establish rapport and would work together effectively during the upcoming school year.

The following week, when the therapist approached the classroom to pick up Dontrell for counseling, Dontrell quietly indicated that he did not want to meet. When the therapist asked him to come out into the hallway to talk privately, Dontrell replied that he wanted to stay in the classroom because he did not want to miss what the teacher was saying. The therapist then explained that the teacher was okay with his leaving the class for therapy sessions—he could make up the work later, and the teacher had agreed to help him with his schoolwork.

---

[1] In this case illustration, all appropriate steps have been taken to disguise the identities of the individuals discussed.

> **Discussion Questions Related to Dontrell**
>
> 1. What is your sense of what transpired in the interaction between Dontrell and the therapist?
> 2. What role does professional language have in this interaction? Why does it have a negative influence on the therapeutic process?
> 3. In what ways can we "unlearn" the professional jargon that has been instilled in us?
> 4. How can cultural mistrust be a protective factor? Why is it important to understand the role of cultural mistrust in our work as helping professionals?
> 5. Dontrell advocated for himself in this situation. What is the role of self-advocacy in therapy? How can you support clients in developing a sense of self-advocacy?
> 6. How would you respond to Dontrell's reactions?
> 7. How would you work to build rapport with Dontrell moving forward?

Dontrell agreed to participate in the session but again responded with silence. The therapist noted that she was surprised by this reaction; she felt that she and Dontrell had made a connection the previous week. Dontrell then shared that he was not comfortable working with the therapist because he did not want to feel like a "case," an experience he did not have with previous counselors. He asked the therapist, "What do you mean by 'treatment'? Does 'psychopathology' mean you think I'm mental?" The therapist assured Dontrell that these words are common terms used in the profession and further explained, "I wanted to share these terms with you." Confused by the lack of rapport in the session, the therapist noted she was just trying to be transparent in sharing the language of clinical work.

LITERATURE REVIEW

As the case illustration shows, it is critical that in our work as multiculturally responsive psychologists, we are aware of the language we bring to our professional relationships. For years, we go through training and develop a new language—the language of our field. This work is important, and the language is important to know, but using jargon with clients, students, research participants, and consultees can interfere with the development of rapport (Mason, 2018) and with their understanding of our work with them. Guideline 3 encourages us to be sensitive to the lived experience of our clients and to the ways in which language frames communication that emerges from that understanding.

Therapists' use of jargon might understandably promote a defensive response, such as intellectualizing instead of getting to emotion. This response occurred in the clinician's work with Dontrell. He may have been anxious about working with a new therapist, and he may have been experiencing a sense of loss because he could not continue to work with his previous therapist in his new school setting (Lavik et al., 2018). Rather than identifying and addressing these concerns, the clinician used jargon, which provided a way for Dontrell to be angry at the new therapist rather than (perhaps unconsciously) being angry at his last therapist because he could not work with him anymore. The language code of the new therapist might have prompted a defensive response for Dontrell: He got angry instead of allowing himself to feel sad. At the same time, the jargon used by the new therapist made Dontrell feel he was viewed as a "case" rather than a person. This understandably interfered with Dontrell feeling as though he could trust the therapist.

The evidence base supports Dontrell's experience. Weist and colleagues (2019) found that participants aged 18 to 25 felt the term "psychopathology" had negative connotations. Interestingly, when asked if the term was appropriate to use when providing mental health services to youth, 51% of the participants who had themselves received mental health services said no, contrasted with 36% of participants who had never received services. Weist et al. concluded that

> receipt of mental health services among young people may sensitize them to negative aspects of the term psychopathology, indicating the need for caution in using this term and other terms that may have negative impacts on mental health service use among youth. (p. 463)

For clinicians, the implication is that using terms such as "psychopathology" can be stigma inducing for young people. This type of language might lead to lower self-esteem and, as in Dontrell's situation, a lack of trust with the provider. The Weist et al. study reflects the first layer of the ecological model, the importance of self-definition in the bidirectional model. As applied here, the implication is that young people can decide the descriptors that they want to use. As applied to language, the key idea is that we can listen to our clients—here, a young person—to hear the language that they use to describe their situations. Clinicians need empathy, a listening ear, and the ability to hold back and be present rather than to rush in and offer a defining label.

Research indicates that building rapport is essential to developing a strong therapeutic connection (Lavik et al., 2018). In their analysis of what adolescents need from therapists to promote change, Lavik and colleagues (2018) identified six themes based on what adolescents told them would help develop rapport with their therapists. These themes included the therapist helping them to

> (1) [face] a scary situation: Attend to the adolescent's starting point, (2) be warm, invested and emotionally engaged, (3) offer live company and presence as a real human being, (4) have integrity as an adult and a professional, (5) know the world of a teenager and get into their stories, and (6) have mutuality as a virtue and treat the adolescent as an equal. (p. 262)

Other research has shown that the type of verbal response mode used in therapy can help develop a working alliance (Sharpley et al., 2000). Communicating empathy and working to understand the client's perspective authentically can further the development of rapport between therapist and client (Sharpley et al., 2000). Efforts to build rapport in this way could have transformed work with Dontrell. The next step for his therapist is "to overcome the adolescents' initial misgivings and skepticism toward therapy through establishing trust and accommodating their developmental desire for autonomy and connectedness" (Lavik et al., 2018, p. 262).

Code Switching

Code switching (CS) refers to

> the practice of moving back and forth between two languages or between two dialects or registers of the same language at one time. Code switching occurs far more often in conversation than in writing. It is also called *code-mixing* and *style-shifting*. It is studied by linguists to examine when people do it, such as under what circumstances do bilingual speakers switch from one to another, and it is studied by sociologists to determine why people do it, such as how it relates to their belonging to a group or the surrounding context of the conversation (casual, professional, etc.). (Nordquist, 2019, para. 1)

Perhaps one way we can understand the clinician's interaction with Dontrell is by considering CS. In this example, CS did not occur between two languages; rather, it occurred between two contexts (i.e., from the clinician's casual language to one that is professional in nature). However, CS was ineffectual: Although the clinician assumed that professionalism would lead to the development of rapport, the opposite was the case. Weist et al. (2019) underscored the reality that perceptions of terminology can lead to negative outcomes. Our job is to work to understand the professional/cultural context in a way that is responsive to those with whom we are working.

CS also applies to dual language experience. It may be that someone uses one language in one situation and another language in another context. For instance, a person might speak Spanish at home with their mom but then speak only English during coursework. CS can also relate to the ways a person expresses themself. In the classroom, an individual might engage with classmates in a reflective way, sharing insights and listening to others. Outside of the classroom, that individual's day-to-day voice is likely to emerge because they express themself in very different ways than they would in the classroom context (Demby, 2013).

The literature explores how CS can call up varying emotional experiences, depending on the language code spoken in the moment (Foster, 1992). These language systems can summon different manifestations of self that are coded in accordance with the language being spoken (Foster, 1996). Hence, if an individual spoke with a partner only in Spanish, and Spanish shaped the nature of the relationship, speaking in Spanish in therapy may prompt getting to issues connected to the partner (Clauss-Ehlers, 2006b). At the same time, to avoid these issues and not talk about the partner, the person might engage in a defensive response by switching the language of the session to English, the language that was not the context of the relationship (Clauss-Ehlers, 2006a; Foster, 1992, 1996).

Because so much of the work that we do as psychologists is based on verbal (spoken and written) and nonverbal communication, it's important for us to be aware of our own processes of CS as well as those of our clients, students, research participants, and consultees. Part of this process involves understanding who owns language:

> For instance, what is the language or terminology that individuals, couples, families, groups, communities, and/or organizations want to use to define themselves? Further, who determines the terminology used and how identities are defined? For those who speak more than one language, how is the language of the psychological interaction decided upon? (APA, 2017c, pp. 34–35)

Our sensitivity to and awareness of these questions is important because language has an inherent connection with who we are, how we identify, and the intersectionality of those identities within a social context.

Language as a Representation of Cultural Values

Language also represents culture. An example mentioned in the literature is the contrast between "I" in the English language and "yo" in the Spanish language (APA 2017a; Clauss-Ehlers 2006a). In English, "I" is capitalized, indicating it is an important focus. The opposite is the case for "yo"—the lower case implies that the individual is less important. These words mirror societal values and worldviews, such as the dominant focus on the individual in many English-speaking societies and the focus on the collective in many Spanish-speaking countries (APA, 2017a; Clauss-Ehlers, 2006a). Culture is representative of language, and as such, the languages spoken by our clients, students, research participants, and consultees tell us a lot about their cultures. It is up to us to listen.

APPLYING MULTICULTURAL GUIDELINE 3 TO CLINICAL PRACTICE

As mentioned earlier in this chapter, it is up to us as psychologists to be committed to understanding the various language systems that are operating in work with our clients. Psychologists need to be aware of the implications of speaking more than one language, the ways in which clients may engage in CS, and what these shifts represent for the clients and their experiences. Relatedly, we too must be aware of the language systems that we bring to work with our clients.

Part of being aware involves being developmentally appropriate in our approaches and our language. Developmentally appropriate communication responds to the specific developmental stages that are presented to us. For instance, a young child might not have the language to express feelings but might be able to demonstrate emotions visually through play. Similarly, because Dontrell is an adolescent, he might already feel that he does not want to talk with someone about his issues. It would be completely developmentally appropriate for him to want to talk about issues with his peers. Given the important connection with peers during adolescence, it is even more important for the therapist to connect with Dontrell as a young adult, not as a label.

Nonverbal communication is a critical component of communication in the practice setting. I (Caroline) recall working with a school-age client who came to meet with me for counseling during my internship. The client would come in, take the office phone off the hook, and post a do-not-disturb sign on the office door. These nonverbal behaviors were screaming to me to recognize that this young person needed time to be listened to and to share. To have ignored these critical experiences of nonverbal communication would have risked this young person not feeling heard, an experience already reflected in so much of this young person's life.

On another level, our role as clinicians working across cultures and languages means we need a pipeline of clinicians versed in different fluencies. A recent comprehensive U.S. Census report, for instance, suggested that the population of the United States speaks 350 languages (U.S. Census Bureau, 2015a). This study identified the vast language diversity across the country. In large metropolitan areas such as New York, Chicago, Dallas, and Los Angeles, more than 150 different languages may be spoken (U.S. Census Bureau, 2015a).

APPLYING MULTICULTURAL GUIDELINE 3 TO TEACHING AND TRAINING

The vast number of languages spoken across the United States is in stark contrast to the lack of linguistically diverse mental health service providers. For instance, 57 million Latino/Hispanic/Latinx people live in the United States, making up 18% of the total U.S. population. This number is expected to grow so that by 2060, the Latino/Hispanic/Latinx population will be 119 million people, encompassing 28% of the total population (U.S. Census Bureau, 2015b). Despite these growing numbers, an APA survey found that only 5.5% of psychologists are able to conduct services in Spanish (B. L. Smith, 2018).

As these data show, we need a greater number of psychologists who are trained to speak languages other than English. In the United States, few graduate or undergraduate programs require learning to speak a language other than English with proficiency. The lack of a second language requirement seems like a disconnection, given the many global service-learning programs that universities are administering worldwide. We need undergraduate psychology programs to start the pipeline, requiring students to take a certain number of credits in another language.

However, linguistic nuances that reflect culture convey that speaking the language is not enough; we also need a cultural translation of language. The cultural translation of language goes beyond the spoken word, grounding verbal and nonverbal symbols in the context of what is being said. Language tells us a lot about culture. It also tells us a lot about identity.

Related to a cultural translation of language are teaching and training efforts that help foster positive nonverbal therapeutic communication. This type of training is particularly important given the nuances presented by nonverbal communication as well as the varied ways in which nonverbal communication can be interpreted across cultures. Given the range of variability and ways that nonverbal language can be interpreted, questions that emerge include "How do trainees address this issue?" and "How do trainees know how to interpret nonverbal behaviors given their meanings can differ by client?" We return to Guideline 3 for an answer. Guideline 3 encourages us to use verbal and nonverbal communication to engage with clients in ways that are sensitive to their experiences. With Dontrell, for instance, the therapist was more focused on communicating from a place that reflected her background. The therapist would benefit from supervision that encouraged her not to use jargon and instead helped her to use verbal and nonverbal language to understand Dontrell's experience more fully. In this way, we can be open to exploring what our clients are communicating to us.

To further learning in the cultural translation of language, we need training sites and supervisors to focus on this area. For instance, training sites such as the NYU/Bellevue Bilingual Treatment Program (BTP) not only trained psychologists to engage in professional practice in Spanish, Mandarin, and Cantonese; trainees also learned the cultural implications of language and their impact on the service delivery process. To have more linguistically diverse therapists, we need this type of training site.

Unfortunately, BTP eventually closed as a training program. Its closure reflects some of the challenges psychologists face in efforts to provide culturally and linguistically focused training and mentoring for students. As shared by Dr. Carmen I. Vazquez, the founder of the BTP Clinic,

> Again, it is so sad that prejudice and a lack of understanding of the role of culture in the provision of mental health services for a diverse population was and is still misunderstood and unsupported. It is clear to me that this ignorance failed to acknowledge that BTP was a successful program that enhanced trainees' competence, benefitted the society in general by helping patients from a diverse background to not only receive appropriate mental health services in a culturally competent manner, but to be better equipped to help them to support their family needs. In other words: healthy families produce healthy members of the society in general, which translates into better functioning for all. Healthier families are better equipped to help and guide their children's emotional needs that if not attended appropriately can escalate to learning and behavioral problems, at times more serious if not attended earlier. BTP provided help and support to Latinx and Asian populations in a competent and compassionate manner. To this day, I cannot understand why such a successful program was dismantled. (personal communication, August 23, 2020)

APPLYING MULTICULTURAL GUIDELINE 3 TO RESEARCH

The community-based participatory research approach (Belone et al., 2016) is a model that resonates with research focused on linguistically diverse communities. In collaborating with the community in which research will be conducted, researchers can get a sense of the linguistic diversity in the community and can develop a research protocol that reflects the languages that are spoken. A limitation of this approach is that measures are often available only in English and may not be translated into the languages reflective of the community in which research is being conducted. Translations of measures of psychological concepts are needed, along with research that includes linguistically diverse normative samples and that identifies psychometric properties, so that they are available for usage in a range of languages. Similarly, we need to conduct more research with linguistically diverse samples so that the generation of knowledge reflects the experiences of communities who speak a range of languages.

In international work, it is important for us as multiculturally responsive psychologists to be aware of linguistic diversity in the countries and regions where we conduct research. Even when the language is English, there may be differences in local terminology, phrases, and expressions. For instance, when conducting research in the United Kingdom, I (Caroline) had to modify the demographic form for youth so that it asked about primary, secondary, and tertiary education rather than elementary, middle, and high school (Clauss-Ehlers, 2020).

In our increasingly global society, we can think about the practice of psychology in other languages. For example, U.S.-trained psychologists often assume that knowledge is shared in English, and most of the peer-reviewed journals published in the United States are in English. As a result, some may fail to understand how psychology is practiced in different linguistic contexts. While we may read peer-reviewed journals published in English, there is a whole world of information in different languages that we might not know about.

Encouraging cross-cultural language immersion experiences is one way to bridge this gap. Given our global society, another way is to collaborate transnationally to learn about psychological contributions in a variety of languages. Translation supports and empathic editing can help provide exposure to the ideas of transnational colleagues.

APPLYING MULTICULTURAL GUIDELINE 3 TO CONSULTATION

"Language within the consultation arena can be an indication of the organization's cultural context" (APA, 2017c, p. 39). As consultants, we can listen to verbal and nonverbal communication within the organizations we work with so that we can obtain information about the organization's cultural context. As we listen for language, questions to consider include: "Which constituencies are more verbal than others?" "Who talks more at the table? Who communicates more when decisions are being made?" "Who is not at the table?" "Who does not seem to have a voice?" In asking these questions, we can get a sense of the patterns of communication in the organization. Is there a hierarchical pattern of communication? Is communication lateral? How does communication occur when there is a crisis? Are some members of the organization more involved in communication than other members? Patterns of communication can tell us about the culture of the organization and the impact of this culture on the organization's diverse constituencies.

Another area of consultation related to language concerns the content that organizations want to communicate about themselves to the world. In the age of technology and social media, organizations may want a consultant to help them communicate a message or create a brand. Consultants can help the organization find the best ways to reach their audience. For instance, I (Caroline) recall being asked to talk about suicide and suicide prevention during finals week on a university campus. The goal of the presentation was to provide coping resources and to let students know about on-campus support services. Only one student showed up for the presentation; the rest of the audience consisted of professionals in the surrounding community. When I asked the organizer at the university how the talk was advertised, the organizer said they had distributed a flyer that read "Suicide Prevention Workshop." This wording was probably a deterrent for students, given the stigma surrounding mental health problems. They might have avoided the presentation because they were concerned that attending would suggest that they had a problem. The organizer and I consulted about advertising the next workshop as something like "Stress Management," which we felt was responsive to students' needs and stigma-related concerns.

CONCLUSION

It is interesting that language is often overlooked in the work that we do, even though it is a central aspect of our work and who we are. The oversight of language diversity is evident in the number of undergraduate and graduate psychology programs with no requirement to learn additional languages and in the lack of practica, externship, internship, and postdoctoral training sites that could provide training and supervision focused on diverse language communities.

Through CS, we can see how language systems can influence experiences of self. The language used in therapy may include one set of verbal symbols that reflect one aspect of a person's world but do not reflect other aspects. For example, in the case illustration presented earlier, the therapist's code switch to professional jargon was not in sync with Dontrell's language system.

Although it reflected the therapist's professional sense of self, it in no way met Dontrell in terms of his sense of self and his experiences.

This gap in both training and linguistically relevant services contributes to mental health disparities. Although the number of people in the United States with limited English proficiency has increased, the training programs in the country do not often offer specialized training focused on bilingual and multilingual language capability. As a result, the United States presently lacks a comprehensive professional pipeline of psychologists who can provide linguistically relevant services. In fact, a survey by the APA (2016) indicated that only 5.5% of psychologists can provide psychological services in Spanish.

We hope that this chapter provides some awareness of the importance of language and the important role of advocacy to build capacity for a linguistically responsive mental health services workforce. In this way, language can be a bridge to greater understanding. In the next chapter, we continue our discussion of the guidelines nested in Level 2 (i.e., the school, community, family context) with a focus on Guideline 4, which encourages us to consider the role of the social and physical environment in our lives.

6

THE IMPACT OF SOCIAL CAPITAL

Multicultural Guideline 4

Guideline 4. Psychologists endeavor to be aware of the role of the social and physical environment in the lives of clients, students, research participants, and/or consultees.

From Multicultural Guideline 3 with its focus on language as a cultural representation, we move into Multicultural Guideline 4 of *Multicultural Guidelines: An Ecological Approach to Context, Identity, and Intersectionality, 2017* (hereinafter referred to as *2017 Multicultural Guidelines*; American Psychological Association [APA], 2017a), the second guideline nested in Level 2 of the model, which emphasizes community, school, and family contexts. Multicultural Guideline 4 emphasizes the impact of social capital and how it may be engaged within a physical environment that is supportive of social, vocational, and psychological opportunities.

Social capital refers to the social networks and resources that are available in the immediate environment and that support "social cohesion, social support, social integration, and/or participation" (Almedom & Glandon, 2008, p. 191). These forms of support and engagement provide a number of the tools we as individuals readily require to build and live our lives effectively

---

https://doi.org/10.1037/0000348-006
Applying Multiculturalism: An Ecological Approach to the APA Guidelines, by C. S. Clauss-Ehlers, S. J. Hunter, G. S. Morse, and P. Tummala-Narra
Copyright © 2024 by the American Psychological Association. All rights reserved.

and resiliently (Uphoff et al., 2013). Social capital influences psychological and physical health status through an interaction with resources that are provided in and by the environment, as well as social contacts and an array of cultural and personal supports (D. Kim et al., 2008). Factors that make up social capital include the socioeconomic distribution and security of a neighborhood, the quality of schools and their accessibility to community members, the environmental and economic impact of businesses and industries on the neighborhood, the availability of food and its nutritional value, and the accessibility of both health care and transportation for residents within a community (Almedom & Glandon, 2008; Clauss-Ehlers et al., 2019; D. Kim et al., 2008; McPherson et al., 2014).

The richer and more diverse the available resources and reciprocal social networks that exist within a community, the greater the likelihood that residents will experience a life that is described as being of quality and that provides both stability and opportunity for all members of the community (Uphoff et al., 2013). In a resource-limited community, greater poverty and associated challenges can result in disadvantage and the increased potential for trauma (McPherson et al., 2014). It is one of our greatest demands as psychologists who emphasize advocacy and social justice as components of our professional practice—and those training within the field—to attend to these potential differences in social capital and acknowledge how they serve to influence the health and welfare of our clients, consultees, research participants, and trainees.

CASE ILLUSTRATION–CAMILA: BALANCING COMMITMENTS IN THE FACE OF ECONOMIC HARDSHIP

Camila[1] is a 20-year-old Latina attending her local urban community college, where she is focusing her studies toward an eventual health care career. Camila, who is of Mexican and Puerto Rican heritage, grew up in a community that included a mix of new immigrants and established families. Both sets of her grandparents immigrated to the United States when they were young, seeking greater employment opportunities than were available at home.

As a third-generation member of the community, Camila is actively involved in promoting opportunities for her fellow residents. When not attending classes or working to meet expenses, she volunteers with a local Latino/Hispanic/Latinx organization that addresses the impact of low resources and

---

[1] In this case illustration, all appropriate steps have been taken to disguise the identities of the individuals discussed.

income on health within the community. Notably, while growing up, Camila spent significant time taking care of her grandparents, particularly while her parents had to work.

Camila's grandfather showed early-onset dementia symptoms, beginning when Camila entered high school. At that time, she was asked to assist her grandmother more regularly and to help care for her grandfather. This situation sensitized Camila specifically to the impact of poverty and low wage employment on health care access as her grandfather's symptoms emerged well before he was eligible for Medicare.

Because Camila's grandfather's symptoms limited his ability to continue to work, her grandmother was suddenly left with much less income for daily needs such as food and transportation. Camila's grandmother became increasingly dependent on the support of her own four children. Luckily, they are all located within the region and are available as needed to assist when called. The reality, however, is that none of Camila's aunts or uncles, nor her own parents, are able to take much time off from work themselves. They have little work flexibility and have to be present at their places of employment to meet financial demands. As a result, Camila and one of her older cousins, Natalia, are often the ones called to step in—to take a leave from school for the day to assist their grandparents with care, including housecleaning, grocery shopping, and cooking.

Because Camila and her parents live on the same street as her grandparents, she is often asked to spend the night or accompany her grandparents to medical appointments. Further, because her older cousin was recently admitted to a state university with a significant scholarship, Camila has become the primary family member asked to take care of her grandparents. She is devoted to doing so, but she also recognizes that providing this level of care is increasingly at the expense of her own educational plans. Camila recognized that her goal of completing her associate degree and then transferring to a 4-year university nearby is challenged by the frequency with which she is required to provide care for her grandparents.

Camila finds herself at times feeling both jealous and resentful of her cousin's opportunities, and she feels angry at her grandfather and his increasing difficulties, which are proving a burden for her and her family. At the same time, Camila feels guilty about having these emotions, which she knows can get in the way of providing the care that is necessary for her grandparents. She loves her grandparents and her family, and she feels bad about the angry feelings she is experiencing. Camila feels progressively trapped between wanting to be a good daughter and granddaughter who cares for the family and wanting to pursue her educational dreams.

> **Discussion Questions Related to Camila**
>
> 1. What are some of the struggles that Camila is dealing with as she transitions into young adulthood?
> 2. As Camila's therapist, how would you build rapport with her?
> 3. This case is potentially challenging to navigate because it reflects competing cultural values. On the one hand, cultural values that focus on the individual might encourage Camila to pursue her education. On the other hand, cultural values that focus on the group or family might lead her to spend more time caring for her grandparents. How would you as the clinician approach this dilemma?
> 4. Camila is working to find a balance. What are the risks to the therapeutic relationship if her therapist doesn't also find that balance in his clinical approach?
> 5. How might you address the resource issues described by Camila in her sessions?
> 6. What issues would be helpful to introduce in supervision regarding supervisee work with Camila?

Recently, one of Camila's friends suggested that she go to the local community mental health center (CMHC) for counseling. Her friend described having a similar experience and shared that the CMHC helped her cope during her difficulties. Camila followed her friend's advice and began working with a counselor, a young graduate student doing a counseling practicum at the site. While working with this individual, Camila has found that her stresses are difficult to share because of her strong sense of family commitment coupled with her overwhelming sense of guilt about negative feelings toward anyone in the family. Although she has not yet shared this with her counselor, Camila also struggles to believe that he is able to understand her difficulties, given he is a non-Latino/Hispanic/Latinx male.

LITERATURE REVIEW

The necessity for, and impact of, available resources within a community are key factors when we consider how individuals establish and take advantage of opportunities that may be available to them. Research has shown that "individuals from disadvantaged backgrounds are disproportionately represented in resource-poor environments" (APA, 2017a, p. 40; see also Reardon et al., 2015). One of the hallmark conveyers of difference and a clear marker of opportunity is socioeconomic status (McLeod et al., 2014; see also Farah & Hackman, 2012). As we attend to barriers to health care access, educational excellence and attainment, and employment, we recognize that social and environmental factors strongly influence these elements of social capital. As Camila's life experience shows, we are called on to recognize how these challenges influence potential outcomes for our clients, students, research participants, and consultees.

A significant literature has developed over the past 2 decades regarding social determinants of health (Kawachi et al., 2008). As defined by Artiga and Hinton (2018), these factors include "socioeconomic status, education, neighborhood and physical environment, employment, and social support networks, as well as access to health care" (p. 1). Artiga and Hinton further added that "addressing social determinants of health is important for improving health and reducing longstanding disparities in health and health care" (p. 1). The World Health Organization defined social determinants of health as "the conditions in which people are born, grow, live, work, and age.... These circumstances are shaped by the distribution of money, power, and resources at global, national, and local levels" (WHO, n.d.-d, para. 1). WHO also offered key considerations when defining social determinants of health:

- ways in which employment opportunities and available jobs for members of the community promote or restrict health
- ways in which exclusion of specific groups and individuals from the social life of the community affects individuals' mental and physical functioning
- addressing availability of programs that support access to health care for all members of a community
- identifying and addressing gender inequities within the community
- addressing availability of evidence-based approaches that promote infant, child, and adolescent development across cognitive, behavioral, and emotional domains
- addressing availability of food and appropriate access to nutritional options
- assessing ways in which globalization affects communities and their health outcomes
- providing access to health care systems that address individuals' physical and mental health needs holistically

- development and implementation of appropriate means to research and assess the processes that affect and impede health outcomes
- outreach and intervention strategies to target factors that influence or diminish mental and physical functioning in the community
- development and implementation of evidence-based policies to promote healthier urban environments

Notably, the literature regarding social capital and social determinants of health is quite varied in terms of potential factors to consider, but overall, the emphasis has been on how available resources and their access to community members strongly influence both physical and psychological health (Berkman, 2009; McPherson et al., 2014; Uphoff et al., 2013). The issue of access to resources is reflected in the work that Camila has taken on, volunteering with an organization that addresses the impact of economic challenge on access to appropriate health care. The importance of access to resources is also apparent in Camila's experience assisting with her grandfather's medical needs and helping her grandmother manage multiple demands associated with the loss of income resulting from her husband's symptoms of dementia.

The intersection of physical health and emotional/behavioral health is strongly noted in the literature (Gask et al., 2018; Mereish & Poteat, 2015). For instance, when discussing the impact of illnesses such as diabetes or high blood pressure, practitioners working with patients often find that they are also addressing feelings of anxiety and/or depression and associated low motivation (Katzmann et al., 2018; Robinson et al., 2018; Sheps & Sheffield, 2001). In the case illustration, Camila does not have a physical health problem; rather, her emotional reaction stems from the intersection of having few resources, physical decline in family members, and policies that do not allow for access to medical coverage until a certain age is reached. Furthermore, the intersection of this experience occurs in the context of an educational opportunity that Camila wants to pursue but is having a hard time doing so.

The interplay among variations in health care, employment, educational and residential challenge, and psychological state is significant. As in the case illustration, feelings of self-worth and efficacy are tied to opportunities for working toward goals (e.g., education), assessing how well significant others are functioning, and meeting daily demands. Intersectional identity influences the availability of social and environmental capital and the interplay with social class (Ryan et al., 2018). Bullock (2013) showed that gender is a particularly salient consideration when addressing the impact of poverty and the resulting reduction in opportunity that occurs. Also at play are considerations of racial and ethnic identity, sexual orientation, religious affiliation, and gender identity. When seeking to engage and advocate for a social-justice approach to their work with persons and systems, multiculturally responsive psychologists need to understand these intersecting—and, at times, hierarchically organized—social and economic considerations, which overlap with and influence how opportunity and the stressors that affect daily life (e.g., educational and health disparities) influence multiple levels of functioning (Garza et al., 2017; Levy et al., 2016).

APPLYING MULTICULTURAL GUIDELINE 4 TO CLINICAL PRACTICE

The case illustration of Camila gives us an interesting opportunity to consider social capital and opportunity within the social and physical environment, in particular, with regard to providing behavioral health care. It is very important that we invest time in understanding where and how our clients live when we are learning about them. It is important to make sense of the neighborhood our clients live in, understand how they pursue their goals and the outcomes that come from that, and consider whether resources for insuring opportunity are available and can be readily pursued (Almedom & Glandon, 2008). Safety challenges, such as bullying, trauma, rejection, and the relationship with police and other safety officers within the community, are also important considerations when making sense of how our clients live and thrive (K. Collins et al., 2010; Wu et al., 2015).

Recognizing that variabilities in opportunity exist, including within low-resource communities (K. Collins et al., 2010), it can be easy at times for mental health professionals to fall into a belief that someone coming from a more impoverished neighborhood is experiencing exposure to trauma or has limited educational options when compared with peers from more economically stable environments (Almedom & Glandon, 2008; Coley et al., 2018). These assumptions may not always be the case (K. Collins et al., 2010). The converse is also not uncommon: Clients who come from affluent backgrounds may be experiencing significant challenges of emotional deprivation in response to efforts required to "keep up standards" they believe they must live within (Coley et al., 2018; Luthar, 2003).

Camila is seeking important help to balance an array of emotional experiences that are secondary to meeting demands placed on her by her family and the environment. She also feels a responsibility toward her family and their needs. She wants to be there to help them. The trainee starting to work with Camila will benefit significantly by spending time exploring with her the intersecting considerations that are at play (Hays, 2016). This process can include an exploration of how Camila's environment simultaneously supports and interferes with her capacity for self-efficacy and determination. It is also important for the trainee to recognize that Camila's life experience is strongly organized around an ethos of family and community. This recognition is key to making sense of her challenges and her pride as a third-generation member of her immigrant Latino/Hispanic/Latinx community (Streit et al., 2020). Camila's response to her biculturalism (i.e., Puerto Rican and Mexican) reflects various roles and expectations. Supporting Camila in feeling confident about discussing the mixed messages she receives, within a more limited range of resources and options than other peers and family members are provided, acknowledges just how deeply her context guides her experiences, emotions, and opportunities (Hays, 2016; S. D. Mills et al., 2020).

Additionally, the case illustration reflects the intersectional aspects of Camila's life, in particular, her role as a Latina within a family structure that may be focused on ideals of *machismo* and *marianismo* (Gil & Vazquez, 1997). This family structure may influence the opportunities that Camila has, such as whether certain opportunities are unavailable, limited, or reduced (Bullock, 2013; Garza et al., 2017; Nuñez et al., 2016; Rosenthal, 2016). The trainee can consider Camila's experience of stress within the family and the stress caused by her family's immigration experience and cultural background, both of which are related to the expectations that are placed on her (i.e., expectations that are both similar to and different from her own goals and desires). Treatment can include working with Camila to form a more integrated sense of possibility and, more directly, balanced engagement with how she approaches the complexity of her goals. The trainee can assist Camila in assessing her values within the context of her culture and family. The trainee can also help guide Camila to reflect on her role as a woman with differing expectations placed on her given where she is positioned within her communities (e.g., the immediate home community and her broader existence with a U.S. city). This focus may help her to recognize options as well as compromises that may be necessary.

APPLYING MULTICULTURAL GUIDELINE 4 TO TEACHING AND TRAINING

A microcosm often exists within the classroom setting. This microcosm allows us to explore and address contextual factors that influence diversity. Guiding trainees and students to recognize that environmental factors play a significant role in understanding the intersectional aspects of self and identity opens the door to a much more nuanced and complex consideration of how differences influence opportunity (Almedom & Glandon, 2008; Hays, 2016). Additionally, discussions about how income disparities influence physical and emotional health serve as a conduit to explore individuals' range of experiences while growing up and through adulthood (D. Kim et al., 2008; Luthar, 2003). This classroom conversation can lead to further discussion of juvenile justice, equity in opportunity and response to challenge within the environment, and trauma (K. Collins et al., 2010). These topics are pertinent when thinking about the interplay between politics and society. They also strongly influence how one comes to understand and then hold empathy toward peers and colleagues (Fisher, 2020; Sue et al., 2019).

Project-based learning opportunities, in which programmatic research is reviewed and considered, are excellent circumstances to explore the intersection among factors such as gun violence, community trauma, and challenges to stability within communities in urban and suburban environments (C. Mills & Ballantyne, 2016). This exploration can include discussion of how these intersections influence self-efficacy related to educational opportunity, choice, and career. By modeling how psychologists attend to policies that have an impact on individual experiences at a societal level, individuals in a teaching role can remind students how a multisystemic approach can support effective outcomes.

Pearrow and Fallon (2019) presented a model for integrating social justice and advocacy into psychologists' training. The model facilitates a necessary aspect of contemporary professional identification and development by emphasizing approaches that activate an investment in learning about and engaging in actions that foster access to the resources required for implementing efficacious processes of self-determination and resilience. Pearrow and Fallon promoted a combination of goal-directed instruction, including multicultural orientation, competence in models and applications of multicultural engagement, and social-justice training. Through didactic, participatory dialogue and group facilitation to engage topics of justice, equity, and intersectionality, trainees are provided with the foundation that will facilitate their efforts in experiential learning, including working with projects and community-based scholarship. Pearrow and Fallon further described a program developed and implemented with counseling and school psychology trainees at the University of Massachusetts Boston. Social-justice curricula and training experiences were embedded in all training and educational engagements throughout that program. Advocacy was a key component of the training: Students in the program learned that their role included "coordination, leadership, and legal action . . . [as] a strategy that is influenced by strategic thinking and relationships" (Pearrow & Fallon, 2019, pp. 4–5). Outcome assessments of the program highlighted a set of successes in regard to development and administrative implementation of recommendations. Direct collaboration with university systems was engaged as a learning component and direct training experience. Notably, this program highlighted an active learning model in which research training, advocacy training, and community integrated practices were modeled and implemented. Students who participated identified a strong personal commitment to social justice as a component of their professional identity.

APPLYING MULTICULTURAL GUIDELINE 4 TO RESEARCH

When thinking about research within communities of varying resources, researchers need to emphasize meeting the community where it sits and understanding how its members regard the goals and methods of the study. This process will often involve understanding available resources and gaps in support that intensify poorer outcomes. An important approach to understanding the dynamics of resource allocation and systemic advantages or challenges that exist within a community is to meet with community members to obtain a sense of their varied experiences with service provision and access (Clauss-Ehlers et al., 2017; Rosenthal, 2016). Such understanding may be accomplished through individual meetings or focus groups, both of which allow researchers to gain a broad sense of the social capital available within that community and the ways in which individuals of varied class backgrounds engage and use such capital (D. Kim et al., 2008).

Camila's case is an excellent starting point to consider conducting research focused on the intersection of limited resources, care for family members with dementia, and means for improving caregiver mental health. Flores and colleagues (2009) conducted interviews with Latina and European American caregivers of family members with dementia to understand the role of *familism* among families affected by physical and mental health issues. They defined *familism* as "the value of the family as an institution, the ideal of family relationships, and the priority placed on reliance on family members rather than more impersonal institutions for instrumental, emotional, and material support" (p. 1056). The concept of familism prompts understanding the ways in which caregivers' choices and burdens affect their own mental health.

Flores et al. (2009) relied specifically on "trained bilingual, bicultural research assistants" (p. 1057) to engage participants in an hour-long semi-structured interview that addressed the participants' experiences as caregivers and the impact of this role on their daily lives. The team used a multimethod qualitative approach to analyze the interviews, focusing on themes related to the rationale behind home caregiving for a family member, understanding the illness within the context of family and community, the model and ethical framework of the care provided, and the emotional considerations underlying choices of care. The researchers explored how familism serves as a framework to contextualize specific values regarding caretaking within a Latino/Hispanic/Latinx context. For instance, research has broadly shown that familism within Latino/Hispanic/Latinx communities serves as a structural outcome related to social status, social inequities, and cultural values.

Flores et al. (2009) came to understand that caregivers take on the caregiving role to privilege the family over the individual. Results indicated that caregivers primarily sought to provide a sense of dignity for their family members who were experiencing cognitive deterioration and other challenges in daily life. With a focus on understanding cultural practices and their ethical value, the researchers suggested several options for clinicians to support caregivers working with Latino/Hispanic/Latinx patients with dementia and their families. Recommendations included developing models for sharing medical information and providing efficacious care within the home setting. The researchers also addressed ways to support and guide caregivers toward self-care and effective stress management strategies. The Flores et al. study illustrates an intersectional research model that explores the intersectionality of multiple reference group identities (e.g., race/ethnicity, disability, age, generation) and an understanding of the values and choices made that determine roles taken on by community members.

APPLYING MULTICULTURAL GUIDELINE 4 TO CONSULTATION

Psychologists who work as consultants within diverse communities are encouraged to commit time to understanding social capital and the ways in which mental health is influenced by an array of social factors that affect choice and decision making. For example, Breland et al. (2013) introduced an integrated health-oriented consultation model that focuses on social capital and its impact on health and psychological functioning. They emphasized the intersection of diabetes and self-care within the community and specifically discussed projects that look at available options for appropriate, nutritional food choices in low-resourced communities. The availability of healthy food options allows individuals at high risk to engage in effective decision making regarding health management and diabetes intervention, a social-justice issue that affects health and mental health functioning for both clinicians and their clients. Food deserts are common in urban settings in which limited investment has taken place and transportation is less readily available, and individuals in these communities are often dependent on small markets and fast food, with few healthier options. Community members may then make poor choices, which can compromise physical health (e.g., hypo- or hyperglycemic episodes, increased risk for stroke, damage to limbs) and accompanying mental health (e.g., anxiety, depression).

Likewise, when the options are low, residents with health challenges such as diabetes may find themselves stressed, frustrated, and unable to manage their specific demands for food and stress management effectively (Breland et al., 2013; Chin et al., 2014). The University of Chicago Pritzker School of Medicine has responded by developing a program to provide individuals with in-session counseling and nutritional guidance when they attend their medical appointments (Peek et al., 2012). Focus groups that explore the need for this program and its outcomes have shown that participants experience greater efficacy regarding self-management of diabetes symptoms, accompanied with stronger HbA1c stability and fewer negative mood symptoms, when they engage in healthier eating and have better food availability. It is apparent that consideration of community opportunities is important when engaging in direct service consultation. When providing guidance to a clinical team seeking to develop an appropriate programmatic intervention for a community, consultants are encouraged to direct efforts toward individuals and toward the settings and contexts within which they live. Directing such efforts in this way will guide how we conceptualize levels of intervention and propose methods of impact that can guide change and improvement in organizational efforts and their outcomes.

A further consideration regarding social capital may be pertinent for a consultant coming into an organization in which employees are representative of a group with low socioeconomic status and have multilayered identities. In considering the multicultural organizational consultation model, Sue (2008) discussed challenges that had developed for a company with many Asian/Asian American individuals in its workforce. Sue noted, in particular, that the executive team was concerned about the feelings of morale and extended motivation of employees. Sue addressed the ways in which stereotypes regarding Asian culture and personality attributes were endemic to the executive group at the company and the ways in which the employees' commitments to their families influenced their ability to meet expectations regarding aspects of company culture that were strongly based in race and class (i.e., mainstream values of commitment to work over family). By addressing these considerations from a framework of social capital and intersectionality, Sue was able to assist changes in executive culture, which in turn fostered greater sensitivity to both intersectional and community cultural demands of the workforce and allowed for revisions in the ways in which employees were reviewed and ultimately promoted.

CONCLUSION

Considerations of diversity and experience are deeply tied to context. Multicultural Guideline 4 focuses specifically on the ways in which social capital requires strong consideration by psychologists in our work with trainees, clients, research participants, consultees, colleagues, and other collaborators. Social capital refers to the extent to which those components of the environment offer opportunity and support an enhanced sense of both security and self-regard.

An awareness of how differences in economic and structural opportunities serve to influence how readily services can be obtained or coursework can be pursued is paramount to making sense of the lives of the individuals we support, teach, and work with. By taking a lead at the level of policy development and implementation, we can more directly confront potential impediments to opportunity and positive outcomes. Being aware of differences in structural and economic opportunities also reminds us of the cultural humility required when engaging with others whose greatest challenges are a lack of basic needs, access, and options.

Level 1 (i.e., bidirectional model of self-definition and relationships) and Level 2 (i.e., community, school, and family context) set the foundation for the third level of the *2017 Multicultural Guidelines:* institutional impact on engagement. Level 3 focuses on the extent to which institutions either encourage engagement in their processes and resources or have systemic barriers that impede involvement. Chapter 7 discusses Multicultural Guideline 5, the first guideline in this level. It addresses institutional barriers and systemic oppression.

PART IV
CONSIDERING THE INSTITUTIONAL IMPACT ON ENGAGEMENT

7
RECOGNIZING INSTITUTIONAL BARRIERS AND SYSTEMIC MARGINALIZATION
Multicultural Guideline 5

Guideline 5. Psychologists aspire to recognize and understand historical and contemporary experiences with power, privilege, and oppression. As such, they seek to address institutional barriers and related inequities, disproportionalities, and disparities of law enforcement, administration of criminal justice, educational, mental health, and other systems as they seek to promote justice, human rights, and access to quality and equitable mental and behavioral health services.

From a focus on the individual, community, school, and family contexts that make up Level 2 of the model, we now shift to Level 3, which is concerned with institutional impact on engagement. This level of the model considers the extent to which institutions encourage inclusiveness or have systemic barriers that interfere with engagement. This chapter focuses on Multicultural Guideline 5, the first guideline in Level 3. Guideline 5 explores questions of engagement through a discussion of institutional barriers and systemic marginalization and examines ways in which these barriers play out in society and the helping professions. This chapter encourages students, trainees, and psychologists to gain an awareness of these barriers and to work to address

---

Contributions to this chapter were made by the following authors: Patricia O'Connor, PhD, Russell Sage College, Troy, NY; Carmen A. Serrano, PhD, University at Albany SUNY, Albany, NY.

https://doi.org/10.1037/0000348-007
Applying Multiculturalism: An Ecological Approach to the APA Guidelines, by C. S. Clauss-Ehlers, S. J. Hunter, G. S. Morse, and P. Tummala-Narra
Copyright © 2024 by the American Psychological Association. All rights reserved.

them in their professional practice. Here we describe and define attributes of institutional barriers and systemic marginalization and how they might occur.

We begin with definitions of *institutional barriers* and *systemic marginalization*. According to Ashcraft (2009), institutional barriers are embedded in an organization and include policies, rules, procedures, and even institutional culture, which may create disadvantages for certain people, most often minoritized persons or those with disabilities. These barriers in turn create a system of marginalization of minoritized groups in particular. For example, in a male-oriented organization there may be no policy regarding flexibility of work hours to accommodate working mothers. Among those who cannot work past a certain time, since most child-care settings are only open during typical 9:00 a.m. to 5:00 p.m. work hours, women may be disadvantaged by not being present after regular work times.

Institutional barriers and systemic marginalization create barriers for success for certain groups of people by limiting the carefully defined margins of participation. An organization that historically was initially designed to support a specific group (i.e., those in the perceived majority) then, either knowingly or unknowingly, functions to prevent higher achievement or mobility of members of the organization who are in the minority, often a group that has been recently added to the organization. Frequently, accommodational changes are not made because of historical ways of functioning or traditions that are embedded in the organizational culture. Ashcraft (2009) suggested that using a problem-solving approach, perhaps with team sessions, can define problem areas, create solutions, and implement these solutions from and for changes that can increase productivity, success, and benefit for a diverse organization. However, the process of engaging in such a team approach requires a commitment on the part of the organization and its members.

The following case illustrates the impact that institutional barriers and systemic marginalization have on lived experience and on engagement with institutions in an ecological context. After the case presentation, we further describe and define attributes of institutional barriers, how they might occur, and then, what we might do to address them.

CASE ILLUSTRATION—ISABELLE: STRUCTURAL BARRIERS TO CREATING A PSYCHOLOGY WORKFORCE

Isabelle[1] was a PhD-level psychology intern at an outpatient health clinic with a focus on community mental health. She was 30 years old and came from a well-respected university with a strong academic background. Isabelle

---

[1] In the case illustration, all appropriate steps have been taken to disguise the identities of the individuals discussed.

grew up in a small urban community, and her family had little money, often scraping by to provide the essentials. Her father worked as a laborer until he was injured on the job. Her mother worked as a nursing home attendant and part-time in private care.

Isabelle's mother had always dreamed of being a nurse or even a doctor. She often talked about the importance of education and caring for others. She frequently commented to Isabelle that the actions of historical figures in the advancement of civil rights supported her ideas of how pursuing her education would allow her to move forward in her goal to care for others. For instance, Isabelle's mother recalled that as a young girl she watched the 1960s' *March on Washington for Jobs and Freedoms*,[2] where the speakers spoke powerfully for each person's agency in their ability to choose and be successful in their work. She noted she might never have even applied for a job as a nursing attendant because of the training requirement. But because she remembered the speeches about women's rights and the rights of people of color, she took a training course and was able to obtain a needed certificate to do the kind of work she liked.

Both of Isabelle's parents were very supportive of her goal of going to graduate school to become a psychologist. When she expressed this idea initially, they were not sure if that was a good idea at that time. This was due to the fact that they were unable to provide any funding for school because Isabelle's father was recovering from his injury and was unable to work—a situation that was likely to continue indefinitely. Fortunately, Isabelle had good grades and high Graduate Record Examinations (GRE) scores, so she was able to obtain a scholarship and an assistantship. This, along with student loans and a full-time job in the evenings cleaning offices, gave her enough money for school, her own living quarters, and expenses. The full-time job, the need to maintain a certain GPA for the scholarship, plus the rigor of graduate school all put a great deal of pressure on Isabelle. As a result, she felt compelled to take one less class each semester to keep up with class assignments and to complete course work.

This was a difficult decision. Isabelle found it painful to watch her cohort move forward at a quicker pace than she was able to, which often left her feeling alone and unsupported. For Isabelle, it was isolating not to have the camaraderie and group knowledge that came about from being in sync with her first-year cohort. When she started the program, she felt she could "learn the ropes" from her first-year group as they shared information with one another and talked about their experiences. In particular, some of Isabelle's group did not have to work and/or had parents who were in academia and

---

[2]See https://www.womenshistory.org/resources/general/march-washington-jobs-and-freedom#:~:text=More%20than%20250%2C000%20people%20gathered, social%20challenges%20confronting%20African%20Americans

thus knew some of the keys to success in graduate school. Without being able to remain in sync with this cohort, Isabelle felt like she was unable to keep up with all the requirements on her own, was losing social connections, and in fact, did miss a scholarship renewal deadline. Additionally, by the time she completed undergraduate and graduate school, Isabelle had over $80,000 in student loans. This created pressure on her to complete her required clinical internship and find a job quickly.

As Isabelle moved into the application process for her predoctoral internship in clinical psychology she was able to join a group of students she called her "new cohort." They designated a meeting time and place to help each other with their applications. At her school, there was an unusual circumstance of specific local internship sites. The department had developed relationships with selected local sites where they preferred to place their students for internships, and this was the program's preferred way for their students to obtain an internship. The relationships with the local sites were important for student funding and the department made every effort to fill their local internship slots. While this was done to guarantee approved internships for their students, these spots were at the low end of the internship pay scale. The option to obtain an external internship was permitted but with the caveat that the department and clinical program specifically could neither guarantee acceptance nor assist since the other internships are managed by the Association of Psychology Postdoctoral and Internship Centers (APPIC) and there was no guarantee for a match between sites and potential interns.

Isabelle believed that she needed an internship setting where she could learn about theoretical applications that were not covered by her very focused program. She also recognized that she needed a higher paying internship site if she was going to be able to stop working at night. Her group of likeminded grad students worked together to support each other through the external internship application process. They read, edited, and made suggestions for each other as they completed their APPIC application packages for the sites they were interested in. Isabelle noted that the members of this particular group were either non-White or from a lesbian, gay, bisexual, transgender, and queer (LGBTQ) cohort that shared similar concerns that she had. Most of these peers had to work outside of the program, and they struggled with the strict format of the program that discouraged breaks, had limited funding opportunities, and had a time limit from admission to graduation to complete their degree. Fortunately, Isabelle was matched with an internship site that met her goals through the APPIC application process. Some of the members of her support group were not so lucky on their first try but were able to get a local, Department approved internship the following year.

Discussion Questions Related to Isabelle

1. What do you imagine Isabelle's racial/ethnic background is and why?
2. How do you think the internship process developed by the department had a negative impact on Isabelle and her peer applicants in her program? What were the potential barriers established by this process that impacted Isabella particularly?
3. How might the department have better supported students like Isabelle, whose intersectional identity and background may contribute to greater challenges with pursuing graduate training?
4. How do limitations discussed in the graduate training program impact the pipeline for a diverse professional psychology workforce?

LITERATURE REVIEW

Institutional barriers and the systemic marginalization that arises from them can be invisible at first glance. As a result, it is surprising to view such marginalization in any setting but shocking when seen in what we presume is a merit- or achievement-based system, as illustrated in the above example. When we think of barriers, we generally envision something that inhibits movement or prevents access to necessary or desired goals. Barriers are generally tangible, visible, and a clear indication of where access stops; such clarity maintains the status quo and consistently keeps certain groups of people on the outskirts of opportunity. Institutional barriers, at first glance, may be seen as part of the naturally evolved and agreed-upon procedures and policies of those institutions.

Upon deeper consideration, however, barriers become recognized as very thinly veiled decisions that favor the privileged and create hurdles for others. For example, an administrative assistant with a primarily certificate-based professional background may be asked to train a new employee who holds a bachelor's degree, a qualification that the organization now requires for a particular job that is supported by the administrative assistant's office. Notably, the administrative assistant may even be able to do the job they are training the new person to take over better than the new employee themselves, yet because they do not hold the requisite college degree, they are passed over for promotion to such a position. The degree requirement for the position creates an institutional barrier for the administrative assistant;

they may never be able to achieve the same financial benefit afforded the people they train for the job. The institutional procedures and policies then work in concert within the system to marginalize those perceived as or deemed less skilled and lesser warranted professionally.

Isabelle's case underscores how socioeconomic factors can have a negative effect on student success in graduate school. More poignantly, we can see these economic factors at play in the following statistics: At the 145 top-ranked schools 74% of students come from families in the top quartiles in reference to earnings and only 3% belong to those in the bottom quartile (Carnevale & Rose, 2004, p. 141; Stephens et al., 2014). These numbers emphasize how students from low-income families are less likely to attend college, and even further, obtain graduate or professional education (U.S. Government Accountability Office [GAO], 2018).

Stephens and colleagues (2014) illustrated how differential access to money, power, and status contribute to inequality. They highlighted how mainstream institutional structures privilege affluent normative values when they stated: "Institutions are not neutral but instead promote particular middle-class understanding of how to be an effective person, student, or worker" (p. 619). In other words, students who were raised in a working-class family with limited resources do not necessarily reflect affluent normative values that are deeply embedded in institutions of higher learning.

Barriers also create a system of marginalization among students of color, especially those with more limited resources. According to the GAO (2018), students of color are more likely to have attended high schools with higher poverty rates and reduced resources. These high schools provide fewer college preparatory courses, such as Advanced Placement courses, that are offered in many middle-class school districts. The study found that "disparities in access were associated with school poverty level for more advanced courses like calculus, physics, and those that may allow students to earn college credit, like Advanced Placement (AP) courses" (GAO, 2018, para. 1).

Systems of marginalization that begin at the undergraduate level are also echoed at the graduate level, as Isabelle's case illustrates. Students from working class families with low resources enter a space that has not specifically been designed for them, and therefore, can face a range of barriers. For example, students may suffer from food insecurity, face mounting student loan debt, and/or consider abandoning their college aspirations to contend with family financial obligations. All challenges that affluent students are able to readily forgo. Institutional mechanisms illustrate the barriers students of color from lower-income families face during the college trajectory; the processes that define the bureaucracy of U.S.-based universities and colleges are often ones difficult for those without familial resources to negotiate independently. Yet, students from these working-class family settings, aware of the social hierarchy, have developed patterns of behavior that underscore toughness, strength, and resilience (Stephens et al., p. 615). Certainly, Isabelle's case illustrates how she was able to ultimately create a supportive community, and sought out mentors, that allowed her to effectively find and match with a suitable doctoral internship.

Recently, numerous institutional barriers that promote systemic marginalization were outlined in American Psychological Association (APA) Division 45's Warrior Path Presidential Task Force (2020) and its final report, *Protecting and Defending Our People: Nakni tushka anowa (The Warrior's Path) Final Report*. Of particular note are barriers that protect the status quo or slow down possible organizational change, such as the organizational requirement of legal review for any changes in by-laws and actions taken by the organization, which is meant to preempt litigation and can lead to parliamentary procedures that slow or end discussion of proposed changes toward stronger equity and engagement with diversity. Such an organizational requirement is a preeminent example of how the barrier protects the institution and not the members; as a result, a barrier that hinders organizational change is upheld and thus maintains the "old ways" of conducting organization business, at the expense of those not within the majority.

Furthermore, as outlined in the *Warrior's Path Final Report*, barriers can also be defined by inertia, bureaucracy, or active resistance to change, and may be different for early career professionals as opposed to those of more senior professional status. For example, it has been shown with this report and other publicly shared documents (see the recent APA Statement of Racism approved by APA Council; APA 2021a) that professional psychology as it has been defined and supported by APA has held a primary focus on Eurocentric views of human behavior, including identifying and promoting mental health treatment and methods that fail to accept the "value of non-mainstream cultural perspectives" (APA Division 45 Warrior Path Presidential Task Force, 2020, p. 16). Merely not acknowledging the value of the "other" cultural perspective creates a spectrum of more subtle to not subtle at all barriers to practice and community engagement.

The impact of institutional barriers in the student experience is also evident in Isabelle's case. Currently many professional psychology students have to overcome high educational costs and associated living expenses, excessive conference costs, professional membership fees that are not always graduated, and increased licensing exam fees. These costs affect students with limited resources, which in turn contributes to a slowing in the pipeline toward a diverse psychology workforce. This is seen readily among groups of diverse individuals who might provide clinical care; engage in educational activities or public policy processes; or conduct necessary research about, with, and for underserved populations (APA Division 45 Warrior Path Presidential Task Force, 2020).

Unfortunately, the institutional barriers do not stop at the student level. Early career professionals often face a potentially stacked deck. Assistant professors, clinicians in training settings, and young researchers may find it difficult to achieve success in their initial efforts due to institutional barriers they can confront professionally, including substantial workloads that may require significant hours for teaching, clinical hours to meet employment setting financial goals, and even minimal clinical supervision or mentorship during their first years in professional practice (Lim & Golub, 2004; Ransdell et al., 2021). For example, assistant professors may be asked to sit on an excessive variety of committees. These additional activities take up a great deal of their precious writing time for publications, which is the gold standard for tenure (Coates, 2020). In another example, a newly licensed bilingual clinician may risk burn out if the clinician is the only person in a clinic setting who shares the client's linguistic background and has a higher caseload of clients as a result.

The impact of institutional racism on the students, trainees, and early career psychologists radiates out to those who need psychological services (see Table 7.1 for a definition of institutional racism). Indeed, the Centers for Disease Control and Prevention (CDC; 2013) noted that the general public is unaware of the institutional barriers that may increase grave public health concerns, such as access to affordable health care, healthy food, or educational and employment opportunities for many underrepresented groups; these barriers have been identified as structural impediments to health and well-being.

Furthermore, this is compounded by the reality identified by the CDC (2013) that the lack of data regarding underserved populations is linked to these structural barriers. The "lack of data" problem exists in multiple disciplines. For example, numerous reports by APA, including those regarding psychologists' careers, have not included information about Native American groups (APA Division 45 Warrior Path Presidential Task Force, 2020) or have lumped together minoritized groups, ignoring the differential impact of such experiences as community-based violence and aggression on Asian immigrants and Asian Americans (APA, 2021a). The group data that are neither collected nor reported create a void that allows a particular group to go uncounted, unnoticed, and thereby not included, becoming invisible.

TABLE 7.1. Levels of Racism

Level	Description
Structural racism	Structural racism results from laws, policies, and practices that produce cumulative, durable, and race-based inequalities, and includes the failure to correct previous laws and practices that were explicitly racist (Yearby, 2020).
Cultural racism	Cultural racism is the individual and institutional expression of the superiority of one's racial and cultural heritage over another (e.g., designing a curriculum that overwhelmingly features the accomplishments of people deemed "superior"; APA Task Force on Race and Ethnicity Guidelines in Psychology, 2019; J. M. Jones, 1972/1997, p. 3).
Institutional racism	Institutional racism results from policies, practices, and procedures of institutions–such as school, health care, law enforcement, and criminal justice systems–that marginalize diverse racial groups (APA Multicultural Guidelines; APA, 2017c; Yearby, 2020).
Interpersonal racism	Interpersonal racism occurs when individuals from socially and politically dominant racial groups behave in ways that diminish and harm people who belong to other racial groups. Interpersonal racism is therefore distinct from bigotry (negative attitudes about an outgroup, not necessarily tied to race) or prejudice (a preconceived opinion that is not based on reason or actual experience; APA, 2017c; Yearby, 2020).
Internalized racism	Internalized racism refers to the acceptance by diverse racial populations of the negative societal beliefs and stereotypes about themselves–beliefs that reinforce the superiority of White people and can lead to the perception of themselves as devalued, worthless, and powerless (C. P. Jones, 2001).

More often the data that are shared and considered "cutting edge" are derived from Western, educated, industrialized, rich, and democratic (WEIRD) societies, and then efforts are made to apply the findings to people of color, people with disabilities, those of different socioeconomic backgrounds, and LGBTQ groups (Henrich et al., 2010). The narrowly obtained data, generalized broadly, fail to capture the nuances of understanding of human behavior, cognition, or biology as they present intersectionality. This in turn, affects the students we train and supervise in psychology, impacting their ability to teach, conduct research, and provide psychological services while presenting with more limited exposure to what may actually work in a multicultural setting. As a result, the professional psychology workforce, with roles as researchers, educators, clinicians, policy makers, and consultants, may approach their demands from an impoverished set of experiences across their training and with limited awareness about intersectional identities and the diversity of human and community experiences. This raises questions such as "Whose problem is it?" and "Who should change it?" Additional questions include "Who is responsible for the institutional barriers and systemic marginalization that exists?" and "Who benefits and who suffers from the maintenance of these systems?"

To respond to these questions and to better understand institutional barriers and systemic marginalization, it is necessary to understand what specifically lies behind these impediments. The APA's (2021a) recent *Resolution on Harnessing Psychology to Combat Racism* outlines five areas of racism to consider. This unanimously approved document carefully defines constructs that are suggested to be employed when developing antiracism strategies (see Table 7.1). It is oriented through an intersectional lens to better understand how different forms of racism interact and magnify the incidence of racism toward and among marginalized people. For example, institutional racism and internalized racism (negative beliefs about others) combine to potentially make it easier to implement racist attitudes (see also C. P. Jones, 2001; J. M. Jones, 1972/1997). These levels of racism may reinforce discrimination and privilege that subsequently provide the foundation for institutional barriers and systemic marginalization.

The interplay and intersectionality of these levels of racism are all utilized within settings and organizations to support their structure in ways that maintain the status quo and privilege for the few. Thus, it is important to understand the words of Arthur Jones: "All organizations are perfectly designed to get the results they get!" (Hanna, 1988, p. 36). Paul Batald4n later rephrased this to state: "Every system is perfectly designed to get the results it gets" (Institute for Healthcare Improvement [IHI], 2015, p.1). This captures how the marginalization of certain groups of people is "baked into" institutional structures. This is the crux of the problem that requires our consideration and is a focus of Guideline 5.

The problem of structural and organizational racism and subsequent marginalization tends to be described as belonging to people of color, who are Black, Indigenous, Asian, or Latinx; those with nonconforming sexual and gender orientations; individuals with disabling conditions; and/or others who experience discrimination. However, another central source of the problem is those who experience privilege, who have the power of that privilege to create and maintain the organizational structures that do not support others who are perceived as different from this privileged group, those who are favored. Until people with privilege recognize and engage with the responsibility their privilege provides, its consequences will continue to be experienced negatively and pejoratively by those who are not considered favored.

Recently, the APA Council of Representatives (COR) unanimously approved an apology resolution that acknowledges the role the American Psychological Association and American psychology have played in perpetuating racism (APA, 2021a). This apology resolution recognizes the problems of organizational and structural racism that exist in the United States, and the subsequent marginalization that has created barriers to success for Black Americans in particular. Within the resolution is the direct recognition that racism within professional psychology has at its foundation the problem of the favored discussed above. The resolution states directly that once this central core challenge to the profession is acknowledged and understood, only then can we move forward to make changes that create a level playing field for mutual success.

APPLYING MULTICULTURAL GUIDELINE 5 TO CLINICAL PRACTICE

The implications of institutional barriers for clinical practice begin at the student level and continue through to professional work. Clinical practice in this context means doctoral level counseling or clinical degrees and, more recently, master's level mental health care providers. The following paragraphs discuss how the barriers in place for students to achieve a clinical degree both precede and go beyond the rigors of graduate work. Ultimately, these barriers interfere with the ability to develop a psychology workforce that can meet the mental health needs of the United States as well as a diverse psychology workforce (Hanson, 2021)

Even before graduate school, for instance, Isabelle was faced with expenses that were difficult for her to manage. For example, entry into a graduate psychology degree often requires that undergraduate students or those with a college degree prepare for the GRE. At the time of this writing, the fee to take the GRE is $205 (see https://www.princetonreview.com/grad/gre-information). However, it is not uncommon for graduate school applicants to take the GRE more than once in an effort to improve their test scores. This cost is exacerbated by the reality that courses that help applicants study for the GRE can start at $1,999 and higher. Many universities continue to require the GRE despite evidence that suggests it is not useful in determining success in graduate school (Miller & Stassun, 2014; S. L. Petersen et al., 2018). Hence Miller and Stassun (2014) stated, "In simple terms, the GRE is a better indicator of sex and skin colour than of ability and ultimate success" (p. 304).

Among student applications, however, the costs of admission do not end with the GRE but continue with graduate school application fees. Just applying to several graduate programs can cost an applicant hundreds or thousands of dollars. While there are fee waiver programs, an applicant may not qualify.

As in the case of Isabelle, suppose the money is available for applications and a student is accepted into graduate school—then the costs of their degree continue to rapidly escalate, with the average cost of obtaining a doctorate in psychology currently falling at $132,200, as reported by the Education Data Initiative (Hanson, 2021). Furthermore, the doctoral level college experience is designed, for the most part, to be a full-time endeavor, and some programs require that students not work outside their program while they are completing their degree. Therefore, it is very common for students to take student loans to cover the costs of their living expenses and books, among other necessities.

The institutional impact of engagement, as described by Multicultural Guideline 5, can be seen with a university system designed for those who can afford to attend. The institutional barriers for doctoral psychology degrees begin with financial barriers and continue through a series of years of unpaid training, low-paid required doctoral internships, and postdoctoral work or low pay for assistant professors. Those who cannot afford to attend without financial support become burdened with student loans that essentially decrease their subsequent income for up to many years after graduation.

This reality is evident in research such as the study by Hsueh and colleagues (2021) that explored clinical psychology PhD student admission experiences. This study specifically explored the admissions experiences of students enrolled in U.S. clinical psychology PhD programs with a focus on race/ethnicity and LGBTQ identity (Hsueh et al., 2021). Results from the study indicated that "racial/ethnic and LGBTQ students considered a programmatic commitment to diversity as more important in application decisions compared to non-Hispanic White and cisgender heterosexual students, respectively" (Hsueh et al., 2021, p. 113). In addition, with regard to finances and financial burden results indicated that "racial/ethnic minority and LGBTQ students identified financial considerations and program outcomes as more important in their decision-making compared with non-Hispanic White and cisgender heterosexual students, respectively" (Hsueh et al., 2021, p. 116).

Ultimately, the cost of becoming a practicing psychologist has an enormous impact on the ability to have a psychology workforce that can adequately meet the mental health needs of the nation and on the ability to provide diversity within the field. More specifically, an inability to readily prepare a diverse pipeline of future practicing psychologists makes it challenging, if not impossible, to ensure culturally responsive care. For those who cannot afford or access resources to pursue an advanced psychology degree, there are limitations on opportunity.

Nevertheless, recent data have shown some shift toward more diversity in the psychologist workforce. APA's Center for Workforce Studies found that more people of color were obtaining psychology degrees (APA, 2020a, 2020b). While this trend has resulted in greater diversity within the psychology workforce, gaps still need to be addressed and progress still needs to be made. For instance, the duality of a positive trend alongside the need for greater change is reflected in study findings that indicate that while 84% of psychologists are White, "in 2018 racial and ethnic minorities represented 26% of psychologists under age 36, compared with 8% of those over age 50" (APA, 2020a, 2020b).

The complexity of this positive trend is further compounded by data presented by the Education Data Initiative (Hanson, 2021) that demonstrate the differential costs of pursuing a doctorate in psychology by race and gender. According to these data, Asian/Asian American doctoral students borrowed $16,838 annually for their program; African American students borrowed $17,479 annually; Latinx students borrowed $20,246 annually; and White/White American students borrowed an average of $18,087 each year. Returning to the point of missing data, however, we see that no data were reported for Native American students or mixed-race students, again demonstrating the limits of our knowledge and awareness of institutional barriers and their impact on engagement.

With regard to gender, results from the Education Data Initiative (Hanson, 2021) demonstrate that both men and women seek to decrease the cost of doctoral study in psychology through research and teaching assistantships. However, results indicate that, on average, men receive greater assistance than women with regard to the cost of completing graduate psychology training. Specifically, 38.7% of men in psychology doctoral programs gain some financial support through research or training assistantships in comparison with 27.1% of women (Hanson, 2021). With regard to the amount of debt, 874 male graduates owed greater than $160,000 in debt in comparison with 1,250 female graduates who owed more than that amount (Hanson, 2021).

Again, the duality of access to resources highlights the complexity of Multicultural Guideline 5 with its emphasis on institutional impact on engagement. On the one hand, for instance, we see a trend toward greater diversification of the psychology workforce by race and ethnicity as evident in APA data (2020a, 2020b). On the other hand, gaps in diversification remain, and we continue to see disparity in terms of who receives what financial resources by race/ethnicity and gender. Hsueh and colleagues (2021) recommended "institutional conversations around recruiting racial/ethnic minorities and LGBTQ trainees" with a focus on greater financial support for students as well as "fostering authentic training environments" (p. 118).

In addressing the complexity of institutional impact on engagement that is at the heart of Multicultural Guideline 5, we encourage taking a both/and approach that involves exploring and being open to positive trends that may be emerging, while also acknowledging and addressing those systemic realities that support the status quo (Clauss-Ehlers et al., 2019). While the example of institutional impact on engagement presented in this chapter reflects that of the psychology student experience, this duality is apparent in other issues where institutional processes can either limit engagement or taint the type of engagement that occurs. Such processes and the level of engagement or disengagement that ensues are paramount in systems of law (Mohamud et al., 2021); health care (Clauss-Ehlers & Tummala-Narra, 2022); education (Ko et al., 2021); and mental health (Guevara Carpio et al., 2022), among many other systemic realities.

APPLYING MULTICULTURAL GUIDELINE 5 TO RESEARCH

Just as institutional barriers interfere with the development of a clinical pipeline of a diverse psychologist workforce, so too do research barriers interfere with the development of a scientific pipeline. For instance, at the very beginning of undergraduate education, psychology students are required to participate in research and to explore the existing literature to learn more about their areas of study. This is where they participate in the projects of graduate students and faculty and write literature reviews that invariably include WEIRD studies (Henrich et al., 2010).

In fact, Henrich and colleagues (2010) contended that most psychology studies are based on findings with WEIRD samples. They stated the following:

> A recent analysis of the top journals in six disciplines of psychology from 2003 to 2007 revealed that 68% of subjects came from the United States, and a full 96% were from Western industrialized countries, specifically those in North America and Europe, as well as Australia and Israel. (p. 3)

More recent research demonstrates that little has changed. For instance, Nielsen and colleagues (2017), in their review of *Child Development, Developmental Psychology,* and *Developmental Science* journals from 2006 to 2010, found that "percentages of participation" in articles published in these journals indicated 90.52% from WEIRD societies, with 57.65% from the United States, 17.95% from English speaking countries, and 14.92% from European countries. This was in stark contrast to the 6.76% of participant representation from non-WEIRD societies, including .63% from Africa, .70% from South/Central America, 4.36% from Asia, and 1.07% from Israel and the Middle East (Nielsen et al., 2017).

We see the trends in the above studies echoed in student research endeavors. In part due to the institutional time limits of graduate training, graduate students must often conduct their research on available populations (e.g., college students), thus expanding the college student population research. For students from diverse backgrounds who try to conduct research in their own communities, it becomes a bit more complicated because time limitations to graduate and complete theses or dissertations suggest a local student population may be the quickest route to program completion. Again, this limits the possible diversity of student research projects. Moreover, by not conducting community-based participatory research (CBPR), and instead focusing on a convenient sample, students miss out on learning research skills and practices endemic to data collection in a community context. As a result of this gap in learning, students may not conduct CBPR in the future as they never gained the requisite skills in their graduate training.

Ultimately, the health and well-being of racial/ethnic minority populations are put at risk by not having data to support appropriate interventions. For example, the Congressional Research Service Report (Bagalman & Heisler, 2016) noted that the lack of a culturally competent workforce is complicated by a basic lack of data with respect to the needs and effective treatment methodologies for American Indian and Alaska Native communities. In another study, Kung (2004) documented cultural barriers related to credibility of treatment among Chinese Americans.

The basic psychological work of researchers, consultants, clinicians, teachers, and even forensic psychologists may be negatively impacted by having a limited research base of information relevant to diverse populations. The APA (2021b) apology resolution outlined specific areas of psychological research that have been used to segregate children of color, have failed to elevate the science behind the adverse social determinates of health for people of color, and acknowledged that Whiteness has been centered in psychological science, scholarship, and practice.

APPLYING MULTICULTURAL GUIDELINE 5 TO TEACHING AND TRAINING

Classroom instructors who are accustomed to having students from middle-class and affluent members of society might misunderstand students who are fully new to the college experience—at either the undergraduate or graduate level. Certain norms are taught to students in secondary schools that groom them for college, which students from working-class families might not be familiar with. Students who were prepared for college might have more awareness of the system as dictated by norms associated with middle-class education. Cabrera and Padilla (2004) referred to this as having awareness of and knowledge about the "culture of college."

Many instructors appreciate students who articulate their ideas in the classroom, demonstrate critical thinking, and express their needs. Yet, some students, for a variety of reasons, might prefer to sit quietly and listen. This may be misunderstood as disinterest, boredom, a lack of intellectual curiosity, or even disrespect. In reality, however, such pensiveness could suggest that "working-class students, guided by norms of hard interdependence, more often learn the importance of 'hanging in there' and of showing respect and deference to authority figures" (Stephens et al., 2014, p. 621). These students may also want to avoid burdening the teacher (Calarco, 2011; Stephens et al., 2014). Becoming aware of how students were or were not prepared for the college transition can inform different teaching styles in which the teacher's normative views of the "good student" could be challenged and adapted to ensure success for all students.

In addition to faculty efforts to get to know their students and how their experience informs their role in the classroom, teaching and training can also commit to an understanding of diversity from a more in-depth, thoughtful perspective. For instance, students of color have shared concerns about a lack of depth in cross-cultural understanding as well as unease with training that seemed to focus on teaching "White students" how to work with people of color while there was nothing taught to students of color about working with White clients (Seward, 2014). This superficial training connected with diverse populations has been described by Trimble and Bhadra (2013) as "ethnic gloss." Trimble and Bhadra defined ethnic gloss as

> an overgeneralization or simplistic categorical label used to refer to ethnocultural groups such as American Indians, Asian Americans, Hispanics, African Americans, and other nationalistic or indigenous groups where unique cultural and ethnic differences found among group members are ignored. An ethnic gloss presents the illusion of homogeneity where none exists, and therefore may be a superficial, almost vacuous categorization that provides little or no information on the existence of numerous subgroups characterized by distinct lifeways and thoughtways. (p. 501)

Professors and trainers who lack an understanding of the complexity associated with between-group and within-group differences may very well replicate institutional barriers to learning in the classroom by teaching and supervising from an ethnic gloss perspective.

APPLYING MULTICULTURAL GUIDELINE 5 TO CONSULTATION

As related to Multicultural Guideline 5, a critical part of the consultation process for psychologists will be their recognition and understanding of power and privilege dynamics within the institutions within which they are serving as a consultant. Here the role of the consulting psychologist, in alignment with Multicultural Guideline 5, is to work with the organization to identify systems and structures that present institutional barriers that can hinder success and engagement.

For instance, in their review, Albritton and colleagues (2019) documented the success of consultations with Head Start and other early childhood teachers in reducing the rate of suspensions and expulsions of their students; however, they identified only three empirical studies. The role of the consulting psychologist as described by Multicultural Guideline 5 is important to understand structures and practices that lead to Albritton et al.'s (2019) conclusion that African American children were more likely to be disciplined. Here the consulting psychologist can work with the educational institution to understand practices and policies that lead to this disparity in discipline procedures.

Part of this consultant's role can involve developing multitiered partnerships with the institution in which the psychologist is consulting. For instance, Eckert and colleagues (2017) reported a unique and effective rural consultation in a diverse elementary school, involving a multilevel partnership with a local nongovernmental organization as well as state and federal resources. In another school-based intervention model, named BRIDGE, mental health professionals act as consultants for teachers in their classrooms, effectively assisting them with their classroom practices (Cappella et al., 2012).

Goforth and colleagues (2017) emphasized the need for a focus on multicultural consultation. Thus, the value of consultation should be recognized, even promulgated, for its effectiveness, but that should occur, for psychologist–consultants using the framework of Guideline 5, in the context of the systemic racism and marginalization that exist within the institution.

CONCLUSION

This chapter explains the institutional barriers in psychology that promote inequities that ultimately impact systems of student training, mental health services, research, and consultation. The potential barriers discussed are not meant to be an exhaustive list but rather a way to highlight, understand, and illustrate how the barriers lead to inequity across reference group identities.

Existing institutional barriers must be managed, redrawn, or removed to allow for the entry and successful trajectory for the potential achievement for all.

The APA Division 45 Warrior Path Presidential Task Force (2020) *Warriors' Path Final Report* and the APA (2021b) apology resolution address issues of institutional engagement as reflected in Multicultural Guideline 5, with implications for practice, research, teaching, training, and consultation. For instance, these initiatives recommend increased funding for students, de-centering Whiteness in science scholarship and practice, ethical research that actively engages communities of color, and collecting and reporting data for specific groups rather than clustering small group data into an "other" category. Institutional barriers within the training and profession of psychology present just one example of the need to allow for greater equity for institutional participants. Barriers can impede people's success and stall a person from moving forward. Identifying and removing barriers to success and adequate support for all participants promotes the success of the institution. We are all stronger when we help each other move upward and forward toward our goals.

8 PROMOTING CULTURE-CENTERED INTERVENTIONS AND ADVOCACY

Multicultural Guideline 6

Guideline 6. Psychologists seek to promote culturally adaptive interventions and advocacy within and across systems, including prevention, early intervention, and recovery.

Following Multicultural Guideline 5, with its emphasis on institutional barriers and systemic marginalization, Multicultural Guideline 6 is the second Level-3 guideline focused on institutional impact on engagement. Its focus is that culture is central to mental health, both in terms of how mental health issues may manifest and in treatment responses to them (Gopalkrishnan, 2018). Culture is also a critical variable in aspects of mental health promotion that include advocacy and prevention, early intervention, and recovery efforts (Gee et al., 2015). At the heart of these concepts is the notion of *culture-centered intervention* (American Psychological Association [APA], 2003; Pedersen, 1997). Culture-centered interventions are mental health interventions that incorporate the role of culture and language in their delivery. Culture-centered interventions reflect an awareness of culture, an integration of cultural values and language in interventions, an understanding of the cultural background of the client or clients receiving services, and an ability to distinguish between pathology and culture (Pedersen, 1997).

https://doi.org/10.1037/0000348-008
Applying Multiculturalism: An Ecological Approach to the APA Guidelines, by C. S. Clauss-Ehlers, S. J. Hunter, G. S. Morse, and P. Tummala-Narra
Copyright © 2024 by the American Psychological Association. All rights reserved.

Psychology as a 21st-century science is developing a solid evidence base that demonstrates the efficacy of culture-centered interventions (Spilka & Dobson, 2015). This science provides empirical evidence that supports the ways in which culture-specific interventions are responsive to diverse individuals and communities seeking services (Bernal & Domenech Rodríguez, 2012). The multiculturally responsive psychologist can provide interventions that are responsive to the cultural background of an individual, group, family, couple, or organization. Culturally competent service delivery systems are thought to increase access and utilization by providing services that reflect people's cultural values and language. The multiculturally responsive psychologist addresses disparities in mental health care and, in so doing, promotes social justice and the human right to mental health treatment (Vera & Speight, 2003).

Mental health stigma is a variable that can influence help-seeking behavior (Shannon et al., 2015). *Mental health stigma* includes stigmatized attitudes associated with having a mental health problem and/or seeking services and stigmatized perceptions of individuals who have mental illnesses (Ahmedani, 2011). Mental health stigma may have an impact on a client's decision to seek or continue with services, parents' decisions to seek treatment for their children, and people's perceptions of individuals with mental illnesses. Guideline 6 is nested under Level 3 (i.e., institutional impact on engagement) because the extent to which services are (or are not) culturally centered, the influence of stigma, and the role of access and utilization inform the individual's, family's, couple's, group's, organization's, and community's level of engagement with institutions and organizations whose charge is to promote mental health.

Returning to the idea that it's important for the field to advocate for diverse ways of knowing, the following case shows how structural barriers interfere with the voices of our transnational colleagues being heard and represented in the research literature.

CASE ILLUSTRATION—JOURNAL PUBLISHING: ADVOCACY EFFORTS FOR GLOBAL INCLUSION IN RESEARCH PUBLICATION

When I, Caroline Clauss-Ehlers, served as editor of the *Journal of Multicultural Counseling and Development* (*JMCD*), we were interested in publishing transnational research. As an editorial team, we felt it was important to include a global perspective that reflected key journal themes of social justice and multicultural counseling. A research group submitted an excellent empirical manuscript with data collected in their country. We were enthusiastic about publishing this contribution. As with all the articles submitted to *JMCD*, we needed to ensure that the authors followed journal submission guidelines. At this point in the process, we noticed that the authors did not have institutional review board (IRB) approval, which is a requirement for journal publication. I reached out to the authors to ask about this omission.

The authors shared that lack of IRB approval had previously been an issue when they had tried to have their work published in other U.S. journals. They said their work was consistently rejected for publication because it did not have IRB approval. The authors shared they did not have IRB approval because IRBs did not exist in their country. Our editorial team began to explore the issue. We learned that many countries do not have IRBs in their institutions of higher education. Instead, we learned that a range of other processes were in place to assure the protection of human subjects who participated in research.

Our editorial team began to talk about the meaning of inclusive research. Some countries did not have review boards—did that mean research coming out of those countries would not be published in journals from countries that required an IRB review process for publication (e.g., U.S.-based journals)? To us, this requirement was a structural inequality: The publication structure in the United States was set up to give some research a review advantage over other research. The result was that ability to share knowledge transnationally was limited and that some studies, such as the one we wanted to publish, could be published only in journals and settings with no IRB requirements. What did this mean for giving a voice to transnational research? What did this mean for disseminating knowledge that reflected global perspectives? We felt a responsibility to advocate for a more inclusive approach to transnational research.

We began to explore how to change publication guidelines so that transnational research would not be excluded in this way. The editorial team spoke with the APA, the American Counseling Association, and the Rutgers IRB (i.e., my home institution). These conversations led us to develop alternative procedures for researchers from institutions without IRBs to provide assurances that all human participants' rights were protected.

These new procedures were put in place, and the authors' work was published. We saw this as an avenue for other transnational work to be published in the journal as well. We hoped our advocacy efforts would serve as a model for other journals interested in being inclusive of transnational scholarship.

> **Discussion Questions: Advocacy Efforts for Global Inclusion in Research Publication**
>
> 1. What transnational issues emerged for the researchers as they attempted to publish their work?
> 2. What are the structural barriers that interfere with the possibility of transnational research being published?
> 3. How does the research process exclude voices of individuals who are not from majority cultures?
> 4. How does the U.S. publication process exclude voices from researchers outside the United States?
> 5. How have structural inequities led to barriers in publishing your own work as a student/trainee or professional?
> 6. How did you deal with those barriers?
> 7. How can psychologists as researchers, educators, and mentors engage in advocacy efforts to promote inclusiveness in the research process?

LITERATURE REVIEW

The science of psychology has an evidence base that demonstrates the efficacy of culturally responsive interventions (Belone et al., 2016; Clauss-Ehlers et al., 2017; Garrett et al., 2001; Hays, 2016; M. T. Kim, 2002; Zane et al., 2016). Culture-centered interventions distinguish between cultural aspects of a situation and pathology. They include efforts to develop rapport within the context of a cross-cultural relationship (Pedersen, 1997).

Advocacy

The important role of advocating for culturally responsive services is a key theme presented in Guideline 6. Advocacy for people from underrepresented groups has a long history in behavioral health (Gee et al., 2015; Weintraub & Goodman, 2010). Table 8.1 presents various mental health advocacy approaches, including culture-centered interventions, systemic mental health advocacy, consumer movement, recovery model, cooperative community,

TABLE 8.1. Advocacy Approaches and Related Definitions

Advocacy approach	Approach description
Culture-centered interventions	Interventions that are culturally informed
	Interventions that incorporate an awareness of culture and cultural values
	Interventions that are responsive to the client's cultural background
	Clinician ability to tell the difference between culture and pathology
	Intervention research adapts interventions to specific communities
Systemic mental health advocacy	Also referred to as "collective mental health advocacy"
	Social movements that work to reform disparities and a lack of access to promote inclusion for people with mental illnesses
	Advocacy efforts to change legal, governmental, and health care systems
Consumer movement	Importance of consumers having a voice in mental health care services, policy, and treatment
	Consumers advocate for services
	Consumers share mental health information with the public
	Notion of recovery connected to the consumer movement
Recovery model	Focus on support/resilience, not just reducing symptoms
	Focus on coping rather than eradicating symptoms
	Emphasis on having control over one's life
	Focus on goals and aspirations rather than being told what one can't do
Cooperative community	Mental health professionals collaborating with others to create awareness and public discourse about mental health issues
	Five advocacy themes defined by Gee et al. (2015, p. 1):
	1. "building consumer and career participation"
	2. "voice and recognition for consumers and careers"
	3. "influencing and improving mental health systems"
	4. "effective collaboration and partnerships"
	5. "building organizational strength"
Prevention	Address behavioral issues before they begin
	Incorporate culture-centered interventions
	Advocacy to convince constituencies to address problems not yet visible
	Fortunate to not know what might have occurred had intervention not been delivered
	Developmental influence to prevent future problems later on in life
	Incorporate in early intervention efforts

(continues)

TABLE 8.1. Advocacy Approaches and Related Definitions (*Continued*)

Advocacy approach	Approach description
Early intervention	Services for infants and children from 0 to 5 years of age
	Ameliorates existing problems and supports developmental milestones
	Preventive aspect is to address concerns before they worsen in the future
	Early intervention goals as defined by Shonkoff and Meisels (2000, pp. xvii–xviii):
	1. "Promote child health and well-being"
	2. "Enhance emerging competencies"
	3. "Minimize developmental delays"
	4. "Remediate existing or emerging disabilities"
	5. "Prevent functional deterioration"
	6. "Promote adaptive parenting and overall family functioning"

prevention, and early intervention. Gee et al. (2015) defined *systemic mental health advocacy* as

> a social movement that seeks to change the disadvantageous policies and practices of legal, government, and health systems from within to develop a more inclusive community for people with mental disorders (also known as collective mental health advocacy; Stringfellow & Muscari, 2003). (p. 1)

Advocacy, as related to the work of psychologists, can be described as "informing and assisting decision-makers . . . who promote the interests of clients, health care systems, public and welfare issues, and professional psychology" (Lating et al., 2009, p. 106, as cited in Cohen et al., 2012, p. 151). Advocacy differs from lobbying, which, in the United States, refers specifically to activities geared toward changing legislation (Cohen et al., 2012). Advocacy is important given its focus on supporting vulnerable groups and responding to gaps in treatment, education, and policy so that individuals and communities are served (Cohen et al., 2012).

For example, after the tragedy of September 11th, 2001, the state of New York enacted a policy that provided free therapy for all individuals who were affected. Initially, only three free psychotherapy sessions were offered to individuals seeking services. Practitioners felt that providing only three sessions in the face of such an enormous tragedy was inappropriate. Of concern was that an individual or family who had just experienced a traumatic loss would connect with a therapist, only to be retraumatized with the loss of the therapist after the three sessions ended. Through advocacy efforts, the professional community came together to request longer treatment for individuals suffering from this trauma. The initial three sessions were extended to a year of free treatment.

This example demonstrates several advocacy elements to think about in our work. One is that the focus is on supporting services, and the delivery of those services, in a professional and healing context. A second element is that the advocacy efforts are focused on one issue—extending treatment. Stakeholder groups and constituencies joined around an issue that was directly defined and communicated—length of treatment. The third element is the importance of stakeholders coming together to promote advocacy efforts. Cohen and colleagues (2012) stated,

> Successful advocacy, therefore, needs to transcend the self-interests of the group advocating for it. To do this we need partners—organizations and individuals who are willing to lend their voices to ours. These might be clients who have benefited from service, legislators, and decision-makers who have first-hand experience of psychological problems and treatment, associations of consumers, or other health care providers who have benefitted or would like to benefit from having their patients seen by a psychologist. (p. 153)

Psychologists as clinicians, educators, researchers, and consultants can engage in advocacy work. Advocacy among psychologists is critical to support funding for research and for educational programs that provide educational access to diverse students. As demonstrated in the example, advocacy can lead to access to mental health services for people and communities who might not otherwise use them.

Advocacy works through multiple steps aimed toward a common goal. Cohen and colleagues (2012) provided 12 advocacy steps for psychology: (1) bring the issue to your association, (2) learn what your association is doing about the issue, (3) let others know you are a psychologist when working on the issue, (4) find out the views of the people you meet with (e.g., legislatures) about your issue, (5) have a discussion ready for those with who you meet, (6) focus on what's important to the person you meet with, (7) understand how policies are made with the person you are meeting with, (8) present an "ask," (9) have an "offer" for your ask, (10) offer help, (11) follow up, and (12) mentor. Although these are important steps, they tend to focus on advocacy-related conversations with a group or individual (e.g., a law-making body, a legislature). This aspect of advocacy is important but certainly not the only avenue.

Advocacy can occur at various levels of a system, whether a mental health delivery system in a city (as in the example) or advocacy for transnational scholarship (as in the case illustration). As psychologists, we are encouraged to advocate for systems change so that interventions are multiculturally responsive to the people they are designed to serve. Unfortunately, it is rare for doctoral training programs to offer courses about advocacy. As a result, we do not necessarily know how to engage in advocacy efforts and incorporate advocacy as a central aspect of our professional and personal identities (Cohen et al., 2012).

Despite a lack of doctoral training in advocacy, advocacy efforts have existed for some time. Since the 1800s, for instance, consumer-run advocacy groups have emerged across the globe. Beers (1908/1981) contributed to the mental health reform movement in the 1900s with the publication of his autobiography, *A Mind That Found Itself*, which was followed by the opening of child guidance clinics focused on prevention and early intervention during the 1910s. In 1963, Congress passed the Community Mental Health Act, which advocated for the deinstitutionalization of mental health systems in the United States. During the Civil Rights Movement (i.e., 1954–1968), civil-rights leaders engaged in efforts to promote mental health services and considered how segregation influenced access to and the use of mental health services (Guevara Carpio et al., 2022; Parham & Clauss-Ehlers, 2016b).

The 1980s and 1990s saw a push toward consumer and recovery movements (Jacob, 2015). Consumers advocated for services and informed the public about the nature of mental health services needed. Critical to the consumer movement was the sense that consumers needed to have a voice in treatment decisions and options and needed to advocate for themselves. The idea that the mental health provider is "the expert" who states the course of intervention and treatment was increasingly rejected as paternalistic (Clauss-Ehlers et al., 2019).

The idea of recovery gained increasing prominence during the consumer movement. For individuals with mental illnesses, recovery is often about "staying in control of their life rather than the elusive state of return to pre-morbid level of functioning" (Jacob, 2015, p. 117). According to Jacob, the recovery model focuses on resilience, coping, and managing life problems rather than complete symptom reduction; it focuses on providing support and forging resilience rather than solely focusing on symptom management.

Early in the 21st century, the central role of culture, race, and ethnicity in the access and use of mental health services was highlighted in the United States through the publication of the Surgeon General's report *Mental Health: Culture, Race, and Ethnicity* (U.S. Department of Health and Human Services [USDHHS], 2001). This report, a supplement to *Mental Health: A Report of the Surgeon General* (USDHHS, 1999), reviewed the status of research regarding experiences of stigma and disparities in mental health care among diverse communities. This groundbreaking work documented that people of color had less access to mental health care and were less likely to receive care than their White/White American counterparts; when care was received, the treatment was often of lesser quality (USDHHS, 2001).

Since the publication of the Surgeon General's supplemental report, a surge of research has built on the knowledge base regarding culture-centered intervention research. The idea of adapting evidence-based treatments within specific community contexts is one means of intervention applicable to diverse community contexts (Bernal & Domenech Rodríguez, 2012). Acknowledging the burden of mental health within a global context is of increasing importance as we come to understand the global prevalence of mental illness (Clauss-Ehlers, Guevara Carpio, & Weist, 2020).

Mental health parity has been an additional ongoing advocacy issue. *Mental health parity* refers to having health insurance plans that provide coverage for mental health-related care that is equivalent to care related to medical and surgical concerns (National Alliance on Mental Illness, 2015). To achieve parity, mental health insurance benefits should be equivalent to the benefits provided for physical health-related problems. In 2008, the Paul Wellstone and Pete Domenici Mental Health Parity and Addiction Equity Act was passed into legislation, a major event that supported mental health parity.

Contemporary 21st-century approaches reflect the early work of the 1900s with their renewed focus on advocacy alongside prevention and early intervention efforts. Gee et al. (2015) described how, as psychologists, we can be part of a "cooperative community" working with consumers, colleagues, and mental health professionals to give voice to mental health concerns. They identified five critical advocacy themes that inform the work of mental health advocates: "building consumer and career participation, voice and recognition for consumers and careers, influencing and improving mental health systems, effective collaboration and partnerships, and building organizational strength" (Gee et al., 2015, p. 1).

Prevention and Early Intervention

Advocacy can include implementing culture-centered interventions in prevention and early intervention efforts (Clauss-Ehlers, 2017; Gardiner & French, 2011; LaFromboise & Malik, 2016). Primary prevention involves efforts to prevent behavioral issues before they begin (Asarnow et al., 2015). Prevention requires advocacy. It may be difficult to convince communities, policy makers, and funders to support prevention efforts for concerns not yet identified or viewed as prevalent (Gardiner & French, 2011). With prevention, we have the privilege of not knowing what might have happened.

Early intervention incorporates prevention to some extent via efforts to address existing issues during early developmental stages. Addressing issues at early onset or early in life (e.g., infancy, toddlerhood) may prevent the development of more serious issues later in life (Chronis-Tuscano et al., 2018; Clauss-Ehlers, 2017). Shonkoff and Meisels (2000) defined early intervention as

> Multidisciplinary services provided for children from birth to 5 years of age to promote child health and well-being, enhance emerging competencies, minimize developmental delays, remediate existing or emerging disabilities, prevent functional deterioration, and promote adaptive parenting and overall family functioning. These goals are accomplished by providing individualized developmental, educational, and therapeutic services for children in conjunction with mutually planned support for their families. (pp. xvii–xviii)

Research has indicated that culturally informed training is critical for successful prevention and early intervention programs (Gardiner & French, 2011).

APPLYING MULTICULTURAL GUIDELINE 6 TO CLINICAL PRACTICE

Culturally Adaptive Interventions

Psychotherapy discontinuation refers to a client's ending treatment before the clinician recommends it. Psychotherapy discontinuation is an enormous problem in the delivery of treatment, with research showing that most clients only attend two therapy sessions and then decide not to return (Swift & Greenberg, 2012). While some research has identified factors that lead to psychotherapy discontinuation (e.g., lack of mental health insurance coverage; Barrett et al., 2008), less is known about the potential for cultural miscommunications that can leave a client feeling unheard and misunderstood, without the clinician even being aware of a problem.

Given that clinical practice involves a conversation, one application of Guideline 6 to clinical work is for clinicians to be aware of cultural aspects of verbal and nonverbal communication relevant for the client. This practice involves being aware of the aspects of verbal and nonverbal communication that have implications for clinical work. For instance, in Latinx cultures, a man looking a woman directly in the eye for an extended period may be interpreted as flirting. A cultural miscommunication can occur when a clinician assumes a client who avoids eye contact is not engaged in therapy; the client may be avoiding eye contact to be respectful. This type of miscommunication might set the stage for psychotherapy discontinuation. For clinicians, being aware of the meaning of nonverbal communication (e.g., eye contact, facial expressions) is an important aspect of effective cross-cultural communication.

E. T. Hall (1959/1973) introduced the concepts of high-context and low-context cultures to help us understand intercultural communication. *High-context cultures* are characterized by a focus on the collective, with a value placed on group rather than individual outcomes. A community focus is central to high-context cultures, and relationships are greatly valued. Individuals in high-context cultures tend to place less emphasis on the direct spoken word for meaning, relying more on nonverbal cues such as gestures and tone. In contrast, *low-context cultures* emphasize the well-being of the individual more than the well-being of the collective. The direct spoken word is a main method of communication, with less attention given to nonverbal communication. According to E. T. Hall's (1959, 1973) theory, people in low-context cultures are less concerned with group relationships and more individually focused than are people in high-context cultures.

The idea of high- and low-context cultures has implications for clinical practice. It is often the case that training programs in the United States focus on clinical work at an individual level, with the spoken word as the main form of communication. This training emphasis reflects a tendency toward the United States being characterized as a low-context culture context. However, the application of values specific to low-context cultures when working with individuals, couples, groups, or families from high-context cultures may result in disconnections during clinical practice.

Advocacy

Relationship-centered advocacy focuses on a mutually supportive professional relationship that occurs within a social-justice framework (Weintraub & Goodman, 2010). Psychologists can engage in advocacy efforts that support those with whom they work. The APA has an entire webpage devoted to ways that psychologists can engage in advocacy (see https://www.apa.org/advocacy). The multiculturally responsive psychologists can integrate advocacy into clinical practice in various ways. Table 8.2 lists opportunities for psychologists to engage in advocacy work in six advocacy areas.

Kozan and Blustein (2018) discussed two ways in which psychologists can incorporate advocacy in their practice: individual-level advocacy and organizational-level advocacy. They found that clinicians who graduated from counseling psychology programs integrated individual-level advocacy in clinical work by engaging in *social justice intentionality*. Such intentionality was evident in their commitment to engaging in advocacy work and to

TABLE 8.2. Key American Psychological Association Areas of Advocacy

Overall theme	Related topics
Health	Health disparities
	Military and veterans
	Physical and mental health
	Substance use disorders
Education and training	Pre-K to Grade 12 education
	Higher education
	Workforce development
Research	Federal funding for psychological research
	Promoting and defending research
Social justice and human rights	Civil rights
	Immigration
	Criminal justice
	Socioeconomic status
Violence prevention	Gun violence
	Interpersonal violence
	Suicide
Practice of psychology	Health care reform
	Medicare reimbursement
	Mental health parity
	Prescriptive authority

Note. This original table is based on the American Psychological Association advocacy priorities (see https://www.apa.org/advocacy).

providing clinical services for people with limited access to them (L. Smith & Lau, 2013). Similarly, social justice intentionality emerged through an understanding of the systemic contextual and environmental barriers clients faced in their lives. Practitioners who participated in Kozan and Blustein's study indicated that they built on client strengths to encourage self-advocacy and that they connected clients with community services.

Organizational-level advocacy in clinical practice involves advocacy within the organization (Kozan & Blustein, 2018). These efforts can help clients connect with existing organizational resources. Alternatively, a clinician can work with clients to advocate for resources when they do not exist. For instance, when I (Caroline) was providing teletherapy to middle school students during the COVID-19 crisis, many shared that they were struggling with math. It was understandably challenging to follow the complexity of math problems in a remote learning environment. I reached out to the school administration to ask if the school could ask the math teachers to provide virtual office hours for students. This level of advocacy within the organization soon proved effective as students began to get the extra math help they needed to succeed.

Multiculturally responsive psychologists can also engage in "advocacy beyond the organization" (Kozan & Blustein, 2018, p. 172). Clinicians can make community contributions outside of their organizations or the private practice setting. For example, multiculturally responsive psychologists might volunteer to participate in a mentoring program for young people who feel isolated during COVID-19. As another example, they might volunteer to provide tutoring for students struggling with a remote learning environment.

Psychologists can be advocates in many ways. Guideline 6 emphasizes advocacy as an important aspect of psychologists' contributions, especially in light of research that suggests many students do not receive training in clinical advocacy skills, even in doctoral programs that have a social-justice focus (Kozan & Blustein, 2018). The risk is that students graduate with a professional and/or personal identity that does not include being an advocate.

Prevention, Early Intervention, and Recovery

It is important that we are aware of cultural differences in perceptions of stigma, help-seeking behaviors, cultural norms, and views of mental health (Turner et al., 2016). These variables can influence whether or not intervention is sought. They can also affect how mental health care systems address mental health care intervention and the nature of care provided. Globally, for instance, mental health care service systems focus on intervening after a crisis or the emergence of an acute mental health issue. Data from the World Health Organization (WHO; 2015) show that an abundance of mental health care systems spend a majority of their budgets on inpatient hospital care rather than on prevention or early intervention.

This gap in service provision, with services that respond to problems after they occur rather than concurrently providing supports to prevent them, does not correspond with what we know about the average age of onset (AAO) for mental health problems. For example, the AAO for mental health issues is during the teenage years: Fifty percent of mental health issues start during this time (Kessler et al., 2007). A proactive alternative to providing hospital beds after an onset of a mental health issue is to provide intervention and supports that foster social and emotional learning, the process through which children and adults acquire and effectively apply the knowledge, attitudes, and skills necessary to understand and manage emotions, set and achieve positive goals, feel and show empathy for others, establish and maintain positive relationships, and make responsible decisions (Collaborative for Academic, Social, and Emotional Learning, n.d., para. 1).

Designing mental health systems of care around a prevention and early intervention model that fosters resilience and coping may ultimately mitigate onset (Chronis-Tuscano et al., 2018).

APPLYING MULTICULTURAL GUIDELINE 6 TO TEACHING AND TRAINING

Surprisingly, very little existing literature focuses on teaching and training future psychologists to deliver and conduct research on culture-centered interventions (Soheilian et al., 2014). Broadly speaking, to foster learning about culture-centered interventions, it is important that graduate programs incorporate a multicultural approach across the curriculum, rather than in one class (Clauss-Ehlers, 2006a). In a curriculum, trainees learn about the application of multicultural content across training domains. Coursework and practicum experiences can consider how to culturally adapt theories and related techniques in work with clients from diverse backgrounds. When multicultural content is embedded throughout the curriculum, trainees are continually considering how to apply cultural content to a range of treatment needs.

Clinical supervision is another important way to promote learning about the delivery of culture-centered interventions (Soheilian et al., 2014). It is important that supervision is a safe place for students to have conversations about issues like racism, discrimination, sexism, and xenophobia. Students may not have a language to engage in conversations about these difficult topics. Supervision can help students develop a voice (and an understanding) that expresses these critical topics. Developing this language and understanding is important for rapport building, and trainees may feel better able to address such topics when clients raise them in treatment.

Trainees are encouraged to record sessions (with client and supervisor permission) and play them back in supervision. Supervisors can encourage trainees to play parts of the session during which the trainee struggled with an intervention. Recording sessions can also be used in a classroom in which role-playing is incorporated as a learning activity (Clauss-Ehlers & Pasquerella, 2017).

Hechanova and Waelde (2017) presented five aspects of diverse cultures for mental health professionals to consider. These elements were discussed in response to disasters in Southeast Asia. They provide a context for conversations about diversity that can start during coursework and supervision and continue through the trainee's transition to professional life. The five elements are emotional expression, shame, power distance, collectivism, and spirituality and religion.

For conversations about emotional expression, trainees can consider the many ways that emotions are expressed. In some cultures, somatic or bodily complaints may be an acceptable way to express emotional content. The statement "I have a headache" may actually mean "I'm depressed." In other cultures, individuals may avoid talking about emotions because they are afraid of the pain that sharing them may cause. It may be difficult for trainees to identify the emotional content raised by their clients. Supervision can help students address and process client emotions rather than avoid them.

The second element, shame, relates to stigma. Is the client ashamed of needing treatment? Is the client experiencing shame because they have not told their family that they are going for treatment? Through conversations that consider how the client may experience shame, a trainee can learn about how to respond when clients present potential barriers to ongoing clinical work.

Power distance is the third element. Power distance refers to power differences between clinician and client. We encourage trainees to recognize that clients may perceive them as the expert and authority. Trainees are encouraged to acknowledge the potential power that comes with this role, rather than to ignore it: Central to the *Multicultural Guidelines: An Ecological Approach to Context, Identity, and Intersectionality, 2017* is an emphasis on a bidirectional relationship that supports a foundation of mutuality between these roles.

Collectivism is the fourth element. Collectivism refers to a worldview that focuses on the greater good rather than the individual (Triandis, 2018). Collectivism resonates with the advocacy principle of promoting the needs of others, rather than those of one's self. Understanding the role of collectivism is particularly important given an emphasis on individual-based therapeutic training in the United States and the recognition that some cultures focus on the family or the group more than the individual.

The last element is spirituality and religion. Understanding a client's spirituality and religion can help trainees better understand the client's coping skills, resilience, and life challenges. This element involves considering ways to acknowledge and respect religious beliefs in the treatment process.

Marsella (2011) used the phrase "society as a patient" to share how client problems result from the surrounding environment rather than at an individual micro level. The society-as-patient framework fits with the *2017 Multicultural Guidelines*' ecological model by considering the therapeutic relationship in the context of multiple environmental systems (APA, 2017a). Training can encourage students to take a contextual, systemic approach to understanding the intersection between individual client issues and the influence and impact of the surrounding environment. Marsella incorporated an advocacy model that encourages clinicians working in diverse cultural contexts to address disparities.

APPLYING MULTICULTURAL GUIDELINE 6 TO RESEARCH

Psychology as a 21st-century science can examine diverse ways of creating new knowledge. Rather than simply engaging in large, randomized studies where one evidence-based practice is statistically supported, researchers can consider how interventions might be culturally adapted (Clauss-Ehlers, 2017; Spilka & Dobson, 2015). It is important that the field values diverse research methods and data collection methods so that specifics related to community experiences are voiced. Such specificity may go unheard when qualitative research that presents overarching trends is the exclusive focus of the field.

As multiculturally responsive research psychologists, we can build on the evidence base to generate knowledge about culture-centered interventions. With a 21st-century scientific foundation already set, it is exciting to consider the next iteration of research on culture-centered interventions. Questions research scientists might ask include: What topics are underrepresented in the literature? How can I collect data from a diverse sample so that findings reflect the experience of this population? What norms are needed so that assessments truly reflect diverse normative data?

A related research approach involves community-based participatory research (CBPR; Belone et al., 2016). CBPR includes an authentic partnership between the research team and the community. Rather than simply take data and leave, the research team collaborates with the community to provide benefits emanating from the research. The community is involved in the research study. For instance, in data collection for a study conducted at a low-resourced school, the school requested that the middle school student body visit the researcher's university campus (Clauss-Ehlers, 2022). The school administration wanted the students to see what a college campus was like so that they could envision college as part of their futures. The researcher organized a campus visit that has continued for years.

APPLYING MULTICULTURAL GUIDELINE 6 TO CONSULTATION

Consultation can focus on the development, promotion, and implementation of culture-centered interventions. Consultation may involve the implementation of culture-centered interventions within a school or organizational setting. It may involve considering ways to adapt an evidence-based practice within a diverse organizational context. Multiculturally responsive psychologists might engage in a needs assessment to determine if community services are responsive to community needs. Throughout these endeavors, we can conceptualize the psychologist as both consultant and advocate, developing a "cooperative community" that advocates for prevention, early intervention, recovery, and systems change.

In keeping with the focus on prevention, early intervention, and recovery presented in Guideline 6, consultation to support building a community mental health care infrastructure is an area where multiculturally responsive psychologists can exert influence. Such consultation is particularly important given research that indicates most people across the globe who have a mental health issue and need treatment do not receive it (Thornicroft et al., 2016). As low-, middle-, and high-income countries explore the extent to which their governments are investing in creating mental health infrastructures, Thornicroft et al. presented a critical question for consultation:

> But what pattern of services and what systems of care best support the provision of the quality and quantity of treatment and care required for people with mental illnesses in the different scenarios (not only high- vs. low- and middle-income countries, but also high- vs. low-resource areas within countries)? (p. 276)

The WHO *World Mental Health Atlas 2017* provides information about mental health systems across the globe (WHO, 2018). It includes data about mental health care systems operating in 177 of the 194 United Nations member states, who "at least partially completed the Atlas questionnaire" (WHO, 2018, p. 2). An analysis conducted by Thornicroft and colleagues (2016) shows that 80% of mental health expenditure in lower-middle-income countries, 50% in upper-middle-income countries, and 30% in high-income countries is spent on care provided through a mental health hospital (e.g., inpatient care). This finding shows how government mental health expenditures prioritize spending on hospital care rather than other inpatient care/daycare and outpatient care/primary care measures. It indicates how more can be done globally to support prevention and early intervention as part of community-based mental health care.

Consultation can address the need for greater expenditure on community-based mental health care infrastructures. Part of this treatment gap is due to stigma, discrimination, and the sense that services are not accessible. Psychology consultants can help implement systems of care that use contact-based interventions that are shown to decrease stigma (Griffiths et al., 2014). As Thornicroft and colleagues (2016) noted, "The implication for community mental health is the need for population-level and community-level platforms to use contact-based interventions to reduce stigma and discrimination" (p. 282).

CONCLUSION

Developing and implementing culture-centered interventions are acts of advocacy. They show clients that mental health professionals are advocating on their behalf to be responsive to their cultural and linguistic experiences. Through advocacy and supporting self-advocacy, we can address systemic issues and barriers such as those that influence access and utilization of services. Guideline 6 encourages us to make advocacy a part of our professional identities.

Multicultural Guideline 6 also encourages us to consider varied approaches to intervention. It highlights the importance and the effectiveness of prevention and intervention efforts, which are often missing from practice, training efforts, research, and consultation. It encourages us to consider employing diverse research approaches and methodologies. Through greater consideration of prevention, early intervention, and recovery models that address stigma and discrimination through community mental health care systems, and a growing culturally informed evidence base, the treatment gap may narrow.

In the next two chapters, we move into guidelines that reflect Level 4 of the ecological model, the domestic and international climate. Chapter 9 focuses on Multicultural Guideline 7, which addresses the impact of globalization on professional identity and engagement as a psychologist.

PART V: PSYCHOLOGICAL PRACTICE WITHIN A DOMESTIC AND INTERNATIONAL CLIMATE

9 UNDERSTANDING GLOBALIZATION'S IMPACT ON PSYCHOLOGY
Multicultural Guideline 7

Guideline 7. Psychologists endeavor to examine the profession's assumptions and practices within an international context, whether domestically or internationally based, and consider how this globalization has an impact on the psychologist's self-definition, purpose, roles, and function.

Multicultural Guideline 7 is the first guideline in Level 4 of the model that focuses on domestic and international climate. This chapter extends from Chapters 7 and 8, which focus on Level 3, Institutional Impact on Engagement, to consider this next layer of sociocultural context. When the Multicultural Guidelines were written, the task force thought it was important to include a guideline specifically focused on global mental health considerations. The previous Multicultural Guidelines focused on the role of psychologists within a U.S. context. Guideline 7 was developed to consider transnational aspects of mental health, including aspects of access and utilization, to expand an understanding of the role of psychology from a global perspective.

The historical focus of psychology within the American Psychological Association (APA) as occurring within U.S. borders is captured by the very name of the association. However, the Americas do not consist solely of

https://doi.org/10.1037/0000348-009
Applying Multiculturalism: An Ecological Approach to the APA Guidelines, by C. S. Clauss-Ehlers, S. J. Hunter, G. S. Morse, and P. Tummala-Narra
Copyright © 2024 by the American Psychological Association. All rights reserved.

the United States, as the APA organizational name may imply, but rather two continents—South America and North America—and four geographical regions, comprising the Caribbean, North America, Central America, and South America. There are 35 countries that make up the Americas (the United States being just one of them), as well as various dependent territories (Nations Online, n.d.). We share this point to underscore the reality that an overfocus on the United States as consisting of the Americas risks overlooking the inherent multicultural reality of what the term *America* actually means.

Considering this redefined context leads us to explore next the growing role of psychologists within a global mental health framework. Global mental health has been described as

> aim[ing] to alleviate mental suffering through the prevention, care and treatment of mental and substance use disorders, and to promote and sustain the mental health of individuals and communities around the world. . . . It prioritizes equity, and is informed by many disciplines, including neuroscience, genomics, social sciences (especially psychology, medical anthropology, and sociology), epidemiology, health services research, and implementation science. (P. Y. Collins, 2020, p. 265)

A global mental health focus is particularly relevant when we consider that while mental health is an important part of health, it is often overlooked in health interventions worldwide. As stated by the World Health Organization (WHO; 2019), "Health is a state of complete physical, mental, and social well-being, and not merely the absence of disease or infirmity. . . . However, mental health remains a neglected part of global efforts to improve health" (p. 2).

This chapter encourages us to consider how psychologists can contribute to psychological endeavors within a global mental health context. The main question presented in this chapter is, How can we work across nations to address the global mental health crisis? Relatedly, another question is, How can we work across disciplines to support interventions that address global mental health? Our focus here is on the international aspect of Guideline 7, with consideration of our current and future "purpose, role, and function" as psychologists who engage in a global context. The following case presentation provides an example of the psychologist's potential role in teaching transnationally.

CASE ILLUSTRATION–GOOD EVENING, GOOD MORNING: TEACHING TRANSNATIONALLY

Just before the COVID-19 shutdown, I (CSCE) was asked by a global outreach program at a large public university to teach a course on adolescent development for high school students in China. The course would be in person, with me lecturing several times a week and providing advisement. This plan suddenly changed in light of the pandemic. Rather than completely canceling the course, it was decided that it would be taught online via Zoom. This was a new experience for me, the teaching assistants (TAs), and the students. The course has now been taught twice in this online format. During this second teaching experience, as our learning community adjusted to a time difference that involved a late-night class for students (e.g., 7:30–10:00 p.m.) and an early morning start for the teaching team (e.g., 7:30–10:00 a.m.), we often found ourselves starting class with "Good evening, good morning!" Several teaching considerations emerged from teaching this precollege adolescent development course in a synchronous format with high school students in China. These emerging learning experiences focused on language, participation, curriculum, and technology.

Language was the first consideration. English was a second language for the students. Many understandably struggled with speaking and writing in English. At the same time, students were committed to participating in English to build their language skills. They specifically wanted to develop their skill in speaking English to support their obtaining a passing score on the Test of English as a Foreign Language (TOEFL) examination that would accompany their applications to postsecondary schools in other countries. This commitment was evident in meetings where, even when a program administrator was available to translate, the students would choose not to use this option. Instead, they relied on their devices, which allowed them to say a word in Mandarin and the device would provide an auditory response in English.

There were several ways the teaching team managed the potentially stressful situation related to language. First, it was suspected that students might be self-conscious about participating on Zoom due to concerns about their English. The teaching team shared this potential stressor with the group, seeking to normalize their potential worries about communicating in English. The teaching team also stressed that students could share when they felt comfortable doing so and reinforced that their skill with English would have no impact on their overall grade for the course. The teaching team also provided students with linguistic options, such as consulting with each other during class or typing their comments in Mandarin into the Zoom chat function. In this way, the teaching team sought to increase participation among students while decreasing stress within the online classroom community.

Technology helped address issues associated with linguistic concerns as well; this, in turn, prompted engagement. Throughout the lectures, for instance, the teaching team would encourage students to share their opinions about relevant topics. These inquiries were often presented to students as close-ended questions so that they could participate with a yes or no response, as indicated by a thumbs up or thumbs down or by sharing an emoji in the chat.

In addition to language, a second consideration for course success focused on student participation and engagement. A preliminary strategy was to share ground rules for the course during the first day of class. These ground rules included letting students know that there was no expectation about English language fluency. The teaching team encouraged students to type a response in Mandarin in the chat if they were uncertain of the answer in English so that they could share their experiences with the larger group.

After working to normalize concerns about language, a second strategy was to give students permission to participate in the course. Given an educational cultural experience that often involves note taking and taking in information given by the instructor, the teaching team created a framework for collaborative learning where students were welcome to share their experiences. This approach was normalized by sharing that class participation and the coconstruction of knowledge are frequently part of the classroom experience in the United States. Students were assured that the nature of their comments would not be graded; rather, their comments were ways that they, too, could explore the information they were sharing.

A third strategy was to create a learning space without the faculty member present. Here, the teaching team, in collaboration with the global outreach program, created a TA discussion group (TADG). The TADG consisted of a 1-hour group with the TAs only that met directly after the lecture. Not only was less formality present with the absence of the professor but the TADG also provided a less formal structure. For instance, the TADG allowed for a space where students could engage in dialogue and experiential activities with one another. This strategy provided a way for students to participate that felt safe and comfortable.

In addition to setting up a structure that supported student participation, course content was another critical area of consideration. Key here was the question of curriculum. Questions that arose for the teaching team included, How is adolescent development defined across cultures? Which literature should be used? How can the course reflect the experiences of the high school students in China? The course took a flexible, culturally adaptive pedagogical approach to respond to these questions. For instance, during each class, the teaching team would consult with students about their experiences and explore how the material presented reflected their understanding of adolescent development and psychology in China.

Case analysis provided another pedagogical approach that prompted reflections based on student experiences. For this strategy, students were given a case that reflected the adolescent theme discussed that week (e.g., the impact of COVID-19 on adolescents, adolescent mental health). After reading through the case as a large group, students would be asked to share their understanding of it from their cultural context.

Similarly, assignments were pulled from the student experience rather than Westernized literature. Students wrote an adolescent experience paper where they talked about an experience that resonated with them. In another assignment, students wrote an adolescent issue paper where they analyzed an issue they felt adolescents experienced within their cultural context. By incorporating such strategies throughout the course, the teaching team sought to cocreate knowledge with the students. This occurred through an ongoing collaboration between the students and the teaching team. The result was often a new understanding of adolescent development that was built on the curriculum and literature and adapted to the students' experience.

Cocreation of knowledge was furthered by the teaching team's commitment to seeking out and incorporating student feedback. Students completed an anonymous informal midsemester evaluation form, for instance, where they shared what they found helpful and what they would like to see changed in the course. The teaching team shared midsemester evaluation feedback with the class and made changes accordingly. For instance, one point of feedback was that it would be helpful to spend time in the TADG analyzing a reading for the week. This change was then subsequently incorporated into the TADG. As a result, students found that they had an important voice in determining course content and the pedagogical approach. Their opinions about content and experience reflected their belief about what would be most effective in moving them toward their educational goals.

The curriculum about romantic relationships during adolescence provides an example of this collaboration. Empirical findings in the U.S. literature discuss how adolescent romantic relationships move from the experience of having one short relationship in early adolescence to having various relationships in middle adolescence and then typically culminating with one longer term relationship during the later adolescent years (Meier & Allen, 2009). Through discussion and collaboration, this framework and how it was understood as a process seen during adolescence shifted as students talked about the nature of adolescent romantic relationships in China. Students talked about being discouraged from engaging in romantic relationships and instead focused on their studies. The concept of "puppy love" was often used by students to describe infatuations and the desire to be in a romantic relationship while simultaneously recognizing that these types of experiences were not necessarily supported.

A final teaching consideration stemmed from recognizing and then leveraging the strengths of technology. At a most fundamental level, the Zoom platform provided a way for the course to happen. Technology further provided a way for students to connect as they emerged from 2 years of dealing with the COVID pandemic. For instance, the final paper consisted of a group project where students were placed into groups of three to four to work together. Where applicable, the teaching team put students who indicated they wanted to get to know one another more into the same group. In this way, technology served as an interpersonal means of connecting students through their collaborative work on their projects.

Technology further addressed language and participation concerns through various interactive Zoom-based features. Each lecture, for instance, included polls where a question was presented and students would indicate their responses anonymously. The entire class could see the percentage of students who chose each possible answer. Seeing differing responses provided a wonderful springboard to discuss diverse understandings of course material.

Students were encouraged to put on their social scientist hats by participating in polls that inquired whether they agreed with a hypothesis. For example, the lecture on how adolescent romantic relationships reflect a developmental milestone included the presentation of four slides, each with a separate hypothesis, followed by a poll where students voted as to whether they agreed with the hypothesis. Poll findings were then reviewed in the context of a discussion about research findings related to the hypothesis.

Another technological strength was provided by the online learning platform that included course content. Discussion boards for each class encouraged

Discussion Questions Related to Good Evening, Good Morning: Teaching Transnationally

1. What are culturally responsive ways that we can engage in teaching transnationally?
2. What are the challenges instructors might face in presenting a curriculum in a culturally syntonic way?
3. What are important considerations for instructors to be aware of when teaching transnationally?
4. How would you incorporate them?
5. What are some ways that you would like to incorporate teaching transnationally in your pedagogical practice?

students to share their experiences and indicate aspects of the weekly topic they wanted to focus on in class and the TADG. The recorded lectures were posted on the learning platform each week so that students could revisit the class, listening to content as needed.

LITERATURE REVIEW

Our discussion of global mental health as a context for psychological intervention starts with prevalence rates associated with mental health issues worldwide. This is a timely and pertinent discussion given recent data that indicate that the COVID-19 pandemic led to a 25% increase in depression and anxiety worldwide (WHO, 2022). In response to these significant increases in depression and anxiety, 90% of the countries surveyed by WHO said they were including mental health considerations as part of their COVID-19 planning response (WHO, 2022).

In recent years, mental health has been seen as being connected to "achieving global development goals" through its inclusion as a part of the WHO Sustainable Development Goals (WHO, n.d.-b). The WHO (2019) *Special Initiative for Mental Health (2019–2023): Universal Health Coverage for Mental Health* introduced a global effort to "scale-up mental health care" so that people across nations have access to mental health services as a result of making mental health care a part of universal health coverage. Efforts include two strategic action plans: (a) Advancing Mental Health Policies, Advocacy and Human Rights; and (b) Scaling Up Interventions and Services Across Community-Based, General Health and Specialist Settings (WHO, 2019). The special initiative goal is to provide access to mental health care for 100 million more people across 12 countries by 2023. To date, eight countries are involved in the special initiative: Bangladesh, Ghana, Jordan, Nepal, Paraguay, the Philippines, Ukraine, and Zimbabwe (WHO, n.d.-c).

Despite increased understanding and awareness of the impact that mental health has on health and well-being, people continue to experience mental health stigma and have limited access to mental health prevention and intervention (WHO, 2019). The need for global investment to address mental health is evident in prevalence data that show how many people are affected by mental health and substance abuse issues worldwide. While it is beyond the scope of this chapter to provide an in-depth analysis of global mental health prevalence, Table 9.1 presents some key data points that underscore the nature of global mental health. In considering these data, it is also important for us to note that prevalence is likely underreported due to stigma,

TABLE 9.1. Mental Health Prevalence Data Point Considerations

Mental health consideration	Prevalence data	Population consideration	Source
Mental health disorders, substance use disorders, and neurological disorders	These disorders combined account for 10% of the global disease burden	Global	WHO Special Initiative for Mental Health (n.d.-c; 2019)
Suicide	800,000 per year	Global leading cause of death for young people	WHO Special Initiative for Mental Health (n.d.-c; 2019)
Depression	280 million people	Global	WHO (2021b, 2022)
Bipolar disorder	45 million people	Global	GBD 2017 Disease and Injury Incidence and Prevalence Collaborators (2018)
Mental health disorder	1 in 7 young people between the ages of 10 and 19; contributes to 13% of GBD	Global	WHO (2021a)
Mental health disorder	15% of adults age 60+	Global	WHO (2017)
Major depressive disorder	Led to 49.4 million DALYs	Globally in 2020	COVID-19 Mental Disorders Collaborators (2021)
Anxiety disorders	Led to 44.5 million DALYs	Globally in 2020	COVID-19 Mental Disorders Collaborators (2021)

Note. DALY = disability-adjusted life years; GBD = global burden of disease; WHO = World Health Organization.

as well as data collected before the COVID-19 pandemic. For instance, more recent research that examined the impact of COVID-19 on 204 countries and territories indicated that the pandemic led to significant increases in depression and anxiety disorders globally (COVID-19 Mental Disorders Collaborators, 2021). The long-term impact of COVID-19 on young people who lived through the pandemic is unknown, with ongoing predictions about future effects on well-being still developing (Garagiola et al., 2022).

Table 9.1 relates prevalence data to the global burden of disease (GBD) and disability-adjusted life years (DALYs). The GBD refers to research examining "both the *prevalence* of a given disease or risk factor and the *relative harm* it causes" (Institute for Health Metrics and Evaluation, n.d., para. 2). A DALY measures the health loss a person experiences. This is done by examining the estimated number of years of having a healthy life that are lost. These lost healthy years could be due to "premature death or living with disability due to illness or injury" (Australian Institute of Health and Welfare, n.d.).

The *2030 Agenda for Sustainable Development* (United Nations General Assembly, 2015) began with the goal to

> end poverty and set the world on a path of peace, prosperity and opportunity for all on a healthy planet. The 17 Sustainable Development Goals demand nothing short of a transformation of the financial, economic and political systems that govern our societies today to guarantee the human rights of all. (United Nations, 2020, para. 1)

The *2030 Agenda* goals for global mental health promotion were as follows:

> 26. To promote physical and mental health and well-being, and to extend life expectancy for all, we must achieve universal health coverage and access to quality health care. No one must be left behind. We commit to accelerating the progress made to date in reducing newborn, child and maternal mortality by ending all such preventable deaths before 2030. We are committed to ensuring universal access to sexual and reproductive health-care services, including for family planning, information and education. We will equally accelerate the pace of progress made in fighting malaria, HIV/AIDS, tuberculosis, hepatitis, Ebola and other communicable diseases and epidemics, including by addressing growing anti-microbial resistance and the problem of unattended diseases affecting developing countries. We are committed to the prevention and treatment of non-communicable diseases, including behavioural, developmental and neurological disorders, which constitute a major challenge for sustainable development. (United Nations General Assembly, 2015, pp. 7–8)

> 3.4 By 2030, reduce by one third premature mortality from non-communicable diseases through prevention and treatment and promote mental health and wellbeing. (United Nations General Assembly, 2015, p. 16)

P. Y. Collins (2020) talked about a "'reframed' mental health agenda into the 2030 Agenda for Sustainable Development" (p. 265) that incorporates "four foundational pillars" (p. 265). The first pillar underscores mental health as "a global public good that requires action and intervention beyond the health sector" (p. 265). The second focuses on viewing mental health along a continuum of well-being to illness. It also advocates for prevention in addition to treatment and supports for mental health promotion efforts.

The third pillar corresponds with the Multicultural Guidelines' focus on intersectionality, given its commitment to understanding mental health and related interventions through an intersectionality of knowledge points and experiences. This pillar also incorporates the Multicultural Guidelines' consideration of trauma and resilience from a cross-cultural perspective by examining sociocultural and environmental experiences, along with neurodevelopment and brain biology, in human experiences along a mental health continuum.

Finally, like the Multicultural Guidelines, the fourth pillar reflects the role of advocacy, stating that human rights are a key component of "global mental health action" (P. Y. Collins, 2020, p. 265). This pillar also includes how important it is for the perspectives of people with mental health issues to inform research, practice, and prevention. Each of these pillars will be incorporated accordingly as we move to explore parameters of global mental health for practice, teaching and training, research, and consultation.

Understanding global mental health is also critical, given the unprecedented numbers of refugees and displaced persons throughout the world. Climate change; the war in Ukraine; conflicts in countries such as Ethiopia, Burkina Faso, Myanmar, Nigeria, Afghanistan, and the Democratic Republic of the Congo; and violence have led to 100 million people being displaced by force, numbers that have never been so high, according to the United Nations High Commissioner for Refugees (United Nations, 2022). Psychologists and other practitioners have been called to provide mental health support for ever-growing groups of displaced people (APA, 2010a, 2010b). It is important to recognize the diversity of national origin, ethnicity, language, culture, and religion and the sociopolitical reasons for displacement among refugees and migrants. Displaced people often cope with exposure to severe violence, such as torture, rape, and witnessing the torture and murder of loved ones. They may face massive disruptions to family stability due to separation from family members. Moreover, because there are typically multiple forced relocations for many migrants and refugees, adequate support for coping with trauma and loss is scarce.

Even after relocating to a more permanent destination (e.g., region or country), displaced people can face xenophobia and racism, posing further stress on individuals, families, and communities (APA, 2010a; Tummala-Narra, 2021). The sudden uprooting of one's life that marks displacement leaves many individuals with economic struggles and hardships in the newly adopted country. There is little opportunity to secure documents confirming one's educational and/or employment background, and credentials earned in the country of origin may not be recognized in a different country. Because displaced people suffer multiple exposures to violence, they are more vulnerable to mental health symptomatology, such as posttraumatic stress, anxiety, depression, and psychosis (Rhodes et al., 2016; Tay et al., 2015). Given these challenges, it is essential for psychologists to consider the impact of trauma and loss faced by refugees, as well as how displaced people navigate multiple contexts and cope with trauma and loss (APA, 2010a, 2010b).

Climate change has had a significant impact on the safety and well-being of communities. Despite scientific support for climate change, political divides have contributed to a lack of support for communities and their members:

> Mounting scientific evidence has supported the fact that the Earth's temperature is rising. . . . Human activity has caused a depletion of the ozone layer and natural resources. . . . This affects weather patterns, infrastructure, and health trends. . . . Scientific publications have been greatly debated among politicians. Beliefs and actions regarding climate change have become polarized despite recorded changes in sea levels, temperature, and weather events. (Foley et al., 2022, p. 425)

Climate refugees are

> individuals who are forcibly displaced (within or beyond their nation-state boundaries) by short- and long-term natural disasters and environmental degradation precipitated or exacerbated by the climate crisis. Such short-term disasters consist of typhoons, hurricanes, wildfires, and tsunamis, while long-term environmental changes include desertification, deforestation, rising temperatures, and rising sea levels, among others. (Ayazi & Elsheikh, 2019, p. 3)

The term *climate-induced displacement* refers to people and communities displaced by force, either within or beyond their country boundaries, by natural disasters related to climate change factors (Ayazi & Elsheikh, 2019).

Tuvalu is a nation made up of nine islands in the Pacific Ocean. The experience of Tuvalu underscores the impact of climate change and the reality of climate-induced displacement. Due to climate change, coastal erosion and rising sea levels place Tuvalu at risk of being flooded and submerged in water (Foley et al., 2022). If this happens, Tuvalu will no longer be habitable, resulting in climate-induced displacement, "leading to a potential loss of cultural connection that the population has with its homeland" (Foley et al., 2022, p. 438).

The report *Climate Refugees: The Climate Crisis and Rights Denied* (Ayazi & Elsheikh, 2019) makes four recommendations to support greater protections for climate refugees:

1. Creating a new refugee convention that incorporates considerations related to the experiences of climate refugees or "amending the 1951 Refugee Convention" (p. 3).

2. "Linking scientific research on habitability and climate-induced displacement under the Warsaw International Mechanism for Loss and Damage with national resettlement plans" (p. 3).

3. "Strengthening the links between the Warsaw International Mechanism and the Task Force on Displacement by identifying climate-induced displacement as loss and damages and thus serve as a basis for liability and/or compensation" (p. 3).

4. "Establishing two international insurance pools: (a) one to compensate nations for damages from climate crisis-induced short- and long-term natural disasters (including climate-induced displacement); and (b) one to compensate host nations that resettle climate refugees, with higher premiums for nations with greater historical responsibility for emissions and the destruction of carbon sinks" (p. 3).

APPLYING MULTICULTURAL GUIDELINE 7 TO CLINICAL PRACTICE

The prevalence of mental health issues worldwide, alongside our growing understanding of global mental health, underscores the need for transboundary clinical practice. Guideline 7 encourages us to consider assumptions related to international psychological practice. In thinking about what these assumptions might be, it is important to explore the parameters of working across country borders as an independent professional (as opposed to someone working within a transnational organization), whether as a licensed clinician or, for that matter (and as is discussed further later in the chapter), an educator, consultant, or researcher. Exploring such parameters raises questions such as, Can I work as a health services psychologist in another country? Can I provide teletherapy to a client in another country if I am in the United States? What do I do if the clinically oriented psychology profession is not regulated in the country where I want to provide services? Will I be covered by my malpractice insurance? These are just some of the questions for us to think about if we are considering transboundary clinical or counseling work.

Being aware of such parameters is especially important given that licensed and/or credentialed psychologists may, in fact, be in high demand due to a lack of mental health professionals in a specific region. In keeping with the Multicultural Guidelines, practitioners are encouraged to seek out training if they are going to a country where they are unfamiliar with the cultural context. In this scenario, it is also helpful to receive consultation and supervision from a psychologist practicing in the same region, if possible. In this way, you, the practitioner, can have hands-on support when cultural issues or questions arise that are unfamiliar. Incorporating this level of cultural humility in transboundary practice is key to being able to understand clients more fully within their cultural context.

In addition to training and consultation, it is important to do the necessary research to be aware of the licensing and registration requirements in the country where you plan to practice (Azar, 2009). Countries can have different requirements, and it is important to find out the specifics for the country where you hope to work. Azar (2009) suggested contacting a country's psychological association to learn about professional practice requirements for the region.

Practicing across country boundaries is further complicated if you want to engage in providing teletherapy while in the United States for someone living in another country. In this situation, Huggins (2016) urged us to be aware of all the authorities involved with that transboundary therapeutic interaction. The first authority Huggins mentioned is the "rules of all boards under which you are licensed/registered/certified" (para. 5), and he explained that no matter where your client may be, you as the practitioner are guided by the practice rules of the states in which you are licensed. He stated, "Your licenses are your licenses all the time" (para. 5). Contacting your licensing board(s) to learn how their specific rules apply to providing teletherapy in another country is an important first step.

In addition to knowing the rules for all the states where you hold licenses, it is critical to know the rules of the nation where you are practicing (Huggins, 2016). For instance, if there is a client in New Zealand for whom you want to provide psychotherapy, you will need to find out the rules and parameters of practice in New Zealand, in addition to those of your state(s) of license in the United States. This is true whether you are living in the country and providing psychological services or providing psychotherapy services via teletherapy from the United States to another country.

A frequent erroneous assumption is the belief that jurisdiction is determined by where the client lives, meaning their legal place of residence. The reality is, however, that the place that has jurisdiction refers to the place where your client "is located" when the session is taking place (Huggins, 2016). For instance, if you are providing teletherapy to a client who lives in a country where you have gone through a process of approval to provide services, and that client travels to another country, and you have a teletherapy session while the client is in that other country, the jurisdiction that has authority is that other country where the client has traveled to because that is where they are located at the moment of the session. It is important to inquire how this process is viewed for the relevant countries in such a situation; similarly, this is a concern for some states within the United States, although not all of them.

Another complication to the issue of working in another country is that some countries do not regulate the provision of psychotherapy. While you might assume this means it is okay to practice in that country, there are important risks and protections to be considered. Questions presented by Huggins (2016) in this area include the following:

1. What would happen if the client died of suicide? What would the role of the family be? Could the family sue you, the practitioner? (And the answer here is yes.)

2. How would you manage a client who is suicidal, given that you are an unregulated professional in this setting? What would this mean in terms of your ability to reach out to a hospital or law enforcement authorities for support?

3. What if you believe that a client needs to be hospitalized? Will the hospital talk with you as an unregulated professional within that country?

The answers to such questions when in an unregulated country with regard to professional psychological practice involve consulting with others to determine best practices and how to set the necessary parameters that are required to be in place to support and guide your practice. Huggins said of his work in Japan, a country that does not regulate the provision of therapy:

> Without clear licensing or certification requirements, however, the task of determining what policies and procedures I needed in my practice became something I had to discover through a due diligence process. That will be true for every jurisdiction we decide to work in that doesn't regulate our practices, or that simply doesn't provide clear rules for what we are required to do. (para. 21)

Another question concerns whether your U.S.-based liability insurance will cover your work as a psychologist in another country. We recommend contacting your insurance company to ask if your malpractice insurance policy will cover you providing psychotherapy and other psychological services in a different country. According to Huggins (2016), some insurance companies will provide coverage, and others will not. If the company does provide coverage, Huggins suggested that practitioners find out the extent and parameters of that coverage. In addition to understanding professional parameters for transboundary clinical work, there are several factors to consider when conducting clinical work in a different country, whether through provision of live, in-person treatment services or via teletherapy. Being aware of the community context is an important way to gauge attitudes about mental health–related stigma. Does the community support those who seek mental health services or not? Understanding attitudes about mental health treatment is important because it has implications for how your clients may feel about themselves when seeking treatment and their potential reluctance to continue with treatment. Moreover, an awareness of cultural perceptions will affect how you assist a client with their experience of people in their community who do not support the client in seeking treatment. Being aware of mental health–related stigma can help you, the practitioner, have a sense of empathy about just how difficult it may be for a client to work with you professionally. Cultural values are another dimension to be aware of when engaging in transboundary clinical work. An individualistic culture like the United States values the person individually and specifically. We see this as a culture that rewards individual achievement and acclaim as a principal goal. Notably, this individualistic cultural value is embedded in U.S.-based psychology training programs, which largely focus on individual issues through what is typically individual psychotherapy and with a primary conceptualization of issues from within an individualistic frame (e.g., personality) rather than larger ecological dynamics (e.g., structural racism).

The individualistic focus is different from that taken by collectivist cultures, which value the contributions of the group or family above those of the individual. I (CSCE) recall an experience during my internship that focused on bilingual intervention with English- and Spanish-speaking clients. An individual client came in for a session that was conducted in Spanish. The client confirmed an appointment for the following week. That next week, the client, unbeknownst to the trainee, returned with several family members whom he had invited to the session. This example highlights a specific feature of a collectivist culture, where the client was invested in seeking answers for problems through a larger, shared lens that directly engaged the participation of others in his life rather than focusing on his perspective alone.

Another consideration is to examine culturally relevant approaches to therapeutic work. This may involve moving away from traditional skills learned in graduate school as a trainee to explore different models and approaches that better reflect community needs and values. This approach reflects the decolonizing aspect of training discussed later in the teaching section (Cullen et al., 2020). When the individual who brought family members to his session first came in for therapy, there was an individual focus on treatment. Realizing the relevance of the family context as culturally syntonic to treatment, the clinic made the shift to incorporate a family systems approach. This was helpful not only for this client but also for the many clients after him who were interested in working with their families rather than individually.

Taking an adaptive approach to treatment involves listening for cues that are often given to us by our clients and, on hearing them, incorporating shifts as appropriate. This is also where supervision is recommended. It is important to have supervisory support if you are shifting your approach in ways that you may not have engaged in before. One possibility is to seek supervision from a mental health professional from the community. In this way, the supervisor is a mentor who can help you adapt interventions in ways that fit with cultural values and understanding.

APPLYING MULTICULTURAL GUIDELINE 7 TO TEACHING AND TRAINING

Our case in this chapter, *Good Evening, Good Morning!* discussed four key learning experiences that emerged from teaching transnationally in an online format: language, participation, curriculum, and technology. As we think about teaching across borders, this section explores the larger pedagogical perspective we can take to facilitate transnational learning experiences like the four mentioned previously.

A key pedagogical aspect of teaching transnationally, as described in the case, was a focus on all classroom participants co-creating knowledge. This reflects the first level of the Multicultural Guidelines, with its focus on a bidirectional relationship between, in this example, faculty, TAs, and students. This educationally oriented bidirectional relationship is characterized by mutual respect, sharing, and collaboration among faculty, TAs, and students.

The collaborative approach was essential in a transnational context where the material presented did not necessarily correspond with the student experience in China. For instance, in a discussion group about the college and university application process, the teaching team learned that Chinese high school students and U.S. high school students applying to college or university go through very different processes. The teaching team learned from the students in China that the Gaokao is the national college entrance examination, administered once a year in China. The students shared that their score on the Gaokao was the only criteria that would be considered for entrance to university in China. Further, that score determines the ranking of colleges for which the students are eligible (Wang, 2021). In learning about this process from the students, the teaching team had greater awareness and understanding of the pressure and stress students were experiencing.

In their work on team teaching English as a foreign language among students in Japan, Tajino and Smith (2016) discussed the concept of "team learning" (p. 14), which "is based on a belief that classroom interaction should not be seen as something solely in teachers' hands, but as a co-production of all the participants in the classroom" (p. 15). As demonstrated in our teaching example, in team learning, teachers, as well as students, view themselves as learners (Tajino & Smith, 2016). Hence, with a value-centered team learning model, the classroom community of teachers and students learn together. This shared classroom learning experience, with its bidirectional focus, as found in the Multicultural Guidelines, enhances "intercultural understanding and intercultural communication skill development" (Tajino & Smith, 2016, p. 20). A team learning approach allows for multiple voices and the multiple intersectional experiences reflected in those voices to be heard. This reflects the fourth pillar of the "reframed" mental health *2030 Agenda* (United Nations General Assembly, 2015), given its commitment to advocacy that encourages all classroom participants to engage in the learning process.

With regard to training doctoral students in clinical psychology, there is much to learn from psychology programs engaged in decolonizing efforts (Cullen et al., 2020). Such programs are working to address colonization, which refers to the historic and current systemic privilege of some groups over others. Critical theorists have discussed how psychology has a history of colonization that continues, as evidenced by the discipline's focus on individualism rather than the larger structural issues highlighted in the Multicultural Guidelines' layered approach (Dudgeon & Walker, 2015). *Processes of decolonization* are defined as

> those which seek to disrupt hierarchical relationships in three broad ways: (a) by acknowledging and interrogating the colonial social contexts in which individuals and institutions exist; (b) by advocating for social change; and (c) by amplifying marginalized voices, perspectives and forms of knowledge. (Cullen et al., 2020, p. 212)

For their study, Cullen and colleagues (2020) interviewed academics from institutions in Australia, Canada, Costa Rica, Ghana, Iraq, Italy, Palestine, South Africa, and the United States who were engaged in decolonizing their clinical psychology programs. Three key themes emerged from their analysis: decolonizing personhood, decolonizing institutions, and decolonizing curriculum. With regard to decolonizing personhood, clinical psychology programs can be aware of the extent to which they provide "cultural safety" (Cullen et al., 2020, p. 215). For instance, training programs can be thoughtful about providing space for students to explore their identities and experience of self. Part of ensuring cultural safety in clinical psychology programs is to have a diverse staff, faculty, and student body, as well as a curriculum that reflects diverse experiences.

Cocreating knowledge with a valued-centered team learning model, as discussed earlier, contributes to having multiple voices heard in clinical psychology training programs. "Decolonising teaching practices was just as important as decolonising teaching content" (Cullen et al., 2020, p. 217). This finding fits with the Multicultural Guidelines' bidirectional approach of a give and take between faculty and students, where teaching practices are a partnership rather than a hierarchy. Training programs and supervision can encourage students to voice their perspectives further and do so within a "culture of safety."

The last theme, decolonizing curriculum, emphasizes the importance of looking at the historical context where clinical psychology trainees are being taught. For instance, many of the Australian academic participants said their students lacked knowledge about "the invasion of Australia, the frontier wars and the stolen generations" (Cullen et al., 2020, p. 218). Decolonizing the curriculum involves bringing the political context into the classroom. In this way, students can understand the impact of political situations on issues such as access to quality mental health services.

Incorporating the role of advocate in supervision with trainees is an important skill. Supervisors can encourage trainees to build advocacy skills. Skill development can include working with trainees to build awareness of systems issues, use supervision to discuss systemic inequities and find solutions, and develop a language about how to advocate for clients.

APPLYING MULTICULTURAL GUIDELINE 7 TO RESEARCH

Chapter 8 presented the case of differing human subjects protections across countries, with some countries having an institutional review board (IRB) while others do not. The case study in Chapter 8 talked about advocacy efforts to support the publication of global research, given some of the barriers that might arise. A key barrier, for instance, was how many journals require manuscript submissions to go through an IRB review process at their home institutions, a process that can leave researchers in countries with no formal IRB structure at a loss as to how to publish their work.

In this chapter, we continue the conversation about global research considerations. This discussion is particularly relevant at this point, given the global experience of the COVID-19 pandemic, which has had an impact across nations (P. Y. Collins, 2020). Understanding the parameters of conducting transnational research is also relevant, given recommendations for countries to develop partnerships to design larger systemic epidemiological studies that address global mental health issues (Wainberg et al., 2017).

Despite these recommendations, however, Wainberg and colleagues (2017) underscored the lack of mental health researchers conducting research in low or middle-income economy countries (LMICs). This lack of capacity means that mental health research risks not having empirical evidence from LMICs documented in the literature.

The Swiss Commission for Research Partnerships (KFPE; Swiss Academy of Sciences [SCNAT], 2018) has a guidebook for developing and implementing "transboundary and intercultural" research partnerships (p. 3). The guidebook presents 11 principles that recognize research partnership as "a continuous process of sound knowledge generation, building mutual trust, mutual learning and shared ownership" (p. 3). The principles also apply to research partnerships between countries with differing levels of economic resources. They state,

> The KFPE's 11 principles underscore this process. However, there are many types of research in partnership; these have different requirements in terms of interaction, communication, and mutuality. This is particularly the case when cooperation takes place between poor and rich countries. In other words, the principles may have to be applied selectively depending on the partnership. (p. 3)

In addition to the 11 principles, seven questions ask about varying aspects of transboundary research relationships. The questions seek to help people understand the research process and consider factors that might support or interfere with transboundary research partnerships. The questions also aim to encourage those involved in transboundary research partnerships to think about what facilitates positive collaboration and how knowledge generated from the research can support positive societal outcomes (SCNAT, 2018). Table 9.2 summarizes KFPE's 11 principles and seven questions. The KFPE

TABLE 9.2. Swiss Commission for Research Partnerships (KFPE) Principles and Questions

KFPE 11 Principles	KFPE 7 Questions
Set the agenda together	Why work in partnership?
Interact with stakeholders	How to ensure cohesion?
Clarify responsibilities	What form of collaboration?
Account to beneficiaries	Which foci and priorities?
Promote mutual learning	Who to involve?
Enhance capacities	Where to create relevance?
Share data and networks	When to consolidate outcomes?
Disseminate results	
Pool profits and merits	
Apply results	
Secure outcomes	

Note. This is an original table based on the principles and questions presented in Swiss Academy of Sciences (2018).

principles and questions provide an important framework for us to understand transboundary research in general as well as when conducting transboundary research where there are differences in wealth between nations.

The first question—"Why work in partnership?"—is a critical foundation question when we consider conducting transboundary research to address global mental health concerns. Transboundary research partnerships can support building research capacity when they involve collaborations between "countries with a high density of research and researchers, and countries with a low such density" (SCNAT, 2018, p. 20). Such partnerships can address power imbalances between countries and seek to generate new knowledge, build research capacity, provide mentoring and career opportunities, and lead to innovations at a societal level.

The second question, however, "How to ensure cohesion?" makes us aware of the many constituency groups (e.g., government, donors, community groups, researchers, and organizations involved in the research) that may have differing views and agendas related to the research collaboration. This question helps us think through how the research partnership can work in alignment. It encourages us to anticipate potential divisions to keep the research moving forward. To deal with and minimize the possibility for such division, suggested strategies include the partnership being based on "joint ownership" between partner countries, having collaborative relationships between the academic side and the societally based side of the research, avoiding "power-based decisions" through "informed decision-making," and having allies that can speak to unspoken concerns and act as "early warners" (SCNAT, 2018, p. 21).

The third question, "What form of collaboration?" encourages us to consider what the collaboration will look like. The KFPE guidebook (SCNAT, 2018) states that transboundary research partnerships often start with one project that subsequently leads to other research endeavors. What began as a single, time-limited study may turn into an ongoing partnership that builds a long-term research program. This leads to the fourth question: "Which foci and priorities?" This area of inquiry helps us think about the overall research partnership goals. The KFPE guidebook presents three goals: knowledge (e.g., the research), capacity (both individual and institutional), and impact (e.g., contributions to society). Question 4 aims to help the transboundary research partnership team be aware of and anticipate possible conflicts between these three goals. The guidebook presents two options to deal with conflict in this area: (a) prioritize one or two goals from the outset of the project, encourage involved constituents to be a part of that process, and have goals communicated to the group; and (b) keep the three goals, but divide the research process into different phases, with each phase more strongly connected to a specific goal (e.g., the dissemination phase may be connected with the impact goal; SCNAT, 2018).

The fifth question, "Who to involve?" specifically speaks to research-related constituency groups that will be potentially involved beyond the main research partnership. The four social orientations presented in the guidebook (SCNAT, 2018) include related scientific communities, agencies, "users and beneficiaries of the research outcomes" (p. 27), and the public. Like the second question about how to foster cohesion, Question 5 encourages us to anticipate the influence that various constituencies may have on the research process. A "broker" is someone who may be able to create linkages between various groups involved in the research. Cultural brokers, for instance, may be able to create bridges between researchers and the community agency in ways that make the larger community aware of the research project (Clauss-Ehlers, 2020).

Relatedly, though not addressed in the guidebook (SCNAT, 2018) per se, it is important that transboundary researchers examine specific aspects of the research process within a global context. S. Petersen's (2017) work presented recommendations for human subjects review boards (HSRBs) that are involved in the international research review process. S. Petersen (2017) noted that HSRBs may assume that individuals can provide informed consent without looking at the larger context in which consent is provided. One example is an individual who lives in a totalitarian society where deference is required. Here, the question of informed consent becomes more complicated:

> If a potential participant lives under totalitarian rule and deference to authority is expected or even demanded and threatened, the notion of refusal becomes untenable. If a society has had such circumstances for a long time, the participant may be relatively oblivious to the possibility of refusal. Voluntariness may be a construct nuanced by the culture in such a way that even when hearing there is no demand to comply, the notion is so foreign that refusal will never occur. (S. Petersen, 2017, p. 171)

Working with vulnerable populations in transboundary research partnerships presents other important considerations. S. Petersen (2017) observed that women may not be seen as a vulnerable population in developed nations. However, "when women are in severely subservient roles, they are vulnerable" (p. 172). Guideline 18 of the *International Ethical Guidelines for Biomedical Research Involving Human Subjects* (Council for International Organizations of Medical Sciences [CIOMS], 2016) states:

> Despite the current general presumption that favours the inclusion of women in research, in many societies women remain socially vulnerable in the conduct

of research. For example, they may suffer negligence or harm because of their submission to authority, their hesitancy or inability to ask questions, and a cultural tendency to deny or tolerate pain and suffering. When women in these situations are potential participants in research, researchers, sponsors and ethics committees must take special care in the research design, assessment of risks and benefits, as well as the process of informed consent, to ensure that women have the necessary time and appropriate environment to make decisions based on information provided to them. (p. 69)

In a related example, the *International Ethical Guidelines* discuss the dynamic of informed consent and authorization: In some cultures, the spouse or a community official may be the entity that provides women permission to be invited to participate in research. The *International Ethical Guidelines* state that being granted this permission cannot take the place of the women themselves providing consent. Rather, "The women must have adequate time and a proper environment in which to decide to enroll" (p. 70).

Question 6, "Where to create relevance?" refers to thinking in advance about the kind of impact the transboundary research seeks to elicit. Considering the societal impact your research will have involves thinking through research goals and the problem your research intends to address. A related goal, as described by KFPE, is to think about the community group where "the research results should trigger outcomes" (SCNAT, 2018, p. 29). Conducting a needs assessment is one strategy that can be used before research implementation to get a sense of how the community or constituency group defines the issue. From there, the research can be developed in ways that reflect the community's definition of the problem (Clauss-Ehlers et al., 2017).

Finally, Question 7, "When to consolidate outcomes?" refers to how research findings can be generated as outcomes for the scientific community, governments, and society. KFPE (SCNAT, 2018) cautions against short-lived outcomes where the research is not fully incorporated in terms of planned impact. To prevent a short-lived outcome, it is first recommended that the transboundary research partnership team actively engages across academic disciplines and with community constituency groups to further the research impact. Second, it is recommended that what might have begun as a single project be consolidated into a larger research program with a longer-term vision of how the research can address the identified problem. The third recommendation is capacity development at individual and institutional levels. For instance, building research skills develops individual capacity, and developing a network of partnerships can help sustain the transboundary research partnership.

APPLYING MULTICULTURAL GUIDELINE 7 TO CONSULTATION

Consultation is highly relevant to global mental health, given that the field involves working across national boundaries and building collaborations with a range of constituency groups. Recent work on social justice for children and young people included regional and country case studies from Brazil, China, Colombia, Cuba, Ethiopia, India, Israel, Mexico, Norway, Pakistan, Palestine, Peru and other Latin American countries, Rwanda, Scotland, South Africa, and the United States (Clauss-Ehlers, Sood, & Weist, 2020). In each chapter, authors talked about how the country they were writing about was moving forward in social justice efforts while simultaneously leaving significant support gaps. A review of the country case studies revealed several common themes. Themes and related action strategies reflected ways to support a social justice infrastructure for children and young people (Clauss-Ehlers, Sood, & Weist, 2020). While these themes and action strategies emerged from work across countries on social justice issues often more broadly defined than mental health (e.g., education, child labor, poverty), they have implications for global mental health consultation efforts.

An application of the first theme, "share lessons learned across countries," encourages countries to share knowledge about best practices in addressing global mental health. Action strategies applicable to a global mental health context include hosting international conferences for networking and capacity building and building communication across countries using technology. The second theme, "share resources across countries," captures the importance of sharing what we know. Consultants can organize international conferences to further dialogue, support practitioners with training on cultural adaptations of interventions, and consult with research collaboration teams in efforts to scale up research (Clauss-Ehlers, Sood, & Weist, 2020, p. 482).

The third theme that emerged concerned the importance of sharing public policy models. Country case studies often talked about how important it was to look to neighboring countries to see how they were addressing a specific problem. Consultants can serve as brokers between nations and promote communication about factors related to policy success and failure. Consultants can help governments explore how mental health policies in other countries might apply to their home countries.

Finally, the fourth theme, "develop a pipeline of professionals focused on social justice issues for children and young people," applies to global mental health. Consultants can serve as brokers who work with multiple constituency groups such as colleges, universities, professional associations, schools, and more to provide clinical, teaching, and research mentoring. In this way, efforts are designed to build global mental health capacity.

CONCLUSION

As we continue to navigate a global pandemic, we see the interconnectedness of nations in their struggle against it. Similarly, global mental health speaks to the prevalence of mental health issues across nations. Research shows that COVID-19 has significantly increased mental health issues, and nations are grappling with how to create the capacity to respond. Trainees, early career psychologists, mid-career psychologists, and seasoned psychologists are all encouraged to consider how they can contribute to addressing global mental health issues.

Multicultural Guideline 7 invites us to move beyond a domestic, U.S.-centric focus to reimagine our roles as practitioners, educators, trainers, researchers, and consultants within a global context. This chapter has highlighted the complexities of working across nations, not to overwhelm the reader but to do the opposite—encourage the reader to explore ways to conduct transboundary clinical work with the knowledge of what the parameters of practice entail.

Teaching and training can invite team learning experiences by cocreating knowledge where all classroom participants are viewed as learners. Team learning creates a backdrop for educators to provide collaborative educational opportunities. As educators embark on this work, they are reminded of the Multicultural Guidelines' model of a bidirectional relationship between the teaching team and student. It is through this shared collaboration that mutual learning can occur.

Multicultural Guideline 7 stretches us to think about research in different ways. We are encouraged to think about key principles in working across nations, with a specific focus on the understanding that nations are likely to have differing economic resources. Unlike specific research methods discussed in other chapters, research in this chapter was strategic in its consideration of specific skills needed to anticipate the division within the transboundary research relationship and the balance between science generation, capacity, and impact. Research capacity is developed when countries working together on one project launch other related projects that eventually lead to a research program. Psychology researchers are also encouraged to move beyond the comfort of their discipline to develop partnerships with faculty from other disciplines. Similarly, consultation involves engaging in a relationship with the organization or entity in which the consultation is occurring. An awareness of sociocultural variables and institutional barriers, coupled with an ability to promote constituency understanding of them, promotes multiculturally informed consultation.

To conclude, Multicultural Guideline 7 points a pathway to transboundary work as clinicians, educators, researchers, and consultants. Given the global mental health prevalence data, there is clearly a need for transboundary clinical work, teaching, building research capacity through partnerships, and consulting. Chapter 10 builds on this work with its focus on developmental stages and the life transitions that are at the core of Guideline 8. This is the second guideline that falls under Level 4 with its focus on psychological practice in domestic and international contexts.

10
THE INTERSECTION BETWEEN DEVELOPMENT AND BIOSOCIOCULTURAL CONTEXT
Multicultural Guideline 8

Guideline 8. Psychologists seek awareness and understanding of how developmental stages and life transitions intersect with the large biosociocultural context, how identity evolves as a function of such intersections, and how these different socialization and maturation experiences influence worldview and identity.

This chapter follows from Chapter 9 with its focus on the second guideline organized under Level 4, which addresses psychological practice within domestic and international contexts. Multicultural Guideline 8 in *Multicultural Guidelines: An Ecological Approach to Context, Identity, and Intersectionality, 2017* (hereinafter referred to as *2017 Multicultural Guidelines*; American Psychological Association [APA], 2017a) is the second guideline under this fourth layer; it addresses the intersection between development and the biosociocultural context. Multiculturally responsive psychologists are guided to consider how development of the individuals who compose the groups they work with regularly (e.g., clients and patients, consultees, students and trainees, research participants) is readily intertwined with and deeply influenced by the political and social experiences that occur in their lives.

---

https://doi.org/10.1037/0000348-010
Applying Multiculturalism: An Ecological Approach to the APA Guidelines, by C. S. Clauss-Ehlers, S. J. Hunter, G. S. Morse, and P. Tummala-Narra
Copyright © 2024 by the American Psychological Association. All rights reserved.

This consideration includes being able to recognize that the developmental intersection with history and circumstance is bidirectional across all aspects contributing to how we develop biologically and socioculturally as humans, including the genetic and epigenetic interactions that are directed and manipulated by the social and environmental contexts in which we are born and grow up (Losin et al., 2020; Roth, 2013; Worthman & Costello, 2009). Additionally, culture and its interactions with biobehavioral development play profound roles in our becoming mature individuals, setting the tone of the environment from before birth (Provenzi et al., 2018) and guiding the ways in which our bodies and minds unfold and mature across time (Hunter & Rendall, 2007). These factors influence how we are both vulnerable and viable, depending on the opportunities and traumas that occur during our lives (Holden et al., 2012; Kirmayer & Ryder, 2016).

We are regularly engaged by a range of experiences and demands, across internal and external systems, that serve to modulate how we make sense of, form schemas about, and enact our goals within our complex world. This engagement serves as a strong reminder for all psychologists working with individuals, groups, and systems that multilayered considerations are necessary when supporting efforts toward change, growth, acceptance, and resilience. To capture this experience with regard to health, Engel (1977, 1978) proposed a biopsychosocial model for medicine and mental health. The biopsychosocial model was readily adopted and has informed practice and research actively. However, this model was adopted without the full recognition of a need to consider the myriad multicultural variables and their influence on development and health. Nor did the model necessarily make sense of the varieties of contexts that humans develop within and the ways in which their cultural experiences and identities represent an independent source of influence developmentally across their lives (Hilty, 2015). Recognizing the need to take broader social and psychological development into consideration, Hilty (2015) proposed a biopsychosociocultural model that recognizes the influence of diversity and culture on development and intervention. This broader perspective is discussed directly in the *2017 Multicultural Guidelines*, specifically with regard to considering mental health care and research within their layered ecological model.

Building from this set of considerations, Multicultural Guideline 8 specifies that multiculturally responsive psychologists consider that we live in a time of challenging, regularly changing circumstances, both locally and globally. Many different sources of information impinge on us simultaneously, keeping us constantly aware of the difficulties, strife, and traumas that occur across the globe and influencing how we make sense of both our position and ourselves within this complex world. We are often bombarded by many sources of information, across all our senses, that seek to inform us of what is most of concern; at times, however, we have very little opportunity to fully step back and independently make sense of or integrate all these stimuli. As a result, we are often unsure where and how we should feel and may have difficulty determining the most appropriate response, if that is even possible. This precariousness is for many a source of trauma and uncertainty, leading to worry and vulnerability to anxiety or depression (e.g., Holden et al., 2012). To counteract this challenge of information overload and its impact on our sense of safety and security and to mediate our emotional and cognitive experience, many of us seek sources of information that counteract the negative onslaught that we are so often fed: stories and images, videos and films, and short snippets of brief pleasure that allow us to engage with our positive beliefs and ideas and to think, for a short period, about what we find pleasant and enjoyable (The Media Insight Project, 2014; Thompson et al., 2019).

This seeking of information is our constant dance with the array of social media and websites that have come to fill our smartphones, tablets, and computer screens. This is our diet, now multiple times a day, of current society and its vagaries. In addition, it affects how we see ourselves, across our development from childhood into adulthood, affecting our emotional and cognitive development and how we form a sense of who we are and what is possible in our lives.

CASE ILLUSTRATION–DAWOUD: IDENTITY CONFLICT CONNECTED TO POLITICAL STRUGGLE

A family therapist was asked to work with Dawoud,[1] who is currently 15 years old, to help him understand and address his ongoing anger and dysphoria, which are affecting multiple aspects of family life. Dawoud is struggling with his interactions with his parents and grandparents in particular, but he also shows significant sadness and anger at home and school. Dawoud lives with his father, Assaf, who is his primary custodial parent in the United States, and his older brother, Lior, who is often away at college. They have been together as a household of three for 10 years now—since Dawoud's mother, Miryam, returned to her family's village in Gaza to care for her aging parents. Notably, Dawoud has a complex heritage ethnically and religiously. His father,

---

[1]In this case illustration, all appropriate steps have been taken to disguise the identities of the individuals discussed.

a physician, is Israeli American and Jewish. His mother is Palestinian and Christian, raised in Jordan.

The therapist learns that Dawoud's parents met when Assaf was treating children in Gaza while working for the organization Doctors Without Borders and Miryam was a translator associated with his mission. Of note, Assaf grew up with his immigrant parents in New York. They came to the United States in part because of regional tensions and a desire to raise their children in the United States because they felt more opportunities were available. Miryam was raised among a mix of Muslim and Christian relatives in Amman, Jordan, following her parent's decision to return to Gaza at the time of the First Intifada (i.e., the initial uprising by Palestinians against the Israeli occupation of the West Bank and Gaza territories that began in December 1987 and lasted until the signing of the Oslo Peace Accord in 1993). Since the Second Intifada, challenges have escalated in Palestine and Israel, and it is now difficult for individuals who reside in Gaza to leave the country through Israel, particularly individuals who hold perceived histories of concern politically (e.g., ties to Hamas, a family member who was arrested by the Israeli police). This situation contributed to Miryam's worries about her parents and led to her return to Gaza.

When discussing concerns about Dawoud's mood and its etiology with his father as part of the initiation of treatment, the therapist is informed that following their courtship in Gaza, Assaf and Miryam married in East Jerusalem with the blessing of both families. They moved to New York and later Chicago; they were all together until Dawoud was 5 years old and his older brother Lior was 8. Following a series of health changes faced by her parents and worries about obtaining appropriate care outside Gaza, Miryam made the decision to return to Gaza to live with and take care of her parents. As the political situation between Israel and the Palestinians living in Gaza deteriorated, her ability to leave became tenuous, as did her U.S. family's ability to visit her.

As part of their work, Dawoud informs the therapist that he speaks weekly with his mother and maternal grandparents in Gaza City. It has been this way for as long as he can recall now. He and his father report feelings of significant depression about the loss of Miryam's presence in their lives, both physically and emotionally. Although Dawoud is typically a strong student overall, his grades fluctuate across the year in response to his mood. This fluctuation is particularly apparent when he is worried about his mother's and grandparents' safety; these worries occur in tandem with news reports about renewed conflicts between Gazans and the Israeli armed forces. At these times, Dawoud struggles to focus on his schoolwork and, understandably, questions its relevance. The result is a drop in grades followed by intense pressure to improve academic performance to get back on track. This pressure then contributes to greater emotional volatility in the home.

Assaf's U.S.-based family tries to be supportive, especially Dawoud's paternal grandparents. However, Dawoud shares with the therapist that tensions arise at times, particularly around differing religious holidays and associated gatherings that take place during the year. Additionally, Israeli relatives in Assaf's family frequently travel to the United States to visit, causing tension for both Dawoud and Lior, who recognize that their mother and her family are forbidden to come. Dawoud and Assaf together relate one difficult incident that occurred in response to Dawoud's decision not to participate in a Bar Mitzvah (i.e., the Jewish coming-of-age ritual held for 13-year-old males; 12- and 13-year-old females participate in a Bat Mitzvah) at the family's synagogue. They further share a more recent disagreement around plans for a cousin's upcoming Confirmation (i.e., a Reform Jewish ceremony where adolescents finishing their religious education confirm their commitment to Judaism and the Jewish people). Dawoud firmly avows that he will not attend the ceremony, stating that he is very angry about his American family's association with Judaism, given the religion's perceived—and often mixed—messages regarding Israel and Palestine. He further relays to the therapist that his anger is associated with daily media reports indicating ongoing U.S. political support for Israel at the expense of the Palestinian people and the U.S. government's decisions regarding Gaza and the West Bank territories, where occupation of Palestinian lands by the Jewish settlement movement continues to grow, with Israeli government support.

Assaf relates to the therapist that he and Miryam try, each in their own way, to be accommodating to Dawoud's struggles and frustrations. They are empathic about the choices he has been making to dissociate himself from his family's practice of Judaism and to reject participation in rituals himself, in response to his anger and frustration about the Israeli–Palestinian situation and its impact on his life. He reports that both he and Miryam see that he is struggling to reconcile the differing cultures he comes from and to understand how values so readily appear to clash. They suspect that this struggle is related to Dawoud's being an adolescent and seeking to make choices of his own. Nonetheless, Assaf shares that he feels at a loss regarding how best to guide Dawoud through this struggle while acknowledging his own desire to keep his son affiliated with his family, who are both local and present for him, and hence a potential source of emotional support.

Assaf reports that Dawoud's Israeli American grandparents have tried to be understanding as well. He describes them as fully committed to allowing

Dawoud to come to an understanding of who he is religiously, ethnically, and politically, yet they are "terrified of being shut out" by Dawoud and of potentially "being disrespected for being Jewish." Assaf also shares that they have tried to see this commitment to Dawoud's coming to an understanding of self as related not only to the situation at hand but also to his being an adolescent seeking to make sense of who he is in the world. When the paternal grandparents attended a session, they shared that while they care deeply for him and share his pain regarding his mother's inability to be physically present in his life, they are tied to their own religious faith and its emphasis on family. They wish that Dawoud would feel more comfortable with this tradition and see it as a source of support.

This conflict around religion in the family has led to some tensions in the relationship that Assaf has with his parents, who struggle to accept Dawoud's choices about being present at family events and functions. Assaf reports that he tries to mediate this situation to some degree: He and Dawoud remain in contact as much as possible with Miryam and her parents, all of whom have asked how they can best support and be available to Dawoud and help him make sense of his tricultural heritage and to make peace with his life and situation.

Discussion Questions Related to Dawoud

1. Taking an intersectional perspective allows us to look at how identities are interwoven with one another, rather than focusing on one identity over (or instead of) the other. How would you address the complexity associated with Dawoud's identities?
2. How would you address the feelings Dawoud shares about his life experiences?
3. It is not unusual that trainees and professionals want to provide an answer to a problem to "fix" a client's situation. How would you respond to a situation with no easy answer and no "quick fix"?
4. What are some developmental considerations Dawoud faces as a 15-year-old?
5. How are these developmental considerations connected with reference-group identities?
6. How would you address issues of loss Dawoud had faced because his family members are separated from one another?
7. Moving forward in your work with Dawoud, what would you focus on?

The therapist continues to meet with Dawoud and learns, through his tears, how very angry he is at the lack of control he feels about the situation with his mother and, more directly, with the political and cultural challenges that affect his family so intensely. Despite efforts made diplomatically across the last 10 years, endeavors to have his mother return to the United States and bring his grandparents have failed, and he feels abandoned by his mother because of the country he lives in. With the political situations in the United States, Israel, and Palestine, Dawoud feels increasingly hopeless that his mother will be an in-person part of his life. He tells the therapist that this challenge has led to his difficulties with peers at school and at his synagogue. He often feels isolated and alone because of his uncertainties about how to understand who he is in the context of what is going on in the world. Dawoud states clearly that he wants to see his mother again and to feel like a family.

LITERATURE REVIEW

Many psychological theories, and their consequent interpretations within practice, education, and consultation, address the self and the array of relationships others hold within and across communities and cultures. Numerous theories also address how these relationships contribute to the acquisition of understanding and knowledge (Callaghan & Corbit, 2018; Ji & Yap, 2016). Recent theories are quite sophisticated in their considerations of the diversity of human lives (Vignoles et al., 2016). Multiculturally responsive psychological practice is now engaged in substantial considerations regarding ways to define and support diversity, along with sensitivities toward cultural, socioeconomic, ethnic, racial, sexual, and gender identity (APA, 2017a; Fisher, 2020; Sue, 2008; Tummala-Narra, 2016). Simultaneously, society has become more willing to experiment with new models of understanding individuals and their lives while attempting to remain cohesively tied to older models of identity and gender roles. As a result, significant challenges have emerged in professional practice, as best seen with the range of viewpoints that are at play in professional psychology itself, both within and across generations. For example, structural and political discussions regularly occur among the APA's membership itself (e.g., the debate regarding how to address the choices made by senior leaders within the APA with regard to interrogations of prisoners in Guantanamo Bay; Carey, 2018).

The history of professional psychology itself is replete with shifts and struggles regarding how to conceptualize, operationalize, and then actively address variations in how individuals and their lives are engaged with and then guided toward change (Casas et al., 2017). Moving from a personhood heavily dichotomized across camps addressing behavioral and psychodynamic models of development to the reengagement with the underlying cognitive processes that support and engage how we think, feel, and behave and then to a growth in multilayered models of self and community, professional psychology has increasingly come to wrestle with the areas in which it has both contributed significantly to the potential for a positive life and served to undermine that opportunity (Casas et al., 2017).

Guideline 8 connects our understanding of the lifelong adventure of identity and self-concept with research regarding how we become who we are and how we best capture changes across time (APA, 2017a; Vespa, 2009). As discussed in the *2017 Multicultural Guidelines*, while we have a limited literature base regarding intersectionality within a framework of development and historical periods, we are becoming more aware of the way that identity is formed both within and across generations and how one's identity is a fluid process at different times developmentally, given the influences that occur (Vespa, 2009; Vignoles et al., 2016). Gender and race influence one's foundational understanding of self to varying degrees at different developmental periods; similarly, political, racial, cultural, and religious identity may be important at others.

Multicultural Guideline 8 is therefore based on both our current circumstances and the accumulation of experiences we have had across multiple generations of contextual variation. It focuses on personhood as situated with an array of influences that are biological (e.g., adolescence, aging), psychological (e.g., self, emotions, capacities), environmental (e.g., neighborhood where living, socioeconomic circumstance), and sociocultural (e.g., race, ethnicity, religion). Although lifespan researchers have paid minimal attention to intersectionality from the perspective of lifespan development within an interaction of both time and context, they increasingly appreciate that how one sees oneself primarily can change over time (Vespa, 2009). Dr. David Satcher, the former United State Surgeon General, spoke of this understanding when he stated,

> Not all members that society groups into a given category will share the same culture. Many may identify with other social groups to which they feel a stronger cultural tie, such as a Mexican American who identifies primarily as being Catholic, gay, Texan, or a teenager. (Office of the Surgeon General, Center for Mental Health Services, National Institute of Mental Health, 2001, p. 9)

Our sense of self and how that is best captured can, may, and most often does change as we progress through time, circumstances, and life experiences. What is most certain about who we are at one point in time may be modified or altered as we age, have children, support elderly parents or relatives, or live among a chosen family of friends. Similarly, as societal expectations change, expectations about ourselves that are key to framing how we self-identify may change as our life choices change. For example, prior to the U.S. Supreme Court decision to allow legal same-gender marriages (*Obergefell v. Hodges*, 2015), many progressive gay men and lesbian women were disinclined to replicate heteronormative relationship models for their partnerships. However, the decision upended their view of marriage, as it was no longer believed to be a far-off possibility. We witness this process daily, in regard to both the strengthening of opportunities that LGBTQ+ individuals or women now have and the continued challenges these opportunities contribute to, given political and national battles against progress and change (e.g., efforts to remove and restrict abortion laws, efforts to prevent transgender individuals from being fired from their place of employment in the United States; see Liptak, 2020; Nash et al., 2019).

Additionally relevant to these considerations is the recognition that our lives are further complicated developmentally and socially by advancements in technology that influence how we make sense of ourselves, our experiences, and how our lives are anticipated to unfold. These enhancements and additions to how we come to know and understand the world provide increased sources of information that simultaneously focus our attention and distract us from other stimulation that occurs around us. These technologies, as we engage them, further influence the ways in which we interact with and make sense of our lives and the people and experiences that define daily existence. Our experiences, including the types of information we most like or seek to avoid, are tracked and coded as trends and then aggregated with a broad range of sources of similar information to provide a profile about who we are—who and what we like to watch on the screen or television and when we like to watch, what we are open to eating, what we wear, what music engages us and whether we listen during the day or night, and how our moods reflect our choices and purchases. We are increasingly coming to understand that these sources of information about the multiple aspects of our identities are used to develop key marketing decisions that are highly personalized and targeted, at the right time, under the right conditions (Bodó et al., 2019; The Media Insight Project, 2014; Walrave et al., 2018).

We think about this issue now because it is emerging in psychological research as a necessary consideration when making sense of the relationship between development and self—how culture is transmitted and understood and when it becomes global in its representation. Psychologists are asked to address how we hold and make sense of the multiple identifications about who we are, given that across our lives we have many layers of being that influence our identities. Psychologists working in professional practice that involves supporting individual, group, or societal change now confront a broad range of potential classifications that become important for understanding how we view and understand ourselves (Hutchinson, 2016; Matz et al., 2017). These identifications have a developmental cycle that is tied not only to our immediate environments and circumstances but also to our historical moments and current societal trends (Matz et al., 2017). As a result, they influence how we exist and understand our cultural contexts and ourselves across all aspects of how we develop and mature—biologically, psychologically, socially, and culturally. Examples are bandied about readily: As one example, we hear or see references frequently in the media about differences among generations, from the "Boomers," a term referring to individuals born just as World War II was ending and through 1964 as the declared ending point, to "Generation Z," individuals born in the years ranging from 2000 to now (Charlesworth & Banaji, 2019; Twenge et al., 2015). These discussions of generations frame how we as citizens understand our role in our current culture and setting.

The Boomer generation has a broad set of connotations, both positive and negative, that are regularly addressed across media. Individuals within this demographic are characterized as the "middle-aged generation," with its oldest members entering their mid to late 70s (Macunovich, 2002; Phillipson et al., 2008). Known for living in a time of great economic prosperity within the United States, the Boomer generation also experienced the array of vast upheavals historically associated with the 1960s and early 1970s (e.g., the Vietnam War, the civil rights movement) that led to significant changes regarding race and gender during the Johnson presidential administration. Sexual identity and orientation were readily and openly discussed (Phillipson et al., 2008), women had the opportunity to take a pill to prevent pregnancy (Macunovich, 2002), drug use was prevalent and even encouraged (Macunovich, 2002), and our political structures worldwide began to shift from a general conservativism to a liberal communitarianism (Macunovich, 2002; Phillipson et al., 2008). Many of the political and social battles that are continuing now, in this present moment in the 21st century, reflect changes related to the start of the Boomer generation and others. These changes serve as a foundation to make sense of our current time and its vacillating responses to multiculturalism, globalism, and diversity (Twenge et al., 2015). Moreover, they exist as a framework for making sense of the ways in which we present and experience our lives, across all domains of who we are and across age and identity.

APPLYING MULTICULTURAL GUIDELINE 8 TO CLINICAL PRACTICE

Awareness of the developmental trajectories of identification of self is an important element in clinical work. As clinicians, we are asked to assist our clients in determining the best ways of understanding who they are at a given point in time and to do so with a recognition of what they can understand given their developmental status (e.g., child, adolescent, emerging and young adult, aging adult). It is not unusual to find that our clients take on and share with us a set of differing roles and identifications during some periods, such as adolescence. For example, in therapy a young Black/African American/Black American female who is beginning to explore her feelings of attraction and sexual orientation directly may comfortably share concerns about identifying as a lesbian, bisexual, or heterosexual person. Our role as multiculturally responsive clinicians within this interaction is one of supportive consideration. We can guide discussion as it unfolds. With our clients, we can work toward ways of making sense of these possible identifications and what it might mean at the present time if one or another were correctly applied.

In the case illustration, the clinician working with Dawoud is asked to make sense with him of what it means to be a 15-year-old tricultural male (i.e., Palestinian, Israeli Jewish, American) wrestling with questions concerning his family structure, loss, and religious identity. The clinical process of identifying answers to these questions is informed by Dawoud's multicultural background. The clinician can work with Dawoud to consider each element of who he is. Therapy can address the loss of his mother in his daily life and the pressures of being strongly placed within his paternal family. Such exploration is necessary but perhaps insufficient for fully accommodating Dawoud's range of emotional responses and the frustration with his experiences. Because Dawoud is actively engaging daily with media that represents the conflicts and challenges within and among his cultural backgrounds, he is acutely aware of the contradictions that situate among these identities.

Therapists may see a similar path when working with parents of an Asian/Asian American adolescent with high-functioning autism spectrum disorder (ASD), a neurodevelopmental disorder that affects awareness of self within a world of others and often limits one's ability to communicate ideas, feelings, and shared experiences (*DSM-5*; American Psychiatric Association, 2013b). In the context of Guideline 8, we might explore how this adolescent with ASD makes sense of both the ways in which they are different from their peers and where the ways in which they are similar to them. Clinical work with this adolescent might subsequently explore strategies for managing those perceived differences and similarities within the home, along with consideration and discussion of goals for the future. Because of their background as an Asian/Asian American possibly with familial expectations regarding academic success or socialization, we are further challenged to make sense with this individual of the ways in which they experience these expectations and their place within the family. Our work is multilayered, and we must give great attention to the individual's developmental level and capacity for understanding.

In the case illustration, Dawoud's challenges with understanding and making sense of himself are well noted. These challenges can be located in the recognition that strong aspects of Dawoud's background (i.e., as an Israeli and Palestinian American adolescent who is raised Jewish and has parents who are Christian and Jewish) are complex and situated in an uneasy balance. As Dawoud struggles with the loss of his mother's physical presence because she cannot leave Gaza and tries to understand what that means for him as an adolescent leaving his childhood behind, he is caught between two cultures.

As clinicians, it is important for us to recognize the many layers of messages Dawoud receives in his life and the ways in which they have an impact on his developing sense of self. For instance, despite his knowing that coexistence between the two cultures is possible (e.g., through his parents' marriage), Dawoud is bombarded daily with negative statements in the media and when engaging with members of his own family. He also sees the intransigence of politics play out in his own life. He is deeply torn and uncertain how to bridge that gulf.

Recognizing that identity is transitional in some domains is a key developmental step, one that unfolds in different ways as we move through adulthood and older age. The literature offers little direct guidance about the best means for addressing the complicated considerations that a multinational identity requires; it is at present an area of increasing focus and consideration. As we navigate clinical waters, it becomes necessary to build approaches to interpreting what has been found empirically (Cohler & Michaels, 2012; Erikson, 1967/1994) and to recognize that our understanding of intersectional identities is an unfolding task.

APPLYING MULTICULTURAL GUIDELINE 8 TO TEACHING AND TRAINING

We teach a diverse student population in the United States, at the primary and secondary levels as well as at the postsecondary levels (U.S. Department of Education, 2017). Our current framework for working with diversity in the educational setting remains one that is moving forward more slowly than the identities put forward by our students require. We are asked to engage with and make sense of the best ways to build a collaborative and accommodating learning setting (U.S. Department of Education, 2017). This engagement can lead to tensions in the ways in which students and trainees have engaged with educational administrations. At times, this engagement has led to strong moves forward in inclusive and engaged pedagogy (Juvonen et al., 2018). At other times, however, this engagement has occurred with less success and greater feelings of distrust (Ulie-Wells et al., 2020).

As psychologists whose work is meant to foster a greater understanding of ways to engage and address these tensions, we are still at times grappling with the right means to move the educational setting forward. The focus of much of this effort is to work within educational settings so that they can serve as inclusive settings that challenge preconceptions and misunderstandings regarding identity and self. The future is open for psychologists to use the current multicultural guidelines to build new pedagogical models that foster trust. New pedagogical models can build a capacity for honesty, which allows for the development of a safe space that can challenge errors in understanding and belief while encouraging a dialogue about different worldviews, intersectional identities, and shared purpose.

Williams (2009) examined the success of a program developed to instruct emerging adolescent girls in prosocial development, self-efficacy, and leadership while understanding intersectional aspects of their identity. The Smart-Girl Program is an example showing that creation of a safe space educationally (i.e., through the use of afterschool programs run by the local YWCA and public schools) can engage effective maturation of these developing young individuals toward a more self-assured adulthood that fully embraces knowledge of their experiences and opportunities. Using a group format and multiple sessions across the year, Williams examined the ways in which the curriculum and its activities and discussions assisted diverse middle school girls to better make sense of their intersectional identities—as persons with racial, ethnic, cultural, gender, and socioeconomic components defining who they are within their immediate environment. Developmental level was an intersectional consideration in the program, which addressed the ways in which age and maturity affect self and position within the daily environment. Over the course of 8 years of development and implementation, the program used an experiential model in which differing explorations of identity and positionality, power, and privilege were considered. It provided participants with opportunities to develop their voices, to define their own understanding of their identities, and to address conflicts that might arise in response to social interactions, given intersectional considerations. Programs similar to this one, adapted for variations of intersectional consideration, are being developed and used broadly in educational settings (e.g., understanding how age-peer models impact disability status as an intersectionality consideration; Locke et al., 2012).

APPLYING MULTICULTURAL GUIDELINE 8 TO RESEARCH

How our intersectional identities unfold and develop over time is widely open to investigation (Azmitia & Thomas, 2015). Developmental aspects of intersectional identities are of particular interest across domains of behavioral health, personality, equity, and social justice, to name just a few (Azmitia & Thomas, 2015; Galliher et al., 2017). The World Health Organization (WHO; n.d.-a) has discussed existing global relationships and the ways in which identity development is often a process that occurs over time and differs according to setting and custom. The WHO recommended cultivating avenues for peoples to recognize and emerge as who they are across all aspects of identity. We can take this further and engage with the need to address the layered components of identity, including developmental level and aging: An imperative has been placed within the social sciences, and psychology more specifically, on research that considers intersectionality and its mediators.

Studies of minority group identity have focused primarily on racial and ethnic groups (Nandi & Platt, 2015). Building on this important literature, Guideline 8 addresses identity formation across time with regard to the broad and full intersectionality we hold (see Table 1.1). Exploring key current models and then building forward from them by engaging a multicultural framework is an identified area of need. This led to a frank, detailed discussion among the task force developing the *2017 Multicultural Guidelines,* as we needed to identify useful starting points for thinking about the ways in which developmental level intersects considerably with the multiple aspects of identity that are commonly considered. In the time since the publication of the *2017 Multicultural Guidelines,* studies have highlighted the importance of viewing identity much more broadly and to engage more effectively the complexities that may mediate how individuals and cultures, together and separately, address lifespan demands and concerns across the biopsychosociocultural perspective.

Ferrer and colleagues (2017) emphasized the necessity of considering race, ethnicity, cultural position, socioeconomic status, and aging within a framework of an intersectional life-course perspective. Their model, one that holds broad applicability, emphasizes the need to consider how positioning within one's array of identities shifts across the lifespan. For example, one's status as an immigrant during childhood influences early experiences, which remain influential but may have different impact as one moves into adulthood and then older age. How one situates within one's cultural milieu, along with how one's cultural milieu is influenced by gender identity or professional opportunity, mediates how one experiences a sense of self-identity and how choices regarding experiences (e.g., socially, educationally, vocationally) may unfold. Incorporating ethnographic analysis, Ferrer et al. (2017) described a multistep process for engaging participants to understand historical experiences across their lives and to consider the ways in which these experiences influence their current position as aging members of the community. Focusing on both cultural and personal experiences, they tied participation in the work force to the ways in which individuals come to mediate their economic and personal identities and to maneuver through societal expectations and roles.

From a broad biopsychosociocultural position, work by a number of psychologists studying neurodevelopment within a social, environmental, and identity-based framework has expanded significantly (for reviews, see Chiao, 2018, and H. S. Kim & Sasaki, 2014). Researchers in social neuroscience have introduced a more specific domain of cultural neuroscience to our research lexicon (Chiao, 2018; Rule et al., 2013). As a field, cultural neuroscience is particularly interested in how we come to "understand how culture as an amalgam of values, meanings, conventions and artifacts that constitute daily social realities might interact with—that is, both constructing and being constructed by, the mind and its underlying brain pathways of each individual member of the culture" (Kitayama & Park, 2010, p. 112). Engaging an active mixed-methods approach that is at times interdisciplinary in its scope of investigations, researchers interested in cultural neuroscience (Chiao, 2018; H. S. Kim & Sasaki, 2014; Rule et al., 2013) seek to understand the ways in which culture and its determinants directly influence the epigenetic and microstructural dynamics of brain development and the subsequent reflection of these developmental steps in such phenomena as neural plasticity, cognitive and affective development, and identity and personality growth. Anthropological, sociological, psychological, and neurological factors are all considered of relevance, helping to identify the historical and current influences that drive diversity and, simultaneously, resilience. Considering these factors provides for a richer conceptualization of how we become socially and affectively engaged across phenomena such as attachment and can guide and mediate our understanding of and approach to about life span development.

APPLYING MULTICULTURAL GUIDELINE 8 TO CONSULTATION

When engaged in consultation, multiculturally responsive psychologists strive to understand that multiple and often unique factors affect how individuals and communities "thrive and meet goals" (APA, 2017a, p. 82) across the lifespan. Research has shown that a multitude of influences affect the ways in which individuals engage with one another and interact socially and in terms of shared engagement in work or leisure; studies related to this specific focus have examined how the historical period during which individuals develop serves to define their generational identification and influences their ideas about self, family, and their community (Baltes et al., 1979) and have explored considerations regarding gender and class (Bullock, 2013; Stephens et al., 2014). Multiculturally responsive psychologists in consultation have been particularly attentive to work by Heather Bullock and Hazel Markus. Their work has influenced efforts to provide organizations and industries with an understanding of the layered influences that affect efforts at guiding decision making related to team building, promotion of diverse individuals to leadership positions, and making changes to approaches to equity (e.g., Fiske & Markus, 2012). Importantly, Bullock, Markus, and Fiske have shown that class, gender, and cultural roles require emphasis when addressing inequalities and considering the ways in which they may resist mediation. This work further underscores the challenges one may come to face when considering intersectional influences on community engagement, work attitudes and values, and the understanding of opportunity, or lack therein, that different generations may experience (APA, 2017a).

The principal tasks when thinking about how to best guide and support multiculturally responsive psychological consultation are to engage with the difference in voices and experience that present within an organization or workplace and to attend to and guide an appreciation for how cohort may serve to structure one's views of how the world may work best. As discussed in Chapter 6 of this volume, Sue (2008) showed that when consultants engage directly with individuals to discuss their identities, considering and assessing how varied intersectional aspects of who they are both together and separately may influence assignation and response within an organizational setting. By confronting stereotypes and biases directly and working to bridge the misunderstandings and microaggressions that these biases may bring forth, consultants and the organizations with which they work may experience increased collaboration, effort, and equity.

CONCLUSION

Multicultural Guideline 8 is a reminder that identity is a lifelong developmental process. We grow and change, and with us, so do elements of how we identify. There is much that remains necessary, in terms of both research and how we engage the flexibility we hold, to make full sense of what it means to be multicultural and work as multiculturally engaged clinicians, teachers, consultants, and researchers across a strongly biopsychosocioculturally informed science and practice. We have strong expectations that the next generations of psychologists to further operationalize and guide how identities are conceptualized and held across time, and how this operationalization will inform the ways in which we build forward a true multiculturally responsive, antiracist, and inclusive practice of professional psychology.

In the next chapter, we move into the fifth and last layer of the ecological model, outcomes. Like the other layers, two guidelines fall under this layer. Chapter 11 explores outcomes that can emerge through culturally informed work in psychology, the overall focus of Multicultural Guideline 9.

PART VI OUTCOMES

11
CONDUCTING CULTURALLY INFORMED WORK IN PSYCHOLOGY
Multicultural Guideline 9

Guideline 9. Psychologists strive to conduct culturally appropriate and informed research, teaching, supervision, consultation, assessment, interpretation, diagnosis, dissemination, and evaluation of efficacy as they address the first four levels of the *Layered Ecological Model of the Multicultural Guidelines*.

Chapter 11 presents Multicultural Guideline 9, the first guideline that focuses on outcomes presented in Level 5 of *Multicultural Guidelines: An Ecological Approach to Context, Identity, and Intersectionality, 2017* (hereinafter referred to as *2017 Multicultural Guidelines*; American Psychological Association [APA], 2017a). Specifically, the outcome in Multicultural Guideline 9 is to encourage psychologists to engage in professional endeavors that are culturally informed and responsive. These endeavors include our roles as researchers, educators, supervisors, and consultants. As a result, Multicultural Guideline 9 encourages an overall focus on the work of the multiculturally responsive psychologist through culturally appropriate assessment, interpretation, diagnosis, teaching and supervision, research endeavors, dissemination of research, consultation, and evaluation of efficacy in our work across these domains.

---

https://doi.org/10.1037/0000348-011
Applying Multiculturalism: An Ecological Approach to the APA Guidelines, by C. S. Clauss-Ehlers, S. J. Hunter, G. S. Morse, and P. Tummala-Narra
Copyright © 2024 by the American Psychological Association. All rights reserved.

Given that Multicultural Guideline 9 is the first guideline to consider outcomes, it makes sense that we would explore what is meant by this term. Crowley (2017) described *outcomes* as "the end result of the therapeutic process, the impact on your life and outlook." Outcomes may vary for clients. For instance, Crowley (2017) discussed various outcomes that clients might experience: "feeling better," "having more confidence/greater self-esteem," "having a better understanding," "changes or improvements," and "the power of being heard." Multicultural Guideline 9 considers the outcomes of a range of psychological endeavors, in addition to client outcomes. Such outcomes encompass client outcomes, outcomes that result from research, teaching and training outcomes, and consultation outcomes.

While outcomes are critical to well-being and the overall impact of psychological intervention in practice, research, teaching, and consultation, it was interesting to note that when we put the phrase "definition psychology outcomes from a multicultural perspective" in a Google Scholar search, the results revealed no specific references that defined psychological outcomes through a multicultural lens. This got us thinking about what we mean by outcomes. When we are exploring the outcomes of what results from a psychological intervention, how do we understand those from a multicultural lens?

One way to think about outcomes from psychological practice is to understand them within the various domains of what we do. In practice, we focus on outcomes for clients and the therapeutic process. For teaching and training, outcomes can relate to learning, awareness, skills, and insights among trainees as well as to the development of knowledge in the classroom and one's professional development. For research, outcomes can involve developing new knowledge, greater awareness of an issue, collaboration with a community, and developing and implementing interventions supported by research. Finally for consultation, psychological outcomes might include new ways that an organization understands its dynamics, relates to its employees, and builds and retains a workforce.

In Chapter 11, we encourage you to consider outcomes of psychological endeavors within a multicultural context. The question is, How are psychological outcomes informed by a multiculturally responsive approach? At their core, we return to the core of the layered ecological model with its focus on the bidirectional relationship in which all constituencies involved in the psychological endeavor engage in partnership in which each is open and willing to be informed and transformed. Table 11.1 presents questions to consider related to outcomes from psychological endeavors. The questions are posed to introduce a dialogue into the literature and are focused on how we can understand outcomes in a multiculturally responsive way.

TABLE 11.1. Questions to Consider in Support of Multiculturally Responsive Outcomes From Psychological Endeavors

Psychological endeavor	Questions to consider
Practice	Who defines the desired goals or outcomes of therapy?
	How is empathy expressed from a multicultural perspective?
	How are movements away from desired outcomes (e.g., a setback, a relapse) acknowledged and supported in therapy?
	How is the development of clinical rapport informed by a multiculturally responsive approach?
Teaching and training	How is knowledge constructed together?
	How are diverse perspectives in the classroom incorporated into learning?
	Who defines the learning goals and outcomes?
	How is disagreement with those goals processed and managed?
Research	Who is the research being conducted for—the researcher, the community, or the field?
	Who defines the desired outcomes from the research project?
	How are those desired outcomes communicated?
	Who benefits from their communication?
Consultation	Who defines the desired outcomes from consultation?
	Who is listened to when project concepts in the organization are explored?
	How do consultation results benefit the organization in an equitable way?

The case illustration presented in this chapter demonstrates research outcomes through involvement in a community-based participatory research approach (CBPR) in a transnational research project. CBPR involves a "collaborative effort between community partners and research institutions to engage in research that benefits community" (Sandoval et al., 2012, p. 681). The aim is to develop culturally centered interventions that are directly informed by and responsive to the needs of the community through collaboration that directly involves an authentic community partnership. CBPR has been amply documented in the literature and shows promise as an approach to address both health and mental health disparities (Smedley et al., 2003). Through an active partnership with the community, CBPR can be directly responsive to community needs and, as the following case illustration shows, incorporate research methodologies that reflect the community's preferred approach to generating new knowledge (Clauss-Ehlers, 2020).

CASE ILLUSTRATION–DR. ANDERSSON: COMMUNITY-BASED PARTICIPATORY RESEARCH SUPPORTING COMMUNITY CHANGE AND ENGAGEMENT

Dr. Andersson[1] is a community-based researcher interested in conducting an international study. Through contacts with colleagues, Dr. Andersson followed up with professional ties to a local community center in Sweden. She first arranged to meet with the center director to discuss her interests and potential shared goals: She was thinking about implementing a primarily quantitative study focused on adolescent development within a community of immigrants in Sweden. Her proposed research design involved a protocol that included a series of questionnaires for adolescent research participants to complete. Question topics would include mental health issues such as depression and anxiety, experiences of immigration, and resilience. Dr. Andersson and her research team would administer the research protocol once at the community center, after parents or guardians signed consent forms and the youth participants gave assent; the research team would analyze the data using SPSS. Results would be reported in aggregate, with interpretations based on the quantitative data.

After Dr. Andersson proposed this research design, the center director told her that youth in the community would benefit more from research that provides a way for them to tell their stories. The center director shared that a study that provides some type of intervention in which young people could talk about their experiences and identities would be more helpful for the community. The center director further shared that many of their young people are isolated and have experienced trauma. She explained that autobiographical narrative is an approach that has been used with other projects. This approach involves participants writing or talking about their experiences, and these narratives (i.e., autobiographies) become a basis for analysis. The center director shared that an autobiographical narrative approach has resonated with the experiences of the youth involved with the center. She further shared that it contributed to strong research participation and that the youth benefited from sharing their stories.

Dr. Andersson heard the center director's recommendation. Through conversations with a range of community constituencies, she made a decision to change her research approach and methodology to align with the recommendation. For instance, Dr. Andersson and her team decided to ask research

---

[1] In this case illustration, all appropriate steps have been taken to disguise the identities of the individuals discussed.

> **Discussion Questions Related to Dr. Andersson**
>
> 1. What are the components of community-based participatory research (CBPR) identified in this case?
> 2. What is your view about Dr. Andersson changing the focus of the study? In your view, should this change have been made? Why or why not?
> 3. Are there additional strategies Dr. Andersson could have employed to further a CBPR approach?
> 4. What are important considerations for researchers to adhere to when engaging in international research?
> 5. How would you incorporate a CBPR approach in your own work?
> 6. What are some ways that researchers can give back to the communities where their research is implemented?

participants to complete a questionnaire administered before and after an autobiographical intervention. The autobiographical intervention was revised to consist of a series of weekly discussions that allow the youth to talk about their immigration experiences.

Participation in the study was high, with many youths attending every week. The knowledge that the youths gain from their participation provided important insights into their experiences immigrating to Sweden. At the end of the study, the youths shared how much they benefited from participating. They described feeling that the project allowed them to have a voice and a safe space to discuss concerns about their futures. At the request of the center, Dr. Andersson returned the following year to share study results with center staff, youth, educators, and policy makers. The conversation contributed to programmatic considerations for the center itself, and community legislators are considering additional funding for mental health services.

LITERATURE REVIEW

As multiculturally responsive research psychologists, we can give back to communities in several ways. One way is to listen to community concerns and actively hear what the community is expressing as their research interests (Belone et al., 2016). This process can involve collaboration between researchers and communities to construct research projects that reflect the community's expressed need and interest (Clauss-Ehlers, 2020).

A second way that researchers can give back to communities is to offer appropriate therapeutic support to the community, for instance, if the project involves a clinical intervention or trial, as long as we avoid conflicts of interest, such as might occur with pro bono therapies, and we can provide appropriate supportive connections to the community by linking the community with behavioral health providers who are available to assist. Community members who may require such support can use therapy before, during, or after the research.

A third way researchers can provide support to community members is by offering intervention services that might not otherwise exist in the community or that might not be affordable (Clauss-Ehlers et al., 2017). Hence, while we as researchers may be testing the efficacy of an intervention, the intervention itself may provide support to community members (Clauss-Ehlers et al., 2017).

A fourth consideration is that researchers and community members can collaborate to disseminate research results among the community. Sharing research results within the community can promote greater awareness and understanding of an issue. Through such greater awareness and understanding, communities may engage in advocacy efforts to address the issue presented. For instance, as part of a research project focused on well-being among youth, the researcher (Clauss-Ehlers) was asked to present findings in a community forum. The community center at which the research was conducted invited the local public health official to learn more about the impact of factors like isolation, depression, and anxiety among young people in the community. In this way, research had the potential to inform policy and could lead to additional supports and interventions for youth in the area.

Multicultural Guideline 9 encourages us to conduct culturally appropriate and informed professional interventions in practice, teaching/training, research, and consultation. In the case example, Dr. Andersson developed a positive research connection based in part on her willingness to change the focus of the study so that it reflected the needs of youth in the community, as shared by their center director. The result was an intervention that benefited youth in the community and contributed knowledge to the field. This approach demonstrated a multiculturally responsive research (and possible clinical) outcome in that the voices of diverse youth were heard and responded to by the larger community context.

Hence a positive outcome across all four domains of psychological practice is an ability to develop genuine partnerships and collaborations with individuals and communities. Rapport in psychological endeavors is noted by demonstrating a sincere commitment to the client, student, research participant, or consultee; demonstrating that commitment by working to build a sense of trust; and building that trust by being self-reflexive and able to internally confront assumptions and biases. Dr. Andersson demonstrates a genuine interest in the youth at the community center by actively listening to the center director and engaging in conversations with community stakeholders. Her willingness to take in the feedback she received ultimately led to a more community-focused, collaborative research project that also supported young people.

APPLYING MULTICULTURAL GUIDELINE 9 TO CLINICAL PRACTICE

Assessment

When both developing and implementing assessments, test developers and administrators should not assume that a test can be uniformly implemented across diverse populations. Doing so might prevent psychologists from understanding cultural differences and could lead to a biased interpretation of what a test result means. The following paragraphs discuss two testing concepts, validity and norming, within a cultural framework. This discussion aims to illustrate the nuances and complexities related to the application of testing concepts when working with diverse populations.

Validity refers to the ability of an assessment or test to measure what it is actually supposed to measure. However, as described by Solano-Flores (2011), tests are "cultural artifacts" (p. 3), meaning that tests are constructed according to "instructional and accountability practices . . . created with the intent to meet certain social needs . . . written in the language (and the dialect of that language) used by those who develop them . . . [and with] content [that] is a reflection of the skills, competencies, forms of knowledge, and communication styles valued by a society" (p. 3). Solano-Flores (2011) discussed how culture and language are viewed as sources of measurement error by professional organizational testing documents where "current testing practices address culture as a threat to validity rather than the essence of validity" (p. 3).

To make culture part of the formal definition of validity, Solano-Flores and Nelson-Barber (2001) presented the concept of cultural validity. They stated that culture should be incorporated as a critical aspect of tests and the test-taking process. They contended that those who develop tests and those who use them should consider cultural validity as strongly as they would other types of validity. They defined the concept of cultural validity as

> the effectiveness with which . . . assessment addresses the socio-cultural influences that shape student thinking and the ways in which students make sense of . . . items and respond to them. These socio-cultural influences include the sets of values, beliefs, experiences, communication patterns, teaching and learning styles, and epistemologies inherent in the students' cultural backgrounds, and the socioeconomic conditions prevailing in their cultural groups. (p. 555)

Solano-Flores (2011) encouraged test users to ask the following four questions to engage the perspective of cultural validity:

1. To what extent are the testing practices consistent with current thinking in the culture and language sciences?

2. How accurately are culturally and linguistically diverse populations specified, and how properly are they represented throughout the entire process of test development?

3. To what extent does the process of test development take into consideration ways in which students from different cultural backgrounds interpret items?

4. To what extent are test review practices based on multiple sources of information, and how well are various forms of data analysis and data representation used in combination to examine how culture influences student performance? (p. 17)

In keeping with the concept of cultural validity, a critical concern in psychological research is whether assessment instruments have used norming samples that are representative of diverse populations (Suzuki et al., 2021). *Norming* has been defined as "the process of constructing norms or the typical performance of a group of individuals on a psychological or achievement assessment" (Renbarger & Morgan, 2018). For research psychologists engaging in the development of assessment measures, it is critical that an intersectional approach that incorporates diverse samples is employed so that the assessment measure is representative of diverse populations (Suzuki et al., 2021).

This is particularly important given the practice of norm-reference assessments where tests "compare an individual's score against the scores of groups [that are used to, for example] . . . help educational stakeholders such as administrators, teachers, and parents make informed educational decisions about an individual student and the student's progress" (Renbarger & Morgan, 2018). A lack of diverse representation through norming can lead to individual student scores being compared to a group score that is not reflective of their reference group identities (e.g., race and ethnicity not being represented in the group that the individual is being compared with). The risk is that individuals receive scores that are not based on their true abilities and are not reflective of experiences in domains such learning/education and mental health status (Nielsen et al., 2017).

Hence, it is important for the practicing psychologist engaging in assessment to consider whether the test and resulting score(s) are the result of testing biases that interfere with validity, such as cultural validity (Solano-Flores, 2011). For instance, a neuropsychological test may include the question "What color is a banana?" Whereas the expected answer might be "yellow" in a North American context, in a Latin American context the response is often "green." The Latin American individual labeling the banana as green would be marked as incorrect, which would be reflected in the final test score (Clauss-Ehlers, 2019b). Similarly, testing procedures might include the instruction to work as quickly as possible. In some cultures, the cultural value of doing (i.e., working fast to achieve more) is not valued (Kluckhohn & Strodtbeck, 1961) as much as taking the time to complete the task at one's own pace (Kluckhohn & Strodtbeck, 1961). If the test taker doesn't realize that part of the task is to work fast and loses points for not working quickly as a result, the person may get a score that doesn't accurately reflect their level because they did not work quickly (Ardila, 2007).

In another example, some tests may require test takers to name objects that simply do not readily exist in their cultural context. For instance, the Boston Naming Test (Kaplan et al., 1978) requires the respondent to provide labels for pictured items, such as a pretzel. While pretzels are well known in the United States, the pretzel is an unknown entity in many countries (Clauss-Ehlers, 2019b), and the test taker loses points when unable to identify the pretzel (Ardila, 2007). This has implications not only for items for which points are lost or additional points are not acquired (i.e., extra points for speed of completion) but also for the cumulative effect of losing points. Points lost for not being able to name objects and not describing an object as the test requires add up.

In addition, speed is a testing condition that may conflict with cultural values. The test taker, for instance, may be told to work as quickly as possible. They may gain additional points for completing items correctly within a quicker time frame. On the other hand, the test taker may lose out on the opportunity to gain such additional points if tasks are not completed, and completed correctly, within that quicker time frame. Ardila (2007) discussed how the speed element on tests "are frankly inappropriate" and described how "speed and quality are contradictory, and good products are the results of a slow and careful process" (p. 28). This cumulative effect can lead to a significantly lower score that subsequently results in a lower classification on the test's scale (Ardila, 2007). While speed may reflect a cultural value of production and mastery in mainstream American culture, it may not in cultures that value a reflective process orientation.

Psychotherapy

Research shows racial disparities in access and utilization of mental health services (García & Courtney, 2011; Smedley et al., 2003). For example, individuals in the service sector may experience disparities in services, especially culturally and linguistically responsive services. In addition, mental health stigma and individual beliefs about mental health may interfere with service utilization (DeFreitas et al., 2018; García & Courtney, 2011; Hankerson et al., 2015). Problems with the service delivery (e.g., lack of services in the client's language, limited office hours, difficulties getting transportation to the clinic, long waiting lists, long waits for appointments and intakes, bureaucratic insurance payment procedures, no sliding fee scale for those without insurance) contribute to lower rates of accessing and utilizing mental health services (Miranda et al., 2008).

The Institute of Medicine makes a distinction between disparities in access to care and disparities that result from discriminatory behaviors among clinicians (Smedley et al., 2003). Both types of disparities can increase the risk that a client will leave the therapeutic relationship before the therapy has been completed and is ready for termination (Office of the Surgeon General, Center for Mental Health Services, National Institute of Mental Health, 2001). To provide successful interventions, psychologists can foster trust in therapeutic relationships that outweighs the client's distrust of the psychologist's ability to relate to their culture and life circumstances. The reflexivity presented in Chapter 1 applies here. Being self-aware and introspective about assumptions and biases is critical in building rapport and the bidirectional relationship that is at the first level of the layered ecological model. With cultural humility, practitioners can be reflexive about what they may not know about the client's background and can be transparent with clients about gaps in their knowledge.

The concept of cultural humility reminds us that an understanding of culture and of the intersectionality of reference group identities is an ongoing, lifelong process of learning and commitment. As multiculturally responsive psychologists, we can further develop rapport by being sensitive to and aware of the language used in interactions. For instance, using professional jargon and keeping a distant stance, perhaps because of the incorrect assumption that this approach appears professional and neutral, may lead to a lack of trust and an inability to build rapport in the counseling relationship. As therapists, we can be thoughtful about the words we use within the therapeutic conversation. For instance, as mentioned in Chapter 5, recent research found that youth between the ages of 18 and 25 who had received mental health services had significantly greater negative perceptions of the term "psychopathology" than youth who had not received mental health services (Weist et al., 2019). Such negative perceptions might lead to internalized stigma, lower self-confidence, and isolation, thereby negatively affecting both the client and the therapeutic interaction.

APPLYING MULTICULTURAL GUIDELINE 9 TO TEACHING AND TRAINING

It is often the case that courses on diversity or multicultural considerations are stand-alone classes in curricula for college students and in graduate coursework. This kind of model risks sending the message that issues of diversity are to be focused on in one course and not throughout the curriculum. In contrast, when a multicultural approach is taken throughout undergraduate and graduate curricular experiences, trainees are aware of the importance of reference group identities across all aspects of their professional roles (Clauss-Ehlers, 2006b). For instance, courses on assessment and testing, family therapy, career counseling, theories of counseling and clinical care, couples therapy, community interventions, ethics, and group counseling can integrate multicultural considerations with regard to working with diverse communities. Clinical experiences including practica, externships, predoctoral internships, and postdoctoral fellowships can also serve this purpose (APA, 2015b; Rivera Mindt et al., 2010).

Teaching and Learning Through Research Participation

Graduate and undergraduate students can actively learn about the research process and outcomes through engagement in research on their campuses. By way of example, students on the research team were actively involved in developing a parenting curriculum with presentations each week geared toward the needs of parents. They were enthusiastic and interested in moving right to developing a curriculum for parents who would be attending the parenting center at which the curriculum was to be implemented.

While initially the focus was on conducting research to determine the "best" curriculum for the parenting program, the research team decided it would be important to consult with the community directly to determine the kinds of workshops that would help the most with parenting skills. The researchers went out into the community and asked parents what they would want to hear if they went to a workshop on parenting. The research team learned that the parents wanted workshops focused on themes that the researchers wouldn't necessarily have thought of. Parents shared that they wanted time to learn about self-care, they wanted to learn about setting limits in a positive way, and, most of all, they wanted to have time to speak with other parents about their experiences.

The research team took this information and incorporated it into the workshop curriculum: The workshops directly reflected what parents from the community said they wanted to hear. Parents attended the center and completed an intervention research protocol while participating in the workshops. Some parents asked for a referral to the organization's counseling services. The student researchers noted that the conceptualization of the study could have gone a very different way had it not incorporated parent feedback.

This brief example shows multiple ways in which outcomes from psychological endeavors were multiculturally responsive. First, the students learned about conducting authentic research that involves the community through their engagement on the research team (i.e., who defines the desired outcomes from the research project? See Table 11.1). Next, the psychological intervention provided to parents directly reflected their feedback and interests. Parents established a sense of trust, so much so that several were open to asking for a referral for counseling (i.e., who defines the desired goals or outcomes of therapy?). The students learned about teaching because they were open and able to respond to feedback and to shift goals to incorporate diverse parent perspectives (i.e., how are diverse perspectives in the classroom incorporated into learning?). Finally, consultation was multiculturally responsive in that the organization consulted with the community to incorporate their perspectives and provided a much-needed service (i.e., Who is listened to when project concepts in the organization are explored?). This example shows how we can have multiple positive outcomes based on the various roles we engage in and the partnerships created through them.

Supervision

It is imperative to provide a role model for students by providing an atmosphere in which they can engage in ongoing conversation and learning about the impact of multicultural factors on their clients' experiences. Additionally, supervisors can model cultural humility by demonstrating how they too may not be fully aware of a client's cultural experiences (Mosher et al., 2017; Upshaw et al., 2020). This process can involve being open to learning and identifying a lack of knowledge so as to better understand their client's cultural background.

For example, consider a real world-example that involved coleading a therapy group with Latinas experiencing depression (Vazquez & Clauss-Ehlers, 2005). The women were actively engaged in the lives of their families and employed. During one group session, group coleaders focused on the women's individual needs, such as self-care and maintaining dental appointments. The following week, none of the women attended the group meeting. Through supervision, group leaders learned that, while the focus of the group was to empower the women, empowerment needs to occur within a culturally relevant context that aligns with the women's cultural values (Vazquez & Clauss-Ehlers, 2005). The supervisor encouraged the coleaders to return to the women and focus on the idea of taking care of one's self to be able to take care of others. This approach resonated with the women. They did not feel they had to choose between their loved ones and their own needs. Rather, the intervention was *culturally syntonic* in its understanding of finding a balance between self and the collective. Here, the term culturally syntonic refers to an intervention or technique that was responsive to and thoughtful of the women's cultural values and the sociocultural environment.

APPLYING MULTICULTURAL GUIDELINE 9 TO RESEARCH

Multicultural Guideline 9 encourages us to undertake culturally informed research that is appropriate for clients with diverse cultural beliefs and values. One way to accomplish this is to understand the limitations of randomized controlled trials (RCTs) in providing evidence-based treatments for culturally diverse populations (Sexton et al., 2011; Wampold & Bhati, 2004). RCTs are the gold standard for both psychological and medical researchers.

Although RCTs have treatment and control groups, they have been criticized for not being fully responsive to and reflective of the diversity of populations in which the methodology is implemented (Sexton et al., 2011). One consideration regarding RCTs concerns "methodological diversity in research" (Sexton et al., 2011, p. 388). The view here is that in efforts to decrease the possibility of error, a hallmark of the RCT approach, the intricacies of working with communities may be lost (Clauss-Ehlers et al., 2017; Sexton et al., 2008). In contrast, for instance, the autobiographical narrative approach taken by Dr. Andersson captured the nuances and specifics of the experiences of the research participants. Similarly, since the sample of participants in an RCT is often not a representative sample of the population due to limitations in participants' diversity, results from RCTs may not be applied more generally.

Some argue that the RCT approach found in the literature would be better balanced with the inclusion of an evidence-based case study approach (Clauss-Ehlers et al., 2017). A benefit of the latter approach is that it can be adapted to the community in which the research is being conducted. In their work with parents of young children in a diverse community context, for instance, Clauss-Ehlers and colleagues (2017) spoke with community members to learn what they wanted to know about parenting before devising any intervention. Workshops and related themes were organized only after having conversations with parents in the community.

A related benefit of the evidence-based case study approach is its capacity to "decrease the gap between research and practice" (Clauss-Ehlers et al., 2017, p. 172). For instance, through their evidence-based parenting intervention study, Clauss-Ehlers et al. (2017) learned that parents valued hearing about the experiences of other parents, rather than simply listening to workshops delivered by "experts." The evidence-based case study approach allowed this practice implication to emerge, with clinical implications not only for workshop development but also for the importance of a peer support model in which parents support other parents.

In addition to diversifying research methodology, a CBPR involves actively collaborating with the community and its members to develop authentic research partnerships (Belone et al., 2016). Part of community collaboration involves actively partnering and seeking feedback from the community about the type of research question and related methodology that would be helpful. This process involves researchers putting their agendas aside and being open to the possibilities that what the community is reporting will be most helpful for them. This was apparent, for instance, in Dr. Andersson's partnership with the center director and the community. Dr. Andersson took in the feedback given to her about how to construct the study. She recognized the value of what the center director told her regarding the importance of the community's youth being able to talk about their immigration experiences. Dr. Andersson's openness to adjusting her research plans so that they aligned with community needs furthered relationships and addressed any potential for cultural mistrust.

A related aspect of CBPR involves addressing sampling biases by recruiting a sample reflective of the community's population. The psychology literature has a bias toward samples in research studies in which research participants are not representative of most of the world's population (Nielsen et al., 2017).

For instance, in their analysis of developmental psychology journals, Nielsen and colleagues (2017) discussed how the field depends on a narrow group of participants and advocated for greater diversification of samples. They use the acronym WEIRD to demonstrate that developmental psychology journals are highly biased toward samples that include the following characteristics among participants: "Western, educated, industrialized, rich, and democratic" (Nielsen et al., 2017, p. 31).

A CBPR approach that collaborates with the community to collect data that represent the diversity of the population leads to results that have high cultural validity, as they reflect the culture of the population being studied. We saw consistent recruitment and engagement, for instance, in the study Dr. Andersson tailored in collaboration with the center director and the community. Through a partnership with the center director and surrounding community agencies, a team of community leaders was able to recruit a diverse sample. Hence, Dr. Andersson's responsiveness to understanding the importance of youth to share their experiences through an autobiographical approach led to ongoing participation in the intervention by research participants.

APPLYING MULTICULTURAL GUIDELINE 9 TO CONSULTATION

When addressing consultation within diverse communities, it is important to keep in mind many of the considerations discussed previously in this chapter. Multicultural consultation incorporates an understanding of sociocultural influences and constituencies (Goforth et al., 2017). By recognizing that institutions and work settings may have a number of different constituencies engaging together, multiculturally responsive consulting psychologists become familiar with the range of similarities that exist within a particular work culture as well as the areas in which cultural differences situate and influence strengths and challenges at play in the organization.

Kirmayer and colleagues (2003) presented a model of mental health services for multicultural societies through cultural consultation. They evaluated the development of a cultural consultation service (CCS) for mental health professionals and primary care practitioners. The goal of their evaluation research was to determine if the delivery of mental health services improved for diverse urban clients, including refugees, immigrants, and underrepresented groups who were being seen at a mainstream clinic.

The implementation of the CCS was evaluated through both quantitative (e.g., nature of case referred) and qualitative (e.g., participant observation) methodologies. The outcome of the study demonstrated that the cases referred to the CCS presented language barriers and highlighted the cultural complexity of providing appropriate diagnoses and treatment options. This was evident in the finding that the CCS recommended changing/reassessing treatment in 70% of cases, implementing added treatment (e.g., therapy, medication) in 48% of cases, and changing a diagnosis in 23% of cases (Kirmayer et al., 2003).

Kirmayer and colleagues (2003) discussed how cultural consultation can involve pulling together resources as the team organizes different areas of expertise. They described "culture brokers," who are members of the team that possess a "cultural understanding" related to the client's experience (p. 151). They found that this level of understanding facilitates rapport and can address the cultural complexities associated with treatment issues. For instance, after the tragedy of the September 11th World Trade Center attacks, an Ecuadorian mother sought psychotherapy for herself and her children. She had lost her husband, the children's father, in the World Trade Center disaster. The concern for the family was that their loved one's body had not been found. The family expressed a sense of denial that their loved one had died, while acknowledging the devastation of the disaster.

The family shared concerns about having a funeral service without a body and what that would mean for their loved one's afterlife. While the clinician focused on mental health issues such as trauma, grief, and denial, it was important to incorporate the family's priest into the treatment process. The priest served as a culture broker who worked with the family and the mental health practitioner to address complicated issues of grief related to not having a body present to mourn and to whom to say goodbye. The collaboration between the mental health professional and the priest furthered supported the family's grieving process by providing them collaborative resources rather than having the family choose between seeing only the mental health professional or talking only with the priest.

CONCLUSION

A concluding question: If you are interested in conducting research in a diverse community context of which you are not a member, how do you approach the community to discuss your potential study and involvement? This question—as well as its application to practice, teaching/training, and consultation—is central to Multicultural Guideline 9. The implications of this work are enormous. For psychologists and students of psychology, for instance, research is integrally a part of professional training and, for many, a key part of our daily lives as professionals. How can we rely on the literature when it does not effectively engage with the variations of identity and self that our clients, students, and trainees represent?

Multicultural Guideline 9 brings forward opportunities to rethink the role that practice, teaching and training, research, and consultation can play and to consider how we can bring elements of research with diversity into our clinical practice and educational endeavors. In the practice arena, Multicultural Guideline 9 encourages us to incorporate cultural and linguistic interventions in clinical activities. It is hoped that this directive will at least begin to address significant mental health disparities, leading to better access and utilization as an outcome.

Teaching and training can further address disparities in mental health access and utilization through the provision of comprehensive multicultural curricula in undergraduate and graduate programs. Through personalized learning that encourages students to develop skills aligned with key multicultural psychology concepts (e.g., domestic and transnational focus, cultural competence and cultural humility, bidirectional relationships; see Chapter 1), a future pipeline of multiculturally responsive psychologists may address the treatment gap and work toward eliminating mental health disparities.

With regard to research, Multicultural Guideline 9 guides us to think from a perspective that is qualitatively driven while recognizing the continued importance of focusing on quantitative questions within our studies. Looking directly at focus groups and case studies can be a way to bring breadth to training and practice, to enter into relationships with the communities with which we work and learn directly from them, to guide how and when we ask pertinent questions, and to devise a range of methodologies to answer them. Similarly, consultation involves engaging in a relationship with the organization or entity in which the consultation is occurring. An awareness of sociocultural variables and institutional barriers, coupled with an ability to promote constituency understanding of them, promotes multiculturally informed consultation.

In summary, Multicultural Guideline 9 shows how multicultural outcomes become a synthesized aspect of our work as psychologists, building new approaches to study and practice. We now turn to Chapter 12, the last chapter devoted to a specific guideline. Chapter 12 addresses the second guideline in Level 5, with a focus on decreasing trauma and increasing resilience.

12
APPLYING A STRENGTH-BASED APPROACH TO PSYCHOLOGY
Multicultural Guideline 10

Guideline 10. Psychologists actively strive to take a strength-based approach when working with individuals, families, groups, communities, and organizations that seeks to build resilience and decrease trauma within the sociocultural context.

This chapter presents Multicultural Guideline 10, the second guideline that falls under Level 5 (American Psychological Association [APA], 2017a) which concerns outcomes. Whereas Chapter 11 focused on outcomes related to conducting culturally informed work as psychologists, this chapter examines resilience and trauma within a cultural context. In doing so, this chapter emphasizes ways that we can support increased resilience and mitigate trauma. A strength-based approach (SBA) is the basis of this work.

An SBA in practice "emphasizes mental health, adaptive functioning, and human strengths" (APA, 2017a, p. 88). Hence, an SBA involves engaging in collaborative partnerships with clients, students, research participants, and consultees. Through such partnerships we can work together toward outcomes such as building resilience and decreasing trauma. Returning to the focus on professional relationships that are at the heart of this book, an SBA captures

---

https://doi.org/10.1037/0000348-012
Applying Multiculturalism: An Ecological Approach to the APA Guidelines, by C. S. Clauss-Ehlers, S. J. Hunter, G. S. Morse, and P. Tummala-Narra
Copyright © 2024 by the American Psychological Association. All rights reserved.

the essence of the bidirectional relationship with its focus on mutual collaboration between providers and clients (please recall that, for the purposes of our book, the term *providers* refers to practitioners, educators, researchers, and consultants, and the term *clients* refers to clients receiving psychological services, students, research participants, and consultees). This approach is different from psychological models that have taken deficit approaches that emphasize a focus on pathology and underfunctioning (Clauss-Ehlers, 2004, 2008; Padesky & Mooney, 2012). "With a strength-based approach, the psychologist operates from a perspective that acknowledges challenges while also identifying positive ways in which diverse individuals, families, groups, communities, and organizations address life experiences" (APA, 2017a, p. 88).

SBAs are increasingly seen in our field. They are evident in the consumer movement, the recovery movement, positive psychology, family support services, humanistic psychology, trauma psychology, and spiritual psychology (Guevara Carpio et al., 2022; Harvey & Tummala-Narra, 2007; Park & Peterson, 2008; Seligman, 2019; Vieten & Lukoff, 2022). We also see SBAs taken in prevention efforts that build on assets and resources to prevent the development of problems in the future (Clauss-Ehlers et al., 2013; Hirst et al., 2013). Within this framework, clients contribute solutions and share or create their own life narrative, rather than simply receiving services (Hook & Andrews, 2005; Pattoni, 2012).

Building on SBAs, we are increasingly understanding resilience from a sociocultural context. Longitudinal studies have altered the understanding of resilience from a deficits model to a strengths-based perspective. For instance, Stephan Collishaw and colleagues' (2016) longitudinal study on young people whose parents have depression demonstrated what they described as "mental health resilience" (p. 49) among young people with familial risk. These researchers assessed parents with major depressive disorder, coparents, and their children three times over the course of 4 years. Study findings indicated that while "Adolescent mental health problems are common, [they are] not inevitable, even when parental depression [was] severe and recurrent" (Collishaw et al., 2016, p. 45). Of the adolescents who participated in the study, 20% indicated, "good sustained mental health" (p. 45). Factors associated with good sustained mental health included parental expression of positive emotions, coparenting support, good social relationships, self-efficacy, and regular exercise. The authors discussed how the findings highlight the importance of providing prevention programs that incorporate a range of protective factors.

In positive psychology, the focus shifts from pathology to hope, optimism, love, vocation, perseverance, and courage (APA, 2017a). This is not to say, however, that challenges and related traumas are ignored, not talked about, or not identified (Pattoni, 2012). The opposite is actually the case. A misconception about SBA practice is that it focuses on strengths at the cost of attending to issues, when in fact this approach identifies, acknowledges, and incorporates challenges and trauma in treatment but does so from an understanding and acknowledgment of the capacities that clients and providers bring to the interaction in efforts to address concerns (Hirst et al., 2013).

CASE ILLUSTRATION-NORA: ADDRESSING SOCIOCULTURAL VARIABLES IN TEACHING AND SUPERVISION

Supervision focused on a case presentation of Nora,[1] a mother who recently lost custody of her 4-year-old child to protective services. The child was placed in foster care after a call came in stating there was no heat, food, or furniture in Nora's apartment. Nora was actively using opioids, and it came out later that she was addicted to them.

A third-year doctoral student was assigned to work with Nora as part of her practicum placement. From the outset, she openly shared in supervision how she did not understand how this parent could choose addiction over the well-being of her child. The student felt so strongly about her view that she found it challenging to develop rapport while working with Nora.

When the supervisor asks what the strong feelings were about, the student shared that she just did not understand how a parent could be in this situation. The student, also a parent, confided that she blamed Nora for her problems because she felt they stemmed from poor judgment and bad decision making. The student's steadfast position made it increasingly difficult to make a therapeutic connection, to the point that the supervisor thought about reassigning the case to another practicum student.

Before referring the case to someone else, the supervisor guided the trainee to better ask Nora more directly about her own life experiences. She encouraged her to be open and ask what led Nora to use opioids and not be able to care for her family. The student was reluctant but approached the session with this line of inquiry in mind. She asked Nora what made her start to use opioids and how usage escalated to this point.

The student did not expect the response she received. Nora shared how her stepfather sexually abused her growing up. She told the student how she

---

[1]In this case illustration, all appropriate steps have been taken to disguise the identities of the individuals discussed.

repeatedly went to her mother to share what was going on and to ask for help. Nora talked about how her mom said she was making up the sexual abuse—that she liked to "cause problems" and did so for attention. She described how alone she felt as a child and how the abuse continued for many years. She shared that as soon as she was old enough, she left home to make a life for herself. Nora confided that she wanted something better for herself and that she was motivated to remove herself from an ongoing traumatic situation.

Over the next several sessions, something begins to change. The student found herself listening and empathizing as Nora continued to share her experience. Nora talked about meeting the father of her 4-year-old, an older man who made her feel safe and comforted almost instantly. She described how the relationship was going well until she became pregnant, which was when the physical abuse began. Nora shared that she knew she needed to leave the relationship out of fear for herself and her unborn child. She left when space at a nearby shelter became available.

Nora described to the student how she received supports and services at the shelter. She delivered her beautiful, healthy baby and was feeling hopeful about this next phase of her life. The shelter helped her secure housing and employment. Day care was provided for her baby. Life had improved. It felt like things were moving on the right path. Then the accident happened.

Discussion Questions Related to Nora

1. What assumptions do we bring to the work we engage in with our clients?
2. How can we gain awareness of the assumptions and biases we have about our clients and the situations they present to us?
3. What is the role of cultural resilience and trauma in working with Nora?
4. What are your thoughts about how the supervisor worked with the student?
5. Have you ever been in a clinical situation where you found it difficult to work with someone? What made it difficult for you? How did you manage those feelings? What was the outcome?
6. If you were the supervisor in this scenario, how would you have responded?

Nora shared that she was hit by a taxi when crossing the street. The driver left the scene and was never identified. Nora explained how her multiple injuries were initially treated with pain medication. She described how the medicine not only helped the pain but also made her feel better in a way she had never felt before. It was as if the medicine provided a way to heal all the years of abuse and hurt she endured. This was how the addiction began.

LITERATURE REVIEW

Historically, the resilience literature has focused on resilience as an individual concept focused on the "process, capacity or outcome of successful adaptation despite challenges or threatening circumstances . . . good outcomes despite high-risk status, sustained competence under threat and recovery from trauma" (Masten et al., 1990, p. 426). A large body of resilience research has taken a trait-based approach to resilience, focusing on individual factors that promote the ability to overcome adversity. Such factors identified in the research include motivation, internal locus of control, problem-solving skills, emotional self-regulation, self-esteem, intelligence, and reading skills, among other variables (Kumpfer, 1999).

While this literature contributes to our understanding of resilience, an individualized approach to resilience may leave addressing the problem, and overcoming the challenge, way too much up to the individual. For children in schools confronting racism, for instance, the implication of an individualized approach to resilience is that children are responsible for overcoming such racism, rather than locating racism in the context of the school system (Ulie-Wells et al., 2020). This then puts the onus of change on the child and the family rather than on an oppressive system:

> McGee and Stovall (2015) pose a challenge to the current research trend of attributing the survival of black students at traditionally white institutions primarily to grit, perseverance, and mental toughness, noting that research on the aforementioned qualities often fails to properly acknowledge multiple forms of suffering. (p. 491)

The practitioner can engage in social activism and advocacy on behalf of their clients and in partnership with them, understanding how the surrounding sociocultural context may or may not promote resilience. The practitioner can also encourage client self-advocacy in response to structural oppression.

Similarly, the concept of grit focuses on the individual's ability to overcome challenges and be a survivor (Duckworth et al., 2007). McGee and Stovall (2015) "challenge the construct of grit to consider the extent to which the mental health concerns of black students go undetected" (p. 491). A focus on individual factors and ability to have grit and overcome challenge shifts the responsibility away from the institutions in which these experiences are being perpetuated and risks placing blame on the individual. Ulie-Wells et al. (2020) stated the following:

> When the focus for change is on the oppressive forces of the institution and the way relationships may be reproduce those forces, it necessarily shifts the question away from "how resilient" a person is. This keeps attention concentrated on the cause of racial oppression, not its symptom. (p. 182)

Positive psychology as a 21st-century science is shifting the focus from a solely individual focus on resilience to an evidence-base that supports sociocultural aspects of resilience and related interventions (Clauss-Ehlers, 2008; Pedrotti et al., 2009; Seligman, 2019). Psychology as a 21st-century science is encouraged to consider the concept of resilience as being supported by "external resources, sociocultural factors, and affirming systems" (APA, 2017a, p. 89). A body of emerging research demonstrates the ways in which larger contextual factors promote cultural resilience (Clauss-Ehlers, 2004). These studies locate SBAs within a sociocultural context (Gallardo & Curry, 2009; Sheely-Moore & Bratton, 2010).

This approach allows for culturally adapted interventions that incorporate the intersectionality of race, ethnicity, ability status, sexual orientation, age, culture, language, gender, gender identity, socioeconomic status, religion, spirituality, immigration status, education, and employment, among other variables (Clauss-Ehlers et al., 2019). Rathod and colleagues (2018) conducted a review of the meta-analytic literature on cultural adaptation for mental health intervention. They found "a growing evidence base to suggest that culturally adaptive interventions are effective" (p. 176). However, they presented recommendations such as research to ascertain what is effective, a review on adaptation frameworks, and economic evaluations to demonstrate value to policy makers (Rathod et al., 2018).

Culturally focused resilient adaptation considers how "resilience processes lie in the environmental context in addition to individual traits" (Clauss-Ehlers, 2004, p. 35). This includes how culture and cultural background factors influence resilience among individuals, couples, groups, families, and within organizations and communities (Clauss-Ehlers, 2008). For instance, this approach examines how "cultural values, norms, supports, language, and customs" can promote resilience outcomes (Clauss-Ehlers, 2004, p. 36). The culturally focused resilience adaptation model (CRA) moves beyond individual traits as the only aspect of resilience to understand how the surrounding sociocultural context intersects with a range of variables to promote resilience. In the face of adversity, CRA is defined as a "dynamic, interactive process in which the individual negotiates stress through a combination of character traits, cultural background, cultural values, and facilitating factors in the sociocultural environment" (Clauss-Ehlers, 2004, p. 36).

Tummala-Narra (2007) examined resilience from a cross-cultural perspective from both "within and across cultural contexts" (p. 36). In taking this cultural contextual approach, resilience considers not only individual factors and developmental stage but also "salient qualities of family, social support network, and community and by prevailing cultural beliefs and values" (p. 36). The *role of community in resilience* considers how the broader community context can either support resilience or undermine it (Tummala-Narra, 2007, 2016). As an example of the community context supporting resilience, for instance, within a week of the shut down due to COVID-19, New York City had overcome potential barriers related to providing counseling services online for children and adolescents who received this service as part of their individualized education program (IEP). Through these efforts, children and adolescents were able to receive counseling services remotely even though New York City schools were physically shut down (Clauss-Ehlers & Tummala-Narra, 2022). In this example, the surrounding community context mobilized to provide access to supports dedicated to promoting resilience and well-being.

On the other hand, communities can present contexts that not only undermine resilience but also traumatize members. Tummala-Narra (2007) discussed how the Catholic Church undermined resilience and limited access to a prior support network for people when they came forward to report having been sexually abused:

> This seems to have been the case, for example, when the disclosures of children who were being sexually abused by parish priests were ignored by family and church, and, later still, when their delayed complaints were scorned by church officials who opted to protect abusive priests from public scrutiny. Today, as many of the now-adult children who were abused come forward in search of recognition and restitution, they and their families find themselves unable to attend church, participate in religious ceremony, and/or rely on the church for moral guidance and support (Harris, 2003; Shepard, 2003). (Tummala-Narra, 2007, p. 37)

Cultural beliefs can influence, or even mediate, connections with the larger community context (Tummala-Narra (2007, 2016). The extent to which community connection may or may not occur, may have a subsequent impact on resilience. Many Western cultures (e.g., the United States) may have cultural values that support an individualistic, achievement-oriented approach to life (Tummala-Narra, 2007, 2016). In this approach, competition with others may be valued, and a sense of accomplishment may be measured in terms of one's individual accomplishments, irrespective of those of the larger community or support network. Such accomplishments, and values of independence and competition, may be viewed as traits that promote resilience within this cultural belief context.

In contrast, for those in collectivistic cultures (e.g., India, Mexico), values of interdependence, supporting the larger group, and placing the needs of the group before one's own needs may be more highly valued (Tummala-Narra, 2007, 2016). Within this cultural/contextual framework, strategies that promote well-being and resilience may include family members, community members, and surrounding community supports. Not do so may be experienced as being unresponsive to cultural values and norms.

An example is when the coauthor (Clauss-Ehlers) was on internship at the Bilingual Treatment Program (BTP) at the NYU Bellevue Hospital Center. A Spanish-speaking Latino client came in for an intake and counseling services. The intake was conducted, and a therapy appointment was set for the following week. When the client arrived for the appointment 7 days later, he showed up with five family members who he wanted to participate in the session with him. We might imagine that it felt culturally dystonic for this client, who was from a collectivistic culture, to talk about the struggles he faced apart from his family. In this moment, it was important to recognize the cultural belief system that promoted the client's resilience, understand the cultural disconnection between an individual therapeutic approach and providing counseling support for the client, and shifting in the moment to provide a family therapy intervention.

Trauma

We often talk about being resilient in response to traumatic situations. Just as we consider the cultural context of resilience, so too can we explore how experiences and understandings of trauma are influenced by the surrounding culture (APA, 2017a; Buse et al., 2013, p. 15; Wilson, 2007). Herman (1992) defined *psychological trauma* as

> an affiliation of the powerless. . . . Traumatic events overwhelm the ordinary systems of care that give people a sense of control, connection, and meaning. . . . Traumatic events are extraordinary, not because they occur rarely, but rather because they overwhelm the ordinary human adaptations to life. Unlike commonplace misfortunes, traumatic events generally involve threats to life or bodily integrity, or a close personal encounter with violence and death. They confront human beings with the extremities of helplessness and terror, and evoke the responses of catastrophe. (p. 33)

Just as resilience can be considered from a cultural perspective, so too can trauma and traumatic responses. We encourage you the reader to understand trauma within the cultural context in which it is experienced. This means that, in our roles as psychologists, we seek to understand how culture influences the interpretation, meaning, and understanding of traumatic experiences. Questions we can ask are: How does culture influence the interpretation of the traumatic experience? What cultural meanings are brought to an understanding of the traumatic experience? How can services be culturally responsive to traumatic experiences?

One example in the literature incorporates gender roles, cultural values, and racial/ethnic background in understanding the meaning and significance of Miranda's traumatic experience (as described in Clauss-Ehlers et al., 2004). Miranda lost her husband in the World Trade Center attack. Despite her husband's being on the top floors of the Tower, she blamed herself for not telling him to get out before the Towers collapsed. Miranda truly felt it was her responsibility to have warned her husband so that he could get out of the Tower.

There could be several clinical responses to this scenario. At an extreme deficit-approach, a clinician might label Miranda as being delusional because she could not understand that no one could get out of the building if the plane hit the Tower floors below. On another level, the clinician could simply focus on the reality that there was no way out given the plane had already struck below where Miranda's husband was located in the building.

A third interpretation is to understand Miranda's experience from a cultural context. In doing so, our exploration of how *marianismo* and the role of wife and mother are highly valued can help us understand Miranda's experience (Gil & Vazquez, 1997; Vazquez & Clauss-Ehlers, 2005). The concept of marianismo states that a woman's duty is to her husband and family. Within this context, the woman's role is to protect the family at all costs, including self-sacrifice. The fact that Miranda had not been able to act in accord with the cultural value of marianismo was central to her interpretation of the trauma.

Parallel to our focus on understanding resilience within the larger sociocultural context, trauma can also be understood within an ecological framework (Ungar, 2013).

APPLYING MULTICULTURAL GUIDELINE 10 TO CLINICAL PRACTICE

Guideline 10 encourages practitioners to "recognize that resilience may be defined in distinct ways across sociocultural contexts, and that resilience and coping may be expressed in individual and collective forms" (APA, 2017a, p. 92; Comas-Díaz, 2012; Harvey & Tummala-Narra, 2007; Tummala-Narra, 2016).

Hence, as practitioners, it's important for us to understand our own worldviews with regard to how we perceive resilience and traumatic stress. When helping clients navigate their way through traumatic stress, we are encouraged to remember that resilience accounts for multiple areas of functioning, such as self-concept, self-esteem, self-efficacy, optimism, problem solving, performance competencies, and the ability to access resources (Kumpfer, 1999). In keeping with a sociocultural approach to resilience, we can work with clients to identify those contextual factors that support resilience such as social support, worldview, and language (Clauss-Ehlers, 2008).

As practitioners, it is also important for us to be aware of and understand traumatic stress factors that are not necessarily considered precipitants for posttraumatic stress disorder (PTSD). A major change between the *DSM-IV* and the *DSM-5* is that PTSD was no longer classified under anxiety disorders. Instead, it was put under a new category: Trauma and Stressor-Related Disorders. In another change, there was also expansion with regard to the types of events that were considered traumatic for Criterion A (e.g., events experienced and how they were experienced). Some of these events can be described as including death and/or being threatened with death, serious injury and/or being threatened with serious injury, sexual violence and/or being threatened with sexual violence, What is lacking from the types of events that are considered precipitants of PTSD, however, are experiences of traumatic stress that are "rooted in exposure to violence based on sexism, racism, xenophobia, religious discrimination, poverty, heterosexism, homophobia, transphobia, social class discrimination, and ableism" (APA, 2017a, pp. 92–93; Clauss-Ehlers & Akinsulure-Smith, 2013).

We encourage a broader understanding of PTSD in your clinical practice, one that considers social injustice factors as precipitants of PTSD (Carter, 2007; Clauss-Ehlers & Akinsulure-Smith, 2013). This broader approach is supported by a body of research that indicates a correlation between social injustices and mental health issues (Carter et al., 2013; Clauss-Ehlers & Akinsulure-Smith, 2013; Parham & Clauss-Ehlers, 2016a, 2016b). Such social injustices may relate to race, ethnicity, gender, ability status, sexual orientation, immigration status, gender identity, religious identity, and socioeconomic status, among other variables. By not considering linkages between social injustices and mental health issues, the practitioner risks failing to meet clients where they are at. This can result in not truly hearing the client experience, focusing on individual factors related to the trauma only, and, in so doing, risks blaming the client for the trauma experienced.

A practice goal for *Multicultural Guideline 10* is to encourage practitioners to gain an understanding of their clients' social injustice-related trauma. This process involves clinicians being able to engage in conversations that explore the client's cultural history (see teaching and training, next section) and acknowledge trauma related to experiences of social injustice such as racism and discrimination. By not engaging in these conversations, the practitioner may locate the source of the client's trauma at the individual level only; undermine the impact of the social injustice-related trauma to the client, both directly and indirectly; and fail to identify the client's inherent resilience in being able to face social injustice-related trauma (Tummala-Narra, 2007).

The disconnection between the practitioner and the client that can result from taking an individualistic approach to trauma may result in a lack of trust the client has towards the clinician. This may in turn lead to premature termination or not sharing important material in sessions. In an analysis of the field's understanding of PTSD, Tummala-Narra (2007) reminded us that "PTSD was formulated in Western cultures that generally value the aim of individual control of one's circumstance and destiny" (p. 39). The analysis continues to indicate that PTSD is an expected response to traumatic situations, implying that "under normal circumstances, individuals do or should have control over their fate" (p. 39).

Not all cultures necessarily believe that individuals can control their destinies. In many cultural contexts, fate plays a role in outcomes. This idea is echoed by research that indicates there are "cultural variations in fate attributions" (Norenzayan & Lee, 2010, p.702). An important role in understanding trauma and resilience is to approach the client experience from a standpoint of seeking to understand what is "normal" for them and how cultural history defines and influences the client's viewpoint (Tummala-Narra, 2007).

Mindfulness is another area of practice has been consistently integrated into Western psychotherapeutic practice over the past 2 decades (Kirmayer, 2015). Mindfulness has been largely connected with the practice of cognitive psychology, due in part to its focus on reducing stress and increasing one's ability to focus. Research has indicated that our brains change in response to meditative practice, a find that has furthered support and interest in the practice of mindfulness (Kirmayer, 2015). Mindfulness strategies have been found to be effective in responding to a range of mental health concerns such as self-acceptance (Ma & Siu, 2020), compassion fatigue (Brown et al., 2017); and mental health during COVID (Matiz et al., 2020), among many other mental health-related concerns.

Although we may consider mindfulness as a part of Western psychotherapeutic practice, it provides a meaningful example of what Kirmayer (2015) described as "cross-cultural transmission" given its Buddhist origins. Kirmayer (2015) discussed how Western mental health practice have focused on Buddhist principles of awareness and being nonjudgmental, when in fact, Buddhism has larger ethical and moral parameters for living one's life. This adaptive practice is referred to as "cross-cultural transmission" or "borrowing" whereby there's an "assumption that mindfulness practices will be effective across contexts because they are based on universal aspects of human functioning" (Kirmayer, 2015, p. 449).

At the same time, while recognizing the universal connections in a practice such as mindfulness, it's also important for practitioners to recognize and understand potential frameworks to adapt such practices to the context in which they are working (Agger, 2015). It is anticipated that being able to adapt principles, such as mindfulness, to the cultural context addresses trauma and, in so doing, promotes resilience. In Western mental health practice, for instance, Kirmayer (2015) described how mindfulness interventions are more likely to reflect *vipassana* or insight aspect of mindfulness with their focus on breathing techniques without any focus on Buddhist teachings. In contrast, other cultures might focus more on *samatha* (e.g., "concentration, calmness, and stability;" Kirmayer, 2015, p. 448) or *jhana* (e.g., "absorption;" p. 448).

APPLYING MULTICULTURAL GUIDELINE 10 TO TEACHING AND TRAINING

We would suggest that much of teaching and training involves reengaging the field in new ways, ways that create a bridge between the history of the field and new directions as presented in this chapter. Teaching and training can empower students to support their clients. We describe this as a sociocultural approach to teaching and training. The sociocultural approach to teaching and training allows us to collaborate with our students and trainees to build capacity by focusing on building strengths, supporting cultural resilience, and understanding trauma from a cultural perspective. The paragraphs that follow focus on several areas that can be included in a sociocultural approach to teaching and training: building the relationship as part of SBA interventions, not always needing to know, self-awareness, analytic reflection, vicarious traumatization, and self-care.

Building the Relationship as Key to Strength-Based Interventions

We encourage supervisors to have their students focus on building rapport in the clinical relationship as a critical strength-based intervention. We know from research that having a positive relationship with clients is a critical factor in building outcomes (M. H. Davis, 1996; Kohut, 1959; Kottler, 1991; Wampold, 2000). Acknowledging client issues while incorporating an SBA may be a challenge. If students (or supervisors) have been trained in a deficit model approach, it may feel uncomfortable to be considering strengths rather than focusing on specific symptoms and symptom reduction. Additionally, if you as a trainee have a very different experience from your client, as is the case in the trainee's work with Nora, and you judge your client's experience from your point of reference, without considering and seeking to understand their perspective, your approach may further perpetuate a system of oppression for your client. In focusing on strengths, the conversation turns to what the client brings to the solution. This can also be a shift for you as a trainee (or supervisor) if your training experience has been focused on imparting experience, rather than co-creating solutions jointly.

Not Always Needing to Know

Creating an authentic collaboration means that we do not always have to have the answers to what's being talked about in therapy. It is understandable that trainees (and seasoned professionals) want to demonstrate their knowledge and awareness of work with clients. In saying you aren't sure what the best answer is or the best approach to take, you open up the possibility for collaborative exploration. In this way, client and provider are engaged in an active conversation, with both parties contributing (Pattoni, 2012). It was only when the trainee working with Nora was responsive to her supervisor's feedback to be open to asking, and hearing, about Nora's experiences, that a therapeutic partnership began to unfold.

Hence, the idea of *not always needing to know* as it relates to teaching and training is that trainees are encouraged to be open to learning and recognize that they do not need to have all the knowledge and skills at the outset of their training experience. To support this, supervisors are encouraged to create safe spaces in supervision so that trainees can be open to identifying and exploring areas of growth. These dynamics also reflect cultural humility in the way that they embrace a process of learning and understanding, rather than having to have the "right" answer.

Trainees are also encouraged to look beyond the boundaries of a clinical diagnosis. In clinical training, for instance, trainees may understandably be eager to develop a language related to diagnosis. This may show up as a focus on diagnostic criteria while excluding consideration of other contextual factors, such as cultural context, that have an impact on the client's experiences. Trainees and supervisors are encouraged to take a broader approach to understanding clients by not relying exclusively on a diagnosis but also considering the larger contextual factors and reference group identities that have an impact on the client's lived experience. This broader perspective aims to support SBAs in that it considers the client in a holistic manner, and not as simply being defined and described by a diagnosis.

Self-Awareness

Self-awareness is a key teaching and training value throughout this book. Self-awareness, in a nondefensive way, allows us to see where we may have not considered a possible client experience, and better understand how our own experiences may interfere with truly seeing and hearing the client. We see the value of self-awareness emerge, for instance, in the trainee's interactions with Nora. When the trainee begins to truly hear Nora (e.g., the active listening concept presented in Chapter 1)—and acknowledged her own privilege—she was able to engage in a way that acknowledged the importance of a bidirectional relationship (Clauss-Ehlers et al., 2019). We believe that providing a safe learning environment, whether it be in supervision or in the classroom, is critical to encouraging this level of self-awareness.

Classroom and Supervision Environment

Providing psychotherapy is vastly different from core tasks in other professions. Psychotherapy is largely influenced by gray areas where there's often no right or wrong answer for a specific situation. What works for one person, couple, group, or family, may not work for another. This is unlike science where specific formulas lead to desired outcomes.

In addition to the gray area is the expansive power we have in the practitioner role. Our awareness, knowledge, skill, and insight influence our approach in ways that are hopefully responsive to our clients, although sometimes they may not be. This is very different from a science experiment in which following the directions is a critical indicator of the outcome rather than the person conducting it. As multiculturally responsive practitioners committed to cultural humility, it's important to constantly reexamine practice and engage in an ongoing reformulation of the "directions," so to speak.

It is these gray areas of psychological practice that make teaching, training, and supervision so important. It's absolutely critical that supervision and classroom environments provide a safe space for students and trainees to explore their reference group identities and how they inform the practitioner role. It's hoped that a safe environment allows students and trainees to give voice to areas of growth and take greater ownership of the work they need to be engaged in as future multiculturally responsive practitioners.

In their research titled "Creating a Healthy Classroom Environment in Multicultural Counseling Courses," Brooks and colleagues (2017) discussed the significance of transformative learning that refers to "the expansion of consciousness through the transformation of basic worldviews and specific capacities of the self" (p. 6). An atmosphere of "attunement" where instructors and students are open to hearing about "voiced and unvoiced" experiences contributes to multicultural awareness and humility (Brooks et al., 2017, p. 4).

Important and difficult conversations around topics such as race and racism might be avoided without a healthy learning environment. Such avoidance can result in students and trainees not engaging in the important process of exploring biases and how might play out in clinical settings. Without the skill of being able to participate in difficult conversations, students and trainees may themselves avoid such dialogues with clients, thus invalidating the client experience—a dynamic that doesn't support resilience.

In creating an equitable academic culture, it's important to acknowledge that difficult classroom/supervision conversations may lead to negative perceptions among students. Such negativity and defensiveness may lead to negative reactions towards multicultural content and the instructor teaching it. This dynamic can be particularly salient for faculty of color engaged in teaching multicultural counseling courses (Brooks et al., 2017). Ahluwalia and colleagues (2019) found that while faculty of color are committed to teaching multicultural counseling courses, they report being the recipients of anger from students and receiving negative student evaluations. Student negativity risks decreasing a focus on multicultural conversations, which limits student/ trainee learning experiences. In addition, negative evaluations can have implications for promotion and tenure for junior faculty of color who teach multicultural counseling courses (Ahluwalia et al., 2019; Brooks et al., 2017).

In their research with graduate students enrolled in a multicultural course in a CACREP-accredited program, Brooks and colleagues (2017) identified key themes that students reported to reflect a healthy classroom environment for multicultural training. These themes included "reflection with vulnerability" (p. 12; e.g., being able to be vulnerable with self and others in the classroom community); cultural awareness, particularly in terms of race, oppression, and privilege; and transfer of learning, meaning that students were able to apply what they learned in the classroom to other experiences and conversations.

As a doctoral practicum supervisor, I (Clauss-Ehlers) have learned that creating a safe space that invites "reflection with vulnerability" for multi-culturally responsive practice involves faculty modeling. Faculty are encouraged to hear student perspectives and be curious about them, inviting students to further self-reflect on their experiences. This, in turn, influences peer support in that supervisees can follow the instructors lead, providing thoughtful feedback to one another. In this sense, supervision becomes an atmosphere in which knowledge, skills, and awareness are cocreated.

Instructors can further encourage the three themes identified in the work of Brooks and colleagues (2017) through group discussions that encourage trainees to be open to feedback. This context can support having difficult discussions as they are framed through a perspective of learning and growth, rather than as a judgment. In creating a safe environment to explore multicultural competence and humility, it is hoped that our trainees will transfer their learning client interventions that involve being open to difficult material raised by clients such as race and racism. Not only may this address trauma and promote resilience for clients in multiculturally responsive ways, it may also forge resilience and a sense of self-efficacy among trainees.

Advocacy

Trainees can address trauma and promote resilience through advocacy skills. It is not uncommon for trainees to share how their clients are traumatized by the systems in which they have to function. Traumatic system experiences often involve racism, discrimination, not being given a voice about treatment, and not given adequate treatment supports to make healthy transitions, among many other institutionally based traumas.

Students and trainees may feel stuck in these situations—as might their clients. On the one hand, trainees have a student status in their placements. I'll often describe this position as akin to being a house guest—trainees are a guest at their placement sites. On the other hand, it is critical that trainees learn to voice concerns as part of client safety and well-being, ethical practice, and professional identity development.

Supervisors and instructors can support the development of advocacy skills by encouraging trainees to voice concerns about the situations they observe. The supervision group can serve as a resource that brainstorms how to address the issues presented. Trainees are encouraged to be open about what strategies feel comfortable for them and which don't fit the context of their placements. Through a parallel process, the instructor models advocacy for student/trainees, which they subsequently model for their clients with interventions such as asking clients about why certain situations are the way they are, what supports might be needed, and who in the system could serve as an ally in efforts to fill gaps in service. By modeling an advocate role, students/trainees encourage clients to engage in self-advocacy.

Vicarious Traumatization and Self-Care

Bearing witness to trauma in the helping professional role can have an impact on emotions and sense of well-being. *Vicarious traumatization*, also known as compassion fatigue, refers to "the emotional residue of exposure that counselors have from working with people as they are hearing their trauma stories and become witnesses to the pain, fear, and terror" that those who have experienced trauma have lived through (American Counseling Association [ACA], n.d.). Supervisors can talk with trainees about vicarious traumatization. They can support supervisees to understand key trauma symptoms such as preoccupation, avoidance, and hypervigilance that may result in reaction to hearing client experiences of trauma.

In understanding the impact of vicarious trauma that can result from working with people who have experienced trauma, supervisors are also encouraged to talk with trainees about the importance of self-care, or engaging in practices that provide an outlet or relief from working with trauma. The World Health Organization (WHO; 2013) defines *self-care* as "the ability of individuals, families and communities to promote, maintain health, prevent disease and to cope with illness and disability with or without the support of a health care provider."

We encourage you as supervisors to incorporate discussions about self-care into supervisory sessions. Such discussions can encourage us to identify activities that help decrease stress and present a break from hearing trauma narratives. As supervisors, you can also encourage trainees to build social networks so that they have friends they can turn to when it is important to engage in activities outside the scope of work.

APPLYING MULTICULTURAL GUIDELINE 10 TO RESEARCH

Several potential areas for future research emerge from Guideline 10. While SBA is gaining traction in the literature, the evidence base regarding its effectiveness is just beginning to develop. Research can identify factors that promote SBAs, particularly with regard to interventions geared to support diverse communities. One possibility is to incorporate SBAs in community-based interventions and evaluate their efficacy (Pattoni, 2012).

Another strand of inquiry is research that seeks to clarify whether resilience is more or less remarkable with cumulative as opposed to single-incident traumas. A question here is the extent to which the dose effect accurately reflects traumatic experience. The *dose effect* refers to "the finding that more frequent and severe trauma exposure leads to worse psychological outcomes"; APA, 2010a, p. 26). Research demonstrates that youth exposed to war and those with refugee status experience "elevated symptoms of posttraumatic stress disorder (PTSD), depression, anxiety, somatic complaints, sleep problems, and behavioral problems" (APA, 2010a, p. 26). The dose effect states that the greater the exposure to trauma, the greater the extent of mental health issues (APA, 2010a; Ellis et al., 2008). However, the dose effect does not explain situations such as two siblings experiencing a war together, with one sibling developing PTSD and the other not having a traumatic reaction (Clauss-Ehlers & Akinsulure-Smith, 2013).

More recent understandings of traumatic stress suggest that the experience of trauma and mental health reactions is not necessarily a proportional relationship. This literature suggests that the dose effect is too narrow in our understanding of PTSD, which is much more complex (APA, 2010a; Bonanno & Mancini, 2008). To this end, the APA (2010a) report *Resilience and Recovery After War: Refugee Children and Families in the United States* describes how the dose-effect approach does not account for children who demonstrate resilience and do not develop PTSD despite having lived through war trauma; does not account for how a traumatic experience may differentially have an impact on people according to their developmental stage in life; and does not account for differing PTSD prevalence rates that can range from 7% to 75% (Allwood et al., 2002; APA, 2010a).

Research is needed to explore the complicated nature of trauma and traumatic reactions. Such research can investigate the role of individual, cultural, contextual, and developmental factors that influence responses to trauma. By way of example, *trilateral migration trauma* was recently introduced as a new term to address gaps in trauma literature by examining "multiple potential points of trauma—and their potential influence on one another—that children and families may experience during forced migration" (Clauss-Ehlers, 2019a, p. 335). *Forced migration* refers to people who must leave their homes and nations due to concerns for their own safety and/or not being able to meet basic needs such as food and water. The trilateral migration trauma model examines three phases of a forced migration experience: departure, migration, and relocation (Clauss-Ehlers, 2019a).

Research can address the intersectionality between resilience and SBAs. We will recall that this approach does not mean that issues are ignored or minimized. Rather, the approach acknowledges critical challenges. Further investigation is needed with regard to relationships between resilience and SBAs and how they coalesce to address life challenges.

APPLYING MULTICULTURAL GUIDELINE 10 TO CONSULTATION

In our role as consultants, we can be aware of the impact of trauma and responses to trauma on a community level. Such awareness is important so that we can engage in community-based interventions that address trauma and promote cultural resilience. Services that respond to trauma need to be sensitive to the cultural needs and values of the community. As an example of consultation/organizational supports that were not effective, consider the following: In the face of the September 11 attacks on the World Trade Center, New York City set up crisis centers on the streets of the city. Such centers were a place for people to go for help in response to the crisis that was unfolding throughout the city. It appeared that these centers remained largely unused. While this seems surprising given the level of crisis and loss occurring throughout the city, incorporating a cultural understanding of trauma helps us to understand this level of underutilization. The outside nature of services provided was quite public and did not necessarily account for stigma-related concerns (Clauss-Ehlers et al., 2004). This meant that people did not feel comfortable accessing services, because they were too publicly visible. Further, the outside setup of services, along with the fact that they were organized throughout the city, reminded some people of the police states that they had fled from in their countries of origin, causing further distance from the possibility of accessing services (Clauss-Ehlers et al., 2004).

This example shows the importance of understanding cultural factors associated with trauma so that communities are motivated to access mental health services. In our roles as consultants, it is important for us to be aware of the sociocultural factors that need to be considered when designing and implementing support services. To omit doing so, as illustrated in this example, risks a lack of utilization of services.

CONCLUSION

This chapter brings us full circle to consider the nature of outcomes related to our work as clinicians/clients, educators/students/trainees, researchers/research participants, and consultants/consultees. It is a culmination of the *2017 Multicultural Guidelines* with a discussion of Guideline 10, the last guideline presented. The *2017 Multicultural Guidelines* present a new paradigm for how we can understand our work as multicultural mental health professionals. Multicultural Guideline 10 engages this paradigm with its focus on SBA in our work as clinicians, educators, researchers, and consultants. Key to this approach is building collaborative relationships with those with whom we work. In the clinical and education domain, this involves creating knowledge and solutions jointly, further supporting the bidirectional relationship presented in Multicultural Guideline 1, while also acknowledging and addressing structural barriers and institutional oppression that have an impact on clients.

Through these collaborative relationships, our work can engage in understanding the role of resilience and trauma within a sociocultural context. This work involves understanding culturally focused resilient adaptations and how trauma is informed by cultural values, meanings, and experiences. We encourage supervisors to integrate discussion about vicarious traumatization into the supervisory process. Relatedly, we encourage supervisory sessions to help students identify ways that they can engage in self-care.

We now move forward to our final chapter, Chapter 13, which focuses on implications of prior chapters with regard to future directions for multicultural psychology and our role in them.

PART VII

FUTURE DIRECTIONS IN MULTICULTURAL PSYCHOLOGY

13 WHERE DO WE GO FROM HERE?

Looking Towards the Future in Multicultural Psychology

This book began with a discussion about *Multicultural Guidelines: An Ecological Approach to Context, Identity, and Intersectionality, 2017* (hereinafter referred to as *2017 Multicultural Guidelines*; American Psychological Association [APA], 2017a). It included a description of how the APA Task Force on Re-Envisioning the Multicultural Guidelines for the 21st Century was formed and how it built on the historical contribution made by the *Guidelines on Multicultural Education, Training, Research, Practice, and Organizational Change for Psychologists* (hereinafter referred to as *2002 Multicultural Guidelines*; APA, 2002). You the Reader was the case presented in Chapter 1 of this volume. You the Reader oriented you to the book by asking you to consider your personal and professional development. Discussion questions related to the case asked you to consider challenges and commitments to contributions as a multiculturally informed psychologist.

APA policy stipulates that the shelf life for any APA guideline is 10 years. The preceding chapters have taken us on a journey related to the 10 guidelines that make up the *2017 Multicultural Guidelines*. In this concluding chapter, we consider where the field will be when the multicultural guidelines are expected to be revised and rewritten (APA, 2017a). Given the world's

---

https://doi.org/10.1037/0000348-013
Applying Multiculturalism: An Ecological Approach to the APA Guidelines, by C. S. Clauss-Ehlers, S. J. Hunter, G. S. Morse, and P. Tummala-Narra
Copyright © 2024 by the American Psychological Association. All rights reserved.

climate and the unexpected events that are currently occurring, it's hard, if not impossible, to predict what things will look like at that time. So many unexpected global events have ensued during this first quarter of the 21st century. Perhaps the only certainty is that more unexpected outcomes and uncertainty will continue to emerge on the global stage.

Given our lack of knowledge as to what the future holds, we can share what we hope for the future and what we hope for the profession. Our hope for the next version of the *Multicultural Guidelines* is that the multicultural psychology field will have grown so much that our *2017 Multicultural Guidelines* will be truly out of date. Our hope for the next version of the APA *Multicultural Guidelines* is that a group of psychologists who are as committed and passionate as the members of our task force will form the new working group to develop the next version. To move forward in these areas, our field needs research and writing to support the multicultural evidence base across all domains of professional psychology. To move forward in these areas, we as practitioners, educators, supervisors, researchers, and consultants need to support the next generations of psychologists to be multiculturally responsive and attuned; we can do so through our training, interventions, assessments, and models of consultation practice and through active engagement of multimethod approaches to multiculturally responsive research. Table 13.1 presents benchmarks to consider in the upcoming years; we are hopeful you are encouraged to embark on the benchmarks.

TABLE 13.1. Professional Benchmarks for Multicultural Psychology in the Upcoming Years

Professional domain	Benchmarks for professional domain trajectory
Practice	• Consider ecological context in multicultural psychological practice
	• Incorporate Indigenous psychological practices
	• Incorporate an intersectional approach
	• Engage in multiculturally responsive practice with individuals, groups, families, couples, and communities
	• Further the psychologist's role as advocate
	• Address the role of stigma across cultures, both domestically and internationally
	• Develop therapeutic approaches that are responsive to current global trends (e.g., impact of climate change among diverse communities)
	• Incorporate prevention science as an intervention tool among diverse communities
	• Provide psychological services that reflect the languages spoken in the community the psychologist is serving
	• Forge partnerships with countries to build an international community of psychologists

TABLE 13.1. Professional Benchmarks for Multicultural Psychology in the Upcoming Years (*Continued*)

Professional domain	Benchmarks for professional domain trajectory
Teaching and training	• Build a pipeline of future generations of multicultural psychologists by being inclusive in recruitment, admissions, training, and retention • Incorporate multicultural practice considerations across coursework, not just in one specialized course • Provide supervision that is culturally and linguistically responsive to the diverse needs of the communities the trainee is working with • Encourage undergraduate and graduate programs to have a second language requirement • Develop American Psychological Association–approved doctoral training sites that offer training that reflects the needs of diverse populations (e.g., the former Bilingual Treatment Program at the NYU/Bellevue Hospital Center) • Support and train students and early career psychologists to conduct multicultural research • Train students in the publication process so that they can share their work and grow in the field • Provide transnational training opportunities (e.g., service learning) to encourage students to learn about psychology from multiple perspectives • Provide mentoring and advisement that supports student professional growth and identity
Research	• Expand the evidence base focused on multicultural prevention, intervention, and outcomes research • Incorporate diverse ways to generate new knowledge (e.g., qualitative and case study approaches in addition to quantitative approaches) • Augment funding streams and grant opportunities that support research in multicultural psychology • Engage in research focused on adapting scientific findings to specific community contexts • Focus on community-based participatory research endeavors • Publish research generated by a global network of social scientists
Consultation	• Engage in culturally and linguistically focused consultation • Take a community-based approach to consultation practice • Develop new multicultural models for consultation practice • Further develop best practices in multicultural consultation • Build an evidence base that reflect best practices in multicultural consultation

The development of the *2017 Multicultural Guidelines* came out of APA's process of reconsidering how to address diversity and inclusion given the literature that has emerged since the *2002 Multicultural Guidelines* development process (APA, 2002, 2003). In 2015, APA developed two separate task forces whose aim was to update the multicultural guidelines. Developing task force groups to revise the guidelines is in alignment with APA policy to have practice guidelines updated every 10 years. The two task force groups that APA created were the Task Force on Re-Envisioning the Multicultural Guidelines for the 21st Century, the set of guidelines that are the focus of this book, and the Task Force on Guidelines Focused on Race/Ethnicity (APA, 2019a). The Board for the Advancement of Psychology in the Public Interest (BAPPI) presented the following rationale for developing two task force groups:

> In the intervening years, there has been enormous domestic and global change affecting the lives of individuals, communities, countries and society at large, as well as the development of substantial new multicultural conceptual and empirical scholarship. BAPPI has determined that the wealth of scholarship specific to race/ethnicity as well as the scholarship focused on other identity groups warrants splitting the *2002 Multicultural Guidelines* into two sets of guidelines going forward: one focused on "pan" or "umbrella" multicultural guidelines that captures universal concepts based on the scholarly literature across a broad cross-section of identity groups (e.g., age, disability status, race, ethnicity, gender, religion/spirituality, sexual orientation and gender diversity, social class, language, immigration status), and the other focused specifically on the race/ethnicity-related scholarly developments since the *2002 Multicultural Guidelines* were adopted. (APA, 2015a, para. 2)

The Task Force on Re-Envisioning the Multicultural Guidelines for the 21st Century, which formed the basis for this book, considered how intersectionality and identity among psychologists and clients, students, trainees, research participants, and consultees are influenced by an array of biopsychosocial, cultural, and environmental factors. Similarly, the task force working on race and ethnicity guidelines focused providing "aspirational guidance for the development of racial and ethnocultural responsiveness for psychological practice" (APA, 2019a, p. 3) by engaging the wealth of research regarding race and ethnicity conducted since 2002. The *APA Guidelines on Race and Ethnicity in Psychology* (APA, 2019a) were approved and then published in 2019. Our view, which is shared with BAPPI and the APA Council of Directors, is that these two sets of guidelines complement and strengthen one another in their contributions to the field.

As discussed in previous chapters, clinical case examples and relevant literature show how each of the 10 multicultural guidelines recognizes that our identities and related experiences are complex constructions that arise within an array of structural contexts. As a result, transactions that occur between psychologist and client (i.e., "client" refers to client, student, trainee, research participant, and consultee) provide guidance and direction for works that support growth and change, and they elicit a multidimensional understanding of who we are within the environments in which we are situated.

What remains necessary, as the 2017 Multicultural Guidelines themselves are understood and considered, is how best to build forward from this iteration of the guidelines. The process involves defining and elaborating on what it means to maintain a position of cultural humility that subsequently directs humane practice and collaborative professionalism. Each iteration of the multicultural guidelines is based on scholarship that reflects how the world has come to understand aspects of reference group identities that are used to define us. We can see that these considerations can be incorrect, incomplete, and, at times, in error. We recognize within our roles as psychological professionals that our efforts are not monolithic or even deterministic. Instead, by understanding and working with the array of identities each of us holds, and considering them simultaneously, we strive toward a humanistic goal of understanding one another while recognizing that we are also always learning from each other.

CASE ILLUSTRATION–EDUARDO: INDIVIDUAL OR FAMILY-BASED TREATMENT? CULTURALLY SYNTONIC CONSIDERATIONS

Eduardo[1] is a 50-year-old Ecuadorian man who began to experience panic attacks after witnessing a drive-by shooting. Because he was reluctant to seek mental health services, Eduardo's family encouraged him to have a mental health consultation at their neighborhood hospital clinic. Their recommendation was based on what they were seeing in daily interactions with Eduardo: He appeared increasingly anxious, a symptom that manifested in not wanting to leave the house or be in public places. Eduardo started to express feelings of fear, accompanied by shortness of breath, when he had to leave the house and take the subway to work. To avoid these experiences, Eduardo started to miss work and stay at home for long periods. He was absent from work so much that he lost some of his income. Eduardo's family made an appointment for him to be seen at the bilingual (English/Spanish) mental health clinic affiliated with their neighborhood hospital.

---

[1]In this case illustration, all appropriate steps have been taken to disguise the identities of the individuals discussed.

Eduardo arrived on time, on his own, for his first appointment. He was assigned a bilingual clinician. In talking with the clinician, Eduardo seemed reluctant to share information about himself or his family. Instead, he talked about seemingly nonrelated experiences such as the weather and asked the clinician about her background. The clinician was concerned about building rapport and questioned whether Eduardo would return the following week.

To the clinician's surprise, Eduardo returns for his session the following week. Even more surprising, he arrives for his scheduled session with five family members. He asks if they can join him in the session, and the clinician agrees. The hospital clinic does not have a family-focused clinic, so working with the family is a departure from the individual therapy services that are typically provided.

Eduardo presents very differently during the family session. He is much more open and talkative. He describes the events of his day leading up to the drive-by shooting and begins to share some of his emotional reactions. Family members are supportive. They clearly love Eduardo and respond to his experience with empathy and concern. At certain points in the session, there is even laughter when *chistes* (i.e., jokes) are shared in the room. Toward the end of the session, Eduardo asks if family members can return the following week. The clinician agrees, and a follow-up appointment is confirmed.

Discussion Questions Related to Eduardo

1. What do you think are the cultural values that were at play in Eduardo's reactions to individual and family therapy?
2. What would you say are the cultural norms that had an impact on Eduardo's feeling more comfortable talking when family members were present than when he was alone?
3. How did Eduardo create a culture-centered intervention for himself and his family?
4. What are your thoughts about how the clinician responded?
5. What role does advocacy play in this case illustration?
6. What are some of the opportunities for advocacy that you would engage in related to this case?
7. If you were the clinician in this scenario, how would you have responded?

A SUMMARY OF THE 10 MULTICULTURAL GUIDELINES

Building on the questions presented in the case of You the Reader (Chapter 1, this volume), this section presents a summary of the 10 multicultural guidelines. Text boxes present key themes in professional domains of practice, teaching/training, research, and consultation that emanate from the summary of each guideline.[2]

Before we summarize the 10 multicultural guidelines, we will recall that Chapter 2 focuses on the overall foundation for understanding and engaging with the *Multicultural Guidelines: An Ecological Approach to Context, Identity, and Intersectionality* (APA, 2017). Through its focus on the layered ecological model, an application of Uri Bronfenbrenner's (1977, 1979) developmental-socioenvironmental theory that addresses the range of transactional ecological influences that impact social, emotional, behavioral, and cognitive functioning across the lifespan, the *2017 Multicultural Guidelines* address how we, as intersectionally defined individuals, interact and ultimately collaborate to affect the movements that occur both within and exterior to our daily lives. The chapter provides a detailed consideration of the ecological model, in particular, and how it reflects the array of influences we experience, as applied across the individual guidelines. With this consideration, you as the reader have had the opportunity to effectively become more knowledgeable about the guidelines and how they can be applied across the array of practices that define professional psychology.

Key to the chapter is the focus on the five layers of the ecological model and how they are adapted to guide our understanding of the multiple influences that impact our lives. Through the use of the case study regarding Dr. Roberto and Dr. Claudia, the chapter allows the 10 guidelines and their applicability to community-based participatory research to come to life. By considering how immigrants and the development of their lives within current U.S. society unfolds, the chapter's questions regarding the levels of influence that are present throughout the guidelines provide the foundation required for then delving more deeply into each of the guidelines and their applicability to professional practice as you read further through this book.

Taking this review of the guidelines now in hand, with references back to the structure of the ecological model and the five layers that define it,

---

[2]The implications for professional domains presented throughout this chapter are adapted from "APA *Multicultural Guidelines* Executive Summary: Ecological Approach to Context, Identity, and Intersectionality," by C. S. Clauss-Ehlers, D. A. Chiriboga, S. J. Hunter, G. Roysircar, and P. Tummala-Narra, 2019, *American Psychologist*, 74(2), pp. 232–244 (https://doi.org/10.1037/amp0000382). Copyright 2019 by the American Psychological Association.

we recommend reviewing that specific case, as well as others encountered throughout this book, and reflecting again on the implications of the guidelines for directing your professional efforts as a psychologist.

Multicultural Guideline 1

> Psychologists seek to recognize and understand that identity and self-definition are fluid and complex and that the interaction between the two is dynamic. To this end, psychologists appreciate that intersectionality is shaped by the multiplicity of the individual's social contexts.

Multicultural Guideline 1 underscores that identity is fluid and complex and is shaped through multiple processes, such as developmental transitions, interpersonal processes, and social structures. The Guideline encourages psychologists to move away from overgeneralizations and simplistic approaches that can diminish an individual's or community's complex experiences of identity. It is important that psychologists respect one's self-definition and experience of identity. Further, approaches to intersectionality should center analyses of power, privilege, marginalization, and oppression that may accompany certain sociocultural locations and experiences. Notably, exposure to discrimination and stereotyping within and outside of one's sociocultural communities has a significant influence on identity development.

Within clinical practice, a client's identity should be explored, bearing in mind the therapist's assumptions and socialization. Therapists can explore the dynamics of the therapeutic relationship with an understanding of the client's and therapist's social, political, economic, and historical contexts. Clinical training curricula can be expanded to include diverse perspectives on human development, identity, and mental health from a strength-based approach. Psychological research can include diverse methodologies to investigate the complexity of identity and intersectionality. Researchers can extend existing studies with various sociocultural communities or groups by examining life experiences associated with mental health issues. With regard to consultation, it is important that consultants educate others about the complexity and intersectionality in both interpersonal and organizational contexts and take a collaborative approach that integrates a clear understanding of the sociocultural experiences of the consultee(s).

Overall, Guideline 1 calls for psychologists to integrate nuanced understandings of identity and intersectionality in all aspects of the profession. Developing collaborations with individuals and communities is critical for understanding how heterogeneity of sociocultural experience shapes identity. New knowledge gained through research and practice that center the

> **Implications of Multicultural Guideline 1**
>
> **Clinical Practice**
> - Practitioners "strive toward attunement to life experiences, transitions, and identity labels, and how identity experience may change over time and context" (Clauss-Ehlers et al., 2019, p. 235).
> - Practitioners ask clients to "describe their identities and labels, rather than relying on preconceived conceptualizations" (Clauss-Ehlers et al., 2019, p. 235).
>
> **Teaching and Training**
> - Teaching and training helps students/trainees understand intersectionality and how intersectional identities can play out for client(s).
> - Students/trainees learn to be aware of and attune to their own biases and preconceived notions about client(s).
>
> **Research**
> - Research psychologists conduct intersectional research that attends to "structural dynamics resulting in social identities through the use of qualitative and quantitative research designs as well as interdisciplinary research teams" (Clauss-Ehlers et al., 2019, p. 235).
> - Researchers engage in contextual research practices that include community collaboration.
>
> **Consultation**
> - Consultants understand dynamics and concerns that arise from disparities and discrimination.
> - Consultants address organizational issues related to reference-group identities.

complexity of identity can help modify existing psychological theories that tend to neglect the perspectives of socioculturally marginalized individuals and communities.

Multicultural Guideline 2

Psychologists aspire to recognize and understand that as cultural beings, they hold attitudes and beliefs that can influence their perceptions of and interactions with others as well as their clinical and empirical conceptualizations.

As such, psychologists strive to move beyond conceptualizations rooted in categorical assumptions, biases, and/or formulations based on limited knowledge about individuals and communities.

Multicultural Guideline 2 encourages us to consider the impact of culture and other societal influences on those with whom we interact across professional domains. Awareness extends to all involved and includes our own awareness of cultural and sociopolitical influences. Multicultural Guideline 2 encourages us as psychologists to be aware of our biases and social influences and to consider how they might inform professional perspectives. This awareness can help us determine the aspects of biases and personal values that

---

Implications of Multicultural Guideline 2

Clinical Practice
- Practitioners are aware of their own stereotypes and how they can have an impact on assessment, diagnosis, and treatment processes.
- Practitioners consider how their worldviews and reference group identities have an impact on perceptions of treatment and assessment processes.

Teaching and Training
- Students/trainees identify preconceived notions and biases they bring to professional interactions.
- Students/trainees learn about the role of cultural humility in their work.

Research
- Researchers hear how research participants identify so that they do not overgeneralize experiences.
- Research considers the interaction of cultural worldview with the phenomenon being studied.
- Culturally informed empirical studies embody a collaborative approach and the researcher's reflections about the research process and reference group identities.

Consultation
- Consultants create safe spaces for supervision and consultation, including safe spaces to talk about issues related to racism, sexism, ableism, and other forms of discrimination.
- Consultants process and work through their own experiences of privilege and power.

lead to making negative attributions (e.g., stereotypes, false categorizations) about clients, trainees/supervisees, data observations/interpretations, and consultees.

Multicultural Guideline 2 urges us to consider whether we are operating from a deficit model instead of taking a strength-based approach. Shallow or otherwise, culturally inappropriate characterizations of clients, communities, organizations, or any other entities that we as psychologists may encounter in a professional capacity need to be identified. Such identification can occur through self-reflection notes and reports, supervisor evaluations, peer reviews, and client/research participant feedback. When false attributions are found to be present, they should be appropriately addressed to eliminate their influences on our professional work. Bias identification is done through ongoing dialogue with peers, clients, and research team members and in partnership with the communities we engage in via domains of professional practice.

Multicultural Guideline 3

> Psychologists strive to recognize and understand the role of language and communication through engagement that is sensitive to the lived experience of the individual, couple, family, group, community, and/or organizations with whom they interact. Psychologists also seek to understand how they bring their own language and communication to these interactions.

Multicultural Guideline 3 recognizes the role of language and communication in the various realms of individual, interpersonal, and online experiences among clients, students/trainees, research participants, and consultees. Both verbal and nonverbal communication are necessary for the establishment of rapport and the maintenance of working alliances between psychologists and the people they serve. Communication can occur through spoken or written language or through nonverbal cues.

We are likely to encounter challenges when language barriers exist. Multicultural Guideline 3 implies that language barriers must be taken into account when a psychologist considers how to structure therapeutic intervention, chooses tests for assessment procedures, obtains informed consent, teaches/supervises trainees for whom English is a second or third language, and generally conveys information in an honest and comprehensible way. The words we use to explain situations, treatment recommendations, and tests can influence how clients perceive them. We as psychologists are encouraged to rethink using professional jargon that might further misunderstanding or create professional distance in the therapeutic relationship. At the same time, we as psychologists are encouraged to hear the client's language,

> **Implications of Multicultural Guideline 3**
>
> **Clinical Practice**
> - Practitioners learn the importance of using developmentally appropriate language.
> - Practitioners form collaborative relationships with interpreters and follow interpreter guidelines.
> - Practitioners seek to understand that language may be experienced differently, even when a shared language experience exists (i.e., whether monolingual, bilingual, or multilingual).
> - Practitioners are aware of the limits of assessment and how test items and norms may not represent the population in which the test is being administered.
>
> **Teaching and Training**
> - Students/trainees consider cultural translations of language.
> - Students/trainees learn languages other than English.
> - Students/trainees receive supervision about the use of jargon with clients and the potential for misunderstanding or distance in the professional relationship.
>
> **Research**
> - Researchers use local terms in research protocols.
> - Researchers are aware of the role of language in informed consent.
> - Researchers are knowledgeable about informed consent procedures for those who are unable to read.
>
> **Consultation**
> - Consultants work to be attuned to the language of the organization to further awareness of dynamic issues.
> - Consultants act as conveners, seeking to bring organizational constituencies together, often through communication and clarification to address misunderstandings.

seeking to learn specific terms and details that describe their experiences. Communication between clients and significant figures can provide information that may be critical to understanding clients' thoughts, emotions, and relationships with others. Social media is becoming an increasingly popular mode of communication and can play an important role in the lives of clients, students/trainees, research participants, and consultees.

Multicultural Guideline 4

Psychologists endeavor to be aware of the role of the social and physical environment in the lives of clients, students, research participants, and/or consultees.

Multicultural Guideline 4 emphasizes the role of social and physical factors in an individual's environment and how these factors influence development. Consequently, Multicultural Guideline 4 focuses on the importance of social, physical, and environmental factors as they relate to psychological practice with individuals, families, couples, groups, and/or communities.

As psychologists, our thorough understanding of the social systems in which people live illuminates social barriers as well as support systems, such as affirmative sexual and gender identity institutions. We as psychologists can be informed about people's physical environments and related resources that are accessible to them, such as public transportation, personally owned cars, grocery stores, other resources for basic physical needs, accommodations that reflect disability status, safe neighborhoods, sufficient accommodations, schools, psychological services, and health care. For instance, people coming from a low socioeconomic status may have trouble acquiring food, warmth, or access to health care and education, all of which will have a strong impact on psychological and physical health.

Similarly, identifying a client as a "minority" in the social environment can potentially result in feelings of alienation. For instance, people in urban settings have likely been exposed to a wider, more heterogeneous group of people than people living in rural settings. Not only do cities contain a larger and more diverse population than most rural settings, but they also tend to have greater proximity to a range of cultural attractions, including museums, concerts, plays, and other events that can have an impact on an individual's perspective of the world. Rural settings may offer a more homogeneous population and greater distance between inhabitants, limiting exposure to different racial/ethnic, cultural, and religious identities.

As multiculturally responsive psychologists, we can identify available resources in the lives of clients to create more positive person–environment interactions. Psychologist and client (whether individual, couple, family, group, or organization) can work together to improve the client's social environments outside of therapy (e.g., at work, at school, at home). We can also incorporate the client's social supports (e.g., friends and family) to assist in treatment. Acknowledging that a client lives in a larger system enables us to have a better sense of the client's experience within the larger context.

> **Implications of Multicultural Guideline 4**
>
> **Clinical Practice**
> - Practitioners strive to be aware of problems of living that may emerge from living in low-resource neighborhoods.
> - Practitioners act as advocates as clients may experience less access to quality institutions for education, health, mental health, housing, transportation, and nutrition, among other areas.
>
> **Teaching and Training**
> - Students/trainees develop an awareness of the client(s) within the context of the physical environment/neighborhood.
> - Students/trainees are aware of biases that lend themselves to blaming the client(s) rather than understanding contextual factors.
>
> **Research**
> - Researchers conduct studies that explore disproportionalities across neighborhoods.
> - Researchers investigate disproportionality in justice and juvenile justice systems.
>
> **Consultation**
> - Consultants consider the role of "social trajectories" related to exposure to adverse environments (Berkman, 2009, p. 34).
> - Consultants engage in consultation related to addressing these disparities (e.g., promoting mental health care access and utilization).

Multicultural Guideline 5

> Psychologists aspire to recognize and understand historical and contemporary experiences with power, privilege, and oppression. As such, they seek to address institutional barriers and related inequities, disproportionalities, and disparities of law enforcement, administration of criminal justice, educational, mental health, and other systems as they seek to promote justice, human rights, and access to quality and equitable mental and behavioral health services.

Multicultural Guideline 5 recognizes that institutional systems such as training and education regulations, research requirements, and consultation practices are only a few that are influenced by inflexible institutional barriers and systemic marginalization. The inequities that individuals face in these systems have significant negative effects on members of diverse communities. Because of our central role in helping individuals cope with negative experiences, as psychologists, we are encouraged to continually recognize and educate ourselves about the impact of structural disparities on our clients (e.g., individual, couple, family, group, organization). Multicultural Guideline 5 also encourages us to advocate for human rights, justice, and equal access to resources. Poverty, race, ethnicity, immigrant status, language differences, disability status, and mental illnesses can create significant barriers to equitable treatment within most institutional systems.

Implications of Multicultural Guideline 5

Clinical Practice
- Practitioners consider institutional disparities and disproportionalities.
- Practitioners "make diagnoses and conduct assessments that are culturally tailored and ecologically relevant" (Clauss-Ehlers et al., 2019, p. 239).
- Practitioners promote social justice, human rights, and access to services.

Teaching and Training
- Students/trainees understand clients in the context of institutional disparities.
- Students/trainees understand their own experiences of power and privilege.
- Students/trainees promote access to services, social justice, and human rights.

Research
- Researchers conduct research focused on issues of access and utilization regarding health and mental health care.
- Researchers examine how the role of stigma influences help-seeking patterns among diverse communities.

Consultation
- Consultants consult with community and nongovernmental groups regarding inequities related to educational, health, and mental health service delivery systems.
- Consultants consult with community groups and law-enforcement agencies regarding disproportionality and discrimination in the legal system.

This guideline focuses on how institutional barriers contribute to and promote continued systemic marginalization. The discussion considers how institutional policies and procedures have embedded barriers that may have deleterious effects and may actually create disadvantages for individuals and marginalized people, including those with disabilities. These constructs were also discussed in terms of levels of racism and the intersectionality of these levels.

The negative effects of institutional barriers and systemic marginalization are clarified in terms of how they impact people in education, research, clinical practice, and consultation. It is important that we, as multiculturally responsive psychologists, remain aware of this disparate treatment and acknowledge the reality of institutional barriers and marginalization of people that prevent their potential success and growth. In education and training, we must recognize that not all students come with the same sets of supports and resources for success. In research, we must recognize that much of the evidence-based treatment is derived primarily from White, educated, industrialized, rich, and democratic (WEIRD) populations. Clinical work is also impacted by the education pipeline and WEIRD research, which has the effect of limiting the number of clinicians from diverse backgrounds and undermines proper mental health treatments for minority populations. Finally, the role of consultant is clarified and how they might work with institutions to identify and understand how their policies and practices may lead to disparities.

Multicultural Guideline 6

> Psychologists seek to promote culturally adaptive interventions and advocacy within and across systems, including prevention, early intervention, and recovery.

Multicultural Guideline 6 suggests that in addition to providing direct services, our support of mental and behavioral health advocacy can potentially increase access to care, decrease stigma, and aid in the development of a functional, culturally competent mental health infrastructure. As multiculturally responsive psychologists, we can engage in collective mental health advocacy that promotes an inclusive community for individuals with mental health issues. Systemic mental health advocacy is designated as

> a social movement that seeks to change the disadvantageous policies and practices of legal, government, and health systems from within to develop a more inclusive community for people with mental disorders (also known as collective mental health advocacy; Stringfellow & Muscari, 2003). (Gee et al., 2015, p. 1)

Collective systemic mental health advocacy aims to empower disenfranchised groups that do not benefit from certain legal, health, and government systems. A "cooperative community" refers to advocacy that goes beyond the therapy room and includes working with clients, students/trainees, research participants, organizations, and other mental health professionals to promote societal changes in health care and mental health care treatment and equity (Gee et al., 2015).

Five key areas of advocacy have been identified in the literature: "building consumer and career participation, voice and recognition for consumers and

---

Implications of Multicultural Guideline 6

Clinical Practice
- Practitioners consider culture-centered interventions as they relate to prevention and early intervention science.
- Practitioners engage in relationship-centered advocacy.

Teaching and Training
- Students/trainees learn about culture-centered approaches to prevention and early intervention science.
- Students/trainees learn about conducting research that represents diverse constituencies.
- Students/trainees learn about their role as advocates in the professional domains of practitioners, educators, researchers, and consultants.

Research
- Researchers contribute to the science of culture-centered interventions.
- Researchers address gaps in the literature by conducting research with participants who reflect diversity across a range of multicultural variables.
- Researchers develop testing and intervention measures that are culturally and linguistically responsive to diverse populations.

Consultation
- Consultants engage in consultative work that fosters the development of culture-centered interventions.
- Consultants engage in advocacy efforts that support access, utilization, and care within a culturally centered mental health system.

careers, influencing and improving mental health systems, effective collaboration and partnerships, and building organizational strength" (Gee et al., 2015, p. 1). Clients are viewed as partners and collaborators, and they work with therapists on both psychological and ecological matters in the context of an authentic relationship. In our role as multiculturally informed psychologists, we can also advocate for systems change within research and scientific communities.

Multiculturally informed advocacy and intervention encompasses prevention and early intervention in schools, family situations, and communities while considering the sociocultural context of the community being served. Early intervention supports primary prevention in its provision of services for children aged 0 to 5 years. Addressing delays in infancy and early childhood can promote child development in current and later years.

Multicultural Guideline 7

> Psychologists endeavor to examine the profession's assumptions and practices within an international context, whether domestically or internationally based, and consider how this globalization has an impact on the psychologist's self-definition, purpose, role, and function.

Multicultural Guideline 7 encourages us to reconsider the growing role of psychologists within a global mental health framework. Global considerations of the work of psychologists involve understanding worldwide prevalence rates of mental health issues. For instance, the World Health Organization (2022) found that the COVID-19 pandemic has led to a 25% increase in depression and anxiety worldwide. Mental health–related stigma continues to be a barrier to service delivery, access, and utilization. The need for global investment in a worldwide mental health infrastructure is evident in such findings.

Both the need for transnational mental health partnerships and services, as well as our growing understanding of that need, introduces questions related to transboundary practice. Doing the research needed to be aware of licensure and registration requirements in a region where you are interested in practicing is an important first step. This research includes being aware of the parameters of practice if you offer teletherapy from the United States to someone in a different country.

With regard to teaching transnationally, whether in-person or online, the role of language, participation, curriculum, and technology are all factors to be considered within a global framework. When conducting transnational research, the Swiss Commission for Research Partnerships (Swiss Academy of Sciences, 2018) presents 11 principles and seven questions to help set the foundation for transnational research partnerships (see Chapter 9).

Implications of Multicultural Guideline 7

Clinical Practice
- Practitioners "aspire to prevent colonization of Indigenous or culture-specific systems of health care" (Clauss-Ehlers et al., 2019, p. 240).
- Practitioners develop partnerships between U.S. mental health systems and primary care systems in other countries.

Teaching and Training
- Students/trainees consider the intersection of domestic and international psychological paradigms in their professional development.
- Students/trainees consider Indigenous and culture-specific systems of care.
- Students/trainees strive to learn about conducting research within international contexts.

Research
- Researchers conduct research that examines mental health practices in other nations to explore the possibility of creating a global mental health paradigm.
- Researchers study the intersection of domestic and international psychology.
- Researchers consult with international organizations to develop local research standards.

Consultation
- Consultants engage in consultative efforts that explore global mental health and behavioral health care systems.
- Consultants examine the impact of a global economy on the provision of services.

Multicultural Guideline 8

Psychologists seek awareness and understanding of how developmental stages and life transitions intersect with the larger biosociocultural context, how identity evolves as a function of such intersections, and how these different socialization and maturation experiences influence worldview and identity.

Multicultural Guideline 8 addresses the relationship between human development and the surrounding environment. As multiculturally responsive psychologists, we are encouraged to understand that people's growth and maturity take place in the context of everything around them (e.g., the family's culture, school experiences, war, financial hardship). People form their unique identities at the intersection of their psychological and physical development and external influences, including local communities.

Taking the time to grasp these multiple influences is part of what helps us perceive an individual in a holistic way and will likely lead to better outcomes. For instance, a client may initially present as a rural, middle-aged White man who may or may not have generalized anxiety. Upon further exploration, you may discover that this person is a professor at a university in a nearby urban city, identifies as female, and is an accomplished jazz musician. Multicultural Guideline 8 encourages you to engage in critical thinking to understand how the client's development took place in relation to the biosociocultural contexts in her history. You might learn that, as the client grew up, she experienced gender identity issues resulting in harsh discrimination and eventual disownment by her family. The client derived inspiration and

---

Implications of Multicultural Guideline 8

Clinical Practice
- Practitioners are aware of the impact that interventions may have on communities and community identity.

Teaching and Training
- Students/trainees learn to consider intervention outcomes among diverse communities.
- Students/trainees learn to conduct research that takes an intersectional approach to data collection, analysis, and interpretation.
- Students/trainees learn how to understand multiple factors that have an influence on human development.

Research
- Researchers strive to incorporate multidimensional aspects of racial/ethnic identity in their research.
- Researchers consider intersectional identities among research participants and consider how they influence interpretation of research findings.

Consultation
- Consultants strive to understand the multiple factors that contribute to life course development.

support from her high school jazz club, whose advising teacher accepted her for her differences and talked with her when she needed someone to listen to her. By keeping in mind the intersection between the client's identity-discovery during the teenage years and the environmental factors, including the people around her, you may develop a deeper comprehension of the client's situation. You may subsequently be able to empathize on many more levels than if you hadn't explored the influential factors that informed the client's history.

Multicultural Guideline 9

Psychologists strive to conduct culturally appropriate and informed research, teaching, supervision, consultation, assessment, interpretation, diagnosis, dissemination, and evaluation of efficacy as they address the first four levels of the *Layered Ecological Model of the Multicultural Guidelines.*

Multicultural Guideline 9 recognizes the importance of conducting culturally appropriate and informed assessment, interpretation, diagnosis, and

---

Implications of Multicultural Guideline 9

Clinical Practice
- Practitioners understand the concept of cultural mistrust.
- Practitioners understand barriers to accessing treatment and work to develop rapport.

Teaching and Training
- Students/trainees learn about barriers to access and utilization of treatment services.
- Students/trainees learn about a range of research methodologies to incorporate in research endeavors.
- Students/trainees are aware of biases and assumptions when consulting with others.

Research
- Researchers recognize the limits of randomized controlled trials with regard to generalizability.
- Researchers explore and learn about community-based participation as a research method.

Consultation
- Consultants strive to identify biases that might affect the organization with which they are consulting.

sharing results and recommendations. As multiculturally responsive psychologists, our understanding of clients' cultural and social identities helps us to avoid perpetuation of institutional discrimination. In fact, our clients' social identities and cultures serve as valuable resources because they illustrate their experiences of privilege and oppression. These experiences may subsequently inform our clients' interpretations of experience and their outlook on assessment, therapy, and life in general. When we as psychologists are cognizant of intrapersonal, interpersonal, and societal-level effects, we can strive to assess and diagnose accurately, including consideration of culture-bound symptoms and testing biases. We can also help clients better integrate results and recommendations into customized treatment.

Multicultural Guideline 10

> Psychologists actively strive to take a strength-based approach when working with individuals, families, groups, communities, and organizations that seeks to build resilience and decrease trauma within the sociocultural context.

Multicultural Guideline 10 urges us to take a strength-based approach to build cultural resilience (i.e., a positive outcome) and decrease trauma (i.e., a negative outcome) within sociocultural contexts. Rather than focusing on pathology as the overarching defining factor for the client, we as psychologists are encouraged to incorporate client background and sociocultural context to identify strengths that promote positive mental health outcomes. Such strengths go beyond individual factors and incorporate cultural values, worldview, community supports, and resources. We as psychologists can identify positive attributes of coping, adaptation, and recovery that individuals, families, groups, and organizations bring to their experiences.

In this sense, the definition of resilience moves beyond personality predisposition to resist adversity and includes consideration of cultural values, worldview, and support of external resources, such as the community, family, religion, and other affirming systems.

A strength-based approach (SBA) forms the basis of work to increase resilience and decrease trauma. Building an SBA involves collaboration, as seen in our field through the recovery movement, family support services, positive psychology, and many other connections, as mentioned in Chapter 12. An SBA approach does not ignore issues and trauma; rather, these are acknowledged with an awareness of the capabilities of clients and providers to address and work through them.

> **Implications of Multicultural Guideline 10**
>
> **Clinical Practice**
> - Practitioners take a strength-based approach to working with client(s).
> - Practitioners examine clients' experiences of trauma and resilience within a community context.
>
> **Teaching and Training**
> - Students/trainees move from a disease-focused to a strength-based approach.
> - Students/trainees strive to incorporate a sociocultural approach to resilience.
>
> **Research**
> - Researchers generate knowledge using diverse research methodologies.
> - Researchers incorporate local terms in research protocols.
>
> **Consultation**
> - Consultants consider the impact of trauma on organizations.
> - Consultants consider systemic factors that influence experiences of trauma and resilience within a sociocultural context.

WHERE DO WE GO FROM HERE?

As discussed throughout this book, we are currently highly connected with and engaged by global considerations and their transactional influences on the United States' politics, policies, and efforts. The population of the United States is known to be highly diverse, with many individuals readily able to identify their ethnic, racial, gender, sexual orientation, socioeconomic status, and educational backgrounds, to name just a few reference group identities. Who we are and how we identify as mental health care professionals, educators, trainers, scientists, and/or consultants are defined by the intersectionality of our reference group identities; we meet our clients similarly, at a place of self-definition within a sociocultural context. This intersectionality serves as a foundation for the initiation and engagement of our professional interactions. Hence, we as psychologists exist within a range of communities in which we seek to engage and influence the successes and opportunities for those with whom we work.

This section considers how future work regarding the Multicultural Guidelines can unfold. We encourage psychologists and other mental health professionals to bring to our work an understanding of how our identities are influenced by multiple factors, how these influences represent strengths, and areas where we seek growth. We are enthusiastic about the field translating the Multicultural Guidelines into new approaches to community-based engagement and consultation. The layered ecological model as a way to assist our colleagues and clients in understanding how we can collaborate across multiple levels of effort is an area ripe for building forward.

Similarly, by engaging the communities we work with from a standpoint of humility, we open the door to new ways of approaching how we build alliances. We can work to sustain these alliances through continual review and exploration. Asking if what is being heard is correct is one opening to checking our privilege and understanding where a client is coming from. Seeking to ensure that the communication is appropriate and understood across both (or all) sides is a building forward in its recognition of experiential influences and related impact.

Working with a community, even if one has personal experience and knowledge of that community, is an opportunity to engage with the range of identities and considerations that situate within that community more broadly. As psychologists who are adept at considering multiculturalism, we need to be ready to listen and ask questions and to be open to multiple viewpoints regarding needs and wants. The task becomes one of thinking multidimensionally with regard to our practice and roles. In doing so, we take into account the varied circumstances and necessary considerations the broader community holds.

TWENTY-FIVE RECOMMENDATIONS FOR TAKING THE MULTICULTURAL GUIDELINES INTO OUR LIVES

We have come full circle from the first chapter of this volume, in which You the Reader was the focus of the case study, to this concluding chapter with recommendations for moving forward. You form the line that extends from our present place of knowledge and understanding to the next levels of growth and skill as new demands and experiences come forward. You are the pipeline for future generations of psychologists and helping professionals. Given this reality, it is imperative that your voices are attended to as a means of driving professional development and efficacious practice into the next generations. Here are 25 recommendations to support your process:

1. Take ownership of the multicultural guidelines in your work and training as a psychologist.

2. Whether as a student, educator, mentor, and/or supervisor, engage the multicultural guidelines in coursework, practica, internships, and fellowship training.

3. Explore how adaptations of the multicultural guidelines may be useful and necessary to support professional practice.

4. Use the multicultural guidelines to demonstrate the scientific evidence base that supports multicultural approaches to the helping professions.

5. Embrace interdisciplinary research. Psychology can benefit from research partnerships with disciplines such as women's studies, sociology, political science, linguistics, history, and law.

6. Engage with the full range of qualitative inquiry. There is no one way to conduct research. Qualitative research can include participant observation, participatory action research, physical and electronic data, ethnography, a variety of case study and narrative approaches, and traditional interview methods. Training programs can demonstrate equal openness to quantitative, qualitative, and mixed-methods doctoral dissertations.

7. Conduct quantitative and qualitative meta-analyses of studies on resilience and trauma constructs from a multicultural framework.

8. Consider how the multicultural guidelines may contribute to changes in research design, hypothesis testing, decisions about appropriate analytic strategies, and interpretations of findings.

9. Promote the development of methodologies to study the complexities of intersectional identities. All too often, researchers resort to collapsing subgroups into broader categories that do not reflect the complex lived realities of reference identity groups to meet statistical power requirements. As researchers, we can learn to pair culturally informed practice in one identity domain (e.g., immigrant status) with culturally informed practice in another (e.g., gay sexual orientation), thus maintaining an adaptive approach in studying multifaceted lived experiences.

10. Prioritize research on populations that have been previously ignored. More research attention on children, young adolescents, older individuals, and people with disabilities across all cultural, linguistic, racial, ethnic,

immigrant, and sexual-continuum groups is needed. We can resist the reliance on convenience samples of college students to make claims about the needs of underrepresented communities.

11. Connect cultural competency research to client outcomes. Many studies of clinician cultural competence rely on clinician self-reflection and self-report. We can take the next step and engage in more outcome-oriented research that helps us better understand the skills that make functional differences in client experiences.

12. Within your research labs or groups, acknowledge that the questions you are asking may need varied approaches to collaboration. In community-based work, for example, while addressing questions of health behaviors and compliance with recommended approaches to managing health care needs, consider how partnering with multiple community groups may foster a stronger understanding of behavioral choices that are being made.

13. Engage in recruitment and retention strategies to diversify programs, departments, and the psychologist workforce. Psychology departments need to be inclusive with regard to students, staff, graduate assistants, faculty, and on-site clinical supervisors. Admissions criteria need to extend to life experience, cultural experiences and living abroad, multilingual competence, and alignment with APA's multicultural and social-justice training goals. This inclusivity needs to apply to senior faculty and administrators as well.

14. Infuse cultural diversity in the curriculum (Mena & Quina, 2019). It's critical to ensure that multicultural issues are incorporated across classes, the curriculum, and training experiences rather than presented in simply one course. Up-to-date research on evolving multicultural constructs such as identity, societal contexts, intersectionality, structural stigma, transnationalism, acculturation, implicit biases, microaggression, intergenerational trauma, intergenerational strengths and resilience, linguistic competence, and the use of translation services must be integrated into coursework. Furthermore, trainers need to ensure that the curriculum centers the experiences of all students in the classroom and in supervisory sessions.

15. Participate in community-engaged programs. Universities can create outreach bridges from the campus to culturally diverse communities so that we can have fluid communication, contact, and collaboration with local people and can engage in prevention practice, research on community mental health needs, and consultation.

16. Ensure that practicum and internship sites are serving underrepresented communities. It is important that we ensure our training programs have affiliations with multicultural clinical sites in community mental health centers and hospitals. Programs will also benefit from requiring service-oriented or social-justice-oriented immersion experiences either before clinical field practica begin or at an early stage of training.

17. Prioritize training for multilingual clinicians. Psychology programs should offer bilingual training tracks. Students who are not bilingual can be trained in the use of interpreters and interpreter-based applications. Monolingual English-only students can be provided with training on language development and communication from various cultural perspectives.

18. Learn from each other as professionals who have both different and similar perspectives. Discuss and assess how the multicultural guidelines address interprofessional engagements and how they may be best moved forward.

19. Learn how to engage in scientific inquiry that takes a multicultural approach.

20. Learn how to engage in the publication process and publish work that supports and/or challenges the multicultural guidelines, as required.

21. Consider how the multicultural guidelines reflect the experiences of the communities you serve. In what ways do they correspond with the experiences you witness? In what ways is new information needed to address what you see?

22. Engage in work as an advocate who advances supports for communities, both domestically and transnationally.

23. Identify gaps in research, intervention, and practice and seek to fill them.

24. Give the field away. Share what you learn with others. Provide a professional translation of your work so that communities can benefit from multicultural psychological science.

25. Imagine how you would like to see the multicultural guidelines build and grow to suit your continued professional development and the development of the communities, organizations, families, couples, and individuals you serve.

CONCLUSION

We return to Eduardo's experience as the book's conclusion. Eduardo was uncomfortable sharing his family experiences individually with a therapist, even though the therapist spoke the same language that he did. Eduardo advocated for himself, asking the clinician if it was okay to have his family join him during sessions. The clinician followed Eduardo's lead and shifted the treatment modality from individual to family therapy. In so doing, the clinician supported his advocacy efforts.

Eduardo came into a community-based hospital clinic that offered individual therapy as the main treatment modality. The clinic did not offer family therapy, which was a more culturally syntonic approach for Eduardo given his cultural value of *familismo* (i.e., the importance placed on family relationships). Furthermore, the mental health stigma that played out for Eduardo centered on his feeling disloyal when he talked about family issues when family members were not present. To discuss family issues without members present might feel like a betrayal.

In understanding the different worldviews that others bring to mental health services, help seeking, and stigma, we as psychologists are more likely to break down barriers to access and utilization. For instance, intuitively, Eduardo's clinician agreed to shift to family-focused treatment. In doing so, the clinician showed she understood that dealing with panic attacks in the context of family therapy was a more comfortable approach for Eduardo. The result of clinician understanding was the provision of better quality care.

The approach taken by Eduardo's clinician increased utilization. She was responsive in a way that motivated Eduardo to return. Had the clinician not agreed to the family therapy, Eduardo might not have come back. By consulting the evidence base for culture-centered interventions, we as psychologists can provide evidence-based culture-centered care. As psychologists who engage in advocacy for their clients, we also model these proactive behaviors. Such advocacy can also be validating within the professional relationship. We learned about self-advocacy from Eduardo's example.

Our hope is that the generation of new knowledge you bring to the field means we have advanced to a science-practitioner evidence base that is so fruitful that completely new guidelines must ensue. We look forward to the work that will emerge in the years to come and the foundation it will lay for this next phase of professional practice, teaching and training, scientific inquiry, consultation, and advocacy.

Finally, we ask this question: If Eduardo comes into your office for another session and, without notifying you first, brings his entire family, what do you do as the clinician in that moment? The answer to this question is what this book is all about. Taking a culture-centered intervention approach involves hearing the needs of your clients, understanding how these needs are derived from the client's cultural context, and being flexible with regard to implementing a culturally adaptive approach in that moment.

AFTERWORD

Every page of *Applying Multiculturalism: An Ecological Approach to the APA Guidelines* reminds readers of the urgent need to confront and address the burgeoning racial and ethnic disparities in both access to and the quality of mental health care. Through case illustrations representing a range of identities characterizing the richness of diversity in American society, the authors deftly illustrate that a conscious commitment to social justice mandates culturally appropriate education for clinicians, educators, researchers, and consultants throughout their careers. The cases highlight the extent to which cultural competence is a dynamic, complex, and continuous process of skills development that is essential to upholding the ethical principles of autonomy, beneficence, and justice.

As a medical ethicist specializing on issues of prisoners' rights, I have observed firsthand the extent to which individuals' beliefs, values, customs, age, disability status, gender and gender identity, sexual orientation, race, ethnicity, languages, religion, and preferences provide a cultural context that informs the relationships among those needing mental health services and health care providers. The inextricable link between cultural competence and ethical decision making by practitioners is grounded in the reality that there is an inherent power differential between caregivers and the individuals they seek to serve and that conscious and unconscious social biases influence interpersonal relationships. The authors have demonstrated the ways in which exercising cultural humility, as a precursor to cultural sensitivity, and acknowledging the ways in which hidden biases hold the potential for affecting respect for persons, fairness, and the promotion of well-being can prevent ethical conflicts arising from an unwarranted, paternalistic imposition of beliefs and values on others. The approach of being respectful of and responsive to cultural beliefs and values improves client, patient, and family outcomes and is especially crucial in communities with longstanding mistrust of the health care system resulting from structural racism and other forms of discrimination.

Mental health care providers are obligated to implement clinical guidelines in a manner that accounts for the cultural identities and lived experience of all patients and clients. Failure to do so undermines patient/client empowerment and the quality of care. Developing meaningful connections with patients/clients, who bring their own biases to clinical encounters, is a vital component of mental health care delivery. Meeting the cultural, social, and linguistic needs of patients/clients necessitates building trust and respect on the basis of a willingness to engage in open and honest communication. Diversifying the profession is key to creating an environment in which patients and clients feel confident that their values and beliefs are understood and respected. However, given the current underrepresentation of diversity among mental health care providers in shaping educational and professional development programs, the guidance contained in this book for fostering multicultural competence is invaluable. The framework offered by the authors for promoting improved cultural competence relies on a multidimensional concept of cultural identity existing at the intersection of privilege, oppression, and unconscious bias. Their vision provides a roadmap for the future and a critical means of shrinking the persistent equity gap in mental health care access and quality.

—*Lynn Pasquerella, PhD*

References

Abbott, D. M., Pelc, N., & Mercier, C. (2019). Cultural humility and the teaching of psychology. *Scholarship of Teaching and Learning in Psychology, 5*(2), 169–181. https://doi.org/10.1037/stl0000144

Adames, H. Y., Chavez-Dueñas, N. Y., Sharma, S., & La Roche, M. J. (2018). Intersectionality in psychotherapy: The experiences of an AfroLatinx queer immigrant. *Psychotherapy, 55*(1), 73–79. https://doi.org/10.1037/pst0000152

Agger, I. (2015). Calming the mind: Healing after mass atrocity in Cambodia. *Transcultural Psychiatry, 52*(4), 543–560. https://doi.org/10.1177/1363461514568336

Ahluwalia, M. K., Ayala, S. I., Locke, A. F., & Nadrich, T. (2019). Mitigating the "powder keg": The experiences of faculty of color teaching multicultural competence. *Teaching of Psychology, 46*(3), 187–196. https://doi.org/10.1177/0098628319848864

Ahmedani, B. K. (2011). Mental health stigma: Society, individuals, and the profession. *Journal of Social Work Values and Ethics, 8*(2), 41–416.

Albright, J. N., & Hurd, N. M. (2020). Marginalized identities, Trump-related distress, and the mental health of underrepresented college students. *American Journal of Community Psychology, 65*(3–4), 381–396. https://doi.org/10.1002/ajcp.12407

Albritton, K., Mathews, R. E., & Anhalt, K. (2019). Systematic review of early childhood mental health consultation: Implications for improving preschool discipline disproportionality. *Journal of Educational & Psychological Consultation, 29*(4), 444–472. https://doi.org/10.1080/10474412.2018.1541413

Allwood, M. A., Bell-Dolan, D., & Husain, S. A. (2002). Children's trauma and adjustment reactions to violent and nonviolent war experiences. *Journal of the American Academy of Child & Adolescent Psychiatry, 41*(4), 450–457. https://doi.org/10.1097/00004583-200204000-00018

Almedom, A. M., & Glandon, D. (2008). Social capital and mental health: An updated interdisciplinary review of primary evidence. In I. Kawachi,

S. V. Subramanian, & D. Kim (Eds.), *Social capital and health* (pp. 191–214). Springer. https://doi.org/10.1007/978-0-387-71311-3_9

American Counseling Association. (n.d.). *Fact sheet #9: Vicarious trauma.* https://www.counseling.org/docs/default-source/trauma-disaster/fact-sheet-9---vicarious-trauma.pdf

American Educational Research Association, American Psychological Association, & National Council on Measurement in Education. (2014). *Standards for educational and psychological testing.* AERA.

American Psychiatric Association. (2010). *Mental health disparities: American Indians and Alaska Natives.* https://www.psychiatry.org/File%20Library/Psychiatrists/Cultural-Competency/Mental-Health-Disparities/Mental-Health-Facts-for-American-Indian-Alaska-Natives.pdf

American Psychiatric Association. (2013a). *Cultural Formulation Interview.* https://www.psychiatry.org/File%20Library/Psychiatrists/Practice/DSM/APA_DSM5_Cultural-Formulation-Interview.pdf

American Psychiatric Association. (2013b). *Diagnostic and statistical manual of mental disorders* (5th ed.). https://doi.org/10.1176/appi.books.9780890425596

American Psychological Association. (n.d.-a). Advocacy. In *APA dictionary of psychology.* Retrieved August 15, 2022, from https://dictionary.apa.org/advocacy

American Psychological Association. (n.d.-b). *Be an advocate for psychology: How to speak up for the issues that matter to you.* https://www.apa.org/advocacy/guide

American Psychological Association. (2002). *Guidelines on multicultural education, training, research, practice, and organizational change for psychologists.* https://www.apa.org/about/policy/multicultural-guidelines-archived.pdf

American Psychological Association. (2003). Guidelines on multicultural education, training, research, practice, and organizational change for psychologists. *American Psychologist, 58*(5), 377–402. https://doi.org/10.1037/0003-066X.58.5.377

American Psychological Association. (2010a). *Resilience and recovery after war: Refugee children and families in the United States.* https://www.apa.org/pubs/reports/refugees-full-report.pdf

American Psychological Association. (2010b). *Resilience of refugee children after war.* https://www.apa.org/pubs/reports/refugees

American Psychological Association. (2015a). *Call for nominations for two APA taskforces.* https://apadiv15.org/2015/04/17/call-for-nominations-for-two-apa-taskforces/

American Psychological Association. (2015b). Guidelines for psychological practice with transgender and gender nonconforming people. *American Psychologist, 70*(9), 832–864. https://doi.org/10.1037/a0039906

American Psychological Association. (2016). *2015 survey of psychology health service providers.* https://www.apa.org/workforce/publications/15-health-service-providers/report.pdf

American Psychological Association. (2017a). *Ethical principles of psychologists and code of conduct* (2002, amended effective June 1, 2010, and January 1, 2017). https://www.apa.org/ethics/code/index

American Psychological Association. (2017b). *Multicultural guidelines: An ecological approach to context, identity, and intersectionality.* https://www.apa.org/about/policy/multicultural-guidelines.aspx

American Psychological Association. (2017c). *Multicultural guidelines: An ecological approach to context, identity, and intersectionality.* https://www.apa.org/about/policy/multicultural-guidelines.pdf

American Psychological Association. (2019a). *APA's race and ethnicity guidelines.* https://www.apa.org/about/policy/summary-guidelines-race-ethnicity#

American Psychological Association. (2019b). *Association rules amended February 2019.* Retrieved August 15, 2022, from https://www.apa.org/about/governance/bylaws/rules.pdf

American Psychological Association. (2020a). *Psychology's workforce is becoming more diverse.* https://www.apa.org/monitor/2020/11/datapoint-diverse

American Psychological Association. (2020b). *Racial/ethnic minority representation among the academic psychology workforce continues to increase.* https://www.apa.org/workforce/publications/minority.pdf

American Psychological Association. (2021a). *APA resolution on harnessing psychology to combat racism: Adopting a uniform definition and understanding.* https://www.apa.org/about/policy/resolution-combat-racism.pdf

American Psychological Association. (2021b). *Apology to people of color for APA's role in promoting, perpetuating, and failing to challenge racism, racial discrimination, and human hierarchy in U.S.* https://www.apa.org/about/policy/racism-apology

American Psychological Association, Division 45: Warrior Path Presidential Task Force. (2020). Protecting and defending our people: Nakni tushka anowa (The warrior's path) final report. *Journal of Indigenous Research, 9*(2021), Article 8. https://doi.org/10.26077/2en0-6610

American Psychological Association, Task Force on Race and Ethnicity Guidelines in Psychology. (2019). *Race and ethnicity guidelines in psychology: Promoting responsiveness and equity.* https://apacustomout.apa.org/commentPracGuidelines/Practice/Race%20and%20Ethnicity%20Guidelines%20For%20Open%20Comment%20V2.pdf

Anders, C., Kivlighan, D. M., III, Porter, E., Lee, D., & Owen, J. (2021). Attending to the intersectionality and saliency of clients' identities: A further investigation of therapists' multicultural orientation. *Journal of Counseling Psychology, 68*(2), 139–148. https://doi.org/10.1037/cou0000447

Ardila, A. (2007). The impact of culture on neuropsychological test performance. In B. P. Uzzell, M. Ponton, & A. Ardila (Eds.), *International handbook of cross-cultural neuropsychology* (pp. 23–44). Psychology Press. https://doi.org/10.4324/9780203936290

Artiga, S., & Hinton, E. (2018). *Beyond health care: The role of social determinants in promoting health and health equity.* https://www.kff.org/racial-equity-and-health-policy/issue-brief/beyond-health-care-the-role-of-social-determinants-in-promoting-health-and-health-equity/

Asarnow, J. R., Rozenman, M., Wiblin, J., & Zeltzer, L. (2015). Integrated medical-behavioral care compared with usual primary care for child and adolescent behavioral health: A meta-analysis. *JAMA Pediatrics, 169*(10), 929–937. https://doi.org/10.1001/jamapediatrics.2015.1141

Ashcraft, C. (2009). *Institutional barriers and their effects: How can I talk to colleagues about these issues?* https://ncwit.org/resources/institutional-barriers-their-effects-how-can-i-talk-to-colleagues-about-these-issues/

Australian Institute of Health and Welfare. (n.d.). *Burden of disease.* https://www.aihw.gov.au/reports-data/health-conditions-disability-deaths/burden-of-disease/glossary

Ayazi, H., & Elsheikh, E. (2019, December). *Climate refugees: The climate crisis and rights denied.* Othering & Belonging Institute. https://belonging.berkeley.edu/climaterefugees

Azar, B. (2009). *International practitioners.* American Psychological Association. https://www.apa.org/gradpsych/2009/03/cover-abroad

Azmitia, M., & Thomas, V. (2015). Intersectionality and the development of self and identity. In R. Scott & S. Kosslyn (Eds.), *Emerging trends in the social and behavioral sciences* (pp. 1–9). Wiley. https://doi.org/10.1002/9781118900772.etrds0193

Bagalman, E., & Heisler, E. J. (2016). *Behavioral health among American Indian and Alaska Natives: An overview.* Congressional Research Service. https://sgp.fas.org/crs/misc/R44634.pdf

Baltes, P. B., Cornelius, S. W., & Nesselroade, J. R. (1979). Cohort effects in developmental psychology. In J. R. Nesselroade & P. B. Baltes (Eds.), *Longitudinal research in the study of behavior and development* (pp. 61–88). Academic Press.

Barrett, M. S., Chua, W., Crits-Christoph, P., Gibbons, M. B., Casiano, D., & Thompson, D. (2008). "Early withdrawal from mental health treatment: Implications for psychotherapy practice": Correction to Barrett et al. (2008). *Psychotherapy: Theory, Research, Practice, Training, 46*(2), 248. https://doi.org/10.1037/a0016184

Baumann, E. F., Ryu, D., & Harney, P. (2020). Listening to identity: Transference, countertransference, and therapist disclosure in psychotherapy with sexual and gender minority clients. *Practice Innovations, 5*(3), 246–256. https://doi.org/10.1037/pri0000132

Beers, C. W. (1981). *A mind that found itself: A memoir of madness and recovery.* University of Pittsburgh Press. (Original work published 1908)

Belkin, M., & White, C. (2020). *Intersectionality and relational psychoanalysis: New perspectives on race, gender, and sexuality.* Routledge.

Belone, L., Tosa, J., Shendo, K., Toya, A., Straits, K., Tafoya, G., Rae, R., Noyes, E., Bird, D., & Wallerstein, N. (2016). Community-based participatory research for cocreating interventions with Native communities: A partnership between the University of New Mexico and the pueblo of Jemez. In N. Zane, G. Bernal, & F. T. L. Leong (Eds.), *Evidence-based psychological practice with ethnic minorities: Culturally informed research and clinical strategies* (pp. 199–220). American Psychological Association. https://doi.org/10.1037/14940-010

Berkman, L. F. (2009). Social epidemiology: Social determinants of health in the United States: Are we losing ground? *Annual Review of Public Health, 30*(1), 27–41. https://doi.org/10.1146/annurev.publhealth.031308.100310

Bernal, G., & Domenech Rodríguez, M. (Eds.). (2012). *Cultural adaptations: Tools for evidence-based practice with diverse populations*. American Psychological Association. https://doi.org/10.1037/13752-000

Bhatia, S. (2019). Searching for justice in an unequal world: Reframing indigenous psychology as a cultural and political project. *Journal of Theoretical and Philosophical Psychology, 39*(2), 107–114. https://doi.org/10.1037/teo0000109

Blasini-Méndez, M. (2019). Interpersonal postcolonial supervision: Facilitating conversations on countertransference. *Training and Education in Professional Psychology, 13*(3), 233–237. https://doi.org/10.1037/tep0000239

Blume, A. W., Morse, G. S., & Love, C. (2020). Human rights and psychology from Indigenous perspectives. In N. Rubin & R. Flores (Eds.), *The Cambridge handbook on psychology and human rights* (pp. 258–272). Cambridge University Press.

Bodó, B., Helberger, N., Eskens, S., & Moller, J. (2019). Interested in diversity. *Digital Journalism, 7*(2), 206–229. https://doi.org/10.1080/21670811.2018.1521292

Bonanno, G. A. (2004). Loss, trauma, and human resilience: Have we underestimated the human capacity to thrive after extremely aversive events? *American Psychologist, 59*(1), 20–28. https://doi.org/10.1037/0003-066X.59.1.20

Bonanno, G. A., & Mancini, A. D. (2008). The human capacity to thrive in the face of potential trauma. *Pediatrics, 121*(2), 369–375. https://doi.org/10.1542/peds.2007-1648

Bowleg, L., & Bauer, G. (2016). Invited reflection: Quantifying intersectionality. *Psychology of Women Quarterly, 40*(3), 337–341. https://doi.org/10.1177/0361684316654282

Breland, J. Y., McAndrew, L. M., Gross, R. L., Leventhal, H., & Horowitz, C. R. (2013). Challenges to healthy eating for people with diabetes in a low-income, minority neighborhood. *Diabetes Care, 36*(10), 2895–2901. https://doi.org/10.2337/dc12-1632

Bronfenbrenner, U. (1977). Toward an experimental ecology of human development. *American Psychologist, 32*(7), 513–531. https://doi.org/10.1037/0003-066X.32.7.513

Bronfenbrenner, U. (1979). *The ecology of human development: Experiments by nature and design*. Harvard University Press.

Bronfenbrenner, U. (1995). Developmental ecology through space and time: A future perspective. In P. Moen, G. H. Elder, Jr., & K. Lüscher (Eds.), *Examining lives in context: Perspectives on the ecology of human development* (pp. 619–647). American Psychological Association. https://doi.org/10.1037/10176-018

Bronfenbrenner, U., & Ceci, S. J. (1994). Nature–nurture reconceptualized in developmental perspective: A bioecological model. *Psychological Review, 101*(4), 568–586. https://doi.org/10.1037/0033-295X.101.4.568

Brooks, M., Alston, G. D., Townsend, C. B., & Bryan, M. (2017). Creating a healthy classroom environment in multicultural counseling courses. *Journal of Human Services: Training, Research, and Practice, 2*(1), Article 3.

Brown, J. L. C., Ong, J., Mathers, J. M., & Decker, J. T. (2017). Compassion fatigue and mindfulness: Comparing mental health professionals and MSW student interns. *Journal of Evidence-Informed Social Work, 14*(3), 119–130. https://doi.org/10.1080/23761407.2017.1302859

Buchanan, L., Bui, Q., & Patel, J. K. (2020, July 13). Black Lives Matter may be the largest movement in US history. *The New York Times*. https://www.nytimes.com/interactive/2020/07/03/us/george-floyd-protests-crowd-size.html

Budiman, A. (2020, August 20). *Key findings about U.S. immigrants*. Pew Research Center. https://www.pewresearch.org/fact-tank/2020/08/20/key-findings-about-u-s-immigrants/

Bullock, H. E. (2013). *Women and poverty: Psychology, public policy, and social justice*. Wiley-Blackwell. https://doi.org/10.1002/9781118378748

Buse, N. A., Burker, E. J., & Bernacchio, C. (2013). Cultural variation in resilience as a response to traumatic experience. *Journal of Rehabilitation, 79*(2), 15–23.

Cabassa, L. J., & Baumann, A. A. (2013). A two-way street: Bridging implementation science and cultural adaptations of mental health treatments. *Implementation Science, 8*(1), 90. https://doi.org/10.1186/1748-5908-8-90

Cabrera, N. L., & Padilla, A. M. (2004). Entering and succeeding in the "culture of college": The story of two Mexican heritage students. *Hispanic Journal of Behavioral Sciences, 26*(2), 152–170. https://doi.org/10.1177/0739986303262604

Calarco, J. M. (2011). "I need help!" Social class and children's help-seeking in elementary school. *American Sociological Review, 76*(6), 862–882. https://doi.org/10.1177/0003122411427177

Callaghan, T., & Corbit, J. (2018). Early prosocial development across cultures. *Current Opinion in Psychology, 20*, 102–106. https://doi.org/10.1016/j.copsyc.2017.07.039

Campinha-Bacote, J. (2018, December 4). Cultural competemility: A paradigm shift in the cultural competence versus cultural humility debate—Part I. *Online Journal of Issues in Nursing, 24*(1). Advance online publication. https://doi.org/10.3912/OJIN.Vol24No01PPT20

Cappella, E., Hamre, B. K., Kim, H. Y., Henry, D. B., Frazier, S. L., Atkins, M. S., & Schoenwald, S. K. (2012). Teacher consultation and coaching within mental health practice: Classroom and child effects in urban elementary schools.

Journal of Consulting and Clinical Psychology, 80(4), 597–610. https://doi.org/10.1037/a0027725

Carey, B. (2018, August 9). Psychologists' group maintains ban on work at military detention facilities. *The New York Times.* https://www.nytimes.com/2018/08/09/health/interrogation-psychologists-guantanamo.html

Carnevale, A. P., & Rose, S. J. (2004). Socioeconomic status, race/ethnicity, and selective college admissions. In R. D. Kahlenberg (Ed.), *America's untapped resource: Low-income students in higher education* (pp. 101–156). Century Found.

Carter, R. T. (2007). Racism and psychological and emotional injury recognizing and assessing race-based traumatic stress. *The Counseling Psychologist, 35*(1), 13–105. https://doi.org/10.1177/0011000006292033

Carter, R. T., Mazzula, S., Victoria, R., Vazquez, R., Hall, S., Smith, S., Sant-Barket, S., Forsyth, J., Bazelais, K., & Williams, B. (2013). Initial development of the Race-Based Traumatic Stress Symptom Scale: Assessing the emotional impact of racism. *Psychological Trauma: Theory, Research, Practice, and Policy, 5*(1), 1–9. https://doi.org/10.1037/a0025911

Casas, J. M., Suzuki, L. A., Alexander, C. M., & Jackson, M. A. (Eds.). (2017). *Handbook of multicultural counseling* (4th ed.). SAGE. https://doi.org/10.4135/9781506304458

Centers for Disease Control and Prevention. (2013, November 22). CDC health disparities and inequalities report—United States, 2013. *Morbidity and Mortality Weekly Report, 62*(3). https://www.cdc.gov/mmwr/pdf/other/su6203.pdf

Centers for Disease Control and Prevention. (2020). *Health equity considerations and racial and ethnic minority groups.* https://stacks.cdc.gov/view/cdc/91049

Charlesworth, T. E. S., & Banaji, M. R. (2019). Patterns of implicit and explicit attitudes: I. Long-term change and stability from 2007 to 2016. *Psychological Science, 30*(2), 174–192. https://doi.org/10.1177/0956797618813087

Chiao, J. Y. (2018). Developmental aspects in cultural neuroscience. *Developmental Review, 50,* 77–89. https://doi.org/10.1016/j.dr.2018.06.005

Chin, M. H., Goddu, A. P., Ferguson, M. J., & Peek, M. E. (2014). Expanding and sustaining integrated health care-community efforts to reduce diabetes disparities. *Health Promotion Practice, 15*(2, Suppl.), 29S–39S. https://doi.org/10.1177/1524839914532649

Cho, S., Crenshaw, K. W., & McCall, L. (2013). Toward a field of intersectionality studies: Theory, applications, and praxis. *Signs: Journal of Women in Culture and Society, 38*(4), 785–810. https://doi.org/10.1086/669608

Chronis-Tuscano, A., Danko, C. M., Rubin, K. H., Coplan, R. J., & Novick, D. R. (2018). Future directions for research on early intervention for young children at risk for social anxiety. *Journal of Clinical Child and Adolescent Psychology, 47*(4), 655–667. https://doi.org/10.1080/15374416.2018.1426006

Chuang, J. A. (2020). Preventing trafficking through new global governance over labor migration. *Georgia State University Law Review, 36*(4). https://readingroom.law.gsu.edu/gsulr/vol36/iss4/6/

Clauss-Ehlers, C. S. (2004). Re-inventing resilience: A model of "culturally-focused resilient adaptation." In C. S. Clauss-Ehlers & M. D. Weist (Eds.), *Community planning to foster resilience in children* (pp. 27–41). Kluwer. https://doi.org/10.1007/978-0-306-48544-2_3

Clauss-Ehlers, C. S. (2006a). Bilingualism. In Y. Jackson (Ed.), *Encyclopedia of multicultural psychology* (pp. 70–71). SAGE. https://doi.org/10.4135/9781412952668.n33

Clauss-Ehlers, C. S. (2006b). *Diversity training for classroom teaching: A manual for students and educators*. Springer.

Clauss-Ehlers, C. S. (2008). Sociocultural factors, resilience, and coping: Support for a culturally sensitive measure of resilience. *Journal of Applied Developmental Psychology, 29*(3), 197–212. https://doi.org/10.1016/j.appdev.2008.02.004

Clauss-Ehlers, C. S. (2017). In search of an evidence-based approach to understand and promote effective parenting practices. *Couple & Family Psychology, 6*(3), 135–153. https://doi.org/10.1037/cfp0000082

Clauss-Ehlers, C. S. (2019a). Forced migration among Latinx children and their families: Introducing trilateral migration trauma as a concept to reflect a forced migratory experience. *Journal of Infant, Child, and Adolescent Psychotherapy; JICAP, 18*(4), 330–342. https://doi.org/10.1080/15289168.2019.1686742

Clauss-Ehlers, C. S. (2019b, April 12). *Multicultural guidelines for the 21st century: A call to the profession* [Paper presentation]. Shine a Light on Mental Health Awareness in New Jersey conference, New Brunswick, NJ, United States.

Clauss-Ehlers, C. S. (2020). Exploration of psychological well-being, resilience, ethnic identity, and meaningful events among a group of youth in Northern England: An autobiographical narrative intervention pilot study. *Adolescent Psychiatry, 10*(2), 92–109. https://doi.org/10.2174/2210676610666200226090427

Clauss-Ehlers, C. S. (2021a). Promoting change amidst systemic oppression: A 21st century call to action for communities and community psychologists. In C. S. Clauss-Ehlers (Ed.), *The Cambridge handbook of community psychology: Interdisciplinary and contextual perspectives* (pp. 3–15). Cambridge University Press. https://doi.org/10.1017/9781108678971.003

Clauss-Ehlers, C. S. (2021b). Rewriting the community psychology narrative: A contextual, interdisciplinary, inclusive, empowerment approach. In C. S. Clauss-Ehlers (Ed.), *The Cambridge handbook of community psychology: Interdisciplinary and contextual perspectives* (pp. 653–664). Cambridge University Press. https://doi.org/10.1017/9781108678971.035

Clauss-Ehlers, C. S. (2022). *The development of the Cultural Resilience Measure* [Manuscript in preparation]. Department of Psychology, Long Island University.

Clauss-Ehlers, C. S., Acosta, O., & Weist, M. D. (2004). Responses to terrorism: The voices of two communities speak out. In C. S. Clauss-Ehlers & M. D. Weist (Eds.), *Community planning to foster resilience in children* (pp. 143–159). Kluwer. https://doi.org/10.1007/978-0-306-48544-2_10

Clauss-Ehlers, C. S., & Akinsulure-Smith, A. M. (2013). Working with forced migrant children and their families: Mental health, developmental, legal, and linguistic considerations in the context of school-based mental health services. In C. S. Clauss-Ehlers, Z. Serpell, & M. D. Weist (Eds.), *Handbook of culturally responsive school mental health: Advancing research, training, practice, and policy* (pp. 135–145). Springer. https://doi.org/10.1007/978-1-4614-4948-5_10

Clauss-Ehlers, C. S., Austin, M., Ahto, L., Samperi, F., Zhao, J., & Su, N. (2017). Application of the parenting research partnership model to an evidence-based case study approach. *Couple & Family Psychology, 6*(3), 171–184. https://doi.org/10.1037/cfp0000081

Clauss-Ehlers, C. S., Chiriboga, D. A., Hunter, S. J., Roysircar, G., & Tummala-Narra, P. (2019). APA *Multicultural Guidelines* executive summary: Ecological approach to context, identity, and intersectionality. *American Psychologist, 74*(2), 232–244. https://doi.org/10.1037/amp0000382

Clauss-Ehlers, C. S., Guevara Carpio, M., & Weist, M. D. (2020). Mental health literacy: A strategy for global adolescent mental health promotion. *Adolescent Psychiatry, 10*(2), 73–83. https://doi.org/10.2174/2210676610666200204104429

Clauss-Ehlers, C. S., & Pasquerella, L. (2017). Application of campus instructional support: Two case studies. *International Journal of Information and Learning Technology, 34*(4), 338–350. https://doi.org/10.1108/IJILT-11-2016-0053

Clauss-Ehlers, C. S., Serpell, Z., & Weist, M. D. (Eds.). (2013). *Handbook of culturally responsive school mental health: Advancing research, training, practice, and policy*. Springer. https://doi.org/10.1007/978-1-4614-4948-5

Clauss-Ehlers, C. S., Sood, A. B., & Weist, M. D. (Eds.). (2020). *Social justice for children and young people: International perspectives*. Cambridge University Press. https://doi.org/10.1017/9781108551830

Clauss-Ehlers, C. S., & Tummala-Narra, P. (2022). Multicultural considerations for health service psychologists and applied psychologists in healthcare settings. In G. J. G. Amundson (Ed.), *Comprehensive clinical psychology: Vol. 2. Professional issues* (2nd ed., pp. 218–229). Elsevier. https://doi.org/10.1016/B978-0-12-818697-8.00169-2

Clauss-Ehlers, C. S., Weist, M. D., Sood, A. B., & Lomaro, C. (2020). Conclusion: Being a change agent for social justice for children and youth. In C. S. Clauss-Ehlers, A. B. Sood, & M. D. Weist (Eds.), *Social justice for children and young people: International perspectives* (pp. 479–490). Cambridge University Press. https://doi.org/10.1017/9781108551830.032

Clauss-Ehlers, C. S., & Wibrowski, C. R. (2007). Building educational resilience and social support: The effects of the Educational Opportunity Fund program among first- and second-generation college students. *Journal of College Student Development, 48*(5), 574–584. https://doi.org/10.1353/csd.2007.0051

Clough, P. T., & Fine, M. (2007). Activism and pedagogies: Feminist reflections. *Women's Studies Quarterly, 35*(3/4), 255–275.

Coates, R. (2020). Rodney Coates outlines a 12-step program for decolonizing academe. *Social Science Space*. https://www.socialsciencespace.com/2020/07/rodney-coates-outlines-a-12-step-program-for-decolonizing-academe/

Cohen, K. R., Lee, C. M., & McIlwraith, R. (2012). The psychology of advocacy and the advocacy of psychology. *Canadian Psychology, 53*(3), 151–158. https://doi.org/10.1037/a0027823

Cohler, B. J., & Michaels, S. (2012). Emergent adulthood in lesbian and gay lives: Individual development, life course, and social change. In C. J. Patterson & A. R. D'Augelli (Eds.), *Handbook of psychology and sexual orientation* (pp. 102–117). Oxford University Press. https://doi.org/10.1093/acprof:oso/9780199765218.003.0008

Cole, E. R. (2009). Intersectionality and research in psychology. *American Psychologist, 64*(3), 170–180. https://doi.org/10.1037/a0014564

Cole, E. R. (2020). Demarginalizing women of color in intersectionality scholarship in psychology: A Black feminist critique. *Journal of Social Issues, 76*(4), 1036–1044. https://doi.org/10.1111/josi.12413

Coley, R. L., Sims, J., Dearing, E., & Spielvogel, B. (2018). Locating economic risks for adolescent mental and behavioral health: Poverty and affluence in families, neighborhoods, and schools. *Child Development, 89*(2), 360–369. https://doi.org/10.1111/cdev.12771

Collaborative for Academic, Social, and Emotional Learning. (n.d.). *Fundamentals of SEL*. https://casel.org/what-is-sel/

Collins, K., Connors, K., Davis, S., Donohue, A., Gardner, S., Goldblatt, E., Hayward, A., Kiser, L., Strieder, F., & Thompson, E. (2010). *Understanding the impact of trauma and urban poverty on family systems: Risks, resilience, and interventions*. Family Informed Trauma Treatment Center. https://www.nctsn.org/sites/default/files/resources/resource-guide/understanding_impact_trauma_urban_poverty_family_systems.pdf

Collins, L. H., Machizawa, S., & Rice, J. K. (Eds.). (2019). *Transnational psychology of women: Expanding international and intersectional approaches*. American Psychological Association. https://doi.org/10.1037/0000148-000

Collins, P. Y. (2020). What is global mental health? *World Psychiatry, 19*(3), 265–266. https://doi.org/10.1002/wps.20728

Collishaw, S., Hammerton, G., Mahedy, L., Sellers, R., Owen, M. J., Craddock, N., Thapar, A. K., Harold, G. T., Rice, F., & Thapar, A. (2016). Mental health resilience in the adolescent offspring of parents with depression: A prospective longitudinal study. *The Lancet Psychiatry, 3*(1), 49–57. https://doi.org/10.1016/S2215-0366(15)00358-2

Comas-Díaz, L. (2012). Colored spirituality: The centrality of spirit among ethnic minorities. In L. J. Miller (Ed.), *The Oxford handbook of psychology and spirituality* (pp. 197–206). Oxford University Press. https://doi.org/10.1093/oxfordhb/9780199729920.013.0013

Cooper, S., & Leong, F. T. L. (2008). Introduction to the special issue on culture, race, and ethnicity in organizational consulting psychology. *Consulting Psychology Journal, 60*(2), 133–138. https://doi.org/10.1037/0736-9735.60.2.133

Council for International Organizations of Medical Sciences (CIOMS). (2016). *International ethical guidelines for health-related research involving humans*. World Health Organization. https://cioms.ch/publications/product/international-ethical-guidelines-for-health-related-research-involving-humans/

COVID-19 Mental Disorders Collaborators. (2021, November 6). Global prevalence and burden of depressive and anxiety disorders in 204 countries and territories in 2020 due to the COVID-19 pandemic. *The Lancet, 398*(10312), 1700–1712. https://doi.org/10.1016/S0140-6736(21)02143-7

Crenshaw, K. W. (1989). Demarginalizing the intersections of race and sex: A Black feminist critique of antidiscrimination doctrine, feminist theory, and antiracist politics. *University of Chicago Legal Forum, 140*(1), 139–167. https://doi.org/10.4324/9780429500480-5

Crowley, J. (2017, February 21). What are 'outcomes' for clients? *Counselling Directory*. https://www.counselling-directory.org.uk/memberarticles/what-are-outcomes-for-clients

Cullen, K., Rhodes, P., Brockman, R., Hunt, C., & Langtiw, C. L. (2020). Decolonising clinical psychology: National and international perspectives. *Clinical Psychologist, 24*(3), 211–222. https://doi.org/10.1111/cp.12228

Davis, D. E., DeBlaere, C., Brubaker, K., Owen, J., Jordan, T. A., II, Hook, J. N., & Von Tongeren, D. R. (2016). Microaggressions and perceptions of cultural humility in counseling. *Journal of Counseling and Development, 94*, 483493. https://doi.org/10.1002/jcad.12107

Davis, M. H. (1996). *Empathy: A social psychological approach*. Brown & Benchmark.

DeFreitas, S. C., Crone, T., DeLeon, M., & Ajayi, A. (2018). Perceived and personal mental health stigma in Latino and African American college students. *Frontiers in Public Health, 6*, 49. Advance online publication. https://doi.org/10.3389/fpubh.2018.00049

Demby, G. (2013, April 8). *How code-switching explains the world*. NPR. https://www.npr.org/sections/codeswitch/2013/04/08/176064688/how-code-switching-explains-the-world

Demby, G., & Miraji, S. M. (2020, May 31). *A decade of watching Black people die*. NPR. https://www.npr.org/2020/05/29/865261916/a-decade-of-watching-black-people-die

Downey, M. M., & Gomez, A. M. (2018). Structural competency and reproductive health. *AMA Journal of Ethics, 20*(3), 211–223. https://doi.org/10.1001/journalofethics.2018.20.3.peer1-1803

Drescher, J. (2009). When politics distort science: What mental health professionals can do. *Journal of Gay & Lesbian Mental Health, 13*(3), 213–226. https://doi.org/10.1080/19359700902964222

Duckworth, A. L., Peterson, C., Matthews, M. D., & Kelly, D. R. (2007). Grit: Perseverance and passion for long-term goals. *Journal of Personality and Social Psychology, 92*(6), 1087–1101. https://doi.org/10.1037/0022-3514.92.6.1087

Dudgeon, P., & Walker, R. (2015). Decolonising Australian psychology: Discourses, strategies, and practice. *Journal of Social and Political Psychology, 3*(1), 276–297. https://doi.org/10.5964/jspp.v3i1.126

Dunham, Y., Baron, A. S., & Banaji, M. R. (2016). The development of implicit gender attitudes. *Developmental Science, 19*(5), 781–789. https://doi.org/10.1111/desc.12321

Dunham, Y., Chen, E. E., & Banaji, M. R. (2013). Two signatures of implicit intergroup attitudes: Developmental invariance and early enculturation. *Psychological Science, 24*(6), 860–868. https://doi.org/10.1177/0956797612463081

Eckert, M. D., Nishimura, S. T., Oka, L., Barber, S., Fleming, L., Hishinuma, E. S., Goebert, D. A., & Guerrero, A. P. S. (2017). A pilot school-based rural mental health consultation program utilizing an innovative stakeholder partnership at a diverse elementary school. *Rural Mental Health, 41*(4), 263–283. https://doi.org/10.1037/rmh0000083

Elliott, D., & Bowman, E. (2020, August 30). *A father's fight paved way for independent investigation into Kenosha shooting*. NPR. https://www.npr.org/2020/08/30/907559478/a-fathers-fight-paved-way-for-doj-s-open-investigation-into-kenosha-shooting

Ellis, B. H., MacDonald, H. Z., Lincoln, A. K., & Cabral, H. J. (2008). Mental health of Somali adolescent refugees: The role of trauma, stress, and perceived discrimination. *Journal of Consulting and Clinical Psychology, 76*(2), 184–193. https://doi.org/10.1037/0022-006X.76.2.184

Engel, G. L. (1977, April 8). The need for a new medical model: A challenge for biomedicine. *Science, 196*(4286), 129–136. https://doi.org/10.1126/science.847460

Engel, G. L. (1978). The biopsychosocial model and the education of health professionals. *Annals of the New York Academy of Sciences, 310*(1), 169–181. https://doi.org/10.1111/j.1749-6632.1978.tb22070.x

Erikson, E. H. (1950). *Childhood and society*. Norton.

Erikson, E. H. (1994). *Identity and the life cycle*. Norton. (Original work published 1967)

Eriksson, M., Ghazinour, M., & Hammarstrom, A. (2018). Different uses of Bronfenbrenner's ecological theory in public mental health research: What is their value for guiding public mental health policy and practice? *Social Theory & Health, 16*, 414–433. https://doi.org/10.1057/s41285-018-0065-6

Falender, C. A., Shafranske, E. P., & Falicov, C. J. (Eds.). (2014). *Multiculturalism and diversity in clinical supervision: A competency-based approach*. American Psychological Association. https://doi.org/10.1037/14370-000

Farah, M. J., & Hackman, D. A. (2012). SES, child experience, and the neural bases of cognition. In V. Maholmes & R. B. King (Eds.), *The Oxford handbook of poverty and child development* (pp. 307–318). Oxford University Press.

Ferrer, I., Grenier, A., Brotman, S., & Koehn, S. (2017). Understanding the experiences of racialized older people through an intersectional life course perspective. *Journal of Aging Studies, 41*, 10–17. https://doi.org/10.1016/j.jaging.2017.02.001

Fisher, E. S. (2020). Cultural humility as a form of social justice: Promising practices for global school psychology training. *School Psychology International, 41*(1), 53–66. https://doi.org/10.1177/0143034319893097

Fisher-Borne, M., Cain, J. M., & Martin, S. L. (2015). From mastery to accountability: Cultural humility as an alternative to cultural competence. *Social Work Education, 34*(2), 165–181. https://doi.org/10.1080/02615479.2014.977244

Fiske, S. T., & Markus, H. R. (Eds.). (2012). *Facing social class: How societal rank influences interaction*. Russell Sage Foundation.

Fiske, S. T., & Taylor, S. E. (2017). *Social cognition: From brains to culture* (3rd ed.). SAGE.

Flores, Y. G., Hinton, L., Barker, J. C., Franz, C. E., & Velasquez, A. (2009). Beyond familism: A case study of the ethics of care of a Latina caregiver of an elderly parent with dementia. *Health Care for Women International, 30*(12), 1055–1072. https://doi.org/10.1080/07399330903141252

Foley, Z., Storck-Martinez, C., Koguc, G., Guevara Carpio, M., Lomaro, C., & Clauss-Ehlers, C. S. (2022). Psychological impact of climate change on communities. In C. S. Clauss-Ehlers (Ed.), *The Cambridge handbook of community psychology: Interdisciplinary and contextual perspectives* (pp. 425–450). Cambridge University Press. https://doi.org/10.1017/9781108678971.025

Foronda, C., Baptiste, D.-L., Reinholdt, M. M., & Ousman, K. (2016). Cultural humility: A concept analysis. *Journal of Transcultural Nursing, 27*(3), 210–217. https://doi.org/10.1177/1043659615592677

Foster, R. P. (1992). Psychoanalysis and the bilingual patient: Some observations on the influence of language choice on the transference. *Psychoanalytic Psychology, 9*(1), 61–76. https://doi.org/10.1037/h0079325

Foster, R. P. (1996). The bilingual self—Thoughts from a scientific positivist or pragmatic psychoanalyst? *Psychoanalytic Dialogues, 6*(1), 141–150. https://doi.org/10.1080/10481889609539111

Frisby, C. L., & O'Donohue, W. T. (Eds.). (2018). *Cultural competence in applied psychology*. Springer International. https://doi.org/10.1007/978-3-319-78997-2

Fryberg, S. A., Markus, H. R., Oyserman, D., & Stone, J. M. (2008). Of warrior chiefs and Indian princesses: The psychological consequences of American Indian mascots. *Basic and Applied Social Psychology, 30*(3), 208–218. https://doi.org/10.1080/01973530802375003

Gallardo, M. E. (2014). *Developing cultural humility: Embracing race, privilege and power*. SAGE. https://doi.org/10.4135/9781483388076

Gallardo, M. E., & Curry, S. J. (2009). Shifting perspectives: Culturally responsive interventions with latino substance abusers. *Journal of Ethnicity in Substance Abuse, 8*(3), 314–329. https://doi.org/10.1080/15332640903110492

Galliher, R. V., McLean, K. C., & Syed, M. (2017). An integrated developmental model for studying identity content in context. *Developmental Psychology, 53*(11), 2011–2022. https://doi.org/10.1037/dev0000299

Garagiola, E., Lam, Q., Wachsmuth, L., Tan, V., Ghali, S., Asafo, S., & Swarna, M. (2022). Adolescent resilience during the COVID-19 pandemic: A review of the impact of the pandemic on developmental milestones. *Behavioral Sciences, 12*(7), 220. https://doi.org/10.3390/bs12070220

García, A., & Courtney, M. (2011). Prevalence and predictors of service utilization among racially and ethnically diverse adolescents in foster care diagnosed with mental health and substance abuse disorders. *Journal of Public Child Welfare, 5*(5), 521–545. https://doi.org/10.1080/15548732.2011.617277

Garcia, M. A., Morse, G. S., Trimble, J. E., Dasillas, D. M., Boyd, B., & King, J. (2017). A partnership with the people: Skillful navigation of culture and ethics in research. In S. Stewart & R. Moodley (Eds.), *Mental health on Turtle Island* (pp. 199–218). SAGE.

Gardiner, E., & French, C. (2011). The relevance of cultural sensitivity in early intervention. *Exceptionality Education International, 21*(3), 33–49. https://doi.org/10.5206/eei.v21i3.7681

Garrett, M. T., Borders, L. D., Crutchfield, L. B., Torres-Rivera, E., Brotherton, D., & Curtis, R. (2001). Multicultural superVISION: A paradigm of cultural responsiveness for supervisors. *Journal of Multicultural Counseling and Development, 29*(2), 147–158. https://doi.org/10.1002/j.2161-1912.2001.tb00511.x

Garza, J. R., Glenn, B. A., Mistry, R. S., Ponce, N. A., & Zimmerman, F. J. (2017). Subjective social status and self-reported health among US-born and immigrant Latinos. *Journal of Immigrant and Minority Health, 19*(1), 108–119. https://doi.org/10.1007/s10903-016-0346-x

Gask, L., Kendrick, T., Peveler, R., & Chew-Graham, C. A. (Eds.). (2018). *Primary care mental health* (2nd ed.). Cambridge University Press. https://doi.org/10.1017/9781911623038

GBD 2017 Disease and Injury Incidence and Prevalence Collaborators. (2018, November 10). Global, regional, and national incidence, prevalence, and years lived with disability for 354 diseases and injuries for 195 countries and territories, 1990–2017: A systematic analysis for the Global Burden of Disease Study 2017. *The Lancet, 392*(10159), 1789–1858. https://doi.org/10.1016/S0140-6736(18)32279-7

Gee, A., McGarty, C., & Banfield, M. (2015). What drives systemic mental health advocates? Goals, strategies, and values of Australian consumer and carer advocacy organizations. *SAGE Open*. Advance online publication. https://doi.org/10.1177/2158244015615384

Geisinger, K. F. (Ed.). (2013). *APA handbook of testing and assessment in psychology* (Vols. 1–3). American Psychological Association.

Gil, R. M., & Vazquez, C. I. (1997). *The Maria paradox: How Latinas can merge old world traditions with new world self-esteem*. TarcherPerigee.

Goforth, A. N., Pham, A. V., Chun, H., & Castro-Olivo, S. (2017). Acculturation and sociocultural factors in children's mental health services: Applying multicultural consultation frameworks. *Journal of Educational & Psychological*

Consultation, 27(3), 239–244. https://doi.org/10.1080/10474412.2016.1275650

Goodley, D., & Runswick-Cole, K. (2011). The violence of disablism. *Sociology of Health & Illness, 33*(4), 602–617. https://doi.org/10.1111/j.1467-9566.2010.01302.x

Gopalkrishnan, N. (2018). Cultural diversity and mental health: Considerations for policy and practice. *Frontiers in Public Health, 6,* 179. https://doi.org/10.3389/fpubh.2018.00179

Gowin, M., Taylor, E. L., Dunnington, J., Alshuwaiyer, G., & Cheney, M. K. (2017). Needs of a silent minority: Mexican transgender asylum seekers. *Health Promotion Practice, 18*(3), 332–340. https://doi.org/10.1177/1524839917692750

Greene, B. (2010). Riding Trojan horses from symbolism to structural change: In feminist psychology, context matters. *Psychology of Women Quarterly, 34*(4), 443–457. https://doi.org/10.1111/j.1471-6402.2010.01594.x

Greene, B. (2013). The use and abuse of religious beliefs in dividing and conquering between socially marginalized groups: The same-sex marriage debate. *Psychology of Sexual Orientation and Gender Diversity, 1*(S), 35–44. https://doi.org/10.1037/2329-0382.1.S.35

Griffin, C. D., Echegoyén, R., & Hyman, J. (2020). The secret society: Perspectives from a multiracial cohort. *Contemporary Psychoanalysis, 56*(2–3), 282–304. https://doi.org/10.1080/00107530.2020.1777520

Griffiths, K. M., Carron-Arthur, B., Parsons, A., & Reid, R. (2014). Effectiveness of programs for reducing the stigma associated with mental disorders. A meta-analysis of randomized controlled trials. *World Psychiatry, 13*(2), 161–175. https://doi.org/10.1002/wps.20129

Guevara Carpio, M., Chee, N., Swarna, M., & Clauss-Ehlers, C. S. (2022). The consumer recovery movement in the United States: Historical considerations, key concepts, and next steps for action. In C. S. Clauss-Ehlers (Ed.), *The Cambridge handbook of community psychology: Interdisciplinary and contextual perspectives* (pp. 266–288). Cambridge University Press. https://doi.org/10.1017/9781108678971.017

Hall, E. T. (1973). *The silent language*. Anchor Books. (Original work published 1959)

Hall, G. C. N., Berkman, E. T., Zane, N. W., Leong, F. T. K., Hwang, W. C., Nezu, A. M., Nezu, C. M., Hong, J. J., Chu, J. P., & Huang, E. R. (2020). Reducing mental health disparities by increasing the personal relevance of interventions. *American Psychologist, 76*(1), 91–103. https://doi.org/10.1037/amp0000616

Hankerson, S. H., Suite, D., & Bailey, R. K. (2015). Treatment disparities among African American men with depression: Implications for clinical practice. *Journal of Health Care for the Poor and Underserved, 26*(1), 21–34. https://doi.org/10.1353/hpu.2015.0012

Hanna, D. (1988). *Designing organizations for high performance*. Prentice Hall.

Hanson, M. (2021). *Average cost of a doctorate degree.* https://educationdata.org/average-cost-of-a-doctorate-degree

Harris, M. (2003). Unto us a child: Abuse and deception in the Catholic Church. *Psychiatric Services, 54*(10), 1417–1418. https://doi.org/10.1176/appi.ps.54.10.1417

Harvey, M. R., & Tummala-Narra, P. (Eds.). (2007). *Sources and expressions of resiliency in trauma survivors: Ecological theory, multicultural practice.* Haworth Press.

Haynes, S. N., Kaholokula, J. K., & Tanaka-Matsumi, J. (2018). Psychometric foundations of psychological assessment with diverse cultures: What are the concepts, methods, and evidence? In C. L. Frisby & W. T. O'Donohue (Eds.), *Cultural competence in applied psychology* (pp. 441–472). Springer International. https://doi.org/10.1007/978-3-319-78997-2_18

Hays, P. A. (2016). *Addressing cultural complexities in practice: Assessment, diagnosis, and therapy* (3rd ed.). American Psychological Association. https://doi.org/10.1037/14801-000

Hechanova, R., & Waelde, L. (2017). The influence of culture on disaster mental health and psychosocial support interventions in Southeast Asia. *Mental Health, Religion & Culture, 20*(1), 31–44. https://doi.org/10.1080/13674676.2017.1322048

Heft, H. (2022). Lewin's "Psychological ecology" and the boundary of the psychological domain. *Philosophia Scientiæ, 26*(3), 189–210. https://doi.org/10.4000/philosophiascientiae.3643

Helms, J. E., & Cook, D. (1999). *Using race and culture in counseling and psychotherapy: Theory and process.* Allyn & Bacon.

Helms, J. E., Jernigan, M., & Mascher, J. (2005). The meaning of race in psychology and how to change it: A methodological perspective. *American Psychologist, 60*(1), 27–36. https://doi.org/10.1037/0003-066X.60.1.27

Henrich, J., Heine, S. J., & Norenzayan, A. (2010, July 1). Most people are not WEIRD. *Nature, 466*(7302), 29. https://doi.org/10.1038/466029a

Herman, J. L. (1992). *Trauma and recovery: The aftermath of violence.* Basic Books.

Hernandez, P., & McDowell, T. (2010). Intersectionality, power, and relational safety in context: Key concepts in clinical supervision. *Training and Education in Professional Psychology, 4*(1), 29–35. https://doi.org/10.1037/a0017064

Hilty, D. M. (2015). Advancing science, clinical care, and education: Shall we update Engel's biopsychosocial model to a bio-psycho-socio-cultural model? *Psychology and Cognitive Sciences, 1*(1), e1–e6. https://doi.org/10.17140/PCSOJ-1-e001

Hirst, S. P., Lane, A., & Stares, R. (2013). Health promotion with older adults experiencing mental health challenges: A literature review of strength-based approaches. *Clinical Gerontologist, 36*(4), 329–355. https://doi.org/10.1080/07317115.2013.788118

Holden, K. B., McGregor, B. S., Blanks, S. H., & Mahaffey, C. (2012). Psychosocial, socio-cultural, and environmental influences on mental health help-seeking among African-American men. *The Journal of Men's Health, 9*(2), 63–69. https://doi.org/10.1016/j.jomh.2012.03.002

Hook, A., & Andrews, B. (2005). The relationship of non-disclosure in therapy to shame and depression. *British Journal of Clinical Psychology, 44*(3), 425–438. https://doi.org/10.1348/014466505X34165

Hook, J. N., Farrell, J. E., Davis, D. E., DeBlaere, C., Van Tongeren, D. R., & Utsey, S. O. (2016). Cultural humility and racial microaggressions in counseling. *Journal of Counseling Psychology, 63*(3), 269–277. https://doi.org/10.1037/cou0000114

Hook, J. N., Watkins, C. E., Jr., Davis, D. E., Owen, J., Van Tongeren, D. R., & Marciana, J. R. (2016). Cultural humility in psychotherapy supervision. *American Journal of Psychotherapy, 70*(2), 149–166. https://doi.org/10.1176/appi.psychotherapy.2016.70.2.149

Hsueh, L., Werntz, A., Hobaica, S., Owens, S. A., Lumley, M. A., & Washburn, J. J. (2021). Clinical psychology PhD students' admission experiences: Implications for recruiting racial/ethnic minority and LGBTQ students. *Journal of Clinical Psychology, 77*(1), 105–120. https://doi.org/10.1002/jclp.23074

Huggins, R. (2016, June 30). *International online therapy: What to know before you go (and start doing it)*. Person Centered Tech. https://personcenteredtech.com/2016/06/30/international-online-therapy-know-go-start/

Hunter, M., & Rendall, M. (2007). Bio-psycho-socio-cultural perspectives on menopause. *Best Practice & Research: Clinical Obstetrics & Gynaecology, 21*(2), 261–274. https://doi.org/10.1016/j.bpobgyn.2006.11.001

Hunter, S. J. (2021). Promoting adolescent mental health: A transculturally informed approach to engaging developmental neuropsychology in the support of prevention and intervention. In C. S. Clauss-Ehlers (Ed.), *The Cambridge handbook of community psychology: Interdisciplinary and contextual perspectives* (pp. 310–330). Cambridge University Press. https://doi.org/10.1017/9781108678971.019

Hutchinson, A. (2016, April 5). New study shows targeted ads can influence self-perception, boost interest. *Social Media Today*. https://www.socialmediatoday.com/marketing/new-study-shows-targeted-ads-can-influence-self-perception-boost-interest

Institute for Health Metrics and Evaluation. (n.d.). *About GBD*. https://www.healthdata.org/gbd/about

Institute for Healthcare Improvement (IHI) Multimedia Team. (2015). *Like Magic? ("Every system is perfectly designed . . .")*. http://www.ihi.org/communities/blogs/origin-of-every-system-is-perfectly-designed-quote

Iotti, N. O., & Jungert, T. (2020). Children and poverty: A global approach. In C. S. Clauss-Ehlers, A. B. Sood, & M. D. Weist (Eds.), *Social justice for children and young people: International perspectives* (pp. 71–90). Cambridge University Press. https://doi.org/10.1017/9781108551830.006

Jacob, K. S. (2015). Recovery model of mental illness: A complementary approach to psychiatric care. *Indian Journal of Psychological Medicine, 37*(2), 117–119. https://doi.org/10.4103/0253-7176.155605

Jensen, E., Fazio-Ruggiero, K., & Belsham, D. (2021). A public health approach to delinquency and incarceration: A case study. In C. S. Clauss-Ehlers (Ed.),

The Cambridge handbook of community psychology: Interdisciplinary and contextual perspectives (pp. 468–494). Cambridge University Press. https://doi.org/10.1017/9781108678971.027

Ji, L. J., & Yap, S. (2016). Culture and cognition. *Current Opinion in Psychology*, 8, 105–111. https://doi.org/10.1016/j.copsyc.2015.10.004

Jones, C. P. (2001). Invited commentary: "Race," racism, and the practice of epidemiology. *American Journal of Epidemiology*, 154(4), 299–304. https://doi.org/10.1093/aje/154.4.299

Jones, J. M. (1997). *Prejudice and racism* (2nd ed.). McGraw Hill. (Original work published 1972)

Juvonen, J., Kogachi, K., & Graham, S. (2018). When and how do students benefit from ethnic diversity in middle school? *Child Development*, 89(4), 1268–1282. https://doi.org/10.1111/cdev.12834

Kaplan, E. F., Goodglass, H., & Weintraub, S. (1978). *The Boston Naming Test*. Lea & Febiger.

Katzmann, J. L., Mahfoud, F., Böhm, M., Schulz, M., & Laufs, U. (2018). Association of medication adherence and depression with the control of low-density lipoprotein cholesterol and blood pressure in patients at high cardiovascular risk. *Patient Preference and Adherence*, 13, 9–19. https://doi.org/10.2147/PPA.S182765

Kawachi, I., Subramanian, S. V., & Kim, D. (Eds.). (2008). *Social capital and health*. Springer. https://doi.org/10.1007/978-0-387-71311-3

Kessler, R. C., Amminger, G. P., Aguilar-Gaxiola, S., Alonso, J., Lee, S., & Üstün, T. B. (2007). Age of onset of mental disorders: A review of recent literature. *Current Opinion in Psychiatry*, 20(4), 359–364. https://doi.org/10.1097/YCO.0b013e32816ebc8c

Kiang, L., Witkow, M. R., & Thompson, T. L. (2016). Model minority stereotyping, perceived discrimination, and adjustment among adolescents from Asian American backgrounds. *Journal of Youth and Adolescence*, 45(7), 1366–1379. https://doi.org/10.1007/s10964-015-0336-7

Kim, D., Subramanian, S. V., & Kawachi, I. (2008). Social capital and physical health: A systematic review of the literature. In I. Kawachi, S. V. Subramanian, & D. Kim (Eds.), *Social capital and health* (pp. 139–190). Springer. https://doi.org/10.1007/978-0-387-71311-3_8

Kim, H. S., & Sasaki, J. Y. (2014). Cultural neuroscience: Biology of the mind in cultural contexts. *Annual Review of Psychology*, 65, 487–514. https://doi.org/10.1146/annurev-psych-010213-115040

Kim, M. T. (2002). Measuring depression in Korean Americans: Development of the Kim Depression Scale for Korean Americans. *Journal of Transcultural Nursing*, 13(2), 109–117. https://doi.org/10.1177/104365960201300203

Kim, P. Y., & Lee, D. (2014). Internalized model minority myth, Asian values, and help-seeking attitudes among Asian American students. *Cultural Diversity and Ethnic Minority Psychology*, 20(1), 98–106. https://doi.org/10.1037/a0033351

Kirmayer, L. J. (2015). Mindfulness in cultural context [Editorial]. *Transcultural Psychiatry, 52*(4), 447–469. https://doi.org/10.1177/1363461515598949

Kirmayer, L. J., Groleau, D., Guzder, J., Blake, C., & Jarvis, E. (2003). Cultural consultation: A model of mental health service for multicultural societies. *The Canadian Journal of Psychiatry, 48*(3), 145–153. https://doi.org/10.1177/070674370304800302

Kirmayer, L. J., & Ryder, A. G. (2016). Culture and psychopathology. *Current Opinion in Psychology, 8*, 143–148. https://doi.org/10.1016/j.copsyc.2015.10.020

Kit, K. A., Tuokko, H. A., & Mateer, C. A. (2008). A review of the stereotype threat literature and its application in a neurological population. *Neuropsychology Review, 18*(2), 132–148. https://doi.org/10.1007/s11065-008-9059-9

Kitayama, S., & Park, J. (2010). Cultural neuroscience of the self: Understanding the social grounding of the brain. *Social Cognitive and Affective Neuroscience, 5*(2–3), 111–129. https://doi.org/10.1093/scan/nsq052

Kivlighan, D. M., III, Hooley, I. W., Bruno, M. G., Ethington, L. L., Keeton, P. M., & Schreier, B. A. (2019). Examining therapist effects in relation to clients' race-ethnicity and gender: An intersectionality approach. *Journal of Counseling Psychology, 66*(1), 122–129. https://doi.org/10.1037/cou0000316

Kluckhohn, F. R., & Strodtbeck, F. L. (1961). *Variations in value orientations*. Row, Peterson.

Ko, D., Bal, A., Bird Bear, A., Sannino, A., & Engeström, Y. (2021). Transformative agency for justice: Addressing racial disparity of school discipline with the Indigenous Learning Lab. *Race, Ethnicity and Education*, 1–24. Advance online publication. https://doi.org/10.1080/13613324.2021.1969903

Kohut, H. (1959). Introspection, empathy, and psychoanalysis; an examination of the relationship between mode of observation and theory. *Journal of the American Psychoanalytic Association, 7*(3), 459–483. https://doi.org/10.1177/000306515900700304

Korteling, J. E., Brouwer, A. M., & Toet, A. (2018). A neural network framework for cognitive bias. *Frontiers in Psychology, 9*, 1561. https://doi.org/10.3389/fpsyg.2018.01561

Kottler, J. (1991). *The complete therapist*. Jossey-Bass.

Kozan, S., & Blustein, D. L. (2018). Implementing social change: A qualitative analysis of counseling psychologists' engagement in advocacy. *The Counseling Psychologist, 46*(2), 154–189. https://doi.org/10.1177/0011000018756882

Kumpfer, K. L. (1999). Factors and processes contributing to resilience: The resilience framework. In M. D. Glantz & J. L. Johnson (Eds.), *Resilience and development: Positive life adaptations* (pp. 179–224). Kluwer.

Kung, W. W. (2004). Cultural and practical barriers to seeking mental health treatment for Chinese Americans. *Journal of Community Psychology, 32*(1), 27–43. https://doi.org/10.1002/jcop.10077

LaFromboise, T. D., & Malik, S. S. (2016). A culturally informed approach to American Indian/Alaska Native youth suicide prevention. In N. Zane, G. Bernal, & F. T. Leong (Eds.), *Evidence-based psychological practice with ethnic minorities:*

Culturally informed research and clinical strategies (pp. 223–245). American Psychological Association. https://doi.org/10.1037/14940-011

La Roche, M. J. (2021). Changing multicultural guidelines: Clinical and research implications for evidence-based psychotherapies. *Professional Psychology, Research and Practice, 52*(2), 111–120. https://doi.org/10.1037/pro0000347

Lating, J. M., Barnett, J. E., & Horowitz, M. (2009). Increasing advocacy awareness within professional psychology training programs: The 2005 National Council of Schools and Programs of Professional Psychology survey. *Training and Education in Professional Psychology, 3*(2), 106–110. https://doi.org/10.1037/a0013662

Lavik, K. O., Veseth, M., Frøysa, H., Binder, P.-E., & Moltu, C. (2018). 'Nobody else can lead your life': What adolescents need from psychotherapists in change processes. *Counselling & Psychotherapy Research, 18*(3), 262–273. https://doi.org/10.1002/capr.12166

Leong, F. T. L., Leung, K., & Cheung, F. M. (2010). Integrating cross-cultural psychology research methods into ethnic minority psychology. *Cultural Diversity & Ethnic Minority Psychology, 16*(4), 590–597. https://doi.org/10.1037/a0020127

Levy, D. J., Heissel, J. A., Richeson, J. A., & Adam, E. K. (2016). Psychological and biological responses to race-based social stress as pathways to disparities in educational outcomes. *American Psychologist, 71*(6), 455–473. https://doi.org/10.1037/a0040322

Lewin, K. (1936). *Principles of topological psychology*. McGraw Hill. https://doi.org/10.1037/10019-000

Lewis, J. A., Williams, M. G., Peppers, E. J., & Gadson, C. A. (2017). Applying intersectionality to explore the relations between gendered racism and health among Black women. *Journal of Counseling Psychology, 64*(5), 475–486. https://doi.org/10.1037/cou0000231

Lim, J. K., & Golub, R. M. (2004). Graduate medical education research in the 21st century and *JAMA* on call. *JAMA, 292*(23), 2913–2915. https://doi.org/10.1001/jama.292.23.2913

Liptak, A. (2020, August 15). Civil rights law protects gay and transgender workers, Supreme Court rules. *The New York Times.* https://www.nytimes.com/2020/06/15/us/gay-transgender-workers-supreme-court.html

Locke, J., Rotheram-Fuller, E., & Kasari, C. (2012). Exploring the social impact of being a typical peer model for included children with autism spectrum disorder. *Journal of Autism and Developmental Disorders, 42*(9), 1895–1905. https://doi.org/10.1007/s10803-011-1437-0

Losin, E. A. R., Woo, C. W., Medina, N. A., Andrews-Hanna, J. R., Eisenbarth, H., & Wager, T. D. (2020). Neural and sociocultural mediators of ethnic differences in pain. *Nature Human Behaviour, 4*(5), 517–530. https://doi.org/10.1038/s41562-020-0819-8

Luthar, S. S. (2003). The culture of affluence: Psychological costs of material wealth. *Child Development, 74*(6), 1581–1593. https://doi.org/10.1046/j.1467-8624.2003.00625.x

Ma, Y., & Siu, A. F. Y. (2020). Dispositional mindfulness and mental health in Hong Kong college students: The mediating roles of decentering and self-acceptance. *Australian Journal of Psychology, 72*(2), 156–164. https://doi.org/10.1111/ajpy.12269

Machová, K., Kejdanová, P., Bajtlerová, I., Procházková, R., Svobodová, I., & Mezian, K. (2018). Canine-assisted speech therapy for children with communication impairments: A randomized controlled trial. *Anthrozoos, 31*(5), 587–598. https://doi.org/10.1080/08927936.2018.1505339

Macunovich, D. J. (2002). *Birth quake: The baby boom and its aftershocks*. The University of Chicago Press. https://doi.org/10.7208/chicago/9780226500928.001.0001

Mann, M. A. (2006). The formation and development of individual and ethnic identity: Insights from psychiatry and psychoanalytic theory. *The American Journal of Psychoanalysis, 66*(3), 211–224. https://doi.org/10.1007/s11231-006-9018-2

Marsella, A. J. (2011, October). Twelve critical issues for mental health professionals working with ethno-culturally diverse populations. *Psychology International*. https://www.apa.org/international/pi/2011/10/critical-issues.aspx

Mason, E. I. (2018). *Rapport during the assessment process: A survey of school psychologists* [Unpublished doctoral dissertation]. James Madison University. https://commons.lib.jmu.edu/edspec201019/134

Masten, A. S., Best, K. M., & Garmezy, N. (1990). Resilience and development: Contributions from the study of children who overcome adversity. *Development and Psychopathology, 2*(4), 425–444. https://doi.org/10.1017/S0954579400005812

Matiz, A., Fabbro, F., Paschetto, A., Cantone, D., Paolone, A. R., & Crescentini, C. (2020). Positive impact of mindfulness meditation on mental health of female teachers during the COVID-19 outbreak in Italy. *International Journal of Environmental Research and Public Health, 17*(18), 6450. https://doi.org/10.3390/ijerph17186450

Matz, S. C., Kosinski, M., Nave, G., & Stillwell, D. J. (2017). Psychological targeting as an effective approach to digital mass persuasion. *Proceedings of the National Academy of Sciences of the United States of America, 114*(48), 12714–12719. https://doi.org/10.1073/pnas.1710966114

Mazzocco, P. J. (2017). *The psychology of racial colorblindness*. Palgrave/Macmillan. https://doi.org/10.1057/978-1-137-59302-3

Mazzula, S., & Nadal, K. L. (2015). Racial microaggressions, Whiteness, and feminist therapy. *Women & Therapy, 38*(3–4), 308–326. https://doi.org/10.1080/02703149.2015.1059214

McCormick-Huhn, K., Warner, L. R., Settles, I. H., & Shields, S. A. (2019). What if psychology took intersectionality seriously? Changing how psychologists think about participants. *Psychology of Women Quarterly*, *43*(4), 445–456. https://doi.org/10.1177/0361684319866430

McGee, E. O., & Stovall, D. (2015). Reimagining critical race theory in education: Mental health, healing, and the pathway to liberatory praxis. *Educational Theory*, *65*(5), 491–511. https://doi.org/10.1111/edth.12129

McKown, C. (2005). Applying ecological theory to advance the science and practice of school-based prejudice reduction interventions. *Educational Psychologist*, *40*(3), 177–189. https://doi.org/10.1207/s15326985ep4003_5

McLaughlin, E. C. (2020, August 9). How George Floyd's death ignited a racial reckoning that shows no signs of slowing down. *CNN*. https://www.cnn.com/2020/08/09/us/george-floyd-protests-different-why/index.html

McLeod, J. D., Lawler, E. J., & Schwalbe, M. (Eds.). (2014). *Handbook of social psychology of inequality*. Springer. https://doi.org/10.1007/978-94-017-9002-4

McPherson, K. E., Kerr, S., McGee, E., Morgan, A., Cheater, F. M., McLean, J., & Egan, J. (2014). The association between social capital and mental health and behavioural problems in children and adolescents: An integrative systematic review. *BMC Psychology*, *2*(1), 7. https://doi.org/10.1186/2050-7283-2-7

The Media Insight Project. (2014, March 17). *The personal news cycle*. American Press Institute. https://apnorc.org/projects/the-media-insight-project/

Meier, A., & Allen, G. (2009). Romantic relationships from adolescence to young adulthood: Evidence from the National Longitudinal Study of Adolescent Health. *The Sociological Quarterly*, *50*(2), 308–335. https://doi.org/10.1111/j.1533-8525.2009.01142.x

Mena, J. A., & Quina, K. (Eds.). (2019). *Integrating multiculturalism and intersectionality into the psychology curriculum: Strategies for instructors*. American Psychological Association. https://doi.org/10.1037/0000137-000

Mereish, E. H., & Poteat, V. P. (2015). A relational model of sexual minority mental and physical health: The negative effects of shame on relationships, loneliness, and health. *Journal of Counseling Psychology*, *62*(3), 425–437. https://doi.org/10.1037/cou0000088

Merriam-Webster. (n.d.). Language. In *Merriam-Webster.com dictionary*. Retrieved August 22, 2022, from https://www.merriam-webster.com/dictionary/language

Metzl, J., & Hansen, H. (2014). Structural competency: Theorizing a new medical engagement with stigma and inequality. *Social Science & Medicine*, *103*, 126–133. https://doi.org/10.1016/j.socscimed.2013.06.032

Miller, C., & Stassun, K. (2014, June 11). A test that fails. *Nature*, *510*(7504), 303–304. https://doi.org/10.1038/nj7504-303a

Mills, C., & Ballantyne, J. (2016). Social justice and teacher education: A systematic review of empirical work in the field. *Journal of Teacher Education*, *67*(4), 263–276. https://doi.org/10.1177/0022487116660152

Mills, S. D., Fox, R. S., Bohan, S., Roesch, S. C., Sadler, G. R., & Malcarne, V. L. (2020). Psychosocial and neighborhood correlates of health-related quality of life: A multi-level study among Hispanic adults. *Cultural Diversity & Ethnic Minority Psychology, 26*(1), 1–10. https://doi.org/10.1037/cdp0000274

Miranda, J., McGuire, T. G., Williams, D. R., & Wang, P. (2008). Mental health in the context of health disparities. *The American Journal of Psychiatry, 165*(9), 1102–1108. https://doi.org/10.1176/appi.ajp.2008.08030333

Mohamud, F., Edwards, T., Antwi-Boasiako, K., William, K., King, J., Igor, E., & King, B. (2021). Racial disparity in the Ontario child welfare system: Conceptualizing policies and practices that drive involvement for Black families. *Children and Youth Services Review, 120*, 105711. Advance online publication. https://doi.org/10.1016/j.childyouth.2020.105711

Moon, S. H., & Sandage, S. J. (2019). Cultural humility for people of color: Critique of current theory and practice. *Journal of Psychology and Theology, 47*(2), 76–86. https://doi.org/10.1177/0091647119842407

Moradi, B., & Grzanka, P. R. (2017). Using intersectionality responsibly: Toward critical epistemology, structural analysis, and social justice activism. *Journal of Counseling Psychology, 64*(5), 500–513. https://doi.org/10.1037/cou0000203

Morris, E. R., Lindley, L., & Galupo, M. P. (2020). "Better issues to focus on": Transgender microaggressions as ethical violations in therapy. *The Counseling Psychologist, 48*(6), 883–915. https://doi.org/10.1177/0011000020924391

Morrow, S. L. (2005). Quality and trustworthiness in qualitative research in counseling psychology. *Journal of Counseling Psychology, 52*, 250–260. https://doi.org/10.1037/0022-0167.52.2.250

Mosher, D. K., Hook, J. N., Captari, L. E., Davis, D. E., DeBlaere, C., & Owen, J. (2017). Cultural humility: A therapeutic framework for engaging diverse clients. *Practice Innovations, 2*(4), 221–233. https://doi.org/10.1037/pri0000055

Musisi, S., & Kinyanda, E. (2020). Long-term impact of war, civil war, and persecution in civilian populations-conflict and post-traumatic stress in African communities. *Frontiers in Psychiatry, 11*, 20. https://doi.org/10.3389/fpsyt.2020.00020

Nadal, K. L., Davidoff, K. C., Davis, L. S., Wong, Y., Marshall, D., & McKenzie, V. (2015). A qualitative approach to intersectional microaggressions: Understanding influences of race, ethnicity, gender, sexuality, and religion. *Qualitative Psychology, 2*(2), 147–163. https://doi.org/10.1037/qup0000026

Nandi, A., & Platt, L. (2015). Patterns of minority and majority identification in a multicultural society. *Ethnic and Racial Studies, 38*(15), 2615–2634. https://doi.org/10.1080/01419870.2015.1077986

Nash, E., Mohammed, L., Cappello, O., & Naide, S. (2019). *State policy trends 2019: A wave of abortion bans, but some states are fighting back*. Guttmacher Institute. https://www.guttmacher.org/article/2019/12/state-policy-trends-2019-wave-abortion-bans-some-states-are-fighting-back

National Alliance on Mental Illness. (2015, March 31). *Mental health parity: Still a long way to go.* https://www.nami.org/Blogs/NAMI-Blog/April-2015/Mental-Health-Parity-Still-a-Long-Way-to-Go

National Association of Social Workers. (2015). *Standards and indicators for cultural competence in social work practice.* https://www.socialworkers.org/LinkClick.aspx?fileticket=PonPTDEBrn4%3D

Nations Online. (n.d.). *Countries of the Americas.* https://www.nationsonline.org/oneworld/america.htm

Neville, H. A., Gallardo, M. E., & Sue, D. W. (Eds.). (2016). *The myths of racial color blindness: Manifestations, dynamics, and impact.* American Psychological Association. https://doi.org/10.1037/14754-000

Nielsen, M., Haun, D., Kärtner, J., & Legare, C. H. (2017). The persistent sampling bias in developmental psychology: A call to action. *Journal of Experimental Child Psychology, 162,* 31–38. https://doi.org/10.1016/j.jecp.2017.04.017

Nordquist, R. (2019, July 29). *Learn the function of code switching as a linguistic term.* ThoughtCo. https://www.thoughtco.com/code-switching-language-1689858

Norenzayan, A., & Lee, A. (2010). It was meant to happen: Explaining cultural variations in fate attributions. *Journal of Personality and Social Psychology, 98*(5), 702–720. https://doi.org/10.1037/a0019141

Nuñez, A., González, P., Talavera, G. A., Sanchez-Johnsen, L., Roesch, S. C., Davis, S. M., Arguelles, W., Womack, V. Y., Ostrovsky, N. W., Ojeda, L., Penedo, F. J., & Gallo, L. C. (2016). Machismo, marianismo, and negative cognitive-emotional factors: Findings from the Hispanic Community Health Study/Study of Latinos Sociocultural Ancillary Study. *Journal of Latina/o Psychology, 4*(4), 202–217. https://doi.org/10.1037/lat0000050

Obergefell v. Hodges, 576 U.S. ___ (2015). https://www.supremecourt.gov/opinions/14pdf/14-556_3204.pdf

Office of the Surgeon General, Center for Mental Health Services, National Institute of Mental Health. (2001). *Mental health: Culture, race and ethnicity.* https://www.ncbi.nlm.nih.gov/books/NBK44243/

Olkin, R., Hayward, H., Abbene, M. S., & VanHeel, G. (2019). The experiences of microaggressions against women with visible and invisible disabilities. *Journal of Social Issues, 75*(3), 757–785. https://doi.org/10.1111/josi.12342

Owen, J., Jordan, T. A., II, Turner, D., Davis, D. E., Hook, J. N., & Leach, M. M. (2014). Therapists' multicultural orientation: Client perceptions of cultural humility, spiritual/religious commitment, and therapy outcomes. *Journal of Psychology and Theology, 42*(1), 91–98. https://doi.org/10.1177/009164711404200110

Owen, J., Tao, K. W., Drinane, J. M., Hook, J., Davis, D. E., & Kune, N. F. (2016). Client perceptions of therapists' multicultural orientation: Cultural (missed) opportunities and cultural humility. *Professional Psychology: Research and Practice, 47*(1), 30–37. https://doi.org/10.1037/pro0000046

Padesky, C. A., & Mooney, K. A. (2012). Strengths-based cognitive-behavioural therapy: A four-step model to build resilience. *Clinical Psychology & Psychotherapy, 19*(4), 283–290. https://doi.org/10.1002/cpp.1795

Parham, W. D., & Clauss-Ehlers, C. S. (2016a). Celebrating our elders who led us across the bridge: A call to action for the academy. *Journal of Multicultural Counseling and Development, 44*(1), 4–27. https://doi.org/10.1002/jmcd.12034

Parham, W. D., & Clauss-Ehlers, C. S. (2016b). Following inspiration: A conversation with Former First Lady Rosalynn Carter. *Journal of Multicultural Counseling and Development, 44*(3), 156–175. https://doi.org/10.1002/jmcd.12044

Park, N., & Peterson, C. (2008). Positive psychology and character strengths: Application to strengths-based school counseling. *Professional School Counseling, 12*(2), 85–92. https://doi.org/10.1177/2156759X0801200214

Pasquerella, L., & Whitehead, D. M. (2020). Educational access for women and girls as a social justice issue: Ghana as a case study. In C. S. Clauss-Ehlers, A. B. Sood, & M. D. Weist (Eds.), *Social justice for children and young people: International perspectives* (pp. 91–105). Cambridge University Press. https://doi.org/10.1017/9781108551830.007

Patallo, B. J. (2019). The *Multicultural Guidelines* in practice: Cultural humility in clinical training and supervision. *Training and Education in Professional Psychology, 13*(3), 227–232. https://doi.org/10.1037/tep0000253

Pattoni, L. (2012, May 1). *Strengths-based approaches for working with individuals: Insight, 16*. Iriss. https://www.iriss.org.uk/resources/insights/strengths-based-approaches-working-individuals

Pearrow, M. M., & Fallon, L. (2019). Integrating social justice and advocacy into training psychologists: A practical demonstration. *Psychological Services*. Advance online publication. https://doi.org/10.1037/ser0000384

Pedersen, P. B. (1997). *Culture-centered counseling interventions: Striving for accuracy*. SAGE.

Pedrotti, J. T., Edwards, L. M., & Lopez, S. J. (2009). Positive psychology within a cultural context. In S. J. Lopez & C. R. Snyder (Eds.), *The Oxford handbook of positive psychology* (pp. 49–57). Oxford University Press.

Peek, M. E., Wilkes, A. E., Roberson, T. S., Goddu, A. P., Nocon, R. S., Tang, H., Quinn, M. T., Bordenave, K. K., Huang, E. S., & Chin, M. H. (2012). Early lessons from an initiative on Chicago's South Side to reduce disparities in diabetes care and outcomes. *Health Affairs, 31*(1), 177–186. https://doi.org/10.1377/hlthaff.2011.1058

Pelzang, R., & Hutchinson, A. M. (2018). Establishing cultural integrity in qualitative research: Reflections from a cross-cultural study. *International Journal of Qualitative Research, 17*(1), 1–9. https://doi.org/10.1177/1609406917749702

Petersen, S. (2017). Human subject review standards and procedures in international research: Critical ethical and cultural issues and recommendations. *International Perspectives in Psychology: Research, Practice, Consultation, 6*(3), 165–178. https://doi.org/10.1037/ipp0000072

Petersen, S. L., Erenrich, E. S., Levine, D. L., Vigoreaux, J., & Gile, K. (2018). Multi-institutional study of GRE scores as predictors of STEM PhD degree completion: GRE gets a low mark. *PLOS ONE, 13*(10), Article e0206570. Advance online publication. https://doi.org/10.1371/journal.pone.0206570

Peterson, W. (1966, January 9). Success story: Japanese-American style. *New York Times Magazine*, 20–43. https://www.nytimes.com/1966/01/09/archives/success-story-japaneseamerican-style-success-story-japaneseamerican.html

Phillipson, C., Leach, R., Money, A., & Biggs, S. (2008). Social and cultural constructions of ageing: The case of the baby boomers. *Sociological Research Online*, *13*(3), 1–14. https://doi.org/10.5153/sro.1695

Phinney, J. (1996). When we talk about American ethnic groups, what do we mean? *American Psychologist*, *3*(1), 918–927. https://doi.org/10.1037/0003-066X.51.9.918

Ponterotto, J. G. (2010). Qualitative research in multicultural psychology: Philosophical underpinnings, popular approaches, and ethical considerations. *Cultural Diversity & Ethnic Minority Psychology*, *16*(4), 581–589. https://doi.org/10.1037/a0012051

Ponterotto, J. G., Casas, J. M., Suzuki, L. A., & Alexander, C. M. (2010). *Handbook of multicultural counseling* (3rd ed.). SAGE.

Posner, S. F., Stewart, A. L., Marín, G., & Pérez-Stable, E. J. (2001). Factor variability of the Center for Epidemiological Studies Depression Scale (CES-D) among urban Latinos. *Ethnicity & Health*, *6*(2), 137–144. https://doi.org/10.1080/13557850120068469

Provenzi, L., Guida, E., & Montirosso, R. (2018). Preterm behavioral epigenetics: A systematic review. *Neuroscience and Biobehavioral Reviews*, *84*, 262–271. https://doi.org/10.1016/j.neubiorev.2017.08.020

Purdie-Vaughns, V., & Eibach, R. P. (2008). Intersectional invisibility: The distinctive advantages and disadvantages of multiple subordinate-group identities. *Sex Roles*, *59*(5–6), 377–391. https://doi.org/10.1007/s11199-008-9424-4

Ransdell, L. B., Lane, T. S., Schwartz, A. L., Wayment, H. A., & Baldwin, J. A. (2021). Mentoring new and early-stage investigators and underrepresented minority faculty for research success in health-related fields: An integrative literature review (2010–2020). *International Journal of Environmental Research and Public Health*, *18*(2), 432. https://doi.org/10.3390/ijerph18020432

Rathod, S., Gega, L., Degnan, A., Pikard, J., Khan, T., Husain, N., Munshi, T., & Naeem, F. (2018). The current status of culturally adapted mental health interventions: A practice-focused review of meta-analyses. *Neuropsychiatric Disease and Treatment*, *14*, 165–178. https://doi.org/10.2147/NDT.S138430

Rattan, A., & Ambady, N. (2013). Diversity ideologies and intergroup relations: An examination of colorblindness and multiculturalism. *European Journal of Social Psychology*, *43*(1), 12–21. https://doi.org/10.1002/ejsp.1892

Ratts, M. J., Singh, A. A., Nassar-McMillan, S., Butler, S. K., & McCullough, J. R. (2016). Multicultural and social justice counseling competencies: Guidelines for the counseling profession. *Journal of Multicultural Counseling and Development*, *44*(1), 28–48. https://doi.org/10.1002/jmcd.12035

Reardon, S. F., Fox, L., & Townsend, J. (2015). Neighborhood income composition by race and income, 1990–2009. *The Annals of the American Academy of Political and Social Science, 660*(1), 78–97. https://doi.org/10.1177/0002716215576104

Renbarger, R., & Morgan, G. (2018). Norming. In B. Frey (Ed.), *The SAGE encyclopedia of educational research, measurement, and evaluation* (pp. 1158–1160). SAGE. https://doi.org/10.4135/9781506326139.n477

Rennie, D. L. (2004). Reflexivity and person-centered counseling. *Journal of Humanistic Psychology, 44*(2), 182–203. https://doi.org/10.1177/0022167804263066

Rhodes, J. E., Parrett, N. S., & Mason, O. J. (2016). A qualitative study of refugees with psychotic symptoms. *Psychosis, 8*(1), 1–11. https://doi.org/10.1080/17522439.2015.1045547

Rivera Mindt, M., Byrd, D., Saez, P., & Manly, J. (2010). Increasing culturally competent neuropsychological services for ethnic minority populations: A call to action. *The Clinical Neuropsychologist, 24*(3), 429–453. https://doi.org/10.1080/13854040903058960

Robinson, D. J., Coons, M., Haensel, H., Vallis, M., Yale, J. F., & the Diabetes Canada Clinical Practice Guidelines Expert Committee. (2018). Diabetes and mental health. *Canadian Journal of Diabetes, 42*(Suppl. 1), S130–S141. https://doi.org/10.1016/j.jcjd.2017.10.031

Rosenthal, L. (2016). Incorporating intersectionality into psychology: An opportunity to promote social justice and equity. *American Psychologist, 71*(6), 474–485. https://doi.org/10.1037/a0040323

Roth, T. L. (2013). Epigenetic mechanisms in the development of behavior: Advances, challenges, and future promises of a new field. *Development and Psychopathology, 25*(4, Pt. 2), 1279–1291. https://doi.org/10.1017/S0954579413000618

Rule, N. O., Freeman, J. B., & Ambady, N. (2013). Culture in social neuroscience: A review. *Social Neuroscience, 8*(1), 3–10. https://doi.org/10.1080/17470919.2012.695293

Ruth, R. (2012). Contemporary psychodynamic perspectives on multiple minority identities. In R. Nettles & R. Balter (Eds.), *Multiple minority identities: Applications for practice, research, and training* (pp. 163–184). Springer.

Ryan, D. A., Singh, M. R., Hentschke, E. A., & Bullock, H. E. (2018). "Minding the gap": Social psychological insights for strengthening interclass relations and advancing economic justice. *Translational Issues in Psychological Science, 4*(2), 187–197. https://doi.org/10.1037/tps0000158

Sameroff, A. J. (2009). *The transactional model of development: How children and contexts shape each other*. American Psychological Association. https://doi.org/10.1037/11877-000

Sandage, S. J., Rupert, D., Stavros, G. S., & Devor, N. G. (2020). *Relational spirituality in psychotherapy: Healing suffering and promoting growth*. American Psychological Association. https://doi.org/10.1037/0000174-000

Sandoval, J. A., Lucero, J., Oetzel, J., Avila, M., Belone, L., Mau, M., Pearson, C., Tafoya, G., Duran, B., Iglesias Rios, L., & Wallerstein, N. (2012). Process and outcome constructs for evaluating community-based participatory research projects: A matrix of existing measures. *Health Education Research, 27*(4), 680–690. https://doi.org/10.1093/her/cyr087

Schooler, D., Ward, L. M., Merriweather, A., & Caruthers, A. (2004). Who's that girl: Television's role in the body image development of young White and Black women. *Psychology of Women Quarterly, 28*(1), 38–47. https://doi.org/10.1111/j.1471-6402.2004.00121.x

Seeley, K. (2005). The listening cure: Listening for culture in intercultural psychological treatments. *The Psychoanalytic Review, 92*(3), 431–452. https://doi.org/10.1521/prev.92.3.431.66539

Seligman, M. E. P. (2019). Positive psychology: A personal history. *Annual Review of Clinical Psychology, 15*(1), 1–23. https://doi.org/10.1146/annurev-clinpsy-050718-095653

Seward, D. X. (2014). Multicultural course pedagogy: Experiences of master's-level students of color. *Counselor Education and Supervision, 53*(1), 62–79. https://doi.org/10.1002/j.1556-6978.2014.00049.x

Sexton, T., Gordon, K. C., Gurman, A., Lebow, J., Holtzworth-Munroe, A., & Johnson, S. (2011). Guidelines for classifying evidence-based treatments in couple and family therapy. *Family Process, 50*(3), 377–392. https://doi.org/10.1111/j.1545-5300.2011.01363.x

Sexton, T. L., Kinser, J. C., & Hanes, C. W. (2008). Beyond a single standard: Levels of evidence approach for evaluating marriage and family therapy research and practice. *Journal of Family Therapy, 30*(4), 386–398. https://doi.org/10.1111/j.1467-6427.2008.00444.x

Shannon, P. J., Wieling, E., McCleary, J. S., & Becher, E. (2015). Exploring the mental health effects of political trauma with newly arrived refugees. *Qualitative Health Research, 25*(4), 443–457. https://doi.org/10.1177/1049732314549475

Sharpley, C. F., Fairnie, E., Tabary-Collins, E., Bates, R., & Lee, P. (2000). The use of counsellor verbal response modes and client-perceived rapport. *Counselling Psychology Quarterly, 13*(1), 99–116. https://doi.org/10.1080/09515070050011097

Sheely-Moore, A. I., & Bratton, S. C. (2010). A strengths-based parenting intervention with low-income African American families. *Professional School Counseling, 13*(3), 175–183. https://doi.org/10.5330/PSC.n.2010-13.175

Shepard, B. (2003). In search of a winning script: Moral panic vs institutional denial. *Sexualities, 6*(1), 54–59. https://doi.org/10.1177/1363460703006001006

Sheps, D. S., & Sheffield, D. (2001). Depression, anxiety, and the cardiovascular system: The cardiologist's perspective. *The Journal of Clinical Psychiatry, 62*(Suppl. 8), 12–16.

Shin, R. Q., Welch, J. C., Kaya, A. E., Yeung, J. G., Obana, C., Sharma, R., Vernay, C. N., & Yee, S. (2017). The intersectionality framework and identity intersections in the *Journal of Counseling Psychology* and *The Counseling Psychologist*: A content analysis. *Journal of Counseling Psychology, 64*(5), 458–474. https://doi.org/10.1037/cou0000204

Shonkoff, J. P., & Meisels, S. J. (2000). *Handbook of early childhood intervention* (2nd ed.). Cambridge University Press. https://doi.org/10.1017/CBO9780511529320

Siegler, M. (2019). Clinical medical ethics: Its history and contributions to American medicine. *The Journal of Clinical Ethics, 30*(1), 17–26.

Smedley, B. D., Stith, A. Y., & Nelson, A. R. (Eds.). (2003). *Unequal treatment: Confronting racial and ethnic disparities in healthcare*. The National Academies Press. https://doi.org/10.17226/12875

Smith, B. L. (2018). Spanish-speaking psychologists in demand: By learning or perfecting their Spanish, practitioners can better serve a large and growing population. *APA Monitor, 49*(6), 68.

Smith, L., & Lau, M. Y. (2013). Exploring the corollaries of students' social justice intentionality. *Education, Citizenship and Social Justice, 8*(1), 59–71. https://doi.org/10.1177/1746197912461327

Soheilian, S. S., Inman, A. G., Klinger, R. S., Isenberg, D. S., & Kulp, L. E. (2014). Multicultural supervision: Supervisees' reflections on culturally competent supervision. *Counselling Psychology Quarterly, 27*(4), 379–392. https://doi.org/10.1080/09515070.2014.961408

Solano-Flores, G. (2011). Assessing the cultural validity of assessment practices: An introduction. In M. del Rosario Basterra, E. Trumbull, & G. Solano-Flores (Eds.), *Cultural validity in assessment: Addressing linguistic and cultural diversity* (pp. 3–21). Routledge Taylor & Francis Group.

Solano-Flores, G., & Nelson-Barber, S. (2001). On the cultural validity of science assessments. *Journal of Research in Science Teaching, 38*(5), 553–573. https://doi.org/10.1002/tea.1018

Solomonov, N., & Barber, J. P. (2018). Patients' perspectives on political self-disclosure, the therapeutic alliance, and the infiltration of politics into the therapy room in the Trump era. *Journal of Clinical Psychology, 74*(5), 779–787. https://doi.org/10.1002/jclp.22609

Spencer, S. J., Logel, C., & Davies, P. G. (2016). Stereotype threat. *Annual Review of Psychology, 67*(1), 415–437. https://doi.org/10.1146/annurev-psych-073115-103235

Spengler, E. S., Miller, D. J., & Spengler, P. M. (2016). Microaggressions: Clinical errors with sexual minority clients. *Psychotherapy, 53*(3), 360–366. https://doi.org/10.1037/pst0000073

Spilka, M. J., & Dobson, K. S. (2015). Promoting the internationalization of evidence-based practice: Benchmarking as a strategy to evaluate culturally transported psychological treatments. *Clinical Psychology: Science and Practice, 22*(1), 58–75. https://doi.org/10.1111/cpsp.12092

Steele, C. M. (1997). A threat in the air. How stereotypes shape intellectual identity and performance. *American Psychologist, 52*(6), 613–629. https://doi.org/10.1037/0003-066X.52.6.613

Stephens, N. M., Markus, H. R., & Phillips, L. T. (2014). Social class culture cycles: How three gateway contexts shape selves and fuel inequality. *Annual Review* of *Psychology*, *65*(1), 611–634. https://doi.org/10.1146/annurev-psych-010213-115143

Streit, C., Carlo, G., & Killoren, S. E. (2020). Ethnic socialization, identity, and values associated with U.S. Latino/a young adults' prosocial behaviors. *Cultural Diversity & Ethnic Minority Psychology*, *26*(1), 102–111. https://doi.org/10.1037/cdp0000280

Stringfellow, J. W., & Muscari, K. D. (2003). A program of support for consumer participation in systems change: The West Virginia Leadership Academy. *Journal of Disability Policy Studies*, *14*(3), 142–147. https://doi.org/10.1177/10442073030140030301

Sue, D. W. (2008). Multicultural organization consultation: A social justice perspective. *Consulting Psychology Journal*, *60*(2), 157–169. https://doi.org/10.1037/0736-9735.60.2.157

Sue, D. W., Arredondo, P., & McDavis, R. J. (1992). Multicultural counseling competencies and standards: A call to the profession. *Journal of Multicultural Counseling and Development*, *20*(2), 64–88. https://doi.org/10.1002/j.2161-1912.1992.tb00563.x

Sue, D. W., Bernier, J. E., Durran, A., Feinberg, L., Pedersen, P., Smith, E. J., & Vasquez-Nuttall, E. (1982). Position paper: Cross-cultural counseling competencies. *The Counseling Psychologist*, *10*(2), 45–52. https://doi.org/10.1177/0011000082102008

Sue, D. W., Capodilupo, C. M., Torino, G. C., Bucceri, J. M., Holder, A. M. B., Nadal, K. L., & Esquilin, M. (2007). Racial microaggressions in everyday life: Implications for clinical practice. *American Psychologist*, *62*(4), 271–286. https://doi.org/10.1037/0003-066X.62.4.271

Sue, D. W., & Sue, D. (2016). *Counseling the culturally diverse: Theory and practice* (7th ed.). Wiley.

Sue, D. W., Sue, D., Neville, H. A., & Smith, L. (2019). *Counseling the culturally different: Theory and practice*. Wiley.

Suzuki, L., Caso, T., West-Olatunji, C., & Prendes-Lintel, M. (2021). Conducting culturally responsive community needs assessments. In C. S. Clauss-Ehlers (Ed.), *The Cambridge handbook of community psychology: Interdisciplinary and contextual perspectives* (pp. 115–136). Cambridge University Press. https://doi.org/10.1017/9781108678971.009

Swift, J. K., & Greenberg, R. P. (2012). Premature discontinuation in adult psychotherapy: A meta-analysis. *Journal of Consulting and Clinical Psychology*, *80*(4), 547–559. https://doi.org/10.1037/a0028226

Swiss Academy of Sciences (SCNAT). (2018). *Commission for Research Partnerships with Developing Countries* (KFPE). https://kfpe.scnat.ch/en

Szymanski, D. M., Kashubeck-West, S., & Meyer, J. (2008). Internalized heterosexism: Measurement, psychosocial correlates, and research directions. *The Counseling Psychologist*, *36*(4), 525–574. https://doi.org/10.1177/0011000007309489

Tajino, A., & Smith, C. (2016). Beyond team teaching: An introduction to team learning in language education. In A. Tajino, T. Stewart, & D. Dalsky (Eds.), *Team teaching and team learning in the language classroom: Collaboration for innovation in ELT* (pp. 11–28). Routledge Taylor & Francis Group.

Tay, A. K., Rees, S., Chen, J., Kareth, M., & Silove, D. (2015). Pathways involving traumatic losses, worry about family, adult separation anxiety and post-traumatic stress symptoms amongst refugees from West Papua. *Journal of Anxiety Disorders, 35*(1), 1–8. https://doi.org/10.1016/j.janxdis.2015.07.001

Tervalon, M., & Murray-García, J. (1998). Cultural humility versus cultural competence: A critical distinction in defining physician training outcomes in multicultural education. *Journal of Health Care for the Poor and Underserved, 9*(2), 117–125. https://doi.org/10.1353/hpu.2010.0233

Thompson, R. R., Jones, N. M., Holman, E. A., & Silver, R. C. (2019, April 17). Media exposure to mass violence events can fuel a cycle of distress. *Science Advances, 5*(4), eaav3502. Advance online publication. https://doi.org/10.1126/sciadv.aav3502

Thornicroft, G., Deb, T., & Henderson, C. (2016). Community mental health care worldwide: Current status and further developments. *World Psychiatry, 15*(3), 276–286. https://doi.org/10.1002/wps.20349

Triandis, H. C. (2018). *Individualism and collectivism*. Taylor & Francis Group. https://doi.org/10.4324/9780429499845

Trimble, J. E. (2007). Prolegomena for the connotation of construct use in the measurement of ethnic and racial identity. *Journal of Counseling Psychology, 54*(3), 247–258. https://doi.org/10.1037/0022-0167.54.3.247

Trimble, J. E., & Bhadra, M. (2013). Ethnic gloss. In K. D. Keith (Ed.), *The encyclopedia of cross-cultural psychology* (Vol. II, pp. 500–504). Wiley Online Library. https://doi.org/10.1002/9781118339893.wbeccp204

Tummala-Narra, P. (2004). Dynamics of race and culture in the supervisory encounter. *Psychoanalytic Psychology, 21*(2), 300–311. https://doi.org/10.1037/0736-9735.21.2.300

Tummala-Narra, P. (2007). Conceptualizing trauma and resilience across diverse contexts: A multicultural perspective. *Journal of Aggression, Maltreatment & Trauma, 14*(1–2), 33–53. https://doi.org/10.1300/J146v14n01_03

Tummala-Narra, P. (2016). *Psychoanalytic theory and cultural competence in psychotherapy*. American Psychological Association. https://doi.org/10.1037/14800-000

Tummala-Narra, P. (2021). Interpersonal violence and the immigrant context. In P. Tummala-Narra (Ed.), *Trauma and racial minority immigrants: Turmoil, uncertainty, and resistance* (pp. 205–225). American Psychological Association. https://doi.org/10.1037/0000214-012

Tummala-Narra, P., Gonzalez, L. D., & Hailes, H. (2021). Women and immigration. In C. S. Clauss-Ehlers (Ed.), *The Cambridge handbook of community psychology: Interdisciplinary and contextual perspectives* (pp. 511–538). Cambridge University Press. https://doi.org/10.1017/9781108678971.029

Tummala-Narra, P., Li, Z., Chang, J., Yang, E., Jiang, J., Sagherian, M., Phan, J., & Alfonso, A. (2018). Developmental and contextual correlates of mental health and help seeking among Asian American college students. *American Journal of Orthopsychiatry*, *88*(6), 636–649. https://doi.org/10.1037/ort0000317

Turner, E. A., Cheng, H.-L., Llamas, J. D., Tran, A. G. T. T., Hill, K. X., Fretts, J. M., & Mercado, A. (2016). Factors impacting the current trends in the use of outpatient psychiatric treatment among diverse ethnic groups. *Current Psychiatry Reviews*, *12*(2), 199–220. https://doi.org/10.2174/1573400512666160216234524

Twenge, J. M., Sherman, R. A., & Wells, B. E. (2015). Changes in American adults' sexual behavior and attitudes, 1972–2012. *Archives of Sexual Behavior*, *44*(8), 2273–2285. https://doi.org/10.1007/s10508-015-0540-2

Ulie-Wells, J., Bruna, K. R., & Romo, C. (2020). Critical school mental health praxis (CrSMHP): A framework for change. In C. S. Clauss-Ehlers, A. B. Sood, & M. D. Weist (Eds.), *Social justice for children and young people: International perspectives* (pp. 175–193). Cambridge University Press. https://doi.org/10.1017/9781108551830.012

Ungar, M. (2013). Resilience, trauma, context, and culture. *Trauma Violence Abuse*, *14*(3), 255–266. https://doi.org/10.1177/1524838013487805

UNHCR. (2019). *Global trends: Forced displacement in 2018*. https://www.unhcr.org/globaltrends2018/

United Nations. (2020). *The sustainable development goals report 2020*. https://unstats.un.org/sdgs/report/2020/The-Sustainable-Development-Goals-Report-2020.pdf

United Nations. (2022). *UNHCR: A record 100 million people forcibly displaced worldwide*. https://news.un.org/en/story/2022/05/1118772

United Nations General Assembly. (2015, October 21). *Resolution adopted by the General Assembly on 25 September 2015*. https://www.un.org/en/development/desa/population/migration/generalassembly/docs/globalcompact/A_RES_70_1_E.pdf

Uphoff, E. P., Pickett, K. E., Cabieses, B., Small, N., & Wright, J. (2013). A systematic review of the relationships between social capital and socioeconomic inequalities in health: A contribution to understanding the psychosocial pathway of health inequalities. *International Journal for Equity in Health*, *12*(1), 54. Advance online publication. https://doi.org/10.1186/1475-9276-12-54

Upshaw, N. C., Lewis, D. E., Jr., & Nelson, A. L. (2020). Cultural humility in action: Reflective and process-oriented supervision with Black trainees. *Training and Education in Professional Psychology*, *14*(4), 277–284. https://doi.org/10.1037/tep0000284

U.S. Census Bureau. (2015a, November 3). *Census Bureau reports at least 350 languages spoken in U.S. homes* [Press release]. https://www.census.gov/newsroom/archives/2015-pr/cb15-185.html

U.S. Census Bureau. (2015b). *Facts for features: Hispanic heritage month 2017*. https://www.census.gov/newsroom/facts-for-features/2017/hispanic-heritage.html

U.S. Department of Education. (2017). *Improving outcomes for all students: Strategies and considerations to increase student diversity.* https://www2.ed.gov/documents/press-releases/improving-outcomes-diversity.pdf

U.S. Department of Health and Human Services. (1999). *Mental health: A report of the Surgeon General.* https://profiles.nlm.nih.gov/spotlight/nn/catalog/nlm:nlmuid-101584932X120-doc

U.S. Department of Health and Human Services. (2001). *Mental health: Culture, race, and ethnicity—A supplement to Mental health: A report of the Surgeon General.* https://www.ncbi.nlm.nih.gov/books/NBK44243/

U.S. Government Accountability Office. (2018). *K-12 Education: Public high schools with more students in poverty and smaller schools provide fewer academic offerings to prepare for college.* https://www.gao.gov/products/gao-19-8

Valmas, M. M., Himrich, S. J., & Finn, K. M. (2020). Women's experiences of supervision and professional development. *Journal of Psychology Integration, 30*(1), 130–139. https://doi.org/10.1037/int0000182

Vazquez, C. I., & Clauss-Ehlers, C. S. (2005). Group psychotherapy with Latinas: A cross-cultural and interactional approach. *New York State Psychologist, 17,* 10–13.

Vera, E. M., & Speight, S. L. (2003). Multicultural competence, social justice, and counseling psychology: Expanding our roles. *The Counseling Psychologist, 31*(3), 253–272. https://doi.org/10.1177/0011000003031003001

Vespa, J. (2009). Gender ideology construction: A life course and intersectional approach. *Gender & Society, 23*(3), 363–387. https://doi.org/10.1177/0891243209337507

Vieten, C., & Lukoff, D. (2022). Spiritual and religious competencies in psychology. *American Psychologist, 77*(1), 26–38. https://doi.org/10.1037/amp0000821

Vignoles, V. L., Owe, E., Becker, M., Smith, P. B., Easterbrook, M. J., Brown, R., González, R., Didier, N., Carrasco, D., Cadena, M. P., Lay, S., Schwartz, S. J., Des Rosiers, S. E., Villamar, J. A., Gavreliuc, A., Zinkeng, M., Kreuzbauer, R., Baguma, P., Martin, M., . . . Bond, M. H. (2016). Beyond the 'east-west' dichotomy: Global variation in cultural models of selfhood. *Journal of Experimental Psychology: General, 145*(8), 966–1000. https://doi.org/10.1037/xge0000175

Wainberg, M. L., Scorza, P., Shultz, J. M., Helpman, L., Mootz, J. J., Johnson, K. A., Neria, Y., Bradford, J. E., Oquendo, M. A., & Arbuckle, M. R. (2017). Challenges and opportunities in global mental health: A research-to-practice perspective. *Current Psychiatry Reports, 19*(5), 28. https://doi.org/10.1007/s11920-017-0780-z

Walrave, M., Poels, K., Antheunis, M. L., Van den Broeck, E., & van Noort, G. (2018). Like or dislike? Adolescents' responses to personalized social network site advertising. *Journal of Marketing Communications, 24*(6), 599–616. https://doi.org/10.1080/13527266.2016.1182938

Wampold, B. E. (2000). Outcomes of individual counseling and psychotherapy: Empirical evidence addressing two fundamental questions. In S. D. Brown & R. W. Lent (Eds.), *Handbook of counseling psychology* (3rd ed., pp. 711–739). Wiley.

Wampold, B., & Bhati, K. (2004). Attending to the omissions: A historical examination of evidenced-based practice movements. *Professional Psychology, Research and Practice, 35*(6), 563–570. https://doi.org/10.1037/0735-7028.35.6.563

Wang, W. (2021, April 6). Why China's college placement exam is much harder than the SAT. *The Daily Orange.* https://dailyorange.com/2021/04/chinas-college-placement-exam-sat/

Watkins, C. E., Hook, J. N., Owen, J., DeBlaere, C., Davis, D. E., & Callahan, J. L. (2019). Creating and elaborating the cultural third: A doers-doing with perspective on psychoanalytic supervision. *The American Journal of Psychoanalysis, 79*(3), 352–374. https://doi.org/10.1057/s11231-019-09203-4

Weintraub, S. R., & Goodman, L. A. (2010). Working with and for: Student advocates' experience of relationship-centered advocacy with low-income women. *American Journal of Orthopsychiatry, 80*(1), 46–60. https://doi.org/10.1111/j.1939-0025.2010.01006.x

Weist, M. D., McWhirter, C., Fairchild, A. J., Bradley, W. J., Cason, J., Miller, E., & Hartley, S. (2019). Assessing acceptability of the term: "Psychopathology" among youth aged 18–25. *Community Mental Health Journal, 55*(3), 463–466. https://doi.org/10.1007/s10597-018-0306-0

The White House Office of the Press Secretary. (2013, December 4). *Remarks by the President on economic mobility.* https://obamawhitehouse.archives.gov/the-press-office/2013/12/04/remarks-president-economic-mobility

Wilkerson, I. (2020). *Caste: The origins of our discontents.* Random House.

Williams, R. L. (2009). Developmental issues as a component of intersectionality: Defining the Smart-Girl Program. *Race, Gender, & Class, 16*(1–2), 82–101.

Wilson, J. P. (2007). The lens of culture: Theoretical and conceptual perspectives in the assessment of psychological trauma and PTSD. In J. P. Wilson & C. S. Tang (Eds.), *Cross cultural assessment of psychological trauma and PTSD* (pp. 3–30). Springer. https://doi.org/10.1007/978-0-387-70990-1_1

World Health Organization. (n.d.-a). *Gender and health.* https://www.who.int/health-topics/gender#tab=tab_1

World Health Organization. (n.d.-b). *Mental health.* https://www.who.int/health-topics/mental-health#tab=tab_1

World Health Organization. (n.d.-c). *Social determinants of health.* https://www.who.int/social_determinants/en/

World Health Organization. (n.d.-d). *Taking action on the social determinants of health.* https://www.who.int/westernpacific/activities/taking-action-on-the-social-determinants-of-health

World Health Organization. (2013). *Self-care for health: A handbook for community health workers and volunteers.* https://apps.who.int/iris/bitstream/handle/10665/205887/B5084.pdf?sequence=1&isAllowed=y

World Health Organization. (2015). *2014 mental health atlas.* https://apps.who.int/iris/bitstream/handle/10665/178879/9789241565011_eng.pdf

World Health Organization. (2017). *Mental health of older adults.* https://www.who.int/news-room/fact-sheets/detail/mental-health-of-older-adults

World Health Organization. (2018). *Mental health atlas 2017.* https://www.who.int/publications/i/item/9789241514019

World Health Organization. (2019). *The WHO special initiative for mental health (2019–2023): Universal health coverage for mental health.* https://apps.who.int/iris/bitstream/handle/10665/310981/WHO-MSD-19.1-eng.pdf?sequence=1&isAllowed=y

World Health Organization. (2021a). *Adolescent mental health.* https://www.who.int/news-room/fact-sheets/detail/adolescent-mental-health

World Health Organization. (2021b). *Depressive disorder (depression).* https://www.who.int/news-room/fact-sheets/detail/depression

World Health Organization. (2022). *COVID-19 pandemic triggers 25% increase in prevalence of depression and anxiety worldwide.* https://www.who.int/news/item/02-03-2022-covid-19-pandemic-triggers-25-increase-in-prevalence-of-anxiety-and-depression-worldwide

Worthman, C. M., & Costello, E. J. (2009). Tracking biocultural pathways in population health: The value of biomarkers. *Annals of Human Biology, 36*(3), 281–297. https://doi.org/10.1080/03014460902832934

Wu, L., Zhang, D., Su, Z., & Hu, T. (2015). Peer victimization among children and adolescents: A meta-analytic review of links to emotional maladjustment. *Clinical Pediatrics, 54*(10), 941–955. https://doi.org/10.1177/0009922814567873

Yancu, C. N., & Farmer, D. F. (2017). Product or process: Cultural competence or cultural humility? *Palliative Medicine and Hospice Care, 3*(1), e1–e4. https://doi.org/10.17140/PMHCOJ-3-e005

Yeager, K. A., & Bauer-Wu, S. (2013). Cultural humility: Essential foundation for clinical researchers. *Applied Nursing Research, 26*(4), 251–256. https://doi.org/10.1016/j.apnr.2013.06.008

Yearby, R. (2020). Structural racism and health disparities: Reconfiguring the social determinants of health framework to include the root cause. *The Journal of Law, Medicine & Ethics, 48*(3), 518–526. https://doi.org/10.1177/1073110520958876

Yeh, C. J., Inman, A. C., Kim, A. B., & Okubo, Y. (2006). Asian American families' collectivistic coping strategies in response to 9/11. *Cultural Diversity and Ethnic Minority Psychology, 12*(1), 134–148. https://doi.org/10.1037/1099-9809.12.1.134

Yi, K. (2014). Toward formulation of ethnic identity beyond the binary of the White oppressor and racial other. *Psychoanalytic Psychology, 31*(3), 426–434. https://doi.org/10.1037/a0036649

Yoo, H. C., Burrola, K. S., & Steger, M. F. (2010). A preliminary report on a new measure: Internalization of the Model Minority Myth Measure (IM-4) and its psychological correlates among Asian American college students. *Journal of Counseling Psychology, 57*(1), 114–127. https://doi.org/10.1037/a0017871

Zane, N., Bernal, G., & Leong, F. T. L. (Eds.). (2016). *Evidence-based psychological practice with ethnic minorities: Culturally informed research and clinical strategies.* American Psychological Association. https://doi.org/10.1037/14940-000

Index

A

Abbott, D. M., 79–80
Ableism, sociopolitical influences of, 75, 250
Abuse
 in Catholic Church, 225
 reporting of, 26, 36
ACA (American Counseling Association), 9, 235
Active listening, 17
Advocacy, 11
 APA definition of, 14
 approaches to, 138–140
 building skills for, 234
 critical themes in, 143
 in cultural humility, 13–15
 culture-centered. *See* Promoting Culture-Centered Interventions and Advocacy (Multicultural Guideline 6)
 defined, 140
 integrated into training, 109–110
 interventions, 34
 literature review, 138–143
 for mental health parity, 143
 organizational-level, 146–147
 as pillar of *2030 Agenda for Sustainable Development,* 164
 to promote resilience, 223
 relationship-centered, 145–147
 self-advocacy, 91
 for social justice, 107
 steps in, 141
 in supervision, 172
"Advocacy beyond the organization," 147
African Americans. *See* Black/African American/Black Americans

Age
 negative categorizations based on, 74
 and socialization experiences, 70
Ageism, sociopolitical influences of, 75
Ahluwalia, M. K., 233
Alaska Natives, lack of data on, 131
Albritton, K., 133
Almedom, A. M., 101, 107
American Counseling Association (ACA), 9, 235
American Indians, lack of data on, 131
American Psychiatric Association
 Center for Workforce Studies, 129
 Cultural Formulation Interview, 9
American Psychological Association (APA), 4
 2017 Multicultural Guidelines. See Multicultural Guidelines: An Ecological Approach to Context, Identity, and Intersectionality, 2017
 and advocacy engagement, 145, 146
 APA Dictionary of Psychology, 14
 APA Guidelines on Race and Ethnicity in Psychology, 244
 Board for the Advancement of Psychology in the Public Interest, 8–9, 244
 Consultation Psychology Journal, 83
 Council of Representatives, 127
 on dose effect, 235–236
 Guidelines on Multicultural Education, Training, Research, Practice, and Organizational Change for Psychologists (2002 Guidelines), 8

309

310 • Index

historical focus of psychology within, 155–156
multicultural guidelines of, 244
on resilience, 224, 227
Resilience and Recovery After War: Refugee Children and Families in the United States, 236
Resolution on Harnessing Psychology to Combat Racism, 126
on shelf life for guidelines, 241
on strength-based approach, 220
structural and political discussions among members of, 187
survey of psychology services in Spanish, 100
Task Force on Guidelines Focused on Race/Ethnicity, 9, 244
Task Force on Re-Envisioning the Multicultural Guidelines for the 21st Century, 9, 244
on traumatic stress, 228
Warrior Path Presidential Task Force, 123, 134
Antireligious prejudice, sociopolitical influences of, 75
APA. *See* American Psychological Association
APA Dictionary of Psychology (APA), 14
APA Guidelines on Race and Ethnicity in Psychology (APA), 244
APPIC (Association of Psychology Postdoctoral and Internship Centers), 120 (Multicultural Guideline 10), 5, 219–238
case illustration, 221–223
for clinical practice, 227–230
for consultation, 237
for education (teaching and training), 230–235
implications of, 263
literature review, 223–227
for research, 235–236
summary of, 262
Ardila, A., 209–210
Artiga, S., 105
Ashcraft, C., 118
Asian/Asian Americans. *See also* People of color
barriers creating marginalization of, 126
coping with trauma and racism by Vietnamese American woman, 50–53

and cost of pursuing doctorates in psychology, 129
differing roles and identifications for, 191–192
lack of data regarding immigrants, 124
stereotypes of, 54–55
study of morale and motivation in the workforce, 112–113
Assessment(s)
biases in, 77–78, 207, 209–210
Conducting Culturally Informed Work in Psychology (Multicultural Guideline 9) for, 207–210
needs, 176
norm-referenced, 150, 207–209
Association of Psychology Postdoctoral and Internship Centers (APPIC), 120
Assumptions
about clients from low-resource or affluent communities, 107
about racial identity, 58
about sociocultural groups, 59
influencing theory, practice, consultation, education, and research, 50
reflexivity about, 210
self-awareness of, 76
Attunement, in classroom environment, 233
Ayazi, H., 165–166
Azar, B., 167

B

BAPPI (Board for the Advancement of Psychology in the Public Interest), 8–9, 244
Batalden, Paul, 126
Baumann, E. F., 59–60
Beers, C. W., 142
Beliefs
about mental health, 210
communication about, in training, 79
communication of, 76–77
respect for and responsiveness to, 272
that influence connections with community context, 225–226
Bellevue Bilingual Treatment Program (BTP), 97, 226
Benchmarks for multicultural psychology, 242–243
Bernal, G., 13

Bhadra, M., 132
Biases
  in assessment, 207, 209–210
  avoiding. *See* Understanding and Avoiding Psychologists' Biases (Multicultural Guideline 2)
  categorical, 74–75. *See also* Stereotypes
  in clinical practice and empirical inquiry into psychological development, 50
  communication of, 76–77
  confronting, 196
  hidden, 272
  in measurement tools, 77–78
  reflexivity about, 210
  sampling, 214–215
Bidirectional model of self-definition and relationships (Level 1), 28–31. *See also* Recognizing the Fluidity and Complexity of Self-Identity and Social Dynamics (Multicultural Guideline 1); Understanding and Avoiding Psychologists' Biases (Multicultural Guideline 2)
Bidirectional relationships, 11, 15–16
  for strength-based interventions, 230–231
  strengths-based focus in, 18, 220
Biopsychosocial model, 182
Biopsychosociocultural model, 182, 195
Biosociocultural context, intersection of development and. *See* The Intersection Between Development and Biosociocultural Context (Multicultural Guideline 8)
Black/African American/Black Americans. *See also* People of color
  barriers creating marginalization of, 126, 127
  and cost of pursuing doctorates in psychology, 129
  differing roles and identifications for women, 191
  disciplining of children in early childhood education, 133
  intersectionality of racism and sexism for women, 55–56
Blustein, D. L., 145, 146
Board for the Advancement of Psychology in the Public Interest (BAPPI), 8–9, 244
Boomer generation, 190
Boston Naming Test, 209

Breland, J. Y., 111–112
BRIDGE, 133
Bronfenbrenner, U., 21–24, 27–28, 247
Brooks, M., 233, 234
BTP (Bellevue Bilingual Treatment Program), 97, 226
Buddhism, 229–229
Bullock, Heather E., 106, 196

C

Cabrera, N. L., 132
Case analysis, in transnational teaching, 156–160
Catholic Church, 225
CBPR. *See* Community-based participatory research
CCS (cultural consultation service), 215–216
CDC (Centers for Disease Control and Prevention), 124
Center for Workforce Studies (APA), 129
Centers for Disease Control and Prevention (CDC), 124
Chinese Americans, cultural barriers to treatment for, 131
Chiriboga, David, 9
Chronosystem
  as circle of engagement and interaction, 28
  in layered ecological model, 23, 24, 41
CIOMS (Council for International Organizations of Medical Sciences), 175–176
Cisgenderism
  sociopolitical influences of, 75
  and student admissions experiences, 128
Civil Rights Movement, 142
Classism, sociopolitical influences of, 75
Classroom environment, 108–109, 232–234
Clauss-Ehlers, Caroline S., 9, 12, 13, 214, 224–225, 227
Client(s)
  ecological niche of, 31
  holistic consideration of, 232
  implementation of clinical guidelines with, 272
  self-definition of, 29
  use of term, 29n1
Climate change, 165
Climate-induced displacement, 165

Climate refugees, 165–166
Climate Refugees: The Climate Crisis and Rights Denied (Ayazi and Elsheikh), 165–166
Clinical practice
  Applying a Strength-Based Approach to Psychology (Multicultural Guideline 10) for, 227–230
  assumptions and stereotypes influencing, 50
  Conducting Culturally Informed Work in Psychology (Multicultural Guideline 9) for, 207–211
  The Cultural Significance of Language and Communication (Multicultural Guideline 3) for, 95–96
  future professional benchmarks for, 242
  gray areas in, 232–233
  The Impact of Social Capital (Multicultural Guideline 4) for, 107–108
  The Intersection Between Development and Biosociocultural Context (Multicultural Guideline 8) for, 191–192
  outcomes in, 202, 203
  Promoting Culture-Centered Interventions and Advocacy (Multicultural Guideline 6) for, 144–148
  Recognizing Institutional Barriers and Systemic Marginalization (Multicultural Guideline 5) for, 127–130
  Recognizing the Fluidity and Complexity of Self-Identity and Social Dynamics (Multicultural Guideline 1) for, 57–61
  recommendations for, 265
  Understanding and Avoiding Psychologists' Biases (Multicultural Guideline 2) for, 76–78
  Understanding Globalization's Impact on Psychology (Multicultural Guideline 7) for, 166–170
Clinical relationship, as key to strength-based interventions, 230–231
Code switching (CS), 93–94
Cohen, K. R., 141
Cole, E. R., 56
Collaboration
  for addressing sampling biases, 214–215
  in community-based participatory research, 214
  in research, 81
  between researchers and communities, 205–207
  in strength-based approach, 219–220
  in teaching and training, 231–232
  in transboundary research, 174
  in transnational teaching, 159, 170
Collective mental health advocacy approaches, 139
Collectivist cultural value
  and connections with community context, 226
  conversations about, 149
  individualistic cultural value vs., 167
Collins, P. Y., 156, 163–164
Collins, L. H., 11, 12
Collishaw, Stephan, 220
Colorblindness
  leading to disengagement and denial of self, 74–75
  as microaggression, 77
Communication. *See also* Language; Listening
  of biases and beliefs, 76–77
  in building alliances, 264
  cultural miscommunication, 144–145
  cultural significance of. *See* The Cultural Significance of Language and Communication (Multicultural Guideline 3)
  developmentally appropriate, 95
  healthy learning environment for, 233
  nonverbal, 94–99, 144–145
  in training, about experiences and belief systems, 79
  verbal, 94, 98–99. *See also* Language
Community, school, and family context (Level 2), 31–34. *See also* The Cultural Significance of Language and Communication (Multicultural Guideline 3); The Impact of Social Capital (Multicultural Guideline 4)
Community-based participatory research (CBPR), 97–98
  authentic partnership in, 150
  collaboration in, 214
  and students' learning from research projects, 131
  in transnational research project, 203–205

Community context. *See also* Community, school, and family context (Level 2)
  awareness of, in gauging mental health-related stigma, 168
  considerations of, 264
  cultural beliefs influencing connections with, 225–226
  data collection in, 131
  in evidence-based case study approach, 214
  evidence-based treatments within, 143
  for resilience, 225
  for trauma, 225
Community-engaged programs, 266
Community Mental Health Act, 142
Community mental health care
  building infrastructure for, 151–152
  following September 11 attacks, 237
Compassion fatigue, 234
Conducting Culturally Informed Work in Psychology (Multicultural Guideline 9), 5, 201–217
  for assessment, 207–210
  case illustration, 204–205
  for clinical practice, 207–211
  for consultation, 215–216
  for education (teaching and training), 211–213
  implications of, 261
  literature review, 205–207
  and meaning of *outcomes,* 202–204
  for psychotherapy, 210–211
  for research, 213–215
  summary of, 261–262
Consultation
  Applying a Strength-Based Approach to Psychology (Multicultural Guideline 10) for, 237
  assumptions and stereotypes influencing, 50
  Conducting Culturally Informed Work in Psychology (Multicultural Guideline 9) for, 215–216
  The Cultural Significance of Language and Communication (Multicultural Guideline 3) for, 98–99
  future professional benchmarks for, 243
  The Impact of Social Capital (Multicultural Guideline 4) for, 111–113
  The Intersection Between Development and Biosociocultural Context (Multicultural Guideline 8) for, 196
  outcomes in, 202–203
  Promoting Culture-Centered Interventions and Advocacy (Multicultural Guideline 6) for, 150–152
  Recognizing Institutional Barriers and Systemic Marginalization (Multicultural Guideline 5) for, 133
  Recognizing the Fluidity and Complexity of Self-Identity and Social Dynamics (Multicultural Guideline 1) for, 66–67
  types of settings for, 66
  Understanding and Avoiding Psychologists' Biases (Multicultural Guideline 2) for, 82–84
  Understanding Globalization's Impact on Psychology (Multicultural Guideline 7) for, 177–178
Consultation Psychology Journal (APA), 83
Consumer movement, 139, 142
Cooperative community, 138–139, 143, 151, 257
COR (Council of Representatives), 127
Council for International Organizations of Medical Sciences (CIOMS), 175–176
Council of Representatives (COR), 127
COVID-19
  family losses secondary to, 222
  global prevalence of disorders during, 162
  institutional impact on engagement in, 35
  mental health considerations in response to, 161
  need for research on impact of, 64
  online counseling services during, 225
  racial/ethnic health disparities emerging during, 15–16
  students' struggles during, 146–147
  transnational teaching during, 156–161
  violence against/harassment of Asian Americans during, 52
CRA (culturally focused resilience adaptation model), 224–225
Crenshaw, K. W., 3, 55–56
Cross-cultural transmission, 229–230
Crowley, J., 202
CS (code switching), 93–94
Cullen, K., 171–172

Cultural competence, 11–15. *See also specific areas of competence*
  critiques of, 14
  and ethical decision making, 271
  key approaches related to, 12–13
  reflexivity work for, 16–17
  research connecting outcomes and, 266
Cultural consultation service (CCS), 215–216
Cultural context
  and control of destiny, 229
  high- and low-context cultures, 145
  for resilience, 220, 225
  of trauma, 226–227, 230, 237
Cultural contextual approach, 225
Cultural differences, 38
Cultural experiences, influence of, 69–70
Cultural Formulation Interview (APA), 9
Cultural humility, 11–15
  in approaching identity and intersectionality, 61
  consultants, 83
  defined, 61
  defining and elaborating on, 245
  in educational setting, 79–80
  key approaches related to, 12–13
  as precursor to cultural sensitivity, 271–272
  in psychological practice, 77–78
  in psychotherapy, 210–211
  reflexivity work for, 16–17
  for sharing space and time with clients, 43
  in supervision, 66, 213
  in transboundary practice, 166
Culturally adaptive interventions, 144–145, 150, 224–225
Culturally adaptive treatment, 170
Culturally focused resilience adaptation model (CRA), 224–225
Culturally informed work. *See* Conducting Culturally Informed Work in Psychology (Multicultural Guideline 9)
Culturally relevant therapy approaches, 167
Culturally syntonic intervention, 213, 245–246, 268
Cultural neuroscience, 195
Cultural racism, 125
Cultural resilience, 224, 262
Cultural roles
  in addressing inequalities, 196
  and identifications for women, 191–192
Cultural sensitivity
  cultural humility as precursor to, 271–272
  development of cultural humility, in trainees, 80
  and therapeutic, supervisory, and teaching relationships, 73. *See also* Understanding and Avoiding Psychologists' Biases (Multicultural Guideline 2)
The Cultural Significance of Language and Communication (Multicultural Guideline 3), 5, 87–100
  case illustration, 90–91
  for clinical practice, 95–96
  and code switching, 93–94
  for consultation, 98–99
  definitions of language in mental health field, 87–90
  for education (teaching and training), 96–97
  implications of, 252
  and language as representation of cultural values, 94–95
  literature review, 91–95
  for research, 97–98
  summary of, 251–252
Cultural translation of language, 96–97
Cultural validity, 207–209, 215
Cultural values
  and connections with community context, 225–226
  and culture-centered, 135–136, 139
  empowerment aligned with, 213
  language as representation of, 94–95
  respect for and responsiveness to, 272
  theories of identity development based on, 50
  transboundary, 169–170
  and traumatic experience, 227
Culture brokers, 216
Culture-centered intervention approaches, 139. *See also* Promoting Culture-Centered Interventions and Advocacy (Multicultural Guideline 6)
"Culture of college," 132
Cultures, high- and low-context, 145
Curriculum
  decolonizing, 171–172
  infusing cultural diversity in, 266
  in transnational teaching, 158

D

DALYs (disability-adjusted life years), 162–163
Decolonization, 171–172
Defensiveness, 17–18
  among students, 233
  and therapist's use of jargon, 92
Deficit approaches, 220, 231
Development
  biases in clinical practice and empirical inquiry into, 50
  considering differing progress of, 75
  intersection of biosociocultural context and. *See* The Intersection Between Development and Biosociocultural Context (Multicultural Guideline 8)
  multiple levels of experiences of, 31
Developmentally appropriate communication, 95
Developmental-socioenvironmental theory, 21, 247
Disability-adjusted life years (DALYs), 162–163
Disability status. *See also* People with disabilities
  negative categorizations based on, 74
  and socialization experiences, 70
Displaced people, 164–165
Diversity
  conversations about, 148–149
  in curriculum, 266
  lack of standard approach to teaching/training in, 61
  need for education about, 62–63
  and norming, 208–209
  in profession of psychology, 272
  teaching and training for understanding of, 132
  of U.S. student population, 192–193
  and viewpoints about others, 76
Domenech Rodríguez, M., 13
Domestic and international climate (Level 4), 37–39. *See also* The Intersection Between Development and Biosociocultural Context (Multicultural Guideline 8); Understanding Globalization's Impact on Psychology (Multicultural Guideline 7)
Domestic focus, 10–12
Dose effect, 235–236
Dual language experience, 94

E

Early interventions
  approaches for, 140
  defined, 144
  differing cultural perceptions of, 147–148
  literature review, 143–144
Eckert, M. D., 133
Ecological niche, 31
Ecological theory, 22–24, 28
Economic hardship, balancing commitments in face of, 102–104
Education (teaching and training)
  addressing sociocultural variables in, 221–223
  in advocacy skills, 142, 234
  Applying a Strength-Based Approach to Psychology (Multicultural Guideline 10) for, 230–235
  assumptions and stereotypes influencing, 50
  authentic collaboration in, 231–232
  biases in, 69–70
  bi- or multilingual training for clinicians, 267
  building clinical relationship in, 230–231
  classroom and supervision environment in, 232–234
  Conducting Culturally Informed Work in Psychology (Multicultural Guideline 9) for, 211–213
  context of. *See* Community, school, and family context (Level 2)
  The Cultural Significance of Language and Communication (Multicultural Guideline 3) for, 96–97
  as dynamic transaction, 73–74
  future professional benchmarks for, 243
  The Impact of Social Capital (Multicultural Guideline 4) for, 108–110
  institutional barriers in, 121–124
  The Intersection Between Development and Biosociocultural Context (Multicultural Guideline 8) for, 192–194
  outcomes in, 202, 203
  practicum and internship sites, 267
  Promoting Culture-Centered Interventions and Advocacy (Multicultural Guideline 6) for, 148–150

Recognizing Institutional Barriers
and Systemic Marginalization
(Multicultural Guideline 5) for,
131–132
Recognizing the Fluidity and
Complexity of Self-Identity and Social
Dynamics (Multicultural Guideline 1)
for, 61–63
recommendations for, 265–267
recruitment and retention strategies in,
266
self-awareness in, 232
sociocultural approach to, 230
supervision, 212–213
through research participation, 211–212
transnational, 156–161
traumatic dynamics in, 62–63
Understanding and Avoiding
Psychologists' Biases (Multicultural
Guideline 2) for, 78–80
Understanding Globalization's Impact
on Psychology (Multicultural
Guideline 7) for, 170–172
vicarious traumatization and self-care
in, 235
Education Data Initiative, 128–129
Egalitarian colorblindness, 75
Elsheikh, E., 165
Emotional expression, conversations
about, 149
Empathy, 11, 17, 43, 92–93
Engagement
with aspects of clients' identities, 58
with community members who will be
subjects of research, 81
concentric circles of, 28
and diversity of U.S. student
population, 193
influence of assumptions and
viewpoints on, 78
institutional barriers to, 15–16. *See also*
Recognizing Institutional Barriers
and Systemic Marginalization
(Multicultural Guideline 5)
institutional impact on, 128–130.
See also Institutional impact on
engagement (Level 3)
multiple levels of, 22
multitude of influences affecting, 196
with others' experiences, 76
of psychologists in advocacy, 145–147
with range of experiences and demands,
182

with tensions, 43
in transnational teaching, 157–158
Engel, G. L., 182
"Ethnic gloss," 132
Ethnicity
negative categorizations based on, 74
and socialization experiences, 70
Ethnic minorities/groups. *See also*
individual groups
financial support for students of, 130
health and well-being of, 131
psychology degrees obtained by, 129
student admissions experiences of, 128
and traumatic experience, 227
Evidence base. *See* Literature review;
Research
Evidence-based case study approach, 214
Exosystem
as circle of engagement and interaction,
28
in layered ecological model, 23–24
Explicit bias, 75

F

Fallon, L., 109–110
Familism, 110–111
Familismo, 268
Family context. *See* Community, school,
and family context (Level 2)
Farrell, J. E., 77
Ferrer, I., 194–195
Fisher, E. S., 80
Fisher-Borne, M., 13
Fiske, S. T., 196
Flores, Y. G., 110–111
Floyd, George, 35
Fluidity, 41–43
of self-identity and social dynamics.
See Recognizing the Fluidity and
Complexity of Self-Identity and Social
Dynamics (Multicultural Guideline 1)
Focus groups, 26–27, 30, 81, 83, 110,
112, 217
Foley, Z., 165
Food availability, 111–112
Forced migration, 11–12, 236
Foronda, C., 13
Future directions in multicultural
psychology, 241–246, 263–269
case illustration, 245–246
professional benchmarks, 242–243
recommendations for, 264–267

G

Gallardo, M. E., 61
GAO (U.S. Government Accountability Office), 122
GBD (global burden of disease), 162–163
Gee, A., 139–140, 143
Gender
  in addressing inequalities, 196
  and cost of pursuing doctorates in psychology, 129
  and foundational understanding of self, 188
  negative categorizations based on, 74
  and socialization experiences, 70
Gendered racism, 58
Gender identity, minimizing or overemphasizing, 58
Gender pronouns, and identity formation, 55
Gender roles
  models of, 187
  and traumatic experience, 227
Generational differences, 38
  in identity, 54
  media discussions of, 190
Glandon, D., 101
Global burden of disease (GBD), 163
Globalization, 11
  and practice of psychology in other languages, 98
  psychology impacted by. *See* Understanding Globalization's Impact on Psychology (Multicultural Guideline 7)
Global Majority, 10
Global mental health, 156. *See also* Understanding Globalization's Impact on Psychology (Multicultural Guideline 7)
Global Minority, 10
Goforth, A. N., 133
Grit, 223–224
Group identity(-ies), 10, 54
  clients' identification with, 29
  and individual identity, 54
  intersectionality of, 3–4
  openness to learning about, 67
Grzanka, P. R., 56
Guidelines on Multicultural Education, Training, Research, Practice, and Organizational Change for Psychologists (2002 Guidelines), 8

H

Hall, E. T., 145
Haynes, S. N., 77
Health
  social determinants of, 105–106
Health disparities
  in mental health, 143, 210
  in mental health care, 136
  racial/ethnic, 15–16
Health-oriented consultation model, 111–112
Hechanova, R., 148–149
Heft, H., 28
Henrich, J., 130
Herman, J. L., 226
Hernandez, P., 67
Heterosexism, sociopolitical influences of, 75
High-context cultures, 145
Hilty, D. M., 182
Hinton, E., 105
Hispanic Americans. *See* Latino/Hispanic/Latinx Americans
Homophobia, sociopolitical influences of, 75
Hook, J. N., 77
Hsueh, L., 128–130
Huggins, R., 167–168
Human rights, 37, 146, 161
Hunter, Scott J., 9
Hutchinson, A. M., 83

I

Identity(-ies). *See also* Reference group identities; Self-identity
  multiple, making sense of, 189–190
  positioning within one's array of, 195
  reductionist views of, 59
  in research, 63–64
  as transitional in some domains, 192
Identity conflict, political struggle and, 183–187
Identity development/formation. *See also* The Intersection Between Development and Biosociocultural Context (Multicultural Guideline 8)
  factors in, 54
  fluidity of, 49. *See also* Recognizing the Fluidity and Complexity of Self-Identity and Social Dynamics (Multicultural Guideline 1)

influences on, 49–50
intersectionality in, 55–56, 60
in minority groups, 194
models of, 187
theories of, 50
Immigration
community based investigations of parenting and resilience case study, 24–27
identity conflict connected to political struggle case study, 183–187
integration into new home society, 38
navigating professional life and staying true to self case study, 70–73
The Impact of Social Capital (Multicultural Guideline 4), 5, 101–113
case illustration, 102–104
for clinical practice, 107–108
for consultation, 111–113
for education (teaching and training), 108–110
implications of, 254
literature review, 104–107
for research, 110–111
summary of, 253
Implicit bias, 74
Inclusive research, 136–138
Indigenous people. *See also* People of color
barriers creating marginalization of, 126
lack of data on, 131
Individual identity
experiences associated with different aspects of, 57–58. *See also* Recognizing the Fluidity and Complexity of Self-Identity and Social Dynamics (Multicultural Guideline 1)
and group identity, 54
Individualistic cultural value
in approaching trauma, 229
collectivist cultural value vs., 167
and connections with community context, 225–226
Information
personal, technologies tracking, 189
sources of, 182–183
Information overload, 183
Institute of Medicine, 210
Institutional barriers
defined, 118
to engagement, 15–16. *See also* Institutional impact on engagement (Level 3)

marginalization created by, 118. *See also* Recognizing Institutional Barriers and Systemic Marginalization (Multicultural Guideline 5)
Institutional context
engagement in, 34–36
multiple constituencies in, 215
Institutional impact on engagement (Level 3), 34–36. *See also* Promoting Culture-Centered Interventions and Advocacy (Multicultural Guideline 6); Recognizing Institutional Barriers and Systemic Marginalization (Multicultural Guideline 5)
Institutional racism, 122–126
Institutional review boards (IRBs), 137, 172
Insurance, with transboundary practice, 166–167
Interactions
concentric circles of, 28
outcomes deriving from, 39
Internalized racism, 124–126
International climate. *See* Domestic and international climate (Level 4)
International Ethical Guidelines for Biomedical Research Involving Human Subjects (Council for International Organizations of Medical Sciences), 175–176
International work, linguistic diversity in, 98
Internships, 120, 265–267
Interpersonal racism, 125
Intersectional invisibility, 58–59, 65
Intersectionality, 3–4
of development and biosociocultural context. *See* The Intersection Between Development and Biosociocultural Context (Multicultural Guideline 8)
of gender and race, 58
identifying, 31
in identity development, 55–56. *See also* Recognizing the Fluidity and Complexity of Self-Identity and Social Dynamics (Multicultural Guideline 1)
implementing guidelines for, 56
of levels of racism, 126
need for attention to, in teaching and training, 62
of physical health and emotional/behavioral health, 106

as pillar of *2030 Agenda for Sustainable Development,* 163–164
between resilience and strength-based approach, 237
Intersectionality theory, 56
The Intersection Between Development and Biosociocultural Context (Multicultural Guideline 8), 5, 181–197
    case illustration, 183–187
    for clinical practice, 191–192
    for consultation, 196
    for education (teaching and training), 192–194
    implications of, 260
    literature review, 187–190
    for research, 194–195
    summary of, 259–261
Interventions
    community-based, addressing trauma and resilience, 237
    community-based research support for, 206
    considerations for, 59–60
    culturally adaptive, 144–145, 150
    culturally syntonic, 213, 245–246, 268
    culture-centered. *See* Promoting Culture-Centered Interventions and Advocacy (Multicultural Guideline 6)
    differing cultural perceptions of, 147–148
    literature review, 143–144
    mindfulness, 230
    strength-based, 230–231
    trust in therapeutic relationships for success of, 210
IRBs (institutional review boards), 137, 172

J

Jacob, K. S., 142
Jargon, 88, 91–92, 97, 211, 251–252
Jones, Arthur, 126
Journal of Multicultural Counseling and Development *(JMCD),* 136–137
Journal publishing, advocacy for global inclusion in, 136–138

K

KFPE (Swiss Commission for Research Partnerships), 173–176
Kirmayer, L. J., 215–216, 229–230

Kit, K. A., 78
Kitayama, S., 195
Kivlighan, D. M., III, 58
Kozan, S., 145–146
Kung, W. W., 131

L

Language(s)
    as barrier to rapport, 90–91
    as complex, interactive process, 87–88
    for conversation about difficult topics, 148–149
    cultural significance of. *See* The Cultural Significance of Language and Communication (Multicultural Guideline 3)
    cultural translation of, 96–97
    definitions of, applied to mental health field, 87–90
    diagnosis-related, 231–232
    dual language experience, 94
    in identity development, 55
    ownership of, 94
    as representation of cultural values, 94–95
    as source of measure error, 207
    in transnational teaching, 157–158
    in the United States, 96
    used by psychologists, 211
Lating, J. M., 140
Latino/Hispanic/Latinx Americans. *See also* People of color
    balancing commitments in face of economic hardship, 102–104
    barriers creating marginalization of, 126
    community based investigations of parenting and resilience in multigenerational family, 24–27
    community supports among, 226
    and cost of pursuing doctorates in psychology, 129
    culturally syntonic considerations with, 245–246, 268
    empowerment of women, 213
    familism in, 110–111
    machismo/marianismo ideals in, 108, 227
    nonverbal communication among, 144
    in U.S. population, 96
Lavik, K. O., 93

Layered ecological model of the *Multicultural Guidelines*, 21–45, 247, 264. *See also individual levels*
  bidirectional model of self-definition and relationships (Level 1), 28–31
  case illustration, 24–27
  chronosystem in, 23, 24, 41
  community, school, and family context (Level 2), 31–34
  domestic and international climate (Level 4), 37–39
  exosystem in, 23–24
  institutional impact on engagement (Level 3), 34–36
  macrosystem in, 23–24
  mesosystem in, 23–24
  microsystem in, 23–24
  outcomes (Level 5), 39–41
  power/privilege, tensions, and fluidity in, 41–43
  trauma and resilience factors in, 44
Learning
  healthy environment for, 232–234
  openness to, 17–18
  project-based, 109
  team, 170–171
  through research participation, 211–212
Lee, A., 229
Level 1 Guidelines, 4. *See also individual guidelines*
Level 2 Guidelines, 4. *See also individual guidelines*
Level 3 Guidelines, 5. *See also individual guidelines*
Level 4 Guidelines, 5. *See also individual guidelines*
Level 5 Guidelines, 5. *See also individual guidelines*
Lewin, Kurt, 28
LGBTQ+ groups/individuals
  financial support for students, 130
  lack of data regarding, 125–126
  opportunities available to, 189
  student admissions experiences of, 128
Listening
  active, 17
  awareness of biases in, 70
  to recognize self-defined identity, 50
  for verbal and nonverbal communication, 98–99

Literature review
  advocacy, 138–143
  culturally informed work in psychology, 205–207
  cultural significance of language and communication, 91–95
  culture-centered interventions and advocacy, 138–144
  early interventions, 143–144
  fluidity and complexity of self-identity and social dynamics, 54–57
  globalization's impact on psychology, 161–166
  impact of social capital, 104–107
  institutional barriers and systemic marginalization, 121–127
  intersection between development and biosociocultural context, 187–190
  interventions, 143–144
  prevention, 143–144
  psychologists' biases, 73–76
  strength-based approach to psychology, 223–227
  trauma, 226–227
Lobbying, advocacy vs., 140
Low-context cultures, 145

M

Macrosystem
  as circle of engagement and interaction, 28
  domestic and international climate (Level 4), 37–39
  in layered ecological model, 23–24
March on Washington for Jobs and Freedoms, 119
Marginalization
  and intersectional invisibility, 58–59
  in intersectionality theory, 56
  research on participants with multiple marginalized identities, 64
  sociopolitical conditions exacerbating toll of, 57
  systemic, 118. *See also* Recognizing Institutional Barriers and Systemic Marginalization (Multicultural Guideline 5)
Markus, Hazel R., 196
Marriage, same-gender, 189
Marsella, A. J., 149–150
Masten, A. S., 223

McCormick-Huhn, K., 65
McDowell, T., 67
McGee, E. O., 223–224
Meisels, S. J., 140, 144
Mental Health: Culture, Race, and Ethnicity (U.S. Department of Health and Human Services), 142–143
Mental health care service systems, 147, 210
Mental health parity/disparity, 143, 210
Mental health stigma, 136, 161, 210
Mentorship, 79–80, 124
Mesosystem
  as circle of engagement and interaction, 28
  community, school, and family context as, 31–34
  in layered ecological model, 23–24
Microaggressions, 56
  lack of education concerning, 63
  racial, 77
  in therapeutic alliance, 82
Microsystem, 23
  bidirectional model of self-definition and relationships as, 28–31
  as circle of engagement and interaction, 28
  in layered ecological model, 23, 24
Migration. *See also* Immigration
  forced, 11–12, 236
  trilateral migration trauma, 236
Miller, C., 127
Mindfulness, 229–230
Minoritized groups. *See also individual groups*
  identities of, 194
  lack of data regarding, 124–125
  system of marginalization of, 118. *See also* Recognizing Institutional Barriers and Systemic Marginalization (Multicultural Guideline 5)
Minority status people
  identity of, 54, 57
  therapists, experience of cultural humility by, 61
Mixed-methods approach, 65, 81–82
Moradi, B., 56
Morgan, G., 208
Multicultural and Social Justice Counseling Competencies: Guidelines for the Counseling Profession (Ratts et al.), 9

Multicultural Guidelines: An Ecological Approach to Context, Identity, and Intersectionality, 2017 (2017 Multicultural Guidelines; APA), 4
  applying, 18
  evidence base for, 16
  future version of. *See* Future directions in multicultural psychology
  model of, 18–19. *See also* Layered ecological model of the *Multicultural Guidelines*
  overview of, 9–10, 247. *See also individual guidelines*
  recommendations for applying, 264–267
  summary of, 247–263
Multiculturalism, person–environment interactions represented in, 28
Multicultural psychology
  bidirectional relationships in, 11, 15–16
  central task in, 3–4
  cultural competence and cultural humility in, 11–15
  domestic and transnational focus in, 10–12
  future directions in. *See* Future directions in multicultural psychology
  guidelines for, 4–6, 8–10. *See also Multicultural Guidelines: An Ecological Approach to Context, Identity, and Intersectionality, 2017*
  key concepts in, 10–16
Multicultural responsiveness, 3
  and awareness of personal biases and perceptions, 70
  in context of bidirectional relationship, 15–16
  cultural competence and cultural humility for, 11
  domestic and transnational focus for, 11–12
  guidelines for. *See Multicultural Guidelines: An Ecological Approach to Context, Identity, and Intersectionality, 2017*
  reflexivity for, 16–18
Multiple marginalized identities, research on participants with, 64
Murray-García, J., 12–14

N

National Association of Social Workers, 9
Native Americans
　and cost of pursuing doctorates in psychology, 129
　lack of data regarding, 124. *See also* Indigenous people
Negativity, among students, 233
Neglect, reporting of, 36
Nelson-Barber, S., 207–208
Neurodevelopment, 195
Neville, H. A., 77
Nielsen, M., 130–131, 214–215
Nonbinary pronouns, 6
Nondefensiveness, in openness to learning, 17–18
Nonverbal communication, 94–97
　listening for, 98–99
　misunderstood, 144–145
Nordquist, R., 93
Norenzayan, A., 229
Norming, 208–209
NYU/Bellevue Bilingual Treatment Program (BTB), 97, 226, 243

O

Olkin, R., 57
Openness to learning, 17–18
Oppression, systems of, 37
Organizational-level advocacy, 146–147
Organizational racism, 126, 127
Outcomes
　as active area of emphasis in American psychology, 39
　connecting cultural competency research to, 266
　consolidating, in transboundary research, 176
　meaning of, 202–204
　multiculturally responsive, 212
Outcomes (Level 5), 39–41. *See also* Applying a Strength-Based Approach to Psychology (Multicultural Guideline 10); Conducting Culturally Informed Work in Psychology (Multicultural Guideline 9)
Overgeneralization, 81–82
Owen, J., 61

P

Padilla, A. M., 132
Parenting in immigrant families, community based investigations of, 24–27
Park, J., 195
Participation
　in research, teaching and learning through, 211–212
　in transnational teaching, 157–158
Paul Wellstone and Pete Domenici Mental Health Parity and Addiction Equity Act, 143
Pearrow, M. M., 109–110
Pelzang, R., 83
People of color. *See also individual groups*
　and APA *Resolution on Harnessing Psychology to Combat Racism*, 131
　barriers creating system of marginalization for, 122–123
　civil rights of, 35–36
　on faculty, student responses to, 233
　and lack of cross-cultural understanding in training, 132
　lack of data regarding, 125–126
　mental health care for, 142–143
　psychology degrees obtained by, 129
　structural and organizational racism and subsequent marginalization of, 126
People with disabilities
　false perceptions of, 55
　lack of data regarding, 125–126
　microaggressions against, 56
　women, stigmatized or oppressed identities of, 57
Perceptions
　cultural, of interventions, 147–148
　of people with physical disabilities, 55
　of terminology/jargon, 93
Petersen, S., 175
Political aspects of identity, 63
Political struggle, identity conflict connected to, 183–187
Positive psychology, 220–221, 224
Posttraumatic stress disorder (PTSD), 228–229, 236
Power distance, conversations about, 149
Power dynamics, between supervisors and supervisees, 66
Power/privilege process, 41–43

Power relationship, 30–31, 83
Prevention
  approaches for, 139
  differing cultural perceptions of, 147–148
  literature review, 143–144
  strength-based approach to, 220
Primary prevention, 143
Privilege
  of affluent normative values in mainstream institutions, 122–124
  in consulting relationship, 83
  of dominant class identity, 75
  institutional barriers favoring, 121–122
  organizational structures created/maintained by those with, 126
  processes of, 41–42
  systems of, 37
  of teachers and mentors, 79
Processes of decolonization, 171–172
Project-based learning opportunities, 109
Promoting Culture-Centered Interventions and Advocacy (Multicultural Guideline 6), 5, 135–152
  case illustration, 136–138
  for clinical practice, 144–148
  for consultation, 150–152
  for education (teaching and training), 148–150
  implications of, 257
  literature review, 138–144
  for research, 150
  summary of, 256–258
Pronouns
  gender, 55
  nonbinary, 6
Protecting and Defending Our People: Nakni tushka anowa (The Warrior's Path) Final Report (APA Warrior Path Presidential Task Force), 123, 134
Psychologists
  advocacy engagement by, 145–147
  barriers creating systems of marginalization for, 123, 124, 127–129. See also Recognizing Institutional Barriers and Systemic Marginalization (Multicultural Guideline 5)
  biases of. See Understanding and Avoiding Psychologists' Biases (Multicultural Guideline 2)
  cost of pursuing doctorates for, 129
  and disparities in mental health care, 210
  global mental health focus for, 156
  languages spoken by, 96
  privilege of, recognizing, 30–31, 43
  professional roles of, 245
  self-definition of, 29
Psychotherapy
  Conducting Culturally Informed Work in Psychology (Multicultural Guideline 9) for, 210–211
  as dynamic transaction, 73–74
  gray areas in, 232–233
Psychotherapy discontinuation, 144
PTSD (posttraumatic stress disorder), 228–229, 236
Publication guidelines, to include transnational research, 137
Public policy models, 177

Q

Qualitative methods, 65, 265

R

Race
  conversations around, 233
  and cost of pursuing doctorates in psychology, 129
  and foundational understanding of self, 188
  negative categorizations based on, 74
  and socialization experiences, 70
Racial–ethnic competence, 58
Racial identity, avoiding assumptions about, 58
Racial microaggressions, 77
Racial minorities/groups. *See also individual groups*
  disparities in mental health services for, 210
  financial support for students of, 130
  health and well-being of, 131
  psychology degrees obtained by, 129
  and student admissions experiences, 128
  and traumatic experience, 227
Racial stereotypes, internalization of, 55
Racism
  Anti-Asian, Vietnamese American woman coping with, 50–53
  apology from APA and American psychology for perpetuating, 127, 131, 134

324 • Index

conversations around, 233
cultural, 125
gendered, 58
injustice and systemic barriers produced by, 55–56
institutional, 122–126
internalized, 125–126
interpersonal, 125
levels of, 125–126
organizational, 126–127
resilience of children confronting, 223
Resolution on Harnessing Psychology to Combat Racism, 126
sociopolitical influences of, 75
structural, 125–127
toward displaced people, 164–165
Randomized controlled trials (RCTs), 213–214
Rapport
  themes for developing, 93
  therapeutic language as barrier to, 90–91
Rathod, S., 224
Ratts, M. J., 9
RCTs (randomized controlled trials), 213–214
Recognizing Institutional Barriers and Systemic Marginalization (Multicultural Guideline 5), 5, 117–134
  case illustration, 118–121
  for clinical practice, 127–130
  for consultation, 133
  for education (teaching and training), 131–132
  implications of, 255
  literature review, 121–127
  for research, 130–131
  summary of, 254–256
Recognizing the Fluidity and Complexity of Self-Identity and Social Dynamics (Multicultural Guideline 1), 4, 49–68
  case illustration, 50–53
  for clinical practice, 57–61
  for consultation, 66–67
  for education (teaching and training), 61–63
  implications of, 249
  literature review, 54–57
  for research, 63–66
  summary of, 248–249
Recovery, differing cultural perceptions of, 147–148

Recovery model approaches, 139
Recovery movements, 142
Reference group identities, 10
  clients' identification with, 29
  intersectionality of, 3–4
Reflection with vulnerability, 233–234
Reflexivity, 16–18
  about assumptions and biases, 210
  about cultural worldviews, experiences, and theoretical conceptualizations, 76
  about self-identity and its biases, 79
  defined, 65
  on implications of guidelines, 248
  in research concerning identity, 65
Relationship-centered advocacy, 145–147, 257
Relationships
  bidirectional. *See* Bidirectional relationships
  bidirectional model of. *See* Bidirectional model of self-definition and relationships (Level 1)
  factors informing, 271
Religion
  conversations about, 149
  negative categorizations based on, 74
  and socialization experiences, 70
  sociopolitical influences of anti-religious prejudice, 75
Religious aspects of identity, 63
Renbarger, R., 208
Research
  advocacy for global inclusion in publication of, 136–138
  Applying a Strength-Based Approach to Psychology (Multicultural Guideline 10) for, 235–236
  assumptions and stereotypes influencing, 50
  biases in, 69–70
  community-based participatory research, 97–98, 131, 150, 203–205
  on complexity of identity, 62
  Conducting Culturally Informed Work in Psychology (Multicultural Guideline 9) for, 213–215
  The Cultural Significance of Language and Communication (Multicultural Guideline 3) for, 97–98
  evidence base for *2017 Multicultural Guidelines* from, 16
  future professional benchmarks for, 243

Global Majority not represented in, 10
The Impact of Social Capital
 (Multicultural Guideline 4) for,
 110–111
institutional review boards for, 137, 172
on intersectionality, 56
The Intersection Between Development
 and Biosociocultural Context
 (Multicultural Guideline 8) for,
 194–195
issues lacking in, 12
methodologies in, 64–65, 265
outcomes in, 202, 203
Promoting Culture-Centered
 Interventions and Advocacy
 (Multicultural Guideline 6) for, 150
randomized controlled trials, 213–214
Recognizing Institutional Barriers
 and Systemic Marginalization
 (Multicultural Guideline 5) for,
 130–131
Recognizing the Fluidity and
 Complexity of Self-Identity and Social
 Dynamics (Multicultural Guideline 1)
 for, 63–66
recommendations for, 265–267
on resilience, 44
teaching and learning through
 participation in, 211–212
transnational, 136–138, 203
Understanding and Avoiding
 Psychologists' Biases (Multicultural
 Guideline 2) for, 80–82
Understanding Globalization's Impact
 on Psychology (Multicultural
 Guideline 7) for, 172–176
WEIRD samples in, 125, 130–131, 215,
 256
Resilience
advocacy skills in promoting, 234
community context for, 225
culturally focused resilience adaptation
 model, 224–225
defined, 44
and dose effect, 236
evidence base for, 224
in immigrant families, community based
 investigations of, 24–27
increasing, 44
recommendations for research on, 265
research on, 235–236
from sociocultural context, 220

strength-based approach to supporting,
 219. *See also* Applying a Strength-
 Based Approach to Psychology
 (Multicultural Guideline 10)
trait-based approach to, 223
worldviews in perception of, 228
*Resilience and Recovery After War:
 Refugee Children and Families in the
 United States* (APA), 236
*Resolution on Harnessing Psychology to
 Combat Racism,* 126
Roysircar, Gargi, 9
Ruth, R., 61

S

Same-gender marriage, 189
Satcher, David, 188
SBA. *See* Strength-based approach
School context. *See* Community, school,
 and family context (Level 2)
SCNAT (Swiss Academy of Sciences),
 173–176
Self
sense of, 188–189
theories of, 187. *See also* The
 Intersection Between Development
 and Biosociocultural Context
 (Multicultural Guideline 8)
Self-awareness. *See also* Reflexivity
of personal biases. *See* Understanding
 and Avoiding Psychologists' Biases
 (Multicultural Guideline 2)
of religious, spiritual, and political
 aspects of identity, 63
in teaching and training, 232
Self-care, 111, 212–213, 235
Self-definition
bidirectional model of. *See* Bidirectional
 model of self-definition and
 relationships (Level 1)
of identity, stereotyping and, 55
Self-identity. *See also* Identity(-ies)
developmental trajectories of. *See* The
 Intersection Between Development
 and Biosociocultural Context
 (Multicultural Guideline 8)
expectations about ourselves in framing,
 189
recognizing fluidity of. *See* Recognizing
 the Fluidity and Complexity of
 Self-Identity and Social Dynamics
 (Multicultural Guideline 1)

Self-reflection. *See* Reflexivity
September 11th, 2001/World Trade Center attacks, 140–141, 216, 227, 237
Service gap, 147–148
Sex, socialization experiences and, 70
Sexism
  injustice and systemic barriers produced by, 55–56
  sociopolitical influences of, 75
Sexual identity, socialization experiences and, 70
Sexual orientation, 74. *See also* LGBTQ+ groups/individuals
Shame, conversations about, 149
Shin, R. Q., 56, 65
Shonkoff, J. P., 144
Smart-Girl Program, 193–194
Smith, C., 170–171
Social capital
  defined, 101
  factors in, 102
  impact of. *See* The Impact of Social Capital (Multicultural Guideline 4)
Social class
  in addressing inequalities, 196
  privilege of dominant class identity, 75
  and socialization experiences, 70
Social determinants of health, 105–106
Social dynamics, recognizing fluidity of. *See* Recognizing the Fluidity and Complexity of Self-Identity and Social Dynamics (Multicultural Guideline 1)
Social group identity, 54
Social identities
  in intersectionality theory, 56
  marginalized, 58–59
Socialization experiences, 70
Social justice, 37
  addressing disparities in mental health care, 136
  advocacy for, 107
  country efforts toward, 177
  as framework for relationship-centered advocacy, 145–147
  injustice as factor in PTSD, 228
  integrated into training, 109–110
  lack of standard approach to teaching/training in, 61
  need for education about, 62–63
  pipeline of professionals focused on, 177–178

Social justice intentionality, 145–146
Social oppression, identity development and, 54
"Society as a patient," 149–150
Sociocultural groups
  heterogeneity of experience within, 50
  individual and group identities within, 54
  research on, 64
  stereotypes about, 59
Socioeconomic status
  balancing commitments in face of economic hardship, 102–104
  and college classroom instruction, 131–132
  as conveyer of difference, 105
  differing, lack of data regarding, 125–126
  negative categorizations based on, 74
  and success in graduate school, 118–122
Solano-Flores, G., 207–208
Special Initiative for Mental Health (2019–2023): Universal Health Coverage for Mental Health (WHO), 161
Speight, S. L., 13
Spiritual aspects of identity, 63
Spirituality
  conversations about, 149
  and socialization experiences, 70
Standards and Indicators for Cultural Competence in Social Work Practice (National Association of Social Workers), 9
Stassun, K., 127
Stephens, N. M., 122, 132
Stereotypes, 54
  about sociocultural groups, 59
  confronting, 196
  internalization of, 54–55, 74
Stereotype threat, in assessment, 78
Stereotyping
  denial of, 77
  impact of, 76
  leading to inaccurate hypotheses, 81
Stigma
  conversations about, 149
  mental health, 136, 161, 210
  with term "psychopathology," 92, 211
  for women with disabilities, 57
Stovall, D., 223–224

Strength-based approach (SBA). *See also* Applying a Strength-Based Approach to Psychology (Multicultural Guideline 10)
  in bidirectional relationships, 18, 220
  collaborative partnerships in, 219–220
  evidence base for, 235
  holistic consideration of client in, 232
  increasing adoption of, 220
  to interventions, 230–231
Structural humility, 43
Structural racism, 125–127
Subjective self-sameness, 54
Sue, D. W., 12–13, 77, 83–84, 112–113, 196
Supervision
  addressing intersecting identities in, 66–67
  addressing sociocultural variables in, 221–223
  culturally informed, 212–213
  in delivery of culture-centered interventions, 148
  for developing advocacy skills, 234
  discussing self-care in, 235
  as dynamic transaction, 73–74
  environment for, 232–234
  as impetus for reflective engagement, 80
  power dynamics in, 66
  role of advocate in, 172
  safe spaces in, 231–233
  talking about vicarious traumatization in, 235
  traumatic dynamics in, 62–63
Swiss Academy of Sciences (SCNAT), 173–176
Swiss Commission for Research Partnerships (KFPE), 173–176
Systemic marginalization
  defined, 118
  recognizing. *See* Recognizing Institutional Barriers and Systemic Marginalization (Multicultural Guideline 5)
Systemic mental health advocacy
  approaches for, 139
  defined, 140

T

Tajino, A., 170–171
Task Force on Guidelines Focused on Race/Ethnicity, 9, 244
Task Force on Re-Envisioning the Multicultural Guidelines for the 21st Century, 9, 244
Teaching. *See* Education
Team learning, 170–171
Techniques in psychotherapy, considerations in, 59–60
Technological advances, sense of self and, 189
Teletherapy, 89, 166–167
Temporal factors. *See* Chronosystem
Tensions, 41–43
Tervalon, M., 12–14
Theory, assumptions and stereotypes influencing, 50
Thornicroft, G., 151–152
Training. *See* Education
Transboundary practice, 166–167
Transboundary research, 172–176
Transnational focus, 10–12
Transnational research, 136–138, 204–205
Transnational teaching, 156–161
Transphobia, sociopolitical influences of, 75
Trauma
  advocacy skills in addressing, 234
  community context for, 225
  community-level impact of and responses to, 237
  cultural factors associated with, 237
  decreasing, 44
  information overload as source of, 183
  literature review of cultural context of, 226–227
  in positive psychology, 220–221
  processes contributing to experience of, 41–43
  recommendations for research on, 265
  research on, 235–236
  social injustice-related, 228–229
  strength-based approach to mitigating, 219. *See also* Applying a Strength-Based Approach to Psychology (Multicultural Guideline 10)
  trilateral migration, 236
  Vietnamese American woman coping with, 50–53
Trauma and resilience factors in, 44
Traumatic stress
  and dose effect, 236
  worldviews in perception of, 228

Traumatization, vicarious, 235
Trilateral migration trauma, 236
Trimble, J. E., 132
Trump, Donald, 52, 57
Tummala-Narra, Pratyusha, 9, 225, 229
2017 Multicultural Guidelines. See Multicultural Guidelines: An Ecological Approach to Context, Identity, and Intersectionality, 2017
2030 Agenda for Sustainable Development (United Nations General Assembly), 163

U

Ulie-Wells, J., 223–224
Uncertainty, information overload as source of, 183
Underserved populations, lack of data regarding, 124
Understanding and Avoiding Psychologists' Biases (Multicultural Guideline 2), 4, 69–84
  case illustration, 70–73
  for clinical practice, 76–78
  for consultation, 82–84
  for education (teaching and training), 78–80
  implications of, 250
  influence of socialization experiences, 69–70
  literature review, 73–76
  for research, 80–82
  summary of, 249–251
Understanding Globalization's Impact on Psychology (Multicultural Guideline 7), 5, 155–179
  case illustration, 156–161
  for clinical practice, 166–170
  for consultation, 177–178
  for education (teaching and training), 170–172
  implications of, 259
  literature review, 161–166
  for research, 172–176
  summary of, 258
United States
  APA's historical overfocus on, 155–156
  diverse student population in, 192–193
  generational responses to political system in, 38–39
  global transactional influences on, 263
  immigrants in, 12
  languages in, 96
  Latino/Hispanic/Latinx population in, 96
University of Chicago Pritzker School of Medicine, 112
U.S. Department of Health and Human Services (USDHHS), 142–143
U.S. Government Accountability Office (GAO), 122

V

Validity
  of assessments/tests, 207
  cultural, 207–209, 215
Vazquez, Carmen I., 97
Vera, E. M., 13
Verbal communication, 94, 98–99
Vicarious traumatization, 235
Visionary colorblindness, 75
Vulnerability, 76, 233–234

W

Waelde, L., 148–149
Wainberg, M. L., 173
Warrior Path Presidential Task Force (APA), 123–124, 134
WEIRD (Western, educated, industrialized, rich, and democratic) research samples, 125, 130–131, 215, 256
Weist, M. D., 92–93
White/White Americans
  centered in psychological science, scholarship, and practice, 131
  communication of others with, 51, 59
  and cost of pursuing doctorates in psychology, 129
  privilege of, 75
  as psychologists, 129
  in research, 64
  training focused on, 132
WHO. *See* World Health Organization
Williams, R. L., 193
Women
  African American, intersectionality of racism and sexism for, 55–56
  cultural roles and identifications for, 191–192
  with disabilities, stigmatized or oppressed identities of, 57
  Latina, empowerment of, 213
  in transboundary research, 175–176

Work settings, multiple constituencies in, 215
World Health Organization (WHO), 105–106, 147
  on global mental health, 156
  on identity development, 194
  mental health considerations in response to COVID-19 pandemic, 161
  self-care defined by, 235
  Special Initiative for Mental Health (2019–2023): Universal Health Coverage for Mental Health, 161
  World Mental Health Atlas 2017, 151
World Mental Health Atlas 2017 (WHO), 151

Worldviews
  in mental health services, 268
  in perception of and traumatic stress and resilience, 228
  reflexivity about, 76

X

Xenophobia
  sociopolitical influences of, 75
  toward displaced people, 164–165

Y

You the Reader case illustration, 6–8

About the Authors

Caroline S. Clauss-Ehlers, PhD, ABPP, is a professor of psychology in the School of Health Professions at Long Island University, Brooklyn. She attended Oberlin College, graduating with Honors in Government and completed her doctorate in counseling psychology at Teachers College, Columbia University. Born in New York and raised in Venezuela, Dr. Clauss-Ehlers has worked with both English and Spanish-speaking communities throughout her career. She has board certification in couple and family psychology by the American Board of Professional Psychology and is a fellow of APA Division 53: Society of Clinical Child and Adolescent Psychology and Division 43: Society for Couple and Family Psychology. She served as Chair of the APA Task Force on Re-Envisioning the Multicultural Guidelines for the 21st Century and as editor-in-chief of the *Journal of Multicultural Counseling and Development*. Among her honors and awards, APA's Division 43 honored Dr. Clauss-Ehlers in 2022 with the Distinguished Service to Family Psychology Award and in 2018 with the Carolyn Attneave Diversity Award. She was honored by the American Counseling Association (ACA) with the Association for Multicultural Counseling and Development Distinguished Service Award for Exceptional Leadership and Devoted Service to the *Journal of Multicultural Counseling and Development* in 2018 and the ACA Association for Multicultural Counseling and Development, Exemplary Diversity Leadership Award in 2014. As a 2004–2005 Rosalynn Carter Fellow for Mental Health Journalism, Dr. Clauss-Ehlers focused on the stigma of mental illness within Latinx communities. She currently serves as an advisory board member for this program. Her book *Eating Together, Being Together: Recipes, Activities, and Advice from a Chef Dad and Psychologist Mom* is coauthored with her chef husband. Dr. Clauss-Ehlers also writes a blog for *Psychology Today* called "Eating Together, Being Together" that makes connections between cooking and building community. She lives in New York City with her husband and has three children.

Scott J. Hunter, PhD, is senior scientific expert in neurodevelopmental disorders and rare pediatric diseases for WCG Clinical Endpoint Solutions. Previously, for 22 years, he was on the faculty at The University of Chicago (UChicago), where he was professor of psychiatry, behavioral neuroscience, and pediatrics and director of neuropsychology for UChicago Medicine. He served as chair of the department's Equity, Diversity, and Inclusion Committee. A fellowship trained clinical medical ethicist, he was vice-chair for the UChicago Medicine and Biological Sciences Institutional Review Board and faculty with the MacLean Center for Clinical Medical Ethics. Dr. Hunter was 2022 chair of the APA's Board for the Advancement of Psychology in the Public Interest and 2014 chair of the Committee on Professional Practice and Standards with the APA Practice Directorate. A coeditor of four well regarded textbooks addressing neuropsychological development and practice with Cambridge University Press, Dr. Hunter has authored numerous research articles in peer-reviewed publications, as well as served on multiple editorial boards and as chief editor for *Behavioral Sciences*.

Gayle Skawennio Morse, PhD, is a professor of psychology and internship director at Russell Sage College in the Capital District of New York. She currently serves on the APA Ethics Task Force and is a guest editor for a special issue of *The Counseling Psychologist—Considering Indigenous and Native American Perspectives on Mental Health and Well-Being*. She is a licensed psychologist in New York State and consults in complex neuropsychiatric cases. She is also a research member of the Institute for Health and the Environment in the School of Public Health at the State University of New York at Albany. For over ten years she was the director of the Counseling and Community Program at Russell Sage College. She was also the program director of the Crossroads program designed for children and adolescents with severe psychiatric illness for the Office of Mental Health of the State of New York Capital District Psychiatric Center. She was also the previous chair of the APA Board for the Advancement of Psychology in the Public Interest, cochair of the Warrior's Path Task Force, and an APA fellow of Division 35: Society for the Psychology of Women and Division 45: Society for the Psychological Study of Culture, Ethnicity and Race. She has been awarded the Division 35, Section 6 Sweet Grass Award for Service to Community and the coveted Joseph E. Trimble and Jewell E. Horvat Award for Distinguished Professional in Native/Indigenous Psychology. Dr. Morse has published numerous peer review journal articles exploring the health effects of neurotoxins on health, treatment modalities after exposure to environmental toxins for

Gulf War veterans, human rights, ethics, and American Indian health and wellness. She has published many book chapters and several books.

Pratyusha (Usha) Tummala-Narra, PhD, is a clinical psychologist and the director of community-based education at the Albert and Jessie Danielsen Institute and a research professor in the Department of Psychological and Brain Sciences at Boston University. Her research and scholarship focus on immigration, trauma, race, and culturally informed psychodynamic psychotherapy. She is also in independent practice, and works primarily with survivors of trauma from diverse sociocultural backgrounds. Dr. Tummala-Narra serves on the Board of Directors of APA Division 45: Society for the Psychological Study of Culture, Ethnicity and Race and, in the past, has served on the Board of Directors of APA Division 39: Society for Psychoanalysis and Psychoanalytic Psychology; as the chair of the APA Division 39 Multicultural Concerns Committee; and as a member of the APA Committee on Ethnic Minority Affairs, the APA Presidential Task Force on Immigration, and the APA Task Force on Re-Envisioning the Multicultural Guidelines for the 21st Century. She is a fellow of the American Psychological Association and of APA Division 39 and Division 45. Dr. Tummala-Narra is associate editor of the *Asian American Journal of Psychology*, associate editor of *Psychoanalytic Dialogues*, associate editor of *Psychoanalysis, Culture, and Society*, and senior psychotherapy editor of the *Journal of Humanistic Psychology*. She serves on the editorial boards of the APA journals, *Psychoanalytic Psychology*, and *Psychology of Men and Masculinities*. She is the author of *Psychoanalytic Theory and Cultural Competence in Psychotherapy* (2016) and the editor of *Trauma and Racial Minority Immigrants: Turmoil, Uncertainty, and Resistance* (2021), both published by the American Psychological Association.